Constitutionalism, Executive Power, and the Spirit of Moderation

SUNY series in American Constitutionalism

Robert J. Spitzer, editor

Constitutionalism, Executive Power, and the Spirit of Moderation

Murray P. Dry and the Nexus of
Liberal Education and Politics

Edited by
Giorgi Areshidze, Paul O. Carrese, and
Suzanna Sherry

Cover image: Mead Chapel at Middlebury College

Published by State University of New York Press, Albany

© 2016 State University of New York

All rights reserved

Printed in the United States of America

For information, contact State University of New York Press, Albany, NY
www.sunypress.edu

Production, Diane Ganeles
Marketing, Anne M. Valentine

Library of Congress Cataloging-in-Publication Data

Constitutionalism, executive power, and the spirit of moderation : Murray P. Dry and the nexus of liberal education and politics / edited by Giorgi Areshidze, Paul O. Carrese, and Suzanna Sherry.
pages cm.
(SUNY series in American constitutionalism)
Includes bibliographical references and index.
ISBN 978-1-4384-6041-3 (hc : alk. paper)—978-1-4384-6042-0 (pb : alk. paper)
ISBN 978-1-4384-6043-7 (e-book)
1. Constitutional law–United States–History. 2. Courts–United States. 3. Judicial power–United States. 4. Executive power–United States. I. Areshidze, Giorgi, 1983- editor of compilation. II. Carrese, Paul, editor of compilation. III. Sherry, Suzanna, editor of compilation. IV. Dry, Murray, honoree.
KF4541.C66 2016
342.73--dc23
2015019475

10 9 8 7 6 5 4 3 2 1

Contents

Foreword

Truth and the Constitution

Harvey C. Mansfield

It is time to do honor to Murray Dry, longtime teacher of American politics and political philosophy at Middlebury College. Not that his time is running out, but that his time has reached a peak from which he can survey his students and friends with his typical warm-hearted concern, usually so full of energy and urgency, now balanced by calm satisfaction at his attainments and at theirs, in good part owing to him. What a life he has had in the green and (let's not forget) the white of the state of Vermont—a scholar's dream of studying all the year in all one's life at a vacation paradise. Together with Vermont's scenic attractions a little of its liberalism has rubbed off on the professor, though not overmuch. Perhaps today's weary liberalism, sadly in need of refreshment, could find something to admire in his generous soul, which is always looking for what is noble in human beings—and in all of them, unlike some of us who give credit mainly to a pinched few fellow Republicans. Yet his warmth is guided by his loyalty to friends and the forgiveness his conservative ones sometimes require for their excessive frowning, the relief they need from the pain of frequent disapproving. One cannot meet Murray Dry without returning the smile he has for you. His opinions are the persuasions of a man you cannot help liking.

Professor Dry's main work, the one that best reveals the cast of his mind, is his book *Civil Peace and the Quest for Truth*. It is a book of constitutional law, focused on the First Amendment, which, as everyone knows, is the one that issues prohibitions to Congress relating to free speech and to religion. It also deals with the people's rights to assemble and to petition, but these have not been nearly as fertile sources of constitutional interpretation as the first two rights. Most of this interpretation, Professor Dry points out, has considered free speech and religion separately, but he sees them to be related. Free speech may seem to be concerned either with self-expression or with self-government, rarely both, because the two are rival causes; the first is making a statement, the second is making an argument.

Dry sees that in the seventeenth century, when free speech was first espoused as a people's right, it was as the right to speak freely about religion, particularly the established or dominant religion. This right, and the sort of speech that it makes possible, were exercised by political philosophers such as Locke, Spinoza, and Milton who contested the notion of divine government, taken from Scripture, on behalf of the right of humans to govern themselves. Here was the original modern argument for self-government made initially more against divinity than against monarchy. The religious question preceded the political question of who should rule, or rather was the first appearance of the political question. For one cannot answer the questions of which men should rule and how without first showing that in any form of regime, men, and not God, deserve to rule.

Because Dry begins from the relationship between free speech and religious freedom, he is able to engage the study of constitutional law with philosophy. Many professors of constitutional law have what could be described as an enthusiastic nodding acquaintance with philosophy as it stands today in university departments of philosophy, representing an outward assurance of friendship without the pleasure of common study. But today's philosophy does not satisfy Murray Dry. He returns to the original modern philosophy that departments of philosophy take for granted. And further: from the early moderns he is led back to the ancients.

The early moderns made it plain that they were concerned to defend philosophy from the oppression of religion, which they did by changing society as a whole to make it less insistently religious. This is the change that would result from the propagation of doctrines of free speech and religious toleration to all citizens, not just to other philosophers who might be dismissed as a few harmless cranks. That is why the early moderns made so plain the dichotomy between divine rule and human rule. The ancients, Dry could not fail to note, kept a cloak over this difference so that human rule could be seen as compatible with, not hostile to, divine rule. Thus in Plato's *Apology of Socrates*, Socrates is presented not as an atheist but as an investigator for the Delphic Oracle and a follower of his own divinity, his *daimonion*. For him, and for the Socratic tradition, religion was respected as a necessary ally, if not always a friend, of philosophy. The early moderns, too, did not avow their atheism, grossly confident though they were; but they constructed a politics and ethics, together with an epistemology, designed to make a rational religion (known later as deism) to reform Christianity and to substitute for the original irrational version. The substitute Christianity was worldly or "secular" rather than divine or noble, and hostile to the notion of soul dear to the ancient philosophers, which reflected a highmindedness shared with religion. The cloak of the ancients under which they kept their criticism of religion did not hide the sort of fundamental redirection of the soul toward worldly goods, as did the much less sincere religious toleration of the moderns.

To conceive and promote this redirection of the soul, the early modern philosophers made the truth of their philosophy more prominent than earlier philosophers. Philosophy itself was transformed from the task of understanding to that of reform, and in the eighteenth century the *philosophes* in France became a public authority respected in both the *ancien regime* and the revolution against it. With the pen of Thomas Jefferson Americans declared their independence on the basis of rights "endowed by their Creator" and derived from "self-evident truths" concerning "the Laws of Nature and of Nature's God." Murray Dry took note of this event. Here in 1776 was truth declared to be the foundation of a regime, a declaration that could not but be reflected in the First Amendment to the Constitution ratified in 1791. The self-evident truths had to do with liberty and with religion, understood as together.

The reason why most constitutional scholars treat free speech apart from religion is that they regard the question of the truth of religion as settled. It may be settled because the truth of atheism has triumphed or, more likely, because the truth of religion is regarded as safely irrelevant to politics. So most scholars turn their attention to the justice of the Constitution. Is it really just? Today this means, is it in accordance with democratic justice? In *Federalist* 10, James Madison made a distinction between a republic and a democracy, the former as representative of the people, the latter as their direct rule. Today "democracy" as the direct rule of the people, such as it was in the rule of the Athenian *demos*, is lost to sight, and everyone calls a representative republic democracy. A democratic government is said to be one that holds elections, that is, elects representatives so as to avoid the evils of direct rule by the people. Yet the Constitution is widely held to be undemocratic by constitutional scholars, almost as if direct rule of the people were the ideal, though unfortunately not feasible. Democracy has come to mean devotion to equality more than rule of the majority of the people, so that a majority decision in an election against the advance of equality might be considered undemocratic. With such thinking abroad in the land, a new Constitutional convention seems appropriate to a number of constitutional scholars, one that makes the Constitution more democratic in Madison's sense and in opposition to his stated view.

It is striking that in his major work Murray Dry does not scrutinize the question of the *justice* of the Constitution. Looking at its title, justice would seem to be something more than "civil peace" and something less than "quest for truth." Dry wanted to take up the fundamental question of the relationship between philosophy and politics as it first appeared in the Socratic political science of Plato and Aristotle and was later transformed in modern political philosophy. One could say that he left the defense of the justice of the Constitution to another student of Leo Strauss, Martin Diamond. Indeed the two M. D.s make a couple, the one speaking for justice, the other for philosophy. Diamond defended the structure of the Constitution, including its apparently undemocratic features such as the federal system and the separation of powers, and showed that they made the Constitution, not more democratic, but with their qualifications of democracy more successfully democratic. Diamond rediscovered the wonderful merit of *The Federalist* for American political science. He justified Jefferson's praise of it and explained, as would a teacher to a dull class, that there is such a thing as excess and there is virtue in moderation.

Dry, for his part, takes up the First Amendment, which is as much beloved by most scholars as the structure of the Constitution is demeaned by them. He shows, as if coupled with Diamond, that they are as incompetent in regard to what they like as in what they dislike. Instead of explaining *The Federalist*, as did Diamond, a pleasurable task of interpreting an excellent book, Dry burrows into the history of constitutional law, where so many cases challenge one's memory and one's ability to construct analogies. In constitutional law theory focuses on the facts of a single case and seeks relevant similarities and differences with other cases. It is displayed in legal formulations and rival arguments that strain for both reason and precedent, science and common sense, syllogism and rhetoric. Dry loves this tangle of rival distinctions and ever-clarifying persuasion, and he gets his students to love it as well.

There are two definitions of constitution. One is limited government, a government that derives its "just powers from the consent of the governed," in the words of the Declaration of Independence. In this meaning some governments are constitutional, others not. A second definition is the constitution as a way of life (a "regime," or *politeia* in the Greek sense), which every country has, whether good or bad. Starting from the first definition, a limited government would be one with something like the First Amendment, requiring that government not infringe upon the rights of free speech and religion. Government would have the function of seeing to it, with various specifications of enforcement, that these rights are protected. They are protected as formal, regardless (or almost regardless) of their content, or how they are exercised.

The trouble with this picture of rigorous formality protecting possibly wayward, possibly licentious informality is that the actual exercise of rights will affect their protection as formal. If, like republican Rome, the country is divided into nobles and plebs despising one another, each party will do its best to compromise or destroy the rights of the other. Or if the country is characterized by deep divisions of religious belief and practice, like Europe in the seventeenth century, civil war will result from the desire of each party to save the souls of its enemy, regardless of respect for rights in this world. In sum, the first definition of constitution as limited government leads to the necessity of a certain way of life that sustains limited government, the life of respect for speech one disagrees with and of toleration for religions other than one's own.

A new trouble in the argument appears, however. Respect for rights seems to require that the free country's goal be a minimum of civil peace, nothing more. To raise the question of truth—whether free speech is true speech and religion true religion—becomes subversive of the limited, though merely formal constitution to which all have agreed. Yet is it possible for human beings to live, each by themselves or all together in a country, without raising this question? If the quest for truth is removed from a way of life, free speech and religion are debased to something less than their most serious, intended character as the practical essence of freedom. Free speech is debased to the purgative value of venting one's feelings (euphemized as "self-expression") and religion to the need for psychological security from fear of death. Neither of these has to do with our minds; in fact, they require us to throttle our minds and to compel ourselves to be satisfied with thoughtless, unguided feelings. Worse than this, neither debasement requires that we be free; in fact, an authoritarian government of a country and an authoritarian personality for an individual might do a better job of preventing our minds from interfering with our feelings. Authority without freedom knows better how to manipulate feelings because it is concentrated solely on the risks, and cares nothing for the benefits, of freedom. These considerations compel us to acknowledge that civil peace requires, and leads to, a concern for truth.

The usual solution for the problem of civil peace versus truth is the fact/value distinction, or something like it. According to this distinction, truth has to do with fact, and nothing to do with value. Value is declared off-limits to the quest for truth, and this advice or prohibition is said to be based on the truth—very convenient for civil peace—that science cannot discover value. But in fact, since we humans have minds, value has everything to do with truth. It is not open to us as human beings to live contentedly by our feelings as do other animals, and this truth will prevent us from living as they do. We will live either better or worse than they. Truth is not a simple thing. It has an aspect of being self-evident, in the matters we must take for granted when we choose and act on, for example, the necessity of assuming our free will. But it also resists definition even as we assume it, so that truth as we know it is always a quest for truth, not an assumed, dogmatic truth.

In his studies of constitutional law and political philosophy, and in his lifelong teaching at Middlebury, Murray Dry has always kept in mind, and conveyed to his students, both the need for civil peace and the quest for truth. They are at odds, but because both belong to human nature and represent human freedom, they must somehow be coupled.

Editors' note: Harvey C. Mansfield is the William R. Kenan Jr. Professor of Government at Harvard University and senior fellow at the Hoover Institution. Mansfield supported two visits at Harvard for Murray Dry, as a Harvard Law School liberal arts fellow, 1985–1986; and as a visiting professor in the Department of Government, spring 2003. Dry's students and colleagues at Middlebury across generations might recall one or more of the many trips that Mansfield made from Cambridge, Massachusetts to Vermont, to lecture at Middlebury at Murray's invitation. Middlebury students and colleagues also might recall, as we do, the civil dialogue in quest for the truth that occurred between these dedicated educators—in turn sparking dialogue and questing among others, as they intended.

Acknowledgments

The co-editors begin by thanking two colleagues whose efforts have been indispensable to a multifaceted project. Irakly George Arison, Middlebury '00 (who used his given name Irakly Areshidze when he studied with Murray Dry at the College) conceived of this entire endeavor in 2009. He envisioned a conference at Middlebury College to honor Murray as he marked forty years of teaching; an endowed professorship of political philosophy at the college in his name; and a *festschrift* to publish the conference papers as an enduring, public honor to our teacher. George worked diligently and largely anonymously to bring this three-part symphony from idea to action, and we are indebted to him for both his thoughtfulness and industry. James Stoner '77 joined with the three co-editors to form the academic planning committee for the conference, held in late 2010 at Middlebury, and continued with the initial planning of this *festschrift*. Academic custom limits co-editors of a single volume to three colleagues, and Jim graciously volunteered to step from the limelight while continuing to provide guidance and crucial wisdom. One particular matter was larger than we could handle, and if not for Jim's deft statesmanship, the ship might have foundered or been gravely damaged. This quiet role, in addition to his fine chapter, is itself a fitting tribute to Murray's legacy.

Middlebury College's then-President Ronald Liebowitz, a longtime faculty colleague of Murray's, supported in word, deed, and funding the three elements of this project and thus has made possible this fitting tribute to liberal education and the college. The alumni office of the college, especially Meghan Williamson and Gail Borden, superbly planned the 2010 conference on "Political Philosophy and the Constitution" and reached out to Murray's many students and admirers. The Department of Political Science and the Rohatyn

Center for Global Affairs, especially the center's then-director Professor Allison Stanger, provided crucial administrative and logistical support for the conference. We are also thankful to the anonymous donor whose financial support helped bring the volume to completion.

It has been a pleasure to work with the leadership and editorial staff at the State University of New York Press. We should note particular thanks to the two external readers the Press chose to review the draft manuscript; their many fine insights have helped the chapter authors and the editors to improve this book.

The two more senior co-editors close by noting that our junior colleague, Giorgi, has provided much of the energy and administrative oversight for this publishing project, as well as his share of the larger conceptions for the volume. Collegiality and diligence are further legacies that Murray and Middlebury College have given us.

Suzanna Sherry '76
Paul O. Carrese '89
Giorgi Areshidze '04

Introduction

Liberal Education and Politics

Giorgi Areshidze and Paul O. Carrese

We offer these essays on the practice and theory of liberal democratic politics in honor of Murray P. Dry, the Charles A. Dana
Professor of Political Science at Middlebury College. Lawyers, law
professors, and political science professors who were his students
during five decades of teaching at Middlebury—from 1968 onward,
with no signs of slowing yet!—explore diverse but related themes, in
the spirit of Socratic inquiry and the liberal education they encountered in his courses. His own teaching and scholarship are informed
by his study of political philosophy with Leo Strauss and Joseph
Cropsey, and of American politics with Herbert Storing, at the
University of Chicago. The legacy Dry passed to students across several generations was not, however, any doctrine or particular school.
His teaching, scholarship, and legacy embody a particular view of liberal education. In Dry's classrooms this meant the broadly philosophical study of politics from the perspective both of the serious
citizen of a free regime and of the inquiring minds who pursue the
deeper questions raised by politics. He taught us to take seriously the
deepest concerns of human beings and citizens, and to pursue the
truth in both realms. Such liberal study in Dry's courses embraces a
range beyond most conventional political science and even political
theory today—from literature, to philosophy of science, to the origins of America's first principles—but centers on questions of how
communities can govern justly and how individuals can lead a good
life. His courses have encompassed Western political philosophy from

the ancients to the present; American political thought; American institutions; and constitutional law. His students thought it fitting to contribute essays particularly addressing themes of constitutionalism, law, and modern philosophy predominant in his scholarship and teaching.

We note that the academic custom of honoring a distinguished teacher with a *festschrift* typically is reserved for professors at graduate schools who directly send students into academic positions. In the hills of Vermont far from the centers of power in academia or politics, Dry has fostered in students at a small liberal arts college an unusual ambition for graduate study of political science, as well as for legal study that has led to federal judicial clerkships, legal academia, and significant government positions. True to the spirit of liberal inquiry that Dry passes on to his students, the authors represent diverse views about legal and political questions.

In recent decades there has been some thoughtful study, and much tendentious criticism, about Leo Strauss and his legacy in academia and politics, including debate about supposed doctrines taught by Strauss and his protégés. Dry implicitly conveyed to his students that there was no doctrinaire "Strauss-ism" that he could discern, or would convey. Indeed, in his 1994 lecture upon taking up the Dana Professorship at Middlebury College, he spoke of his "vocation" as leading students up the same mountains, decade upon decade, in search of great debates, great ideas, and serious formation of the mind and soul. This activity sought to prepare them for an examined life and responsible citizenship. He identified himself not as a professor but as "a teacher," invoking the guide who assists with, but does not presume to do, the climber's work. The pursuit of truth is the student's burden and ultimate aim, with success measured by the capacity to continue with trekking long after college studies. That said, the guide does recommend mountains, not foothills, let alone molehills; and recommends some mountains as more worthy of climbing than others.

In Dry's courses such recommendations meant study of a range of philosophers spanning the likes of Plato, Aristotle, Aquinas, Machiavelli, Bacon, Spinoza, Kant, Tocqueville, or Nietzsche; and meant studying the American order through such seminal sources as Publius, the Anti-Federalists, Melville, Lincoln, Martin Luther King Jr., or landmark cases of constitutional law. The vistas from these peaks cannot be reconciled, and thus no doctrine is conveyed, but such diverse challenges prepare the intrepid student and citizen for the intellectual and practical treks lying ahead. One wonders, for example, whether students in the Green Mountains had ever encountered much of Spinoza before Dry arrived in the late 1960s, and how vistas may have changed at Middlebury given the challenges posed by that daring philosopher.

Dry's dedication to teaching and the life of his college, and to fostering inquiry into fundamental alternatives about the ends and means of politics, permitted some time for scholarship. He completed the work of his mentor Storing in publishing path-breaking scholarship on the thought of the Anti-Federalists. He developed Storing's view that the American founding was unique for constituting both core principles and a lively debate about them, and he observed how this complex character echoes through our politics.

To his own articles and essays (a list of publications is appended to this volume) he more recently has added two books. His first, *Civil Peace and the Quest for Truth: The First Amendment Freedoms in Political Philosophy and American Constitutionalism* (2004), captures his complex approach to teaching and scholarship over many decades. Current legal-political developments deserve careful study, but this requires investigation of the institutional and philosophical sources that inform more familiar views and issues. Dry's focus is the civil liberties of speech and religion; he notices our tendency to separate the two, when instead we should ponder their intrinsic relation. Moreover, whether we are citizens, scholars, or jurists, we would do well to study the political philosophers who first debated whether a free but decent society could protect diverse speech and religious views. As if this approach connecting constitutional law and political philosophy were not already unusual, Dry further argues that liberal politics could have too much of a good thing. A deepening of the law and culture that achieved "civil peace" through toleration of nearly all views and beliefs might be undermining the capacity for, and priority of, "the quest for truth." Liberalism thus paradoxically calls for moderation—described by Dry as a classical virtue—that can help us to strike the right balance between freedom and the search for truth. Inquiry into Plato, Thucydides, and Aristotle reminds us that speech in a democracy can tend toward opposition to reason or higher inquiry. We may have some grounds for tempering the efforts of modern philosophy to lower and limit the aims of both government and communal authority regarding morals and religion. Can a merely skeptical, and ever-more emotive, political community sustain free speech and religious pluralism for successive generations? Having said this much about *Civil Peace and the Quest for Truth* we leave the reader with this incomplete summary of a weighty and complex argument in part because Harvey C. Mansfield devotes much of his Foreword (which precedes this Introduction) to a philosophical appraisal of Murray's book.

Dry's second book is a sequel in spirit and approach, on *The Same-Sex Marriage Controversy and American Constitutionalism: Lessons Regarding Federalism, the Separation of Powers, and Individual Rights* (2015). Once again Dry combines philosophical and legal analysis to assess a recent moral-political controversy that has largely been framed as a matter of individual rights, and prominently contested in courts of law. Dry first describes the moral arguments about marriage, contrasting the views of traditionalists with those of advocates of same-sex marriage. Here he sees the reasonableness, as a policy matter, of the American principle of liberty developing to incorporate a redefinition of marriage to include two homosexual partners. In the second part he assesses the constitutional and civic propriety of courts of law settling this monumental policy matter of society and politics through interpretation of constitutional texts to the exclusion of, or overriding, the judgments of elected representatives and citizens. Dry concludes that in our constitutional order there is not such a clear legal-judicial warrant for allocating these questions to the courts; republican self-government would be undermined by seeking to settle the controversy in this manner. In both parts of the argument Dry seeks a hearing for the main opposing principles and arguments, and remains open to a reasonable middle ground that gives a proper result in light of a larger, comprehensive assessment of the enduring principles at stake.

The chapters in this volume were commissioned to mirror our teacher's blending of constitutionalism, constitutional law, and political philosophy, particularly his attention to liberal democratic politics and also to the philosophy that both informs and investigates it. It does not surprise us as editors that, as it turns out, the chapters collected here honor our teacher's interest in and commitment to both intellectual and political moderation. We did not cajole the authors to emphasize this theme, nor select the authors with this thread in mind, and there is no unified doctrine of moderation pronounced herein. In the spirit of Dry's explorations of the nexus between liberal education and politics, his students light upon the questions of constitutional, legal, and philosophical balance in diverse ways. To guide the reader's journey, we have structured our exploration of these important themes in three sections. In Part I, "The Role of Courts in Constitutional Democracy," five contributors explore the proper functions and limits of the judiciary and judicial decision-making in constitutional government. Suzanna Sherry argues for the restoration of the original function of the judiciary as an institution intended to limit democratic majorities, concluding that activist courts, properly defined, are healthier for democracy than those passively deferential to popular branches. Karl Coplan assesses recent literature on legal realism that emphasizes the indeterminacy of legal meaning and the arbitrariness of legal outcomes; he then poses provocative questions about the troubling consequences of legal realism for judicial decisions and authority. Ayşe Zarakol studies the role of the judiciary in a comparative perspective, by investigating the elite push toward "judicialization" of politics in Turkey and India as an institutional bulwark against subversive and illiberal popular movements, and wonders what this means for democratic legitimacy. Barbara Kritchevsky explores whether federal courts can provide remedies to individuals who have suffered violations of constitutional rights, arguing that judges should infer a damages remedy from the Constitution itself.

In Part II, "Law and Executive Authority," scholars as well as contributors with experience in the federal executive and judicial branches reflect on the tensions between constitutionalism and presidential leadership in both domestic and international arenas. Sean Mattie focuses on Lincoln's Reconstruction policy to explore a larger lesson about political leadership in a free politics—namely, how the institution of the presidency addresses the demands of necessity while capturing a nobler aspirational element of constitutionalism that only a president can articulate through the exercise of constitutional rhetoric. C. Kevin Marshall, former deputy assistant attorney general under George W. Bush, provides an insider's account of the contests over war-making powers between the judiciary and the executive during a contentious and anxious period for constitutional government. Finally, James A. Morone assesses the continuities and discontinuities in the presidential pursuits of national health-care insurance in the administrations of Truman, Johnson, Clinton, George W. Bush, and Obama, and reflects on the important role of ideas in America's constitutional politics.

Part III, "Liberal Education, Constitutionalism, and Philosophic Moderation" shifts the focus to the relationship between constitutionalism and political philosophy, and especially to the modern modes of philosophy that most directly influenced the American Founders. James R. Stoner Jr. contrasts classical political philosophy and American political thought through comparative examination of Plato's *Republic* and Madison's *Notes of Debates in the Federal Convention of 1787*; these two divergent works pose enduring questions about the best regime, and the dialogue is more salient than modern Americans might appreciate. Peter Minowitz investigates the enduring importance of Adam Smith's concept of the invisible hand, assessing Smith's different formulations of the metaphor and their significance for grasping the moral as well as the economic dimensions of his philosophy. David R. Upham examines the arguments of *The Federalist* concerning the conditions necessary for responsible popular deliberation—as distinguished from impulsive popular or democratic choice—as a precondition for a healthy republican society. Paul O. Carrese explores Tocqueville's arguments for political and philosophical moderation in liberal democracy; Tocqueville's call for a new political science was informed by Montesquieu, but also by classical and medieval philosophy as well as religion, and seeks to temper democratic tendencies toward populism, rationalism, and the soft despotism of administration. Giorgi Areshidze closes the volume with an exploration of the philosophic shortcomings of more recent Rawlsian liberalism and its assertive secularism, by assessing whether its expression in European multiculturalism is sustainable given the strains caused by growing ethnic and religious migration in the European Union; he asks whether the American consensus that religious liberty accommodates both nonestablishment of religion and free exercise of faith is more reasonable and sustainable than the prevailing European options of either enforced secularism or a theory of radical pluralism.

As is true of Professor Dry's range of courses and published writings, our volume tries to understand the historical development of constitutional theory and practice but also to appreciate the underlying foundation of philosophic moderation that is needed for the success of constitutional government. It is a reflection on Dry's teaching and scholarship on the courts, therefore, that the essays in Part I defend a distinctive and significant role for the courts (and especially the Supreme Court) in American constitutionalism, against calls today from both the left and the right to limit judicial power, but also against calls from recent strains of liberal jurisprudence to give too great a role to courts. Part II addresses several pressing questions of executive power in our constitutional order, both historical and contemporary, in the same spirit of assessing constitutional balance. Here the question is what constitutional constraints should guide an office that has grown in power quite substantially since the time of the constitutional founding. We are reminded that Dry's teaching and scholarship together argue for the necessity of understanding the range of views expressed at the founding about our constitutional republic. These include the Hamiltonian principle of a more capable central government, and the Anti-Federalist defense of local liberty and the small member republics, as well as the Jeffersonian spirit that democratic populism should guide the development of the new constitutional order. These chapters on presidential power in both foreign and domestic affairs consider the right balance between the rule of law and the capacity of the executive to pursue new ideals in public debate and legislative advocacy; the old question about tensions between constitutionalism and presidential leadership is alive and well, and our current debates should be more adequately grounded in these enduring ideas. Part III pursues the deeper principles of philosophical moderation that inform constitutionalism, courts, and executive power in both our constitutional republic and in other liberal democracies. These chapters suggest that we should rediscover moderation as the avoidance of extremes—suggesting, for example, that contemporary academic and political discourse should not veer toward thinking that only the latest theories, and only a focus on present concerns and debate, will help us to sustain a constitutional republic and a decent liberal order.

Another extreme that is questioned by these chapters is the view that the American founding, and the principles of our constitutional order, can be reduced to one principle or theory (with differing schools advocating for their favorite principle). The complexity of early modern liberalism, drawing on classical, medieval, and religious principles in the Western tradition, informs the ambition in our constitutional order to achieve a better politics by embracing and balancing various tensions. Regarding this meaning of moderation, we are familiar with the institutional design of balancing powers against one another, but these chapters explore the deliberate balancing or reconciling of principles in our politics—religious liberty and secular reason, liberty and equality, the higher aims of the soul with the practical demands of politics, moral principle and economic interest, popular consent and practically wise deliberation. The Socratic spirit of debate and liberal education is an analogue for the aim of a moderate liberal constitution to encompass and reconcile these various tensions. This old idea of liberal education therefore might be a more useful guide to politics and policy—in a higher sense of utility—than we now tend to appreciate.

We have not thought it proper or possible here to summarize the many dimensions and achievements of Murray Dry's long career—the distinguished fellowships he has held; his several leadership positions in service to Middlebury College; his many dozens of public lectures in Vermont and beyond; his broad contributions to the disciplines of political science and law in America as a valued speaker and contributor to conferences, journals, and many other projects of inquiry, discourse, and civic education. We also could say more about our gratitude to Murray, and about the importance of his dedication to a traditional but very lively conception of liberal education. This would be especially proper given the contrast between Dry's efforts and the deepening emphasis on professionalism, and other kinds of pragmatism and narrowness, in American higher education during the past century (not to mention the new challenge of technophilia). We instead let the chapters speak for themselves on these points, so that Dry's efforts can be judged at least by the aspiration in his students' arguments to find deeper, higher, and enduring meanings about human affairs and politics. In part we can be brief once again thanks to the Foreword contributed by Professor Mansfield, which honors the principles of philosophy and education for which Dry has stood as both teacher and scholar.

Readers find other tributes to Dry's vocation, and his example, in the chapters themselves. Amid the serious prose are moments that, for us, fittingly provoke deep emotion. We close this introduction here, and perhaps err on the side of brevity or concision, also because of the echoes in our ears of Dry's regular exhortation to emulate Lincoln's Gettysburg Address in our writing: to reach for the highest thoughts with the greatest economy. Imagine the several generations of students receiving such a challenge! We know, as we knew all along, that we have not quite achieved that summit with our writing in this volume. Nonetheless, we are eternally grateful for the teacher and friend who posed such challenges to us, and so opened the life of the mind to us.

Part I

The Role of Courts in Constitutional Democracy

Chapter 1

Why We Need More Judicial Activism

Suzanna Sherry

Too much of a good thing can be bad, and democracy is no exception. In the United States, the antidote to what the drafters of the Constitution called "the excess of democracy" is judicial review: unelected, life-tenured federal judges with power to invalidate the actions of the more democratic branches of government. Lately, judicial review has come under fire. Many on both sides of the political aisle accuse the Supreme Court of being overly activist and insufficiently deferential to the elected representatives of the people. Taking the Constitution away from the courts—and giving it back to the people—has become a rallying cry. But those who criticize the courts on this ground misunderstand the proper role of the judiciary. The courts *should* stand in the way of democratic majorities, in order to keep majority rule from degenerating into majority tyranny. In doing so, the courts are bound to err on one side or the other from time to time. It is much better for the health of our constitutional democracy if they err on the side of activism, striking down too many laws rather than too few.

In this chapter, I begin by defining two slippery and often misused concepts, judicial review and judicial activism, and briefly survey the recent attacks on judicial activism. I turn then to supporting my claim that we need more judicial activism, resting my argument on three grounds. First, constitutional *theory* suggests a need for judicial oversight of the popular branches. Second, our own constitutional *history* confirms that the founding generation—the drafters of our

Constitution—saw a need for a strong bulwark against majority tyranny. Finally, an examination of constitutional *practice* shows that too little activism produces worse consequences than does too much. If we cannot assure that the judges tread the perfect middle ground (and we cannot), it is better to have an overly aggressive judiciary than an overly restrained one.

The Judiciary and its Critics

Judicial review, despite some claims to the contrary, is *not* judicial supremacy. Courts are the final arbiter of the Constitution only to the extent that they hold a law *un*constitutional, and even then only because they act last in time, not because their will is supreme. The branches are co-equal when it comes to constitutional interpretation, but all three branches must agree that a law (or other government action) is constitutionally permissible for it to be valid. If Congress believes that a proposed law is unconstitutional it will choose not to enact that law, and no other branch can override Congress's decision. If the president believes that a proposed law is unconstitutional he will veto it, and his view can be overridden only with difficulty (and only by the legislative branch). Judicial review simply ensures that the judiciary has the same opportunity as the other two branches to prevent the government from acting unconstitutionally. Moreover, if the Supreme Court finds something to be *constitutional*, that holding is not binding on the other branches, as the history of the Bank of the United States shows: despite the Court's unequivocal holding in *McCulloch v. Maryland* that the bank was constitutional, the popular branches continued to spar over the question, and ultimately the bank's charter was discontinued.[1]

Indeed, throughout most of American history, judicial review of federal statutes was uncontroversial. *Marbury v. Madison* was not novel, and generated virtually no opposition to its invocation of the Court's power to invalidate federal statutes (its substantive holdings are a different story). Historically, the only major dispute about judicial review was a debate about federalism rather than separation of powers. Few objected to federal judges reviewing the constitutionality of federal statutes, or state judges reviewing the constitutionality of state statutes. But *federal* judges reviewing the constitutionality of *state* statutes? That was a problem. It was, however, merely one aspect of the larger issue of federal power in general; objections to federal judicial interference with state prerogatives were no louder than objections to federal legislative or executive interference with state prerogatives. From *Martin v. Hunter's Lessee* through John Calhoun's interposition and nullification theories to the Civil War, some states periodically resisted *all* federal claims of supremacy. Their constitutional theory—essentially one of polycentric constitutionalism—was never very attractive, and it was definitively rejected with the defeat of the Confederacy and the enactment of the Reconstruction Amendments to the Constitution.[2]

Ultimately, judicial review of state actions serves the same purpose as judicial review of federal actions. It ensures that when a state act is challenged, it is not upheld as valid unless at least one branch of the federal government agrees that it is constitutional. We could have designed a system granting that review power to the federal executive or legislature, but by and large we did not. James Madison actually proposed a congressional veto on state laws, but it was overwhelmingly rejected.[3] Congress has power to preempt state laws by enacting its own statutes, but cannot simply declare a state law unconstitutional. And no one ever seems to have thought that letting the federal executive veto state laws was a good idea.

If judicial review simply allows the courts to participate on an equal footing with the other branches and the states, what is judicial activism? Most accusations of judicial activism can be reduced to a charge that the judiciary has invalidated a statute that the accuser favors. Conservatives bemoan *Roe v. Wade* as judicial activism, and liberals hurl the same charge at *Citizens United v. FCC*. Both sides claim to be limiting their criticism to invalidations that depend on erroneous interpretations of the Constitution, but there is no agreement on what constitutes a good or bad interpretation—or even on the validity of different interpretive methods. If the characterization of a decision as activist depends on the politics of the person doing the characterizing, "judicial activism" is a merely meaningless pejorative.[4]

To avoid this trap, we need a definition of judicial activism with no political valence. It should include the acts of a conservative court striking liberal legislation as well as a liberal court striking conservative legislation. It should not embroil us in an argument over whether the court has properly or improperly interpreted the Constitution. It must, in other words, be objective.

Luckily, it is easy to describe judicial activism in objective terms. Judicial activism occurs any time the judiciary strikes down an action of the popular branches, whether state or federal, legislative or executive. Judicial review, in other words, produces one of two possible results: if the court invalidates the government action it is reviewing, then it is being activist; if it upholds the action, it is not. This definition also has the advantage of recognizing the counter-majoritarian aspect of judicial invalidations as the core distinguishing feature of activism.

Judicial activism, as so defined, is still subject to two different sorts of critiques. First, we can still argue about whether any particular invalidation, or any particular interpretation of the Constitution, is correct. But that requires us to delve into substance rather than simply resorting to name-calling: the problem is not the "activism" but rather the decision itself. The disputes are thus about the *correctness* of the court's decision, not—as is the case with charges of "activism"—about its *legitimacy*. I would welcome such a change in the tenor of debates about the Supreme Court, but it is beyond the scope of this chapter.

The second possible critique is that activism, as I define it, is a bad thing and should be rare. The argument rests on a basic majoritarian premise: in a democracy, the wishes of the majority should generally prevail. We can charitably describe the current attacks on judicial review and judicial activism as making this type of critique.[5] But criticism of judicial *activism*—in theory and for the Supreme Court's modern critics—does not necessarily entail criticism of judicial *review*. Truly unconstitutional statutes should be invalid. The problem, for these critics, is that rather than hewing carefully to the Constitution, the Court erroneously substitutes its own policy preferences for the majority's. These majoritarian critiques of judicial activism fall into three categories.

Some scholars call for theories of constitutional interpretation that would allegedly constrain the courts and limit the circumstances under which judges could invalidate the actions of the popular branches. These scholars would cabin judicial discretion and thus reduce judicial activism. The most prominent such theories are originalism and textualism, but others include minimalism and various translation theories. I have explained elsewhere that all of these grand theories are all doomed to fail in their efforts at constraint because it is not possible to make constitutional interpretation mechanical.

Judges will always have sufficient discretion—especially in the diffi-cult cases that reach the Supreme Court or divide the courts of appeals—to reach more than one plausible conclusion.[6]

Unsurprisingly, moreover, the theories actually constrain no one—neither judges nor scholars. The textualists do not complain when textualist judges interpret the Eleventh Amendment to include "fundamental postulates" that are directly contradicted by the text; the originalists do not complain when originalist judges invalidate limits on corporate campaign contributions without examining his-torical views on whether corporations should have First Amendment rights; the minimalists allow for some maximalism (read: activism), but do not specify the contours except to include cases that reach their favored results.[7]

Other scholars, perhaps recognizing the futility of trying to rein in judicial activism through theories of constitutional interpretation, would instead limit the power of courts to engage in judicial review. These "popular constitutionalists" advocate "taking the Constitution away from the courts" and giving it back to the people or their demo-cratic representatives. This popular constitutionalism comes in many flavors, from mild exhortations, to specific proposals for limiting judicial authority or finality, to arguments that the states and the fed-eral government may ignore the Supreme Court's decisions.[8]

The grand theorists and the popular constitutionalists have in common their preference for majoritarian decision making over counter-majoritarian judicial decision-making, and thus both would prefer less judicial activism. A third response to judicial activism is to claim that it is only superficially counter-majoritarian. In fact, some scholars argue, the Supreme Court ultimately follows the lead of popular majorities, striking down governmental actions only when those actions are contrary to the considered judgment of a majority of Americans. The judiciary thus serves to keep the people's wishes from being frustrated by unresponsive elected officials. Although the Court sometimes makes mistakes and invalidates truly popular laws, it does not adhere to such decisions for long, quickly revising its views and overturning its precedent.[9]

This third group of scholars thus does not explicitly criticize judi-cial activism, but instead trivializes it as irrelevant. Nevertheless, scholarship taking this approach shares with grand theory and popu-lar constitutionalism both a majoritarian outlook and an anti-activist consequence. To the extent that politicians, academics, the public, and, especially, judges, accept judicial review as *descriptively* majoritarian, they will likely come to believe that it is *normatively* better for judges to hew to the majority's will as well. Judges will become more reluctant to invalidate statutes as unconstitutional lest they inadvertently mistake public sentiment.

All of this leads to a deeper question: Why *should* we prefer majority decision-making? This brief survey of the jurisprudential landscape suggests that the apparent preference for majoritarianism, and thus contemporary attacks on judicial activism, might arise from any of several sources. First, there might be confusion (perhaps deliberately fostered by critics of particular decisions) between judicial review and judicial supremacy. Criticism of judicial review thus might stem from a belief that such review implies the superiority of unelected judges over the elected branches. I have argued here that this conflation of judicial review and judicial supremacy is unwarranted. Second, to the extent that criticism of judicial activism rests on the argument that judges are substituting their own policy preferences for those of the majority, it seems to stem from a belief that constitutional adjudication is more akin to political policy making than to legal interpretation. As I have argued elsewhere, I believe that this conflation of law and politics is also mistaken: the process of judging in constitutional cases is constrained in the same ways that it is in other, uncontroversial, cases; judges interpreting the Constitution are not legislators in black robes.[10]

Finally, there are the arguments I address in the remainder of this essay: that constitutional theory disfavors judicial activism; that our particular Constitution and its history privilege popular majorities over unelected judges; and that as a matter of practice, judicial activism is likely to do more harm than good—that is, that the majoritarian branches are more likely to be right, and judges more likely to be wrong, in most cases. After briefly examining the theory and history in support of judicially imposed counter-majoritarian limits on majority preferences, I return to the last, practical, question of whether activism does more harm than good.

Constitutional Theory

The constitutional theory in support of judicial review—and judicial invalidation of popular transgressions against the Constitution—is widely understood, and needs little discussion. I merely sketch its contours here, and suggest the implications we can draw from it.

Our Constitution establishes what is often called a limited or constitutional democracy. In a pure democracy, the majority is entitled to enact its wishes into law. In a constitutional democracy, by contrast, the Constitution places limits on the majority's power. The purpose of the Constitution, then, is to simultaneously empower and disempower popular majorities, to ensure democratic governance but nevertheless place a check on unfettered democratic rule. The Constitution establishes liberty as well as democracy.

The liberty-enhancing purpose is evident in many parts of the Constitution. The most well-known example is that various provisions, including most prominently the Bill of Rights and the Reconstruction Amendments, place explicit limits on what the majority can do. Less appreciated as a source of limits on majority power are the multiple divisions of authority: between the states and the federal government, among the different branches of government, and between the House and the Senate. The historical evidence tells us that the purpose of all these divisions, too, was to keep majorities from too easily implementing their will.[11] Other, more subtle divisions aim toward the same goal, such as the division of responsibility in criminal cases between a judge and two different types of juries. The Constitution also filters the desires of the majority through multiple layers to reduce its impact—the Electoral College filters majority will in the election of the president, and senators were originally appointed by state legislatures rather than popularly elected.

In a constitutional democracy, the role of the judiciary is to enforce the constitutional limits, and to put the brakes on popular tyranny and popular passions. As Alexander Bickel understood, "[t]heir insulation and the marvelous mystery of time give courts the capacity to appeal to men's better natures, to call forth their aspirations, which may have been forgotten in the moment's hue and cry." Henry Hart similarly described the Supreme Court as "the voice of reason, charged with the creative function of discerning afresh and of articulating and developing impersonal and durable principles of constitutional law." The same principles animated the work of John Hart Ely, who, turning a three-paragraph footnote in a Supreme Court opinion into a masterful book of political theory, recognized that legislatures, like citizens, sometimes harbor and act on irrational prejudices;

it is the judiciary's task to root out those illegitimate motives and protect the victims of them.[12]

All of these political theorists—and many others besides—take as their starting point that the Constitution is both majoritarian and anti-majoritarian, and they try to find ways of accommodating both principles. Each proposes a careful and elegant line beyond which the judiciary should not tread, lest it exceed the liberty-protecting function of its role and begin to trespass on democratic authority. Unfortunately, however brilliant the theorist, the project of line-drawing will inevitably fail. Like the grand theories of constitutional interpretation, political theories that are supple enough to confront the ever-changing complexities of modern life and modern government, let alone capacious enough to generate consensus, are necessarily too malleable to provide any real guidance on concrete cases (although it might limit the range of possible interpretations).

So what can we take from constitutional theory? We can accept its basic insight: that judicial activism serves a vital purpose in a constitutional democracy. As Justice Robert Jackson summarized it: "Unrestricted majority rule leaves the individual in the minority unprotected. This is the dilemma and you have to take your choice. The Constitution-makers made their choice in favor of a limited majority rule."[13] We can also learn from the failures of political theory by recognizing that no political or philosophical theory will ever succeed in specifying exactly how much activism is enough and how much is too much. For that task, we must take a more pragmatic approach. After first documenting in the next section the accuracy of Justice Jackson's view of our "Constitution-makers," I will turn in the last section to a more pragmatic analysis.

Constitutional History

Judicial protection from majority tyranny is not just one constitutional theory, it is also one of the motivating goals of *our* Constitution. It is too often forgotten that the founding generation subscribed to a theory of limited democratic governance. Indeed, most people—including many who exhort judges to follow the original understanding of the Constitution—do not realize how strongly counter-majoritarian, even anti-democratic, the founders were. As one historian puts it, summarizing historical consensus:

[A]longside the evils of monarchic tyranny and corruption that American republicans identified were another
set of evils, and . . . the form of government created by
the Constitution was designed to respond to those as well
as to the former set. The other evils were *democratic* tyranny and corruption, the expected results of interactions
between demagogues and the untutored masses. . . . [T]he
proponents of the Constitution, while understanding the
importance of a theoretical relocation of sovereignty in
"the people," held, in the main, a skeptical view of the capacity of the people as a whole to govern themselves. . . . [14]

Both proponents and opponents of the Constitution shared these
views, fearing what Elbridge Gerry of Massachusetts—a representative to the Constitutional Convention who ultimately became
an Anti-Federalist and opposed ratification—called the "excess of
democracy." James Madison, whose views were probably the most
broadly representative and are the most cited today, referred to the
"inconveniencies of democracy" and described the need for an unelected body to "protect the people against the transient impressions
into which they might be led." Edmund Randolph of Virginia, who
attended the Convention and refused to sign the Constitution but
then changed his mind and supported ratification, lamented the
"turbulence and follies of democracy" and argued that the nation's
"chief danger arises from the democratic parts of our constitutions."
Gouverneur Morris of Pennsylvania, a Convention delegate and
strong Federalist supporter of the Constitution, agreed that "the
public liberty [is] in greater danger from Legislative usurpations
than from any other source." Roger Sherman of Connecticut, another strong Federalist and later one of the key players in the adoption of the Bill of Rights, said that the people "should have as little to
do as may be about the government." The influential Anti-Federalist
essayist "Agrippa" wrote that it was "as necessary to defend an individual against the majority in a republick as against the king in a
monarchy." Similarly, the Anti-Federalist Maryland "Farmer" suggested that in democratic governments, "the tyranny of the legislative is most to be dreaded." Nor are these statements isolated or
idiosyncratic; they are representative of the speeches and writings of
both Federalists and Anti-Federalists during the drafting and ratification of the Constitution.[15]

And one significant remedy for legislative excess was judicial activism. Alexander Hamilton, among many others, recognized that the rights protected by the Constitution "can be preserved in practice in no other way than through the medium of courts of justice, whose duty it must be to declare all acts contrary to the manifest tenor of the Constitution void."[16] John Marshall—who argued the case for ratification in the Virginia Convention long before he became chief justice—famously put the theory into practice in *Marbury v. Madison*, invalidating part of a federal statute on constitutional grounds.

If we follow the original, widely shared understanding of the Constitution, then we should read it to grant considerable authority to counter-majoritarian federal judges, and to countenance a great deal of judicial activism. Judicial restraint, not judicial activism, seems to be the more modern invention. Not everyone believes that the contemporary meaning of the Constitution should track the original understanding. If we are free to adjust the balance between liberty and democracy, between judicial activism and judicial deference, on our own terms, how should we do so? The next section turns to that question.

Constitutional Practice

My primary claim is an empirical one: that we are better off erring on the side of too much judicial activism than too little. Although this argument has not previously been raised to evaluate judicial review, it invokes the familiar trade-off between false negatives and false positives. A failure to invalidate a law that should be declared unconstitutional is a false negative, a failure to detect unconstitutionality (sometimes labeled a Type II error). On the other hand, the erroneous invalidation of a law that should be upheld is a false positive, a wrongful attribution of unconstitutionality (sometimes labeled a Type I error). Legal rules frequently depend on the trade-off between false positives and false negatives. For example, the famous maxim that it is better to let ten guilty people go free than to convict one innocent person suggests that in the context of criminal convictions, false positives are much worse than false negatives. In other contexts, especially regulatory contexts, we draw the opposite conclusion, preferring to over-regulate in order to avoid the risk of under-regulation.

In this section, I argue that in the context of judicial review, false negatives are more harmful than false positives.[17]

But how are we to decide whether false negatives or false positives are worse? If there is no consensus on whether a particular law is constitutional or not, we cannot tell whether the attribution of unconstitutionality is true or false. Perhaps we can avoid this problem by evaluating activism as a whole: Is it better or worse for the polity to have too many false negatives or too many false positives? But even then, we cannot determine whether activism as a whole has positive or negative consequences because we generally cannot agree whether a constitutional decision is good or bad for the polity.

There are two related problems here. For many people, as I have noted, the charge of activism reduces to dislike of the decision. On this formulation, activism is bad by definition because it *always* produces bad results. Even if we escape this problem by redefining activism as I have done, we cannot evaluate it because we cannot agree on whether any particular invalidation is helpful or harmful to the polity. It seems that trying to evaluate judicial activism just mires us in the impossible task of trying to specify which judicial decisions are right and which are wrong or which are good and which are bad.

We do have one lens through which to examine the consequences of judicial activism and judicial restraint: we can use hindsight as a tool to identify decisions that are now universally condemned, and thus about which there is no disagreement. If everyone agrees that a decision was wrong and detrimental, we need not come up with any criteria for evaluating judicial decisions—for the purpose of using a particular decision to explore the consequences of judicial activism or judicial restraint, it is enough that there is universal agreement that it *is* bad. We can then ask whether these universally condemned cases are more likely to be false positives or false negatives.[18]

Coming up with a list of universally condemned Supreme Court cases turns out not to be very difficult for the very reason that they are so widely loathed. No one has a good word to say about them, they turn up in law review articles as everyone's favorite bad example, and they form the core of symposiums on the Supreme Court's worst or most maligned cases. They are rejected by modern cases and never cited positively by the Supreme Court, and they are thoroughly discredited if not technically overruled.[19]

A few ground rules are needed to shear off marginal cases and ensure that we really leave ourselves with the worst of the worst.

We should not include cases about which there is significant disagreement as to their soundness—even if some people would include
them among the worst—lest we devolve back into ideological arguments about the validity of particular judicial invalidations. That rule
will exclude cases such as *Lochner v. New York* and *Roe v. Wade*.
Lochner, which invalidated laws limiting the number of hours that
bakers could work, is a favorite target of liberals accusing the Court
of activism, but is often praised by conservatives. *Roe* invalidated laws
limiting abortion, and is hated by conservatives but praised by liberals. Neither generates sufficient consensus to count as universally
condemned, however strongly each is castigated by some. We should
also exclude cases that are too recent to evaluate objectively; but with
the possible exception of *Bush v. Gore*—which I treat separately in the
next paragraph—I doubt that there are any recent cases that have
generated enough consensus to be universally condemned.[20]

Finally, I suggest that we must exclude two universally condemned
cases that had little practical effect. Cases with little practical effect
are of little use in determining whether they produced more harm
than good, because by definition they produced few consequences at
all. Thus the 1857 case of *Dred Scott v. Sandford*, which invalidated
federal regulation of slavery in the territories and held that free blacks
could not be citizens, was made irrelevant with the start of the Civil
War in 1861 and reversed with the adoption of the Fourteenth
Amendment in 1866. The division over slavery was deepening
throughout the 1850s, and *Dred Scott* probably would have made
little difference regardless of which way the Court ruled. *Bush v. Gore*,
besides being too recent, also had no practical effect: no matter what
the Supreme Court held, either a recount in Florida or a decision by
Congress under the Twelfth Amendment would have put George W.
Bush in the White House. These cases should also be excluded
because in both cases, the Court recognized that it was making an
extraordinary decision but thought it was necessary in order to save
the nation from a constitutional crisis. The *Dred Scott* Court
thought—mistakenly, as it turned out—that it could prevent a civil
war by resolving questions of slavery that were tearing the country
apart. The *Bush* Court thought—this time perhaps correctly—that it
could end the weeks-long national nightmare of an inconclusive
presidential election and prevent a possible lacuna in the presidency.
We cannot put much weight on cases decided under such

extraordinary circumstances, because the Court is more likely to make mistakes no matter what it chooses to do.[21]

With these exclusions, the chronological list of universally condemned cases is short (drumroll, please):

- *Bradwell v. State* and *Minor v. Happersett,* which in 1873 and 1874 upheld state laws prohibiting women from, respectively, practicing law or voting in state elections. *Minor* was overruled by the adoption of the Nineteenth Amendment in 1920; *Bradwell* remained good law until 1971, when it was discredited (but not officially overruled) in *Reed v. Reed.*[22]
- *Plessy v. Ferguson,* which upheld racial segregation in 1896 and remained good law until it was discredited (but, again, not overruled) by *Brown v. Board of Education* in 1954.[23]
- *Abrams v. United States* and three other related 1919 cases, which upheld the censorship of political ideas and remained good law until they were overruled by *Brandenburg v. Ohio* in 1968.[24]
- *Buck v. Bell,* which upheld involuntary sterilization in 1927 on Justice Holmes' famous reasoning that "three generations of imbeciles are enough," and remained good law until it was discredited (but, again, not overruled) in 1942 by *Skinner v. Oklahoma.*[25]
- *Minersville School District v. Gobitis,* which in 1940 allowed a school district to force children to salute the flag even though it violated the children's religious principles. *Gobitis* was explicitly overruled only three years later, in *West Virginia State Board of Education v. Barnette,* in which Justice Jackson famously declared: "If there is any fixed star in our constitutional constellation, it is that no official, high or petty, can prescribe what shall be orthodox in politics, nationalism, religion, or other matters of opinion or force citizens to confess by word or act their faith therein."[26]
- *Hirabayashi v. United States* and *Korematsu v. United States,* which upheld, respectively, curfews on Japanese-Americans and their exclusion from the West Coast (followed by forced relocation to concentration camps) during World War II. Neither case has ever been overruled although the convictions have been expunged and the United States has apologized and paid reparations to those affected by the exclusion and relocation orders.[27]

Each of these cases is universally recognized as wrong. Each also did great damage, not only to the particular plaintiffs but to our society. The two cases limiting women's rights—*Bradwell* and *Minor*—helped to keep women in a state of subordination for almost a century. *Plessy* allowed Jim Crow laws to deepen, racism to become more entrenched, and the status of African-Americans to deteriorate for almost sixty years. We are still feeling the effects of the prolonged period of segregation. *Abrams* and its progeny, by allowing government censorship, led directly to the McCarthy witch hunts of the 1950s; the House Un-American Activities Committee (HUAC) ruined the lives of innocent individuals and encouraged friends, families, and neighbors to turn on one another. The decision in *Buck* led to a rash of involuntary sterilizations: Before *Buck*, an average of about 200 people were involuntarily sterilized each year; between *Buck* and *Skinner* that annual average increased tenfold to more than 2,000.[28] *Minersville*, though short-lived, traumatized innocent children and encouraged a Soviet-like attitude toward forced displays of patriotism. *Korematsu* and *Hirabayashi* upheld the most invidious racially discriminatory regime since slavery, forced thousands to abandon their homes and livelihoods, and encouraged (or at least exacerbated) an anti-Asian bigotry that has since dissipated but not disappeared.

And all of these cases have something else in common: in each case, the Supreme Court *upheld* the challenged governmental action rather than invalidating it. Each is an example of a false negative, a failure to engage in judicial activism. Not a single activist case—a false positive invalidating a state or federal law—makes this first-cut list of worst cases.[29] False negatives are more likely to eventually be repudiated than are false positives. The Supreme Court, it seems, is more likely to make the most egregious mistakes by being too cautious rather than by being too aggressive.[30]

When it comes to judicial activism, then, the problem is in the eye of the beholder: some people applaud the same activist cases that others deplore. But when the Court fails to act—instead deferring to the elected branches—it abdicates its role as guardian of enduring principles against the temporary passions and prejudices of popular majorities. It is thus no surprise that with historical hindsight we sometimes come to regret those passions and prejudices and fault the Court for its passivity. History teaches us that it is better to allow a few good laws to be blocked than to permit truly terrible laws to remain on the books as a result of judicial timidity or restraint.

Ideally, the Court should be like Baby Bear: it should get everything just right, engaging in activism when, and only when, We the People act in ways that we will later consider shameful or regrettable. But that perfection is impossible, and so we must choose between a Court that views its role narrowly and a Court that views its role broadly, between a more deferential Court and a more activist Court. Both kinds of Court will sometimes be controversial, and both will make mistakes. But history teaches us that the false negatives—the cases in which a deferential Court fails to invalidate governmental acts—are of much more enduring, and detrimental, significance. Only a Court inclined toward activism will vigilantly avoid such cases, and hence we need more judicial activism.

In evaluating the appropriate role of the judiciary in a democracy, theory can take us only so far. No theory can draw the line between too many and too few judicial invalidations, nor specify parameters or constraints that produce a perfect balance. We are left with the pragmatic task of making the best trade-off between false negatives and false positives, and only an examination of the actual consequences of judicial activism or restraint can inform that decision. What such an examination teaches us is that too little judicial activism is worse than too much. We most regret the cases in which the Supreme Court failed to prevent popular majorities from making serious constitutional mistakes. If we wish to avoid such regrets in the future, we should encourage more judicial activism, not less.

Notes

1. McCulloch v. Maryland, 17 U.S. 316 (1819). For histories of the political disputes over the Bank of the United States, see, for example, Bray Hammond; Daniel Walker, 373–386; John M. McFaul; Robert V. Remini; Sean Wilentz, 202–216, 360–374, 392–403, 436–455.
2. Marbury v. Madison, 5 U.S. 137 (1803); Martin v. Hunter's Lessee, 14 U.S. 304 (1816). On *Marbury*'s benign reception, see, for example, Robert Lowry Clinton, 102; Howard E. Dean, 27; Michael J. Klarman, "How Great Were the 'Great' Marshall Court Decisions?," 87. On the history of polycentric constitutionalism and its relationship to judicial review, see Daniel A. Farber, 38.
3. In the Constitutional Convention, Madison seconded a motion—made by Charles Pinckney of South Carolina—arguing that a federal legislative veto over state laws was "absolutely necessary to a

perfect system." James Madison, 88 (June 8) [hereinafter "Madison's Notes"]. He later explained that his support derived from his view that "[c]onfidence cannot be put in the State Tribunals as guardians of the National authority and interests" (304–305 [July 17]). The proposal was ultimately rejected by a margin of seven states to three (305 [July 17]).

4. Roe v. Wade, 410 U.S. 113 (1973); Citizens United v. FEC, 558 U.S. 310 (2010). For a good description, with examples, of how liberals and conservatives have made "activism" a meaningless pejorative, see Barry Friedman, 343–346.

5. Although it does seem suspicious that some liberals who praised the rulings of the Warren and Burger Courts have more recently become critics of judicial activism and that some conservatives who used to accuse the Court of activism have lately muted their criticism. Judicial activism, it seems, has many fair-weather friends, as do the various responses to it (including popular constitutionalism and grand theories of interpretation).

6. For my own previous description and critique of these "grand theories" of judicial interpretation, see Daniel A. Farber and Suzanna Sherry.

7. On the Eleventh Amendment and its "fundamental postulates," see, for example, Alden v. Maine, 527 U.S. 706 (1999). The dissenting opinion in *Citizens United*, 558 U.S., demonstrates that the majority's invalidation of campaign finance limits is inconsistent with the original intent. As for "maximalism," the quintessential minimalist, Cass Sunstein, writes that "there are times and places in which minimalism is rightly abandoned." Sunstein, 106; see also Sunstein, *One Case at a Time: Judicial Minimalism on the Supreme Court*, 56–60.

8. For some examples of popular constitutionalist scholarship, see Larry D. Kramer; Richard D. Parker; Jamin B. Raskin; Mark Tushnet; Jeremy Waldron.

9. See, for example, Friedman, *The Will of the People*; Michael J. Klarman, *From Jim Crow to Civil Rights: The Supreme Court and the Struggle for Racial Equality*; Jeffrey Rosen; Gerald N. Rosenberg.

10. See Daniel A. Farber and Suzanna Sherry, *Judgment Calls: Principle and Politics in Constitutional Law* (New York: Oxford University Press, 2009).

11. On dividing power as a method of cabining majority tyranny, the classic expositions are James Madison, *Federalist Papers* 10 and 51, in Alexander Hamilton, James Madison, and John Jay, *The Federalist Papers*, ed. Clinton Rossiter, 77, 320. See also Robert A. Dahl, 24 ("A substantial number of the Framers believed that they must erect

constitutional barriers to popular rule"); Jenna Bednar, 217 (detailing Madison's scheme for controlling democratic majorities).

12. Alexander M. Bickel, 26; Henry M. Hart Jr., 84, 99; John Hart Ely.

13. Robert H. Jackson, 79.

14. G. Edward White, 787, 794–795. See also Saul Cornell; Forrest McDonald.

15. "Madison's Notes," 39 (May 31) (Gerry, Sherman), 42 (May 31) (Randolph "turbulence and follies"), 76 (June 6) (Madison "inconveniencies"), 193 (June 26) (Madison "transient impressions"), 339 (July 21) (Morris); *The Records of the Federal Convention of 1787*, 3 vols., ed. Max Farrand, 1:26–27 (Randolph "chief danger"); "Letter from Agrippa to the Massachusetts Convention (Feb. 5, 1788)" in *The Complete Anti-Federalist*, 7 vols., ed. Herbert J. Storing, 4:111 (Agrippa), "Essay by a Farmer (Feb. 15, 1788)," 5:15 (Maryland "Farmer").

16. Hamilton, *Federalist Paper 78*, 466.

17. In almost any situation, the labeling can be reversed: failing to acquit an innocent person can be seen as a false negative, for example, and attributing constitutionality can be seen as a false positive. Because the trade-off is context-dependent, we cannot conclude that false negatives are *always* worse (or better) than false positives. For these reasons, the labels themselves are matters of convenience; the trade-off remains the same regardless of which labels we attach.

18. We could, in theory, also examine cases for which there is universal support, but those cases are even rarer than the cases that are universally condemned. On everything from *Marbury v. Madison* to the New Deal revolution to the First Amendment, there are substantial numbers of modern dissenters. The cases that can most plausibly be viewed as commanding a positive consensus are *Brown v. Board of Education*, 347 U.S. 483 (1954) (which outlawed segregated schools) and *Loving v. Virginia*, 388 U.S. 1 (1967) (which invalidated anti-miscegenation laws). Even assuming that they are universally applauded—an assumption that may or may not be warranted—both were examples of judicial activism, invalidating laws enacted by majoritarian state legislatures. Both cases thus suggest that judicial activism is beneficial, and thus support my thesis to the extent they are relevant at all.

19. See, for example, "Symposium: Supreme Mistakes," *Pepperdine Law Review* 39 (2011), 1: symposium participants selected three of the exemplary cases I use in this chapter (*Plessy, Buck,* and *Korematsu*) plus *Dred Scott*—which, as I explain, is a poor example—and *Erie Railroad Co. v. Tompkins*, 304 U.S. 64 (1938), which is condemned primarily because modern scholars have subsequently invoked it as a way to attack activist judicial review (see *Pepperdine Law Review* 39, 149–153).

See also Jamal Greene, 379 (listing *Dred Scott, Plessy, Korematsu,* and *Lochner*—the last of which is in fact *not* universally condemned).

20. Lochner v. New York, 198 U.S. 45 (1905); Roe v. Wade, 410 U.S. 113 (1973); Bush v. Gore, 531 U.S. 98 (2000). That *Roe* is not universally condemned needs no citation. Praise for *Lochner* includes David E. Bernstein; Michael S. Greve, 232, 272, 324, 338.

21. Dred Scott v. Sandford, 60 U.S. 393 (1856); Bush v. Gore, 531 U.S. 98 (2000).

22. Bradwell v. State, 83 U.S. 130 (1873); Minor v. Happersett, 88 U.S. 162 (1874); Reed v. Reed, 404 U.S. 71 (1971).

23. Plessy v. Ferguson, 163 U.S. 537 (1896); Brown v. Board of Education, 347 U.S. 483 (1954).

24. Abrams v. United States, 250 U.S. 616 (1919); Schenck v. United States, 249 U.S. 47 (1919); Frohwerk v. United States, 249 U.S. 204 (1919); Debs v. United States, 249 U.S. 211 (1919); Brandenburg v. Ohio, 395 U.S. 444 (1969).

25. Buck v. Bell, 274 U.S. 200 (1927); Skinner v. Oklahoma, 316 U.S. 535 (1942).

26. Minersville School Dist. v. Gobitis, 310 U.S. 586 (1940); West Virginia Bd. of Educ. v. Barnette, 319 U.S. 624 (1943).

27. Korematsu v. United States, 323 U.S. 214 (1944); Hirabayashi v. United States, 320 U.S. 81 (1943). Korematsu's conviction was vacated in Korematsu v. United States, 584 F. Supp. 1406 (N.D. Cal. 1984); Hirabayashi's conviction was vacated in Hirabayashi v. United States, 627 F. Supp. 1445 (W.D. Wash. 1986), *aff'd in relevant part,* 828 F.2d 591 (9th Cir. 1987). Reparations were awarded by Act of Aug. 10, 1988, Pub. L. No. 100–383, 102 Stat. 903 (1988) (codified as amended at 50 U.S.C. §§ 1989–1989b).

28. Victoria F. Nourse, 31.

29. Even if you are not persuaded that *Dred Scott* and/or *Bush* should be excluded, the point remains the same. Counting both *Dred Scott* and *Bush,* as well as all of the cases in my list, there are thirteen universally condemned cases. Only two of the thirteen are activist, suggesting that mistakes are more likely when the Court is deferential. And although this list is not exhaustive, it probably contains most—if not all—of the cases that more than a handful of Americans (with or without legal training) would consider abhorrent.

30. I suspect that within twenty-five years we will have another case to add to the list, also a failure to invalidate a law that infringed on both equality and intimate personal liberty. In 1986 in *Bowers v. Hardwick,* 478 U.S. 186 (1986), the Supreme Court upheld state prohibitions on homosexual sodomy. Less than two decades later, in *Lawrence v. Texas,* 539 U.S. 558 (2003), the Court overruled *Bowers,* unequivocally condemning it

as "not correct when it was decided, and . . . not correct today" (560). Although there is currently some controversy about whether the Court was right in *Lawrence*, I believe that discrimination on the basis of sexual orientation—including limitations on what sexual acts consenting adults may engage in—will eventually be as universally rejected as racial discrimination. *Bowers* and *Lawrence* will be the *Plessy* and *Brown v. Board of Education* of a not-too-distant future generation.

Bibliography

Bednar, Jenna. "The Madisonian Scheme to Control the National Government." In *James Madison: The Theory and Practice of Republican Government*, edited by Samuel Kernell, 217–242. Stanford: Stanford University Press, 2003.

Bernstein, David E. *Rehabilitating Lochner: Defending Individual Rights Against Progressive Reform*. Chicago: University of Chicago Press, 2011.

Bickel, Alexander M. *The Least Dangerous Branch: The Supreme Court at the Bar of Politics*. Binghamton, NY: Bobbs-Merrill, 1962.

Clinton, Robert Lowry. *Marbury v. Madison and Judicial Review*. Lawrence: University of Kansas Press, 1989.

Cornell, Saul. *The Other Founders: Anti-Federalism and the Dissenting Tradition in American, 1788–1821*. Chapel Hill: University of North Carolina Press, 1999.

Dahl, Robert A. *How Democratic is the American Constitution*. New Haven, CT: Yale University Press, 2001.

Dean, Howard E. *Judicial Review and Democracy*. New York: Random House (1966).

Ely, John Hart. *Democracy and Distrust: A Theory of Judicial Review*. Cambridge, MA: Harvard University Press, 1980.

Farber, Daniel A. "Judicial Review and Its Alternatives: An American Tale." *Wake Forest Law Review* 415 (2003).

Farber, Daniel A., and Susan Sherry. *Desperately Seeking Certainty: The Misguided Quest for Constitutional Foundations*. Chicago: University of Chicago Press, 2002.

Farrand, Max, ed. *The Records of the Federal Convention of 1787*. 3 vols. New Haven, CT: Yale University Press, 1937.

Friedman, Barry. *The Will of the People: How Public Opinion Has Influenced the Supreme Court and Shaped the Meaning of the Constitution*. New York: Farrar, Straus and Giroux, 2009.

Greene, Jamal. "The Anticanon." *Harvard Law Review* 125 (2011), 379.

Greve, Michael S. *The Upside-Down Constitution*. Cambridge, MA: Harvard University Press, 2012.

Hamilton, Alexander, James Madison, and John Jay. *The Federalist Papers*. Edited by Clinton Rossiter. New York: Mentor, 1961.

Hammond, Bray. *Banks and Politics in America from the Revolution to the Civil War*. Princeton, NJ: Princeton University Press, 1957.

Hart, Henry M. Jr. "Foreword: The Time Chart of the Justices." *Harvard Law Review* 73 (1959).

Howe, Daniel Walker. *What God Hath Wrought: The Transformation of America, 1815–1848*. New York: Oxford University Press, 2007.

Jackson, Robert H. *The Supreme Court in the American System of Government*. Cambridge, MA: Harvard University Press, 1955.

Klarman, Michael J. "How Great Were the 'Great' Marshall Court Decisions?" *Virginia Law Review* 1111 (2001).

———. *From Jim Crow to Civil Rights: The Supreme Court and the Struggle for Racial Equality*. New York: Oxford University Press, 2004.

Kramer, Larry D. *The People Themselves: Popular Constitutionalism and Judicial Review*. New York: Oxford University Press, 2004.

Madison, James. *Notes of Debates in the Federal Convention of 1787*. Edited by Adrienne Koch. Athens: Ohio University Press, 1966.

McDonald, Forrest. *Novus Ordo Seclorum: The Intellectual Origins of the Constitution*. Lawrence: University Press of Kansas, 1985.

McFaul, John M. *The Politics of Jacksonian Finance*. Ithaca, NY: Cornell University Press, 1972.

Nourse, Victoria F. *In Reckless Hands: Skinner v. Oklahoma and the Near Triumph of American Eugenics*. New York: Norton, 2008.

Parker, Richard D. *"Here, the People Rule": A Constitutional Populist Manifesto*. Cambridge, MA: Harvard University Press, 1994.

Raskin, Jamin B. *Overruling Democracy: The Supreme Court vs. The American People*. New York: Routledge, 2003.

Remini, Robert V. *Andrew Jackson and the Bank War*. New York: Norton, 1967.

Rosen, Jeffrey. *The Most Democratic Branch: How the Courts Serve America*. New York: Oxford University Press, 2006.

Rosenberg, Gerald N. *The Hollow Hope: Can Courts Bring About Social Change?* 2nd ed. Chicago: University of Chicago Press, 2008.

Storing, Herbert J., ed. *The Complete Anti-Federalist*. 7 vols. Chicago: University of Chicago Press, 1981.

Sunstein, Cass R. *One Case at a Time: Judicial Minimalism on the Supreme Court*. Cambridge, MA: Harvard University Press, 1999.

———. "Of Snakes and Butterflies: A Reply." *Columbia Law Review* 2234 (2006).

"Symposium: Supreme Mistakes." *Pepperdine Law Review* 39 (2011).

Tushnet, Mark. *Taking the Constitution Away From the Courts*. Princeton, NJ: Princeton University Press, 1999.

Waldron, Jeremy. *The Dignity of Legislation.* New York: Cambridge University Press, 1999.

White, G. Edward. "Reading the Guarantee Clause." *University of Colorado Law Review* 65 (1994).

Wilentz, Sean. *The Rise of American Democracy.* New York: Norton, 2005.

Chapter 2

Legal Realism, Innate Morality, and the Structural Role of the Supreme Court in the U.S. Constitutional Democracy

Karl Coplan

Introduction

"It is emphatically the province . . . of the [courts] to say what the law is."[1] So declared Chief Justice Marshall more than two hundred years ago in *Marbury v. Madison*, in an affirmative and enduring statement of the structural finality of judicial review in resolving questions of constitutional interpretation in the United States' constitutional democracy. Yet Marshall's use of the definite article—"the law"—reflects a certain deterministic assumption about the nature of law that has not withstood the test of time. While nineteenth-century scholars and jurists may have largely shared this deterministic vision of the law, either as a result of natural law assumptions underlying the common law processes or as a matter of the legal formalism that prevailed by the late nineteenth century, the legal realists of the turn of the twentieth century provided a key insight into the nature of the judicial process: law, it turns out, was not determinate at all. Impeccable legal reasoning could be used to support more than one outcome in a large proportion of the cases decided by the appellate courts. According to the realists, rather than declaring what the law is, courts declare "law,"[2] making policy choices in the process. These policy choices are informed more by each individual jurist's background and sense of fairness than by formal reasoning from legal rules.

While legal realism may never have caught on with academics and philosophers as a coherent theory of jurisprudence, its key insights—that law is indeterminate in many cases and that judges make rulings in those cases based on a visceral sense of fairness and justice as applied to the facts of the case—retain wide acceptance among practicing lawyers and legal academics to this day.[3] The legal realists were largely concerned with the practical, lawyerly problem of predicting how a court would rule when presented with a new fact situation. Yet this approach invites a behavioralist inquiry into whether the resolution of indeterminate legal problems might nevertheless be predictable as a matter of human behavior (judges being human after all). Recent psychological research has posited that a sense of fairness and justice may be innate and evolved in human nature—that certain moral precepts are shared across religions, national boundaries, cultures, and ages. The existence of an innate human sense of fairness might seem to support the long-abandoned notion of natural law as a source of legal principles and predictability. The rub is that this same research shows that while people generally recognize shared principles of fairness, different people place different relative values on some of these shared principles. In particular, these studies have shown that, across cultures, people who self-identify as liberals tend to value the moral precepts of group loyalty and respect for tradition and authority less than people who self-identify as conservatives. Because these different political identifications place different relative values on these principles, an innate sense of justice common to humans seems also to be indeterminate and an inadequate predictor of judicial decision making generally.

Moreover, the realists' insight that formal legal reasoning is indeterminate and that judges make policy choices and apply their subjective sense of fairness in resolving the indeterminate cases casts doubt on the fundamental theoretical basis of judicial review in the United States constitutional system. If judges do not declare the law, as Chief Justice Marshall articulated it, but rather choose law out of an indeterminate range of outcomes supportable by legitimate legal reasoning, basing their choices on idiosyncratic notions of policy and fairness, then are not judges making legislative choices that more properly belong with the legislature? If the justification for judicial review is the inherent judicial function of applying the rule of decision required by a superior legal document (the United States Constitution, with its Supremacy Clause) as against an inferior legal document (congressional legislation), does not this theoretical justification fall apart in those cases where accepted constitutional legal reasoning will support more than one outcome, and the judicial choice of outcomes is based on something other than ineluctable legal reasoning? And if this judicial choice of outcomes in those indeterminate cases is based on differing value systems that correlate well with different political alignments, the inherently political nature of this choice of outcomes would also seem to argue strongly that these choices be assigned to the more politically responsive branches of government, and not to unelected judges.

Yet these political arguments against judicial review would ignore the judiciary's (and particularly the United States Supreme Court's) structural role as the final arbiter of constitutional limits on government action. The Constitution, together with accepted modes of constitutional legal reasoning, may fail to provide a determinate answer, and the answer a particular judge or justice gives in those indeterminate cases may correlate well with her own political proclivities (which may be contrary to those of a duly elected legislative majority). Nevertheless, a constitutional form of government requires some body with final say over the interpretation of the Constitution. The alternative—leaving the legislature as the final judge of its own powers—risks rendering constitutional limits on government unenforceable. Although the Framers may not have been legal realists, they anticipated judicial review and understood the value of leaving the final interpretation of the Constitution to judges with life tenure, who would not have to run for reelection, thus removing immediate political advantages from consideration in resolving questions of constitutional interpretation. In doing so, they served a deeply felt social need for neutrality and finality in resolving the inevitable political disputes that would arise from conflicts between states in a federal system, competing branches of government at the federal level, and an empowered citizenry.

In the second section, this chapter explores the competing jurisprudential theories of formalism and realism, the problems posed by the frequent indeterminacy of law, and the synthesis represented by legal process theory. The third section explores possible nonformalist determinants of the judicial decision-making process, specifically the role of moral intuition and the freedom of will of judges. The fourth section then seeks to reconcile the institution of constitutional judicial review with a moral intuitionist understanding of legal realism, based on the structural role of the Supreme Court as the ultimate check and final arbiter of those disputes not entrusted to the political branches. Political acceptance of the Supreme Court's resolution of the 2000 election in its *Bush v. Gore* decision exemplifies political acceptance of this structural role of the Court even when it acts without a firm formalist basis. The final section draws some conclusions about the relationship between a moral intuitionist's understanding of legal realism, accusations of "judicial activism," and the judicial selection process. The chapter then concludes with the suggestion that the Supreme Court's ultimate resolution of the same-sex marriage controversy may provide an appropriate test of the relative strengths of legal formalism and moral intuitionism as competing descriptions of the Supreme Court's decision-making process.

Formalism, Realism, and the Problem of Indeterminacy

The idealized popular conception of law is a formalist one. In this view, law is a set of rules that define enforceable rights and impermissible conduct and establish consequences for the breach of rights and standards of conduct. Application of the law to a given case is an exercise in pure logic: the law is the major premise of a logical syllogism, while the facts of a given case fit (or do not fit) the law's syllogistic rule. Thus, in a negligence case, the law states a major premise: a party who suffers legal damage proximately caused by another party who has failed to exercise reasonable care is entitled to recover his damages. The facts provide the minor premise: Jim Jones ran a red light (breaching his duty of reasonable care) and ran into Sam Smith, breaking his leg (proximately causing injury to Smith). The legal conclusion follows ineluctably: Jones must pay damages to Smith.

Under this view of the law, law and logic dictate one correct, determinate answer to every legal problem. A judge's sympathies, prejudices, policy preferences, and ideology play no part in determining the result in any case: a judge must reach the conclusion demanded by law's "rules" even if the judge considers the result unfair. This idealized conception of the nature of law is embodied in the aphorism that the United States is a "[nation] of laws and not of men"[5]—that is, our nation is governed by a set of legal rules, not by the arbitrary whim of individual decision-makers.

These determinist assumptions about the nature of law have deep roots in American jurisprudence. Blackstone's *Commentaries on the Law of England*, which would have been an essential part of the education of those of the Framers with legal training, did not admit that application of law could result in more than one correct result. In expounding on the imperative that judges adhere to precedent, Blackstone admits of an exception where the prior precedent is incorrect in terms that make clear that law can provide only one "correct" result:

> [T]his rule admits of exception, where the former determination is most evidently contrary to reason; much more if it be clearly contrary to the divine law. But even in such cases the subsequent judges do not pretend to make a new law, but to vindicate the old one from misrepresentation. For if it be found that the former decision is manifestly absurd or unjust, it is declared, not that such a sentence was bad law, but that it was not law.[6]

The deterministic assumption underlying this passage is clear: if law permitted more than one correct result, then the overruling of precedent would constitute a change in the law (a change from one possible correct result to another possible correct result). By rejecting the notion that law can change, Blackstone's description of the common law endorses determinacy. The law always provided one correct result; it just took a later jurist to recognize that an earlier jurist's resolution was "incorrect." Blackstone also recounts a formalist formulation of the concept of law: "lawyers . . . tell us, that the law is the perfection of reason, that it always intends to conform thereto, and that what is not reason is not law."[7]

To be sure, eighteenth-century determinism had natural law underpinnings as much as it was based on legal formalism. Blackstone's *Commentaries* explicitly rely on a theistic natural law as "foundational" law, which common law and legislative acts may not countermand.[8] Much has been written about the American Founders' reliance on natural law concepts, particularly in the Declaration of Independence, which explicitly relies on natural law to justify a rejection of the colonies' legal obligations to Britain.[9] Chief Justice John

Marshall's constitutional jurisprudence has likewise been described as "conclusions from deterministic natural law principles embedded in either the text or spirit of the constitutional document when it was framed."[10]

Natural law is premised on the idea that certain notions of appropriate conduct and interrelationships are universally shared by human beings. These notions are seen as appropriate foundational principles for legal rules governing punishment and compensation. Blackstone considers natural law precepts to be reason's participation in the eternal law, and the eternal law is the law by which God governs the universe. On the other hand, Blackstone also indicates that there may sometimes be overlap between natural law and revealed divine law, as is the case in the Ten Commandments, even the latter merely reinforces through revelation the natural principles of right conduct that are accessible to all reasoning human beings. This view of a nontheistic natural law is shared not only by Thomas Aquinas, but also by most natural law thinkers who consider it to be intrinsic to the human condition and universally shared even without divine inspiration.[11]

By the late nineteenth century, this formalist, natural law concept of legal decision making was the dominant mode of legal thought in the United States. Formalism was thought to cabin judicial discretion and eliminate the influence of politics, ideology, and emotion from the law. Rather, pure detached logic based on preexisting rules would provide a neutral answer for every legal question. Christopher Columbus Langdell incorporated this formalism into legal education, developing a curriculum for Harvard Law School that substituted the casebooks and the Socratic method for lectures and treatises such as Blackstone's *Commentaries*; students were expected to discover the preexisting principles of common law by reading the cases and engaging in Socratic dialogue. The formalists viewed law as a branch of scientific inquiry; pure reason based on scientific evidence would lead to one, and only one, correct result. Although based on pure reason (and not divine revelation), legal formalism continued to incorporate a form of natural law: legal principles were thought to preexist individual factual applications. Judges did not declare the law; rather, they discovered the law. Pragmatism and instrumentalism had no place in formalist legal thought: legal principles, logically applied, necessarily prevailed no matter what the consequences.

Formalists sought to organize legal rules by establishing comprehensive categories of cases. The Supreme Court's anti-economic regulation decision in *Lochner v. New York* can be seen as the high-water mark of the influence of legal formalism.[12] The Court essentially declared that New York's attempt to regulate the hours and working conditions in the baking trade did not fall into the "police power" category, but rather violated substantive rights to "liberty" and "freedom of contract."[13] The Court rejected the New York Legislature's health-based rationale for the regulation, reasoning that the baker's trade was "in and of itself, . . . not an unhealthy one" leaving the adjustment of relative economic power between employer and employee as the only plausible purpose of the legislation—a purpose, in the view of the majority, that was not within the preexisting logical category of legitimate state police power. The determinative factor— that the baker's trade was not "intrinsically unhealthy"—was presumably determined based on pure rational deduction from preexisting principles of law.

By the early part of the twentieth century, influential U.S. legal thinkers began to question the premises of legal formalism, thus planting the seeds of legal realism.[14] Justice Oliver Wendell Holmes famously observed in his 1881 book, *The Common Law*, "The life of the law has not been logic: it has been experience."[15] This contradicted formalism's premise that legal decision making was an exercise in pure rational thought. And, in what was to become the legal realists' critical insight, Justice Holmes observed that common law reasoning "decides the case first and determines the principle afterwards."[16]

Justice Holmes ultimately recognized that common law rules reflected value-laden policy choices. He gave the example of common law decisions that allowed no recovery for competitive business injury, while providing injunctive relief against labor boycotts causing business injury.[17] In his later writings, he rejected the determinism of classical legal formalism and acknowledged the legislative character of judicial decision making: "Behind the logical form lies a judgment as to the relative worth and importance of competing legislative grounds, often an inarticulate and unconscious judgment, it is true, and yet the very root and nerve of the whole proceeding."[18] Holmes likewise rejected the notion of determinacy underlying classical legal formalism, and criticized the idea that legal principles "can be worked out like mathematics from some general axioms of conduct."[19]

Justice Holmes carried his evolving skepticism with him while a justice of the Supreme Court. Recognition that judicial decision making most often reflected political value judgments more appropriately left to the legislature, Justice Holmes was more reluctant than his brethren to disturb legislative judgments. He dissented in *Lochner*, criticizing the majority for seeking to import a political policy choice into constitutional law, famously arguing that "[t]he Fourteenth Amendment does not enact Mr. Herbert Spencer's Social Statics."[20]

Rejecting the absolutism of formalism, Justice Holmes also adopted a more explicitly open-textured, evolutionary approach to constitutional judicial review. In *Missouri v. Holland*, he opined:

> [W]hen we are dealing with words that also are a constituent act, like the Constitution of the United States, we must realize that they have called into life a being the development of which could not have been foreseen completely by the most gifted of its begetters. . . . The case before us must be considered in the light of our whole experience and not merely in that of what was said a hundred years ago. . . . We must consider what this country has become in deciding what [the 10th] Amendment has reserved.[21]

Justice Holmes's legal writings set the groundwork for the legal realist movement of the 1920s and 1930s. Building on Justice Holmes's key (but understated) insights, the legal realists rejected the idea that law provided objective, determinate resolution to all legal disputes. Rather, the realists posited a substantial class of open, indeterminate cases—particularly those cases reaching the appellate courts—in which more than one result was supportable by accepted legal reasoning. The realists argued that judges responded with idiosyncratic notions of fundamental fairness to the appeal of the facts of individual cases, and came up with legal rationalizations for their opinions after the fact. Professor Karl Llewellyn famously compiled a list of paired, opposing rules of statutory construction, leading to the conclusion that, far from being deterministic, common law legal reasoning could be used to support either outcome in many contested issues of statutory construction.[22]

A leading realist, Judge Joseph Hutcheson frankly described the process of judicial decision making as one of judicial hunch followed by a legalistic "apologia": "[T]he judge really decides by feeling, and not by judgment; by 'hunching' and not by ratiocination, [such] ratiocination appear[ing] only in the opinion."[23] Leading realist writer Jerome Frank (later a judge on the United States Court of Appeals for the Second Circuit) generalized from Judge Hutcheson's observation and posited the following:

> The process of judging, so the psychologists tell us, seldom begins with a premise from which a conclusion is subsequently worked out. Judging begins rather the other way around—with a conclusion more or less vaguely formed; a man ordinarily starts with such a conclusion and afterwards tries to find premises which will substantiate it. If he cannot, to his satisfaction, find proper arguments to link up his conclusion with premises which he finds acceptable, he will, unless he is arbitrary or mad, reject the conclusion and seek another.[24]

Judge Benjamin Cardozo similarly confessed that judicial decision making "is not discovery, but creation."[25] To the realists, legal formalism was a pernicious myth and a fairy tale.

Rather than condemning the level of judicial discretion (and judicial policy making) implicit in this view of the judicial process as contrary to democratic governance, however, some legal realists celebrated indeterminacy as an opportunity to bring conscious policy making into the judicial process in pursuit of progressive social change. Jerome Frank argued that a realist acknowledgment of the open-ended nature of judicial decision making should allow more frank and conscious consideration of the social and economic impacts of judicial decisions, that judges should practice equity in the cases before them rather than apply law.[26] Karl Llewellyn argued for a "conception of law as a means to social ends and not as an end in itself," and argued "'[l]aw' without effect approaches zero in its meaning."[27] Other realists, however, were less concerned with changing the nature of judicial decision making than with improving the lawyers' skill at predicting judicial responses to idiosyncratic factual scenarios; to them, legal realism meant a realistic approach to advising clients.[28]

Legal realism influenced United States' legal thought in profound ways. It gave rise to the Critical Legal Theory movement, which embraced realism's indeterminacy premise and argued that judicial lawmaking was no more than an instrumentalist means by which the dominant race, class, and gender maintained its hold on power and wealth.[29]

Perhaps more profoundly, legal realism (as the antithesis to the prevailing natural law formalism) gave rise to a synthesis of sorts in the legal process school of positivism of H.L.A. Hart, Albert Sacks, and Herbert Wechsler. The legal process school accepted realism's posit of the partial indeterminacy of law, rejected formalism's natural law predicates in favor of a positivist definition of law as a construct of human government institutions, and sought to cabin judicial arbitrariness through its recognition of the institutional roles and limitations of lawmaking institutions (including the courts) and adherence to rules-based precedent based on neutral principles.[30] Hart emphatically rejected what he called the "rules skepticism" of the realists. His process theory thus shares with formalism the idea that legal reasoning (application of rules) is the primary driver of legitimate judicial decision making.[31]

Realism also lives on in the political science academy, where, distinct from their cousins in legal academia, the so-called attitudinalists posit that (especially at the Supreme Court level) individual judicial attitudes and policy preferences are a better predictor of judicial votes than legal reasoning.[32] Indeed, in 1994, one political science writer asserted that he was not "[aware of one] political scientist who would take plain meaning, intent of the framers, and precedent as good explanations of what the justices do in making decisions."[33]

While legal academics may avoid the language of realism in their writings, the realist premises of indeterminacy and suspicion that judicial law "declaring" is really judicial policy making continue to pervade the assumptions of lawyers, judges (in moments of candor), and even the very academics who dismiss realism as a valid descriptive theory. It is a cliché among legal academics "that we are all realists now."[34] Certainly, litigators know that the identity of the judge has a profound effect on the odds of winning a case, and will make extraordinary efforts to get their case before an ideologically receptive panel.[35] Judge (now Justice) Sotomayor, speaking candidly before an audience of law students, said, the "court of appeals is where policy is made."[36] Judge Posner of the United States Court of Appeals for the Seventh Circuit recently published a book whose entire premise is frankly realist: that law is indeterminate in many cases, and that in such cases, judges make policy choices or rely on intuitions of fairness to reach results. More importantly, echoing Hutcheson, Frank, and Cardozo, Judge Posner posits that the process of judicial decision making consists first of an initial inclination, followed by testing that inclination against available avenues of formalist legal reasoning. In other words, the decision comes first, and the rationale comes later. Judge Posner concludes that the Supreme Court is a frankly political court, not a court of law, and should be accepted as such.[37]

Intuitive acceptance of the premises of realism persists not only among legal insiders (practitioners, judges, and academics), but among the public as well. A 2001 survey of public attitudes about the Supreme Court revealed that, while respondents shared the idealized vision that the Supreme Court should decide cases without regard to the ideology or political party of the justices, substantial majorities believed that individual judicial ideology (85.1 percent) and individual judicial party affiliation (69.9 percent) in fact had either "some impact" or a "large impact" on justices' decisions.[38]

But normative resistance to the realist premise is even more persistent. The realist premises may seem true, but they cannot be right in a normative sense. Few argue that a judicial branch of government with the power to annul legislation should be ruled by individual policy preferences and partisan loyalties. Acceptance of the realist premises of indeterminacy and judicial idiosyncrasy seems at war with one of the foundations of American constitutional law—the principle of judicial review. Indeed, without judicial review constitutional law does not really exist as a legal discipline at all. But if judges make policy choices, then judges are acting in a political capacity and would seem to have no institutional or structural claim to reject the enactments of the more popularly responsive Congress and state legislatures.

Even more unsettling are the unresolved questions laid bare by realism's premise: if legal rules in the form of constitutional text and precedent do not explain judicial behavior, what exactly does? Are judicial decisions truly rank political choices completely unfettered by law? What is the source of the decisive judicial "hunch" that several realist judges have referred to?

The remainder of this chapter explores the role of moral intuition in explaining judicial decision making, and the implications of this role for the structural efficacy (if not legitimacy) of judicial review in our constitutional system.

Searching for the Determinants of an Indeterminate System of Law: The Role of Moral Intuition and the Conundrum of Free Will

To legal formalists, the realist vision of the judicial process is something of a nightmare: rather than the rule of law, realist judges would rule based on personal whim—at best, legislating from the bench and at worst, arbitrarily deciding cases based on personal partisanship and venality. To borrow from Robert Frost, realist adjudication is like "playing tennis with the net down."[39] There seem to be no objective rules for assessing the quality, or even the legitimacy of judicial decision making.[40] Realist judging by life-tenured judges thus appears to be a form of despotism, not a legitimate institution in a constitutional democracy.

But judging in a realist world is not quite the free-for-all that realist premises might seem to imply. Several thoughtful authors have detailed the genuine constraints on freewheeling policy making by judges. These constraints include the expectation that judges will write an opinion justifying their decisions based on formal legal reasoning relying on text and precedent, the possibility of appellate reversal, judges' reputational concerns (including reputation among fellow judges, the public, and academics), the moderating effects of collaborative decision making on appellate panels, and ultimately, the judge's own self-respect and desire to be a good, impartial judge.[41] For the purpose of considering the Supreme Court's role in reviewing the constitutionality of acts by other government institutions, however, most of these constraints are quite weak: Supreme Court justices in constitutional cases cannot be reversed (apart from the extraordinarily difficult and rare process of constitutional amendment) and are relatively impervious to their reputations among the public, their peers, and particularly among academics.[42] Accounts of the Supreme Court conference process reveal that there is little collaborative decision making in the (usually determinative) initial conference vote.[43] Supreme Court justices now delegate much of the work of opinion drafting to law clerks, blunting the constraints of the need to articulate conventional legal reasons to support decisions. In any event, the premise of indeterminacy is that cogent legal reasoning will most often support more than one unique conclusion, so that the constraints of cogent opinion writing do not often preclude judicial discretion about the result.

This leaves the justices' own self-respect and desire for judicial legitimacy as the principle constraint on the raw exercise of judicial power by Supreme Court justices. Very few judges are avowed instrumentalists, self-consciously exercising judicial power to achieve their personal policy and political preferences. As Judge Posner points out, practically all federal judges are people who see themselves as (and strive to be) "good" judges, that is, judges who decide cases impartially.[44] Most judges, presumably including Supreme Court justices, will consciously seek to avoid making biased or result-oriented decisions.

This sort of judicial self-restraint, however, does little to mitigate or prevent the effects of preconscious or unconscious result biases on the part of judges. Professor Dan Simon has performed a fascinating analysis of the Gestalt psychology of judicial decision making.[45] Professor Simon posits that the judicial "hunch" is in fact the gelling of a complex series of coherent sets of premises and inferences in which the judge considers multiple competing and related premises, eventually selecting the combination of premises most closely aligned with her core beliefs to form a coherent result (that is, one with minimal cognitive dissonance), and in the process rejecting those premises inconsistent with the result reached. At some point, cognitive biases kick in, allowing the judicial mind (like all human minds) to pay more heed to those premises that support the nascent conclusion. Legal reasoning is not irrelevant to this process, but it is not necessarily the determinative factor, as the coherence of the entire factual "story" of the case is also important. Legal premises fall into place along with factual premises in reaching the conclusion. In this way, Professor Simon suggests, a judge can genuinely believe that the result reached is the uniquely correct result and write a formalist opinion that admits of no possible alternative results, even though the result was indeterminate ex ante. One of Professor Simon's key conclusions is that the judge is unaware of this cognitive process and thus unaware of the process by which she reaches her decision.[46]

Professor Simon posits that his analysis is valid for those cases that have "low stakes" for the judicial decision maker—that is, cases in which the decision maker has no ideological or partisan interest in one result or another. But one can question whether there are truly very many cases that are low stakes for the judge—particularly when it comes to constitutional cases in front of the Supreme Court. While judges presumably strive to be good, unbiased judges, judges presumably will also resist reaching results that violate their intuitions of right and wrong. These moral stakes may or may not be conscious, but they undoubtedly affect the receptivity of judges to opposing legal arguments—the unconscious mind will resist accepting coherent sets of premises that contravene the judge's innate sense of right and wrong.[47]

Professor Simon's analysis thus suggests that realist premises are at least partially supported by cognitive psychology. This analysis does not completely reject the role of formalist legal argument and reasoning, however (and neither do the Realists). Rather, competing formalist legal premises constitute but one of multiple sets of premises that the judge unconsciously networks, accepts, and rejects in coming to a judicial hunch. The conscious, rational mind realizes that it has reached a decision, and, after the fact, attributes that decision to deliberative, rational decision making based largely on formalist legal arguments. But the rational mind has not made the decision at all; rather, the unconscious mind has reached the decision through a complex process of accepting and rejecting related premises, both factual and legal. This process is remarkably similar to the process described by psychology's moral intuitionists, who similarly assert that moral judgments are formed at an intuitive level based on preexisting receptivity to certain moral principles, while moral reasoning is invoked only after the fact to justify a moral response reached at the intuitive level.[48]

Indeed, neurological science questions whether the rational, conscious mind is capable of affecting human action at all. To put it bluntly, the formalist model of legal decision making depends on the existence of human free will: a judge rationally weighs the formal legal arguments, picks the "correct" arguments and rejects the "flawed" or "incorrect" arguments, and through an exercise of rational free will, decides the case. One self-described formalist jurist describes the process as an act of conscious will: "[J]urists make conscious efforts to focus on the facts and the law, ignoring their own internal conceptions of right and wrong."[49] But neurologists question whether the conscious mind ever actually wills human action at all. In a famous set of experiments, Benjamin Libet monitored the brain activity of subjects who were asked to "decide" which button to press.

What he found was that, as subjects pushed the buttons, the action-oriented portions of the brain became active before the conscious, decision-oriented portions of the brain. In other words, the action came first, and the conscious "decision" to act came later. Nevertheless, the subjects all subjectively believed that they had made the decision first, before commencing the action.

Libet's experiments (together with confirmatory follow-up research by other neurologists) helped reignite the centuries-old debate about the existence of human freedom of choice.[50] In the legal academy, this renewed skepticism about the existence of human freedom of choice has renewed scholarly debate about the ethics of retributive justice—if lawbreakers do not make choices to break the law, then a retributive theory of justice based on the moral culpability of human actors loses its justification. But no one seems to have made a connection between a lack of human free will and the role of the human participants in a system of justice—that is, if lawbreakers lack rational free will to conform their conduct to the legal and ethical norms, why should equally human lawmakers and judges administering a system of justice be any more responsive to ethical arguments against retributive justice? Or, for that matter, to formalist arguments addressed to human reason? Judges, even justices of the Supreme Court, are human animals. To be sure, there is a world of difference between a decision to take a discrete physical action such as pushing a button and the incremental realization of a dispositive judicial hunch. Libet's startling conclusion—that action precedes consciousness of a decision and that the mind nevertheless believes that the decision occurred first and caused the action—is remarkably analogous to the realist conception of the decision-making process as described by writers from Frank and Cardozo on down to Judge Posner and Professor Simon.

But rejection of human free will is equally inconsistent with the most cynical version of the realist vision of judicial decision making: the notion that judges willfully make decisions consistent with their policy preferences or rank partisan leanings. For if judges lack the free will to implement the rational conclusion of a formalist process of reasoning, they undoubtedly equally lack the free will to decide cases in a way that consciously achieves their personal preferences. That does not mean that personal policy preferences (or result preferences) are irrelevant to the judicial result—it just means that, consistent with Judge Posner's idea that judges strive to be good (impartial) judges, the process by which personal judicial outcome preferences affect decision making is neither conscious nor willful. Determinism thus makes its way back into the lawmaking process, not as the determinism of the legal formalists (who insist that there is one "correct," syllogistic answer to every legal case), but the determinism of the philosophical determinists (now supported by neurological science) that finds all human actions to be deterministic. Under this theory, all human choices are a physical process in the human brain, of which the conscious mind becomes aware only after the choice has already been made.

If judges are thus hardwired to make the choices they do, then perhaps discovery of the nature of that hardwiring might provide a better answer to the realists' question of "what really determines a particular judge's decision in a particular case?" Evolutionary psychologists posit that human moral intuitions are in fact evolved and wired into human beings. An individual's moral sense is thus largely innate. Research on infants as young as six to ten months reveals that children have an innate sense of fairness; they prefer the shape that plays a "helper" role in an animation to the one that plays the "hinderer" role.[51] Rudimentary moral intuitions are also observed in primates, and Darwin himself hypothesized that human moral intuitions were the result of evolutionary processes in a social species.[52] This is not to say that all moral intuition is fixed and innate from birth; rather, psychological anthropologists suggest that human evolution in the context of social, hunter-gatherer groups lead to innate receptivity to certain generalizable moral principles, which are culturally reinforced or rejected during a child's development in much the same way that human children acquire a native language.[53]

Moral psychologist Jonathan Haidt has explored the manifestations of innate morality in the specific context of the moral disagreements underlying the most contentious Supreme Court cases: those involving the fundamental political conflicts of the so-called culture war in the United States.[54] He posits that there are five basic moral intuitions for which human beings have evolved to be receptive: (1) avoidance of harm/care for others, (2) fairness/reciprocity, (3) ingroup/loyalty, (4) authority/respect, and (5) purity/sanctity.[55] Haidt finds that these moral intuitions are shared across cultures, throughout history, and around the world. And Haidt also suggests, like the legal realists, that moral judgments are most often based on moral intuition—this innate grammar of morality—while moral reasoning (like formalist legal reasoning) is a post hoc rationalization for a judgment made at a preconscious level.[56]

If these five moral principles were truly innate and universal, then natural law philosophy and legal positivism, as well as legal realism, might all be reconciled. Judicial decision making might well be indeterminate as a matter of formalist legal reasoning but determinate as a matter of application of innate moral principles to particular social facts, making these rules both universal and immutable (as natural law holds) as well as a creation of human institutions (which themselves are a product of evolutionary biology). It is, however, not quite so simple. Professor Haidt finds that, although receptivity to each of these five ethics is universally shared, they are not universally equally valued. Rather, Haidt finds, individuals who self-identify as political liberals value the ethics of harm avoidance/care and fairness/reciprocity more highly than the other three moral intuitions, while self-identified conservatives value all five ethics more or less equally (thus giving greater relative weight to respect for authority, group loyalty, and purity than liberals do).[57]

To Haidt, this difference in weighting explains the intractability of the most contentious issues of the culture wars (including the issues that become constitutional issues before the Supreme Court). Liberals support same-sex marriage on grounds of fairness and reciprocity and do not understand contrary arguments (found compelling by conservatives) based on respect for authority (tradition) and purity (revulsion against nonprocreative sexual acts). To some conservatives, support for affirmative action may offend notions of group loyalty that strike liberals as frankly racist.[58] Punishment for those who disrespect authority and reject group symbols, as by burning flags or refusing to say the pledge of allegiance, may strike conservatives as morally appropriate while liberals fail to see any harm that would justify the punishment. Nor are the process school theorists free of these cognitive biases; Herbert Wechsler's famous criticism of *Brown v. Board of Education*[59] might be explained as a preference for the conservative ethic of group loyalty (translated into "freedom of association") as opposed to fairness/reciprocity ethic given more relative weight by social liberals (translated into "equality"). The constitution embodies both principles,[60] and judges resolving controversies will ultimately resolve the conflicting values through cognitive processes that result in the least cognitive dissonance for their own fundamental values.

Haidt's moral foundations theory and Professor Simon's cognitive analysis together have important implications for understanding judicial decision making when clashes of values become constitutional issues. Simon posits that formal legal argument is but one of the many premises sorted out by the unconscious judicial mind in reaching a decision. Haidt's analysis would suggest that people in general share a set of innate moral intuitions; these moral intuitions may themselves be seen as part of the system of interrelated premises that go into the unconscious cognitive process of reaching a decision. Simon's analysis of the cognitive drive towards coherent sets of premises suggests that a judge will be inclined to reject sets of premises (including formalist legal argument) that lead to results inconsistent with any fundamental moral intuitions the judge holds. Haidt similarly posits that the triumph of moral reason over moral intuition, while possible, is rare.[61] But formalist legal reasoning does not thus become inoperative to an intuitionist judicial hunch; after all, precedent and legal texts (like the Constitution) are quite literally forms of authority, and rejection of these cognitive premises would presumably offend Haidt's "authority" precept.

This synthesis is neither purely realist nor purely natural law formalism. The realists are correct that formalist law is often indeterminate and that results in such cases will vary with the outlook and makeup of the judges involved. However, the natural law formalists may have been intuitively correct that judges declaring the law were in fact channeling some innate principles of justice (or morality) but incorrect in assuming that these principles were either God-given or the product of pure reason; rather, they may simply reflect a shared, evolutionary, and cultural moral intuition. Unfortunately for the natural law formalists (and consistent with the realists' key insight), these shared principles of justice (or morality) are themselves indeterminate: the result in a given case will depend on how a particular judge is wired to weigh competing innate ethical principles. As even the most casual students of the Supreme Court have observed, different justices will reach starkly different conclusions when addressing the most contentious issues of constitutional law (where constitutional values may themselves conflict with each other). These results, as the attitudinalists have shown, are better predicted based on the ideological (read, innate moral) preferences of the individual justices than by legal argument or reasoning. Supreme Court justices reaching diametrically opposite conclusions will be honestly convinced of their own impartiality. Intellectually neutral observers will note that these justices will support their opposing convictions with impeccable logic and arguments based on accepted modes of legal reasoning.

As a descriptive matter, the formal predicate for judicial review— an impartial court applying determinate constitutional law to assess the legitimacy of actions of coequal branches and federalist states— thus seems simply incorrect. At the end of the day, the identity (and ideology) of the judicial decision makers matters—the choice of ideologically conservative or liberal justices will affect the result. Does this conclusion, patently obvious as it may seem, thus deprive judicial review of its legitimacy in the United States constitutional democracy?

Reconciling Moral Intuitionist Realism with Judicial Review: The Structural Role of the Supreme Court in United States Constitutional Government

A moral intuitionist brand of realism undermines the classic John Marshall formalist justification for judicial review in the United States constitutional scheme. Constitutional law, in particular, is frequently indeterminate, and the result in any given constitutional controversy will often depend on the identity of the justices deciding the case. The classic notion that the Supreme Court is a nonpolitical branch performing the uniquely judicial function of declaring what "the" determinate law is refuted by all objective evidence. If there is nothing uniquely judicial about how the Supreme Court resolves constitutional controversies, then democratic theory seems to require that the democratically elected branches of government make these fundamental choices.

Or not. Perhaps it is no more an indictment of constitutional judicial review as "undemocratic" because judges cannot help making political policy choices in deciding cases than it is to point out (as several political scientists have) that Congress in our evolved democracy is more responsive to the interests of organized lobbying groups than it is to the will of voting constituents. Indeed, some public choice theorists posit that collective decision makers like Congress are struc-turally incapable of making rational decisions in the public interest.[62] Few would suggest that acceptance of public choice theory under-mines the legitimacy of Congress in a constitutional democracy. After all, the theory of the republican form of democracy adopted by the Framers supports the role of Congress as the democratically account-able vehicle for implementing public preferences. The fact that American society, politics, and Congress itself have evolved in ways inconsistent with the Framers' aspirational theories of republican governance does not undercut the legitimacy of Congress as a demo-cratically responsive institution in any fundamental way. The fact that judicial decisions cannot help but reflect the personal moral makeup of justices similarly does not undercut the classic justifica-tion for judicial review in any fundamental way. Just as congressional representatives should strive to serve their constituents and the good of the republic, even when against the interests of organized groups that help finance their campaigns, judges should strive to decide cases according to formalist legal reasoning even when contrary to their ideological and moral preferences. Legal formalism is, after all, an internally consistent theory. As Professor Brian Leiter argues, even the legal realists were not conceptual rule skeptics—they did not question the value of determinate legal rules. Rather, they were empirical rule skeptics; they questioned the practicality of such a system in the real world.[63]

But acceptance of legal formalism even on a theoretical basis requires acceptance of at least the theoretical plausibility of formalist legal determinism. This may be a greater leap of faith than that required to believe that elected representatives will truly represent their constituents. Law may be subject to description in a series of syllogisms, but no legal syllogism satisfactorily explains how to choose among competing syllogisms. It is very hard to find determin-ist legal theoreticians in the academy anymore; most legal theorists accept that law is indeterminate and search for foundational theories that, they hope, will cabin judicial discretion in applying indetermi-nate legal principles.

The formalist determinate justification is not the only justification for judicial review, however. There is a structural justification for judicial review in our constitutional system as well—one that is per-haps more compelling than the formalist reasoning. The genius of the Constitution is not that it implemented a form of perfectly representative democracy that precludes judicial policy making. Rather, the Framers invented a system of government with competing elements of monarchy (the executive branch), republican democracy (Congress), and aristocracy (the judiciary), and explicitly relied on the competition between these branches to prevent usurpation of power by any one of them.[64]

Indeed, the very premise of a written constitution is that some questions of governance and even some policy choices are to be taken off the table of the representative institutions and settled more permanently. Societies need a referee to settle their fundamental disputes without resorting to violence. The judiciary has long served this societal function of providing closure. The legal process school itself is premised in major part on the institutional role of the adjudicative process in resolving disputes and making legitimate legal rules.[65] Indeed, Alexis de Tocqueville long ago observed of American political culture, "There is virtually no political question in the United States that does not sooner or later [turn] into a judicial question."[66] The more transitory and more political branches of government cannot provide this sort of closure, as these branches can only settle these disputes until the next election. One of the innovations of the Constitution was to constitute a judicial branch that was independent of both the executive and the legislature.[67] Much has been written about the structural role that the judiciary plays in protecting the interests of political minorities from abuse by the majoritarian branches of government;[68] less has been written about the judiciary's structural role in providing closure to fundamental disputes among branches of government or even among factions of society. At least one commentator has suggested that the judiciary is the most appropriate branch to resolve interbranch controversies as "the one institution that is permanent, non-partisan, independent of Congress and the president, explains its conclusions publicly, has fact-finding facilities, [and] a long-range viewpoint."[69] Another commentator notes that Supreme Court decisions enjoy persuasiveness because of the structural place of the Supreme Court at the head of the judicial branch.[70]

This structural legitimacy of constitutional judicial review has support in the text of the Constitution itself as well as in *Federalist No. 78*. Article III of the Constitution, after all, grants jurisdiction to the judiciary to hear cases "arising under this Constitution."[71] In *Federalist No. 78*, Alexander Hamilton explicitly endorsed judicial review of legislative acts and gave a structural justification for it in the following universally cited passage:

> The complete independence of the courts of justice is peculiarly essential in a limited Constitution. By a limited Constitution, I understand one which contains certain specified exceptions to the legislative authority; such, for instance, as that it shall pass no bills of attainder, no ex post facto laws, and the like. Limitations of this kind can be preserved in practice no other way than through the medium of courts of justice, whose duty it must be to declare all acts contrary to the manifest tenor of the Constitution void. Without this, all the reservations of particular rights or privileges would amount to nothing.[72]

Not only does *Federalist No. 78* reflect an expectation that the judiciary would exercise power to declare acts of Congress void, but its author must have understood, I would suggest, that in exercising this power of judicial review, judges would exercise discretion in resolving individual cases of constitutional indeterminacy. For, in a later passage, Hamilton indicates that he understood full well that law can be indeterminate and that judges deciding cases must exercise their discretion:

> It has been frequently remarked with great propriety that a voluminous code of laws is one of the inconveniences necessarily connected with the advantages of a free government. To avoid an arbitrary discretion in the courts, it is indispensable that they should be bound down by strict rules and precedents which serve to define and point out their duty in every particular case that comes before them.[73]

Thus, in the same breath as he endorses constitutional judicial review, Hamilton acknowledges that in the absence of a "voluminous code" setting forth rules "in every particular case," judges will exercise an "arbitrary discretion."[74] *Federalist No. 78* thus endorses judicial review even with a frank acknowledgment that indeterminacy exists in law and that judges exercise discretion to make law in the face of indeterminacy.[75]

Judicial review thus derives legitimacy from constitutional text and the expectations of the Founders even in the absence of formalist assumptions about the determinate nature of judicial decision making. It has become one of the structural assumptions of our system of government. And, judicial and academic predictions to the contrary notwithstanding,[76] ten years after the Court's most apparently partisan decision in *Bush*, public approval of the Supreme Court remains high and has consistently exceeded public approval of the elected branches of government for decades.[77]

Indeed, *Bush* itself may be the realist example that proves the structuralist role of the Supreme Court. Conservative justices voted against their ideological leanings to vastly expand equal protection analysis in voting rights cases,[78] apparently motivated by a purely partisan desire to hand the presidency to the candidate of their in-group (their political party). Confounding formalism and legal process "neutral principles," the per curiam decision suggested that its reasoning would not apply to future cases because of the "complexities" of the case. Academic condemnation of the decision was immediate and nearly unanimous: both for its out-of-character interpretation of the Equal Protection Clause of the Fourteenth Amendment as well as for its activist intrusion into the Article II process of selecting the president where the constitutional text clearly puts the responsibility for resolving disputed elections in Congress, not the Supreme Court.[79] Justice Stevens confidently predicted that the legitimacy of the Court would suffer as a result of the decision, in language hinting at parallels to the Court's infamous *Dred Scott v. Sandford* decision.[80]

At the end of the day, the academic criticism of *Bush* does little more than prove the realists' first point: law, especially constitutional law, is indeterminate. Although it is easy to point out the inconsistency of the per curiam's equal protection reasoning with previous positions by the justices who joined the opinion, it is harder to say that the reasoning is facially invalid—a point underscored by the fact that the Court's liberal justices joined the equal protection reasoning, but disagreed solely on the remedy. The concurrence's literalist reliance on its discovery of the Article II clause providing for designation of electors through means chosen by the legislature is likewise not a facially invalid form of legal reasoning, and the dissent's emphatic rejection of this reliance is equally supported by precedent. And the ultimate alignment of the justices seems to prove the realists' second point: choices within the range of indeterminate outcomes in contested cases will depend on the ideological outlook of the judges.

But, despite this setup for a realist challenge to the legitimacy of judicial review by an apparently political court, a strange thing happened once the decision was announced. Even with the control of the presidency at stake, and having indisputably won the popular vote, Al Gore conceded the presidency rather than mount a political attack on the legitimacy of judicial review. Gore could easily have done so by challenging the electoral votes from the State of Florida when the votes were presented to Congress, thus seeking to have the House of Representatives determine the election as provided by the Twelfth Amendment. It may well be that a crude political calculation revealed the futility of such an attempt, but with a popular vote victory and the presidency at stake, it is telling that Gore—and the nation—accepted the Supreme Court's verdict on the election as final with barely a whimper.

Indeed, the most compelling defense of the Supreme Court's role in Bush is not any neutral principle in the majority's exposition of equal protection analysis of differential means of counting votes, nor in the concurring justices' discovery of the "legislature clause" in Article II, but rather in the important structural role the Supreme Court played in promptly resolving the election and avoiding a perceived threat of political chaos if the election were dragged out beyond the meeting of the electoral college.[81] This, incidentally, is the principle justification argued by Judge Posner in defense of the *Bush* decision in his book, *Breaking the Deadlock*.[82]

Some Conclusions and a Challenge

A moral intuitionist understanding of judicial decision making articulates a noncynical version of legal realism, as it accepts legal realism's premise that formal legal reasoning is indeterminate without drawing legal realism's potentially cynical conclusion that judicial decision making in indeterminate cases consists of nothing more than deliberate judicial policy choices. Rather, moral intuitionist legal realism posits that judges act in good faith to make decisions that they honestly believe are supported by determinate legal reasoning, even while the unconscious process resulting in these decisions necessarily reflects the cognitive biases and moral values of individual judges.

While the form and language of constitutional adjudication may thus be a "[nation] of laws and not of men,"[83] the substance of constitutional decision making largely depends on the identities and the moral values of the justices on the Supreme Court at any given time.

It follows then, that the Supreme Court is a political court, at least in the sense that justices make policy choices in constitutional cases that reflect differential weighing of competing social and moral values. It does not follow, however, that constitutional judicial review is an illegitimate usurpation of the legislative functions of the "more politically responsive" branches. The Framers, by enshrining principles in a written constitution and endorsing judicial review of legislation, intentionally took certain issues off of the legislative—and state—tables, contemplating a judicial check on transient majorities. The Constitution, especially as amended by the Bill of Rights, perhaps contains more indeterminacy than was understood by the Framers, but *Federalist No. 78*, at least, reflects an understanding of indeterminacy in law and the reality that judges would apply discretion in cases of indeterminacy. Acknowledgment of this reality—particularly if the discretion is not completely arbitrary but rather reflective of widely shared but not equally weighted moral values—does nothing to detract from the structural role of the Supreme Court as a check on the political branches and as a penultimate arbiter of divisive social issues.

It also follows that accusations of judicial activism from either side of the ideological divide are bankrupt. As has been persuasively argued elsewhere,[84] judicial activism seems to mean nothing more than an outcome in a legally indeterminate case in which the Supreme Court overturns action by a legislature or a state and the accuser disagrees with the result. Under this definition, "judicial activism" includes such universally condemned decisions as *Lochner* and *Dred Scott*, but it also includes currently applauded decisions like *Brown*, as well as liberal landmarks such as *Roe v. Wade* and more recent conservative triumphs such as *Printz v. United States*, *New York v. United States*, *District of Columbia v. Heller*, and *Citizens United v. Federal Election Commission*.[85] Judicial activism thus defined also includes such foundational Marshall Court decisions as *Marbury* itself, which struck down portions of the Judiciary Act of 1789; *McCulloch v. Maryland*, which struck down a Maryland-legislated tax on the national bank and established the so-called implied powers interpretation of the necessary and proper clause; and *Gibbons v. Ogden*, which established the foundation for the modern commerce power while voiding a New York-legislated licensing scheme for steamboats.[86]

Indeed, it was the open-textured, purposivist—and ultimately indeterminate—approach to constitutional interpretation of the Marshall Court in these latter cases that opened the door of indeterminacy a little wider than a strict, textual approach might have and ultimately enabled the evolution of a policy-making Supreme Court. Justice Thomas may pine for an eighteenth-century model of federalism—and may even be willing to try to turn back the clock to limit the application of the commerce power to regulating imports and exports among states[87]—but other conservative justices of the current Supreme Court have all accepted the coevolution of industrial technology, a national economy, cultural diversity, and a purposive, values-weighing constitutional law doctrine, at least to some extent.[88]

But to say that the Supreme Court makes policy choices that reflect individual moral values is not to say that Supreme Court justices enjoy the "arbitrary discretion" of Hamilton's *Federalist No.78*. The constraints on judicial discretion are real, even if weakened at the Supreme Court level. While the Supreme Court from time to time pushes social change ahead of social consensus (as in *Roe* and *Brown*), and at other times constrains social change even after political consensus is reached (*Lochner*), many commentators have noted that the Supreme Court's value imposition is never drastically far from the emerging social consensus.[89] While the Court may have declared a right to be free from punishment for same-sex consensual intimacy in *Lawrence v. Texas*, this right is not out of the mainstream of American views, and Justice Scalia's dissent to the contrary notwithstanding, the Court is nowhere near to extending that right to incestuous relationships, polygamy, or bestiality.[90]

Moreover, the political branches enjoy some ultimate oversight over the court, curbing judicial adventurism. The constitutional amendment process, though rarely evoked and difficult to implement, discourages decisions that will be universally condemned. The threats of court packing, jurisdiction curbing, impeachment proceedings, and outright disobedience by political actors, though rarely implemented, are also effective constraints on "arbitrary" judicial discretion.[91]

Presidents from Franklin D. Roosevelt on down have learned that the most politically expedient way to effect incremental change in constitutional interpretation is through the appointment power. The structure of the Article II Appointments Clause together with the Article III Life Tenure Clause allows for political influence on the general ideological direction of the Supreme Court while ensuring judicial independence. To be sure, growing political acknowledgement of the realist premise that Supreme Court justices make law has led to politicization of the process, but this politicization together with observance of the sixty-vote cloture rule generally tends to assure that, at least in their publicly stated positions, Supreme Court justices will not be terribly far from the current ideological center.[92] Individual judges' ideologies clearly matter to judicial results, and the ideologies of Supreme Court candidates have quite properly become matters of debate in the appointment process; this is part of the constitutional structure that keeps the center of the Court not too distant from contemporary moral values.

And judicial restraint has become the new rallying cry for the political process of appointing Supreme Court justices, albeit a self-serving rallying cry given the ideological relativity of the definition of judicial activism. At some level, the choice of justices who are assertive in their ideology and likely to garner an activist label from their ideological opposites is itself a political choice about the kind of Supreme Court the political consensus desires. The premise of this chapter is that it is impossible to eliminate judicial value-imposition in the context of Supreme Court review of constitutional challenges. But if judicial restraint—that is, moderation in judicial value-imposition—is truly to be desired, then a realist, moral-intuitionist understanding of the judicial decision-making process might provide some insights into the kind of personal qualities likely to promote judicial restraint and moderate judicial value-imposition.

Some of these qualities are obvious. The moral intuitionists have observed that high intelligence correlates with an ability to resist moral judgments based on pure intuition and to apply moral reasoning instead.[93] It follows that the more intelligent jurists will also be more able to resist value judgments based on moral intuition and follow formal legal arguments instead. Other qualities associated with likely judicial restraint might be inferred, such as general respect for authority (one of Haidt's conservative moral values), for adherence to precedent and authoritative text is itself a form of respect for authority. This might suggest that, in general, conservative judges should be less activist than ideologically liberal judges (who place less value on respect for authority and tradition), but this characteristic may itself be counterbalanced by conservatives' relative overweighting of in-group/loyalty values; for a conservative justice may be instinctively more inclined to decide cases in favor of her political party—witness *Bush*—or other group identity. Liberal thinkers' lower valuation of group loyalty may, on the other hand, equate with greater impartiality and open-mindedness in considering the interests of outgroups and political minorities—the structural role of judicial review championed by John Hart Ely, among others. The ideal moderate jurist might then be one who combines a strong sense of respect for authority (receptivity to authority-based arguments) and a weak sense of in-group loyalty, together with personal qualities of intelligence and the ability to defer gratification—if such a person exists.

The natural tendency of the judicial selection process, however, may unfortunately favor judges with a strong sense of in-group loyalty, as service and loyalty to political party are important factors in the selection process.[94] The selection process has also recently favored practicing litigators for initial judicial appointments. Although this may properly bring real-world pragmatism to the bench,[95] this preference may also promote an activist bench. For, rather than a tendency to defer moral judgment, litigators are conditioned by habit to focus on a desired result first, then to deploy the tools of formalist legal reasoning to achieve that result—the very definition of a more activist judicial approach.[96]

Moral intuitionism may also support the value of diversity in a collegial body such as the Supreme Court. Several commentators have pointed out the value of collegiality as a restraint on judicial decision making;[97] Professor Haidt's article on moral intuitionism also points out that diverse perspectives at the stage in which an issue is framed affects moral reasoning and may limit the tendency of moral intuition to adopt the framing and conclusions of members of the in-group.[98] Group-think inherent in a body of like-minded individuals reinforces idiosyncratic views. Professor Cass Sunstein performed a fascinating study on the results of ideologically diverse and ideologically conforming courts of appeals panels and concluded that the presence of just one judge with a different ideological makeup dramatically altered and moderated the results as compared to three-judge panels that were ideologically pure.[99] Justice Sotomayor's choice of phrasing may have been unfortunate when she announced (well before her nomination to the Supreme Court), that "a wise Latina woman with the richness of her experiences would more often than not reach a better conclusion than a white male who hasn't lived that life,"[100] but she may properly be intuiting that a diverse panel of judges representing different ethnic and social groups within American society will be more likely to reach decisions in indeterminate cases that reflect the moral mean of American society rather than one extreme or another.

The thesis of this chapter is that individual moral intuition plays a role at least as important as rule-based legal reasoning in the decision-making process of Supreme Court justices engaged in constitutional judicial review. Like most theses in legal academia, this proposition is endlessly debatable and absolutely unprovable. The cognitive premise of this thesis is that judges themselves are unaware of the exact process by which they reach decisions, so even an interview with a perfectly candid and introspective jurist would not settle the question. No judge is going to allow electrodes to be attached to her brain during the cogitative process to allow scientific examination of the relative activity of the moral intuition neurons and legal reasoning neurons, even if such an experiment were possible.

Nevertheless, some thought experiments are possible to assess the relative weight of moral intuition and formal legal reasoning in a values-fraught constitutional controversy. A district court in California has recently struck down California's Proposition 8, amending the California constitution to forbid the state from recognizing same-sex marriage, as violative of the Fourteenth Amendment's guarantee of Equal Protection, as well as being an unsupported denial of the fundamental right to marry.[101] This issue is likely to make it to the Supreme Court within the coming years. Proponents of a Wechslerian "neutral principles," rules-based approach to equal protection analysis have long read *Brown* to require color blindness in law (absent satisfaction of strict scrutiny), thus rejecting relativist remedial measures such as affirmative action.[102] The gender discrimination corollary is that law must be gender-blind, or satisfy so-called heightened scrutiny.[103] Formalist neutral principles would seem to demand that those who subscribe to color-blindness in race discrimination law must apply heightened scrutiny to the facial gender discrimination of Proposition 8: under Proposition 8 a legal disability turns on the gender of those subject to its prohibition.

The conservative wing of the current Court has accepted and endorsed the color-blindness formulation.[104] Under the gender-blindness corollary, Proposition 8 would be subject to heightened scrutiny regardless of whether one gender or another—or even some other classification entirely—is being benefited or burdened by the discrimination.[105] Without pretending to forecast the results of such a value-laden analysis, neutral principles and formal legal reasoning would demand that these same justices subject Proposition 8 to heightened scrutiny, searching for an "important governmental purpose" with means "substantially related" to that purpose.

We may eagerly await the results of this thought experiment.

Notes

1. *Marbury v. Madison*, 5 U.S. 137 (1803).
2. I use quotation marks around the word "law" here because even the concept of law can, at some level, be indeterminate. Law can mean formal reasoning from rules announced in judicial precedents and statutes, or it can be more broadly defined as the universe of socially accepted sources for discovering principles for deciding cases. See generally, Liam Murphy; and Kenneth Einar Himma.
3. See, for example, Mark Hall and Ronald Wright (advancing a unique method of analytical legal scholarship largely based on the tenets of legal realism); Brian Leiter (recognizing the influence of legal realism on legal academia and culture and advocating for greater acceptance of the theory in the realm of jurisprudential philosophy); Victoria Nourse and Gregory Shaffer (outlining a "dynamic new realism" and recognizing "that law, politics, and society, not to mention markets and governments, cannot be reduced to one another because they interact simultaneously"); Brian Z. Tamanaham (describing the pervasive nature of realism in jurisprudential analysis and describing the theory as a mainstream, nonradical philosophy); and Edmund Ursin (analyzing the self-described decision-making techniques of three preeminient judges and routinely relying on realist theories to support the adequacies of their various methodologies).
4. See *Bush v. Gore*, 531 U.S. 98 (2000).
5. Massachusetts Constitution, pt. 1, art. 30.
6. William Blackstone, ch. 69–70.
7. Note that it is not clear whether Blackstone himself accepted this characterization.

8. According to Blackstone: "This law of nature, being coeval with mankind and dictated by God himself, is of course superior in obligation to any other. It is binding over all the globe in all countries, and at all times: no human laws are of any validity, if contrary to this; and such of them as are valid derive all their force, and all their authority . . . from this original . . . [I]t is still necessary to have recourse to reason: whose office it is to discover . . . what the law of nature directs in every circumstance of life; by considering, what method will tend the most effectually to our own substantial happiness. . . . Upon these two foundations, the law of nature and the law of revelation, depend all human laws; that is to say, no human laws should be suffered to contradict these" (Blackstone, *Commentaries on England*, ch. 41–42).

9. In addition to the recitation that all men "are endowed by their Creator with certain unalienable rights," the Declaration of Independence refers to the colonists' right to assume "the separate and equal station to which the laws of nature and of nature's God entitle them." For analysis of the Founders' reliance on natural law principles, see Bernard Bailyn, 77–79, 185–188; Morton White, 142–184; Helen K. Michael; and "The Role of Natural Law in the American Revolution," review of *Constitutional History of the American Revolution*, by John P. Reid, *Harvard Law Review* 108 (1995).

10. Robert N. Clinton.

11. For example, "The basic requirements of an organized social life are the basic principles of the natural law." Stephen Buckle, 19, quoted in Randy E. Barnett, "A Law Professor's Guide to Natural Law and Natural Rights," *Harvard Law Review* 20, no. 3 (1997): 655; and "[P]eople possess [rights] simply by virtue of their humanity . . . which, as a matter of justice, others are bound to respect and governments are bound . . . to protect." Robert P. George, "Natural Law," *Harvard Journal of Law and Public Policy* 31 (2008).

12. *Lochner v. New York*, 198 U.S. 45 (1905).

13. For a discussion of Lochner as a representation of formalist, categorical reasoning, see Morton J. Horwitz, 29–30.

14. As legal historian Morton Horwitz has pointed out, Holmes was by no means the first legal thinker to question the objectivity and neutrality of natural law–based legal formalism. Indeed, the codification movement of the early nineteenth century—vigorously opposed by the organized bar—was largely a reaction to the popular perception that common law judges indeed "made" the law and that popularly elected legislatures were more appropriate sources of legal rules than judge-made law (ibid., 258).

15. Oliver Wendell Holmes Jr., *The Common Law*.

16. Holmes, "Codes, and the Arrangement of the Law," *American Law Review* 5 (1870). Reprinted with author attribution in *Harvard Law Review* 44 (1931).
17. Holmes, "Privilege, Malice, and Intent," *Harvard Law Review* 8 (1894). Reprinted in *Collected Legal Papers* (New York: Harcourt, Brace, and Company, 1920).
18. Holmes, "The Path of the Law," *Harvard Law Review* 10 (1897). Reprinted in *Collected Legal Papers*, 181. For an analysis of the progression of Justice Holmes' thinking about the nature of law and the underlying policy judgments, see Horwitz, *Transformation of Law*, 109–143.
19. Holmes, "Path of Law," 465.
20. *Lochner v. New York*, 75 (Holmes, J., dissenting).
21. *Missouri v. Holland*, 252 U.S. 416 (1920), 433–434.
22. Karl N. Llewellyn, *The Common Law Tradition*, 521–535.
23. Joseph C. Hutcheson Jr.
24. Jerome Frank, 100.
25. Benjamin N. Cardozo, 166.
26. See Frank, *Law and the Modern Mind*, 157 (arguing judges should be arbitrators doing equity); and ibid., 167 (endorsing judges who are aware that all legal rules are fictions and seek to do justice in each case).
27. Karl N. Llewellyn, "Some Realism About Realism—Responding to Dean Pound," 1236, 1249. See generally William W. Fisher III, Morton J. Horwitz, and Thomas A. Reed, eds., 167 (describing realist program as "purposive adjudication").
28. Felix S. Cohen, 839–840; Holmes, "Path of Law," 458–459. See generally Llewellyn, *American Legal Realism*, 166 (stating that to realists, the virtue of "real rules" is to "enable lawyers to advise their clients more [effectively]").
29. For the seminal works of the Critical Legal Studies Movement, see Mark Kelman; Duncan Kennedy, *Legal Education and the Reproduction if Hierarchy: A Polemic Against the System*; and Roberto Mangabeira Unger. For concise analysis of the underlying theories and summaries of these works, see Duncan Kennedy, "Legal Education as Training for Hierarchy," in *The Politics of Law: A Progressive Critique*; and John M. Finnis.
30. For the seminal works on Legal Positivism, see Henry M. Hart Jr., and Albert M. Sacks; Henry M. Hart Jr. and Herbert Wechsler. See also H.L.A. Hart, "Positivism and the Separation of Law and Morals"; Herbert Wechsler. For concise analysis of these theories and their formation, see Anthony J. Sebok; and David A.J. Richards.
31. As Hart explains: [T]hough every rule may be doubtful at some points, it is indeed a necessary condition of a legal system existing, that not

every rule is open to doubt on all points.... [C]ourts have jurisdiction to settle [cases] by choosing between the alternatives which the statute leaves open, even if they prefer to disguise this choice as a discovery. H.L.A. Hart, *The Concept of Law*, 148–149.

32. See Jeffrey A. Segal and Harold J. Spaeth.

33. Gregory A. Caldeira, review of Segal and Smith, *Supreme Court and the Attitudinal Model, American Political Science Review* 88 (1994).

34. Michael Steven Green (emphasis omitted); see Eric J. Segall, "The Skeptic's Constitution," review of *Remnants of Belief: Contemporary Constitutional Issues*; Daniel J. Solove.
      See generally Brian Leiter, *Naturalizing Jurisprudence*, 21 (claiming "realism is omnipresent in American law schools and legal culture"). For an essay suggesting reconvergence of legal realism in the legal academy and the political science academy, see Thomas J. Miles and Cass R. Sunstein, "The New Legal Realism," *University of Chicago Law Review* (2008).

35. Lawyers routinely go to great extremes to choose sympathetic judges. Prior to the Twenty-eighth Amendment, to provide for assignment by lottery, lawyers seeking to challenge agency rule making would post agents with walkie-talkies in the halls of administrative agencies to inform them when rules were adopted so that their petition could be the first one filed in a favorable circuit. Disputes about which petition was filed first would turn on fractions of a second. Marshall J. Breger, "The Race to the Courthouse Is Over," *Washington Post*, March 16, 1988, A23.

36. Judge Sonia Sotomayor (remarks during a judicial clerkship information panel, Duke University Law School, Durham, NC, February 25, 2005).

37. See Richard A. Posner, *How Judges Think*.

38. John M. Scheb II and William Lyons, 185.

39. Robert Frost, address at Milton Academy, Massachusetts, May 17, 1935.

40. See Posner, *How Judges Think*, 146–152 for a realist perspective and extended discussion of the difficulty of establishing objective measures of judicial job performance

41. Daniel A. Farber and Suzanna Sherry, 87–110. See Posner, *How Judges Think*, 125–158. Note that the "reasoned elaboration" requirement of the judicial process is a key element of the legal process school's constraints on judicial politicization. See Farber and Sherry, 44–45; and Wechsler, "Toward Neutral Principles," 15–20.

42. Posner, *How Judges Think*, 205.

43. See William H. Rehnquist, 254–255, 258.

44. Posner, *How Judges Think*, 61–64, 69, 204.

45. Dan Simon, "A Psychological Model of Judicial Decision Making." For other cogent analyses of the cognitive psychology of judicial decision making, see Edward S. Adam and Daniel A. Farber; and Dan M. Kahan.
46. Dan Simon, "Psychological Model," 30. For other cogent analyses of the cognitive psychology of judicial decision making, see Adams and Farber, "Beyond Formalism"; and Kahan, "'Ideology in'" or 'Cultural Cognition.'"
47. Professor Simon, in a later article, thus notes, "We have also found evidence that supports the proposition that coherence effects interact with the decision-maker's preexisting attitudes, particularly those embedded in the person's enduring value system." Dan Simon, "A Third View of the Black Box: Cognitive Coherence in Legal Decision Making," *University of Chicago Law Review* 71 (2004): 542.
48. Jonathan Haidt, "The Emotional Dog and Its Rational Tail: A Social Intuitionist Approach to Moral Judgment."
49. Timothy J. Capurso, 11.
50. The nature and extent of human freedom of will has fascinated Western philosophers across the centuries, particularly in relation to the moral responsibilities of individuals for their actions. St. Augustine, writing in the fourth century, grappled with the conflict between predestination and the individual autonomy necessary for free will and moral responsibility (*On Free Choice of the Will*). Eighteenth-century moral philosophers Emanuel Kant and David Hume famously disagreed with each other on the nature of human free will. Hume adopted a version of the compatibilist view that human action was subject to predetermined cause and effect like all natural phenomena but that individuals remained responsible for their actions, as human freedom of action allowed for such responsibility, even if such actions were predetermined ("Of Liberty and Necessity"). Kant, on the other hand, postulated the existence of free will as essential to a priori moral reasoning, relegating deterministic views to the standpoint of empirical phenomenology, which he found irrelevant to moral philosophy. See *Critique of Practical Reason*; *Critique of Pure Reason*; and *Groundwork of the Metaphysic of Morals*. For a general discussion of Kant's and Hume's nuanced views on free will, see Lara Denis, "Kant and Hume on Morality," in *Stanford Encyclopedia of Philosophy*. The debate between Hume, an empiricist who believed that moral judgments followed from passion, and Kant, a theorist, who believed that all moral judgment proceeds rationally from first principles of moral thought, anticipates the ongoing debates between formalists and realists in the legal arena and between rationalists and moral intuitionists in the psychology arena.

51. Paul Bloom, "The Moral Life of Babies," *New York Times Magazine*, May 9, 2010, 44(L).

52. See Haidt, "Emotional Dog," 826.

53. Ibid., 827; see also John Mikhail, 753–755.

54. See Jonathan Haidt and Jesse Graham.

55. Jonathan Haidt and Craig Joseph, 367; Haidt and Graham, "When Morality Opposes Justice," 106–109. Haidt builds on earlier theorists who posited three evolved moral ethics, those of autonomy, community, and divinity. Ibid., 106–107 (citing Richard A. Shweder, "In Defense of Moral Realism: Reply to Gabennesch," *Child Development* 61, no. 6 [1990]).

56. Haidt, "Emotional Dog," 817–818.

57. Haidt and Graham, "When Morality Opposes Justice," 108–111.

58. This is not to discount the fact that many conservatives oppose affirmative action on fairness grounds, rather than group loyalty.

59. *Brown v. Board of Education*, 347 U.S. 483 (1954); see Wechsler, "Toward Neutral Principles," 22–34.

60. The Fourteenth Amendment explicitly guarantees equal protection, while a constitutional value in freedom of association has been inferred from the First Amendment guarantees of freedom of speech and the right to petition. See *Boy Scouts of America v. Dale*, 530 U.S. 640 (2000); *Roberts v. U.S. Jaycees*, 468 U.S. 609 (1984); and *NAACP v. Alabama*, 357 U.S. 449 (1958).

61. Haidt, "Emotional Dog," 819.

62. See, for example, Daniel A. Farber and Philip P. Frickey; William N. Eskridge Jr.

63. See Leiter, *Rethinking Legal Realism*, 295–299.

64. See *Federalist no. 51*.

65. See Hart and Sacks, *The Legal Process*, 4: "[E]very modern society differentiates among social questions, accepting one mode of decision for one kind and other modes for others."

66. Alexis De Tocqueville, 310.

67. Colonial and British courts of the eighteenth century were adjuncts of either the legislative branch or the Crown. See Blackstone, *Commentaries*, 147 (describing the English government as consisting of two branches: "the one legislative, to wit, the parliament, consisting of king, lords, and commons; the other executive, consisting of the king alone"); James E. Pfander, 920–922 no. 82.

68. See, for example, Jesse H. Choper, *Judicial Review and the National Political Process: A Functional Reconsideration of the Role of the Supreme Court* (role of judicial review to protect minorities); John Hart Ely, 87–88 (representation-reinforcing theory of judicial review); Jesse H. Choper, "The Supreme Court and the Political Branches: Democratic

Theory and Practice," 830–832; and Antonin Scalia, "The Doctrine of Standing as an Essential Element of the Separation of Powers," 894.

69. James L. Oakes, 1415.
70. See Stephen M. Feldman, 104.
71. United States Constitution, art. 2, sec. 2, cl. 1.
72. *Federalist no. 78.*
73. Ibid.
74. See ibid.
75. See Jonathan T. Molot, 19–27 (arguing that the Framers had a moderately indeterminate view of the law, which supported the need for an independent judiciary).
76. See *Bush v. Gore*, 128–129 (Stevens, J., dissenting).
77. Frank Newport, "Trust in Legislative Branch Falls to Record-Low 36%," Gallup.Com, September 24, 2010; see also Larry D. Kramer, 221–233 (discussing the historically widespread public approval of even the most controversial high court decisions).
78. See Geoffrey R. Stone, "Equal Protection? The Supreme Court's Decision in *Bush v. Gore*" (talk delivered to the Federal Bar Association, Chicago, May 23, 2001).
79. See, for example, Ronald Dworkin, ed.; Vincent Bugliosi; Bruce Ackerman, ed.; Alan M. Dershowitz; and Cass R. Sunstein and Richard A. Epstein, eds.
80. See *Dred Scott v. Sandford*, 60 U.S. 393 (1856).
81. This perceived threat of electoral chaos may be overstated, as there was no actual threat to the security or order of the United States at the time the Supreme Court issued its decision. However, one can hypothesize that in addition to the relatively weak formalist arguments accepted by the justices who joined the per curiam decision, the cognitive premises working in favor of stopping the recount included a prompt resolution of the election, avoidance of immediate chaos (Haidt's avoidance of harm), and the justices' party loyalty (Haidt's in-group/loyalty premise). That the liberal justices accepted the equal protection arguments as well, but differed only in the matter of the appropriate remedy, is consistent with the high value liberals place on fairness (equal protection and equality of results) as well as the comparatively weaker value these justices place on in-group loyalty (party loyalty). A purely partisan Democratic position would be to reject the equal protection arguments and avoid legitimizing any portion of the per curiam decision's reasoning.
82. Richard A. Posner, *Breaking the Deadlock: The 2000 Election, the Constitution, and the Courts.*
83. Massachusetts Constitution, pt. 1, art. 30.
84. See Kermit Roosevelt III, 38–47, 229–236.

85. See *Citizens United v. Federal Election Commission*, 558 U.S. 310 (2010); *District of Columbia v. Heller*, 554 U.S. 570 (2008); *Printz v. United States*, 521 U.S. 898 (1997); *New York v. United States*, 505 U.S. 144 (1992); *Roe v. Wade*, 410 U.S. 113 (1973); *Brown v. Board of Education*; *Lochner v. New York*; and *Dred Scott v. Sandford*.

86. See *Gibbons v. Ogden*, 22 U.S. 1 (1824); *McCulloch v. Maryland*, 17 U.S. 316 (1819); and *Marbury v. Madison*.

87. See *United States v. Morrison*, 529 U.S. 598 (2000), 627 (Thomas, J., concurring); *United States v. Lopez*, 514 U.S. 549 (1995), 584–602 (Thomas, J., concurring); see also *United Haulers Association v. Oneida-Herkimer Solid Waste Management Authority*, 550 U.S. 330 (2007), 349–355 (Thomas, J., concurring) (rejecting Dormant Commerce Clause doctrine).

88. See Antonin Scalia, "Originalism: The Lesser Evil," 864. Justice Scalia has described himself as a "faint hearted originalist" who would allow originalist principles to yield to stare decisis.

89. It has long since been noted that "th[e] [S]upreme [Cou]rt follows th[e ele]ction returns." Finley Peter Dunne, *Mr. Dooley's Opinions* 26 (1901).

90. See *Lawrence v. Texas*, 539 U.S. 558 (2003), 590, 599 (Scalia, J., dissenting). Haidt uses the example of consensual adult incest as an example of universal moral revulsion at conduct that cannot be shown to have any objective harm (Haidt, "Emotional Dog," 814).

91. See Tom Donnelly, 984–1000 (discussing examples of "popular constitutionalism" resistance to Supreme Court decisions, including the impeachment of Justice Chase, President Jackson's refusal to implement the Cherokee Nation decision, and President Franklin Roosevelt's court-packing plan); see also L.A. Powe Jr. (reviewing twentieth-century incidences of popular resistance to Supreme Court decisions, including school desegregation, school prayer, and abortion rights decisions).

92. But see Emily Bazelon, "Sorry Now? What Do the Liberal and Moderate Lawyers Who Supported John Roberts' Nomination Say Today?," *Slate Magazine*, June 29, 2007; Adam Cohen, editorial, "Last Term's Winner at the Supreme Court: Judicial Activism," *New York Times*, July 9, 2007, A16; Editorial, "The Court's Aggressive Term," *New York Times*, July 5, 2010, A16; Michael Doyle, "Who's Activist Now? In Election Spending Case, Conservatives," *McClatchy DC News*, January 21, 2010; Edward M. Kennedy, "Roberts and Alito Misled Us," *Washington Post*, July 30, 2006, B01; Stuart Taylor Jr., "The End of Restraint: Alito, Roberts, and Judicial Modesty," *Newsweek*, February 1, 2010, 16.

93. See Haidt, "Emotional Dog," 823–824; cf. *The Federalist no. 78* (observing that jurists would have to be very smart to know the vast body

of codes and precedent necessary to limit arbitrary discretion). Haidt posits that high intelligence may also be associated with the ability to defer gratification. See Haidt , "Emotional Dog," 823–824 (citing Yuichi Shoda, Walter Mischel, and Philip K. Peake, "Predicting Adolescent Cognitive and Self-Regulatory Competencies from Preschool Delay of Gratification: Identifying Diagnostic Conditions," *Developmental Psychology* 26, no. 6 [1990]).

94. See Farber and Sherry, *Judgment Calls,* 116–117.
95. Ibid.
96. Note that Haidt describes the moral judgment process in these terms—one exercising moral judgment is more like a lawyer than a judge (Haidt, "Emotional Dog," 814).
97. Farber and Sherry, *Judgment Calls,* 91; Posner, *How Judges Think,* 32–33, 143, 256; Harry T. Edwards.
98. Haidt, "Emotional Dog," 823.
99. Cass R. Sunstein, David Schkade, and Lisa Michelle Ellman.
100. J. Sonia Sotomayor.
101. *Perry v. Schwarzenegger,* 704 F. Supp. 2d 921 (N.D. Cal. 2010): 1003.
102. See Richard A. Posner, "The DeFunis Case and the Constitutionality of Preferential Treatment of Racial Minorities"; William Van Alstyne; and Wechsler, "Toward Neutral Principles," 31–35.
103. See *United States v. Virginia,* 518 U.S. 515 (1996), 566–603 (Scalia, J., dissenting) (implicitly applying heightened scrutiny); *Johnson v. Transportation. Agency,* 480 U.S. 616 (1987), 656 (Scalia, J., dissenting) (endorsing gender-blindness standard for Title VII and an analogous equal protection analysis); *Mississippi University for Women v. Hogan,* 458 U.S. 718 (1982); and *Frontiero v. Richardson,* 411 U.S. 677 (1973). But see *Lawrence v. Texas* (Scalia, J., dissenting) (distinguishing *Loving v. Virginia* from same-sex marriage on grounds that antimiscegenation statute was based on white supremacy).
104. See *Parents Involved in Community Schools v. Seattle School District. No. 1,* 551 U.S. 701 (2007).
105. Note that Virginia argued in *Loving v. Virginia* that equal protection did not apply because both blacks and whites were equally disabled by the antimiscegenation law from marrying the other race. The Court rejected this argument, supporting a "color-blind" view of equal protection (8–9). Obviously, more than a glancing exposition of the constitutional issues raised by *Perry v. Schwarzenegger* is beyond the scope of this chapter. For good treatments of the facial, gender-based, equal protection argument, see Mary Anne Case; Mark Strasser; Valorie K. Vojdik.

Bibliography

Ackerman, Bruce, ed. *Bush v. Gore: The Question of Legitimacy.* New Haven, CT: Yale University Press, 2002.

Adam, Edward S., and Daniel A. Farber. "Beyond the Formalism Debate: Expert Reasoning, Fuzzy Logic, and Complex Statutes." *Vanderbilt Law Review* 52 (1999).

Bailyn, Bernard. *The Ideological Origins of the American Revolution.* Cambridge, MA: Harvard University Press, 1967.

Blackstone, William. *Commentaries on the Laws of England.* Vol. 1. Edited by George Sharswood. Philadelphia: Lippincott, 1893.

Buckle, Stephen. *Natural Law and the Theory of Property: Grotius to Hume.* Oxford: Oxford University Press, 1993.

Bugliosi, Vincent. *The Betrayal of America: How the Supreme Court Undermined the Constitution and Chose Our President.* New York: Nation Books, 2001.

Capurso, Timothy J. "How Judges Judge: Theories on Judicial Decision Making." *University of Baltimore Law Forum* 29 (1999).

Cardozo, Benjamin N. *The Nature of the Judicial Process.* New Haven, CT: Yale University Press, 1921.

Case, Mary Anne. "'The Very Stereotype the Law Condemns': Constitutional Sex Discrimination Law as a Quest for Perfect Proxies." *Cornell Law Review* 85, no. 5 (2000).

Choper, Jesse H. "The Supreme Court and the Political Branches: Democratic Theory and Practice." *University of Pennsylvania Law Review* 122 (1974).

———. *Judicial Review and the National Political Process: A Functional Reconsideration of the Role of the Supreme Court.* Chicago: University of Chicago Press, 1980.

Clinton, Robert N. "Original Understanding, Legal Realism, and the Interpretation of 'This Constitution.'" *Iowa Law Review* 72 (1987).

Cohen, Felix S. "Transcendental Nonsense and the Functional Approach." *Columbia Law Review* 35 (1935).

Denis, Lara. "Kant and Hume on Morality." In *Stanford Encyclopedia of Philosophy.* Summer ed. Edited by Edward N. Zalta, 2009.

Dershowitz, Alan M. *Supreme Injustice: How the High Court Hijacked Election 2000.* Oxford: Oxford University Press, 2001.

Donnelly, Tom. "Note. Popular Constitutionalism, Civic Education, and the Stories We Tell Our Children." *Yale Law Journal* 118 (2009).

Dworkin, Ronald, ed. *A Badly Flawed Election: Debating Bush v. Gore, the Supreme Court, and American Democracy.* New York: New Press, 2002.

Edwards, Harry T. "The Effects of Collegiality on Judicial Decision Making." *University of Pennsylvania Law Review* 151, no. 5 (2003).

Ely, John Hart. *Democracy and Distrust: A Theory of Judicial Review.* Cambridge, MA: Harvard University Press, 1980.

Eskridge Jr., William N. "Politics Without Romance: Implications of Public Choice Theory for Statutory Interpretation." *Virginia Law Review* 74, no. 2 (1988).

Farber, Daniel A., and Philip P. Frickey. *Law And Public Choice: A Critical Introduction.* Chicago: University of Chicago Press, 1991.

Farber, Daniel A., and Suzanna Sherry. *Judgment Calls.* Oxford: Oxford University Press, 2009.

Feldman, Stephen M. "The Rule of Law or the Rule of Politics? Harmonizing the Internal and External Views of Supreme Court Decision Making." *Law and Social Inquiry* 30, no. 1 (2005).

Finnis, John M. "On 'The Critical Legal Studies Movement.'" *American Journal of Jurisprudence* 30 (1985).

Fisher III, William W., Morton J. Horwitz, and Thomas A. Reed, eds. *American Legal Realism.* Oxford: Oxford University Press, 1993.

Frank, Jerome. *Law and the Modern Mind.* New York: Brentano's, 1930.

George, Robert P. "Natural Law." *Harvard Journal of Law and Public Policy* 31 (2008).

Green, Michael Steven. "Legal Realism as Theory of Law." *William and Mary Law Review* 46 (2005): 1917.

Haidt, Jonathan. "The Emotional Dog and Its Rational Tail: A Social Intuitionist Approach to Moral Judgment." *Psychological Review* 108, no. 4 (2001).

Haidt, Jonathan, and Craig Joseph. "The Moral Mind: How Five Sets of Innate Intuitions Guide the Development of Many Culture-Specific Virtues, and Perhaps Even Modules." In *The Innate Mind: Foundations and the Future.* Edited by Peter Carruthers, Stephen Laurence, and Stephen Stich. Oxford: Oxford University Press, 2005.

Haidt, Jonathan, and Jesse Graham. "When Morality Opposes Justice: Conservatives Have Moral Intuitions that Liberals May Not Recognize." *Social Justice Research* 20, no. 1 (2007).

Hall, Mark, and Ronald Wright. "Systematic Content Analysis of Judicial Opinions." *California Law Review* 96, no. 1 (2008).

Hart, H.L.A. "Positivism and the Separation of Law and Morals." *Harvard Law Review* 71 (1958).

———. *The Concept of Law.* Oxford: Oxford University Press, 1961.

Hart Jr., Henry M., and Albert M. Sacks. *The Legal Process: Basic Problems in the Making and Application of Law.* Tentative 1958 ed. Edited by William N. Eskridge Jr., and Philip P. Frickey. Westbury: Foundation Press, 1994.

Hart Jr., Henry M., and Herbert Wechsler. *The Federal Courts and the Federal System.* Westbury: Foundation Press, 1953.

Himma, Kenneth Einar. "Substance and Method in Conceptual Jurisprudence and Legal Theory." *Virginia Law Review* 88, no. 5 (2002).

Holmes Jr., Oliver Wendell. "Codes, and the Arrangement of the Law." *American Law Review* 5 (1870).

―――. *The Common Law.* Boston: Little, Brown, 1881.

―――. "Privilege, Malice, and Intent." *Harvard Law Review* 8 (1894).

―――. "The Path of the Law." *Harvard Law Review* 10 (1897).

Horwitz, Morton J. *The Transformation Of American Law, 1780–1960.* Cambridge, MA: Harvard University Press, 1979.

Hutcheson Jr., Joseph C. "The Judgment Intuitive: The Function of the 'Hunch' in Judicial Decision." *Cornell Law Quarterly* 14 (1929).

Kahan, Dan M. "'Ideology in' or 'Cultural Cognition of' Judging: What Difference Does It Make?" *Marquette Law Review* 92 (2009).

Kelman, Mark. *A Guide to Critical Legal Studies.* Cambridge: Harvard University Press, 1987.

Kennedy, Duncan. *Legal Education and the Reproduction if Hierarchy: A Polemic Against the System.* New York: New York University Press, 1983.

―――. "Legal Education as Training for Hierarchy." In *The Politics of Law: A Progressive Critique.* Rev. ed. Edited by David Kairys. New York: Pantheon Books, 1990.

Kramer, Larry D. *The People Themselves: Popular Constitutionalism and Judicial Review.* Oxford: Oxford University Press, 2004.

Leiter, Brian. "Rethinking Legal Realism: Toward a Naturalized Jurisprudence." *Texas Law Review* 76, no. 2 (1997).

―――. *Naturalizing Jurisprudence.* Oxford: Oxford University Press, 2007.

Llewellyn, Karl N. "Some Realism About Realism—Responding to Dean Pound." *Harvard Law Review* 44 (1931).

―――. *The Common Law Tradition.* Boston: Little, Brown, 1960.

Michael, Helen K. "The Role of Natural Law in Early American Constitutionalism: Did the Founders Contemplate Judicial Enforcement of 'Unwritten' Individual Rights?" *North Carolina Law Review* 96 (1991).

Mikhail, John. "'Plucking the Mask of Mystery from Its Face': Jurisprudence and H.L.A. Hart." Review of *A Life Of H.L.A. Hart: The Nightmare and the Noble Dream.* By Nicola Lacey. *Georgetown Law Journal* 95 (2007).

Molot, Jonathan T. "The Judicial Perspective in the Administrative State: Reconciling Modern Doctrines of Deference with the Judiciary's Structural Role." *Stanford Law Review* 53, no. 1 (2000).

Murphy, Liam. "Better To See Law This Way." *New York University Law Review* 83, no. 4 (2008).

Nourse, Victoria, and Gregory Shaffer. "Varieties of New Legal Realism: Can a New World Order Prompt a New Legal Theory?" *Cornell Law Review* 95, no. 1 (2009).

Oakes, James L. "Hans Linde's Constitutionalism and Craft." *Review of Intellect and Craft: The Contributions of Justice Hans Linde to American Constitutionalism.* Edited by Robert F. Nagel. *University of Oregon Law Review* 74 (1995).

Pfander, James E. "Sovereign Immunity and the Right to Petition: Toward a First Amendment Right To Pursue Judicial Claims Against the Government." *Northwestern University Law Review* 91, no. 3 (1997).

Posner, Richard A. "The DeFunis Case and the Constitutionality of Preferential Treatment of Racial Minorities." *Supreme Court Review* (1974).

———. *Breaking the Deadlock: The 2000 Election, the Constitution, and the Courts.* Princeton, NJ: Princeton University Press, 2001.

———. *How Judges Think.* Cambridge: Harvard University Press, 2008.

Powe Jr., L.A. "Are "the People" Missing in Action (and Should Anyone Care)?" Review of *The People Themselves: Popular Constitutionalism and Judicial Review.* By Larry D. Kramer. *Texas Law Review* 83 (2005).

Rehnquist, William H. *The Supreme Court.* New York: Knopf Doubleday, 2001.

Richards, David A.J. "Rules, Policies, and Neutral Principles: The Search for Legitimacy in Common Law and Constitutional Adjudication." *Georgia Law Review* 11 (1977).

Roosevelt III, Kermit. *The Myth of Judicial Activism: Making Sense of Supreme Court Decisions.* New Haven, CT: Yale University Press, 2006.

Scalia, Antonin. "The Doctrine of Standing as an Essential Element of the Separation of Powers." *Suffolk University Law Review* 17 (1983).

———. "Originalism: The Lesser Evil." *University of Cincinnati Law Review* 57, no. 3 (1989).

Scheb II., John M., and William Lyons. "Judicial Behavior and Public Opinion: Popular Expectations Regarding the Factors that Influence Supreme Court Decisions." *Political Behavior* 23, no. 2 (2001).

Sebok, Anthony J. *Legal Positivism in American Jurisprudence.* Cambridge: Cambridge University Press, 1998.

Segall, Eric J. "The Skeptic's Constitution." *Review of Remnants of Belief: Contemporary Constitutional Issues.* By Louis Michael Seidman and Mark V. Tushnet. *UCLA Law Review* 44 (1997).

Segal, Jeffrey A., and Harold J. Spaeth. *The Supreme Court and the Attitudinal Model.* Cambridge: Cambridge University Press, 1993.

Simon, Dan. "A Psychological Model of Judicial Decision Making." *Rutgers Law Journal* 30 (1998).

———. "A Third View of the Black Box: Cognitive Coherence in Legal Decision Making." *University of Chicago Law Review* 71 (2004).

Solove, Daniel J. "The Darkest Domain: Deference, Judicial Review, and the Bill of Rights." *Iowa Law Review* 84 (1999).

Sotomayor, Sonia. "A Latina Judge's Voice." *Berkeley La Raza Law Journal* 13 (2002).

Strasser, Mark. "Equal Protection at the Crossroads: On Baker, Common Benefits, and Facial Neutrality." *Arizona Law Review* 42 (2000).

Sunstein, Cass R., and Richard A. Epstein, eds. *The Vote: Bush, Gore, and the Supreme Court.* Chicago: University of Chicago Press, 2001.

Sunstein, Cass R., David Schkade, and Lisa Michelle Ellman. "Ideological Voting on Federal Courts of Appeals: A Preliminary Investigation." Working paper. University of Chicago John M. Olin Law and Economics. Chicago, 2003.

Tocqueville, Alexis. *Democracy in America.* Translated by Arthur Goldhammer. New York: Library of America, 2004.

Tamanaham, Brian Z. "Understanding Legal Realism." *Texas Law Review* 87, no. 4 (2009).

Unger, Roberto Mangabeira. *The Critical Legal Studies Movement.* Cambridge: Harvard University Press, 1986.

Ursin, Edmund. "How Great Judges Think: Judges Richard Posner, Henry Friendly, and Roger Traynor on Judicial Lawmaking." *Buffalo Law Review* 57, no. 4 (2009).

Van Alstyne, William. "Rites of Passage: Race, the Supreme Court, and the Constitution." *University of Chicago Law Review* 46, no. 4 (1979).

Vojdik, Valorie K. "Beyond Stereotyping in Equal Protection Doctrine: Reframing the Exclusion of Women from Combat." *Alabama Law Review* 57, no. 2 (2005).

Wechsler, Herbert. "Toward Neutral Principles of Constitutional Law." *Harvard Law Review* 73 (1959).

White, Morton. *The Philosophy of the American Revolution.* Oxford: Oxford University Press. 1978.

Chapter 3

Is Judicialization Good for Democracy?

A Comparative Discussion

Ayşe Zarakol

As much as it was characterized by increase in mass participation around the world, the last century has also witnessed the great empowerment of judges.[1] More and more, the judicial branches of governments around the globe have been absorbing power from institutions more explicitly tasked with executive and especially legislative duties. John Ferejohn has noted that this process occurs principally through three mechanisms: by courts imposing limits on the power of legislative institutions, by courts making substantive policy and by courts regulating political activity itself.[2] This siphoning of legislative power by the judiciary is usually called "judicialization."

The spread of judicialization may be linked to the spread of democratization, but the relationship between these two processes is not as straightforward as it has been traditionally assumed. While judicialization is certainly a consequence of the spread of democracy, more judicial power does not automatically mean a more vibrant democracy. This is as much the case in "established" North-Western democracies of the world as it is in the "struggling" South-Eastern democracies; however, the rise in the number of countries in the latter category provide both the urgent incentive and the examples to rethink taken-for-granted assumptions about the role of judges in a democracy. The goal of this chapter is to first revisit the arguments for a powerful judiciary in a democracy with an eye on how those arguments would fare outside of the Western context and second to put assumptions about so-called advanced democracies under new scrutiny given the broader comparative perspective. At stake is a fundamental tension that all democracies must face: finding and managing the proper limits of majoritarian rule without slipping into authoritarianism.

Judicialization as Hegemonic Preservation

From an outside vantage point, there are two immediate problems with the extant judicialization literature. One is the limited nature of its comparative lens. For a very long time it seems, judicialization (as judicial activism) was treated and studied as a unique feature of the American democracy, and until recently it was still the case that legal scholars who worked within the American tradition showed little awareness of the problem of judicialization as a global phenomenon.[3] Especially in the last decade, comparativists[4] have started to observe that most Western democracies[5] have been exhibiting aggressive symptoms of judicialization,[6] but these observations also tend to be geographically and culturally bound to Western contexts.[7] This essay will argue that it does not make sense to limit observations about judicialization to the "established" democracies of the West or even to democracies in general.[8] Focusing on such historically contingent but theoretically unnecessary (at least in the way we have thus far conceived it to be) correlation patterns may skew our understanding of the phenomenon of judicialization.

The second problem flows from the first. Because judicialization has been studied either mostly in the context of what are considered established democracies or as driven by international law regimes, it is generally not treated as particularly problematic in the context of democratization. With some notable exceptions,[9] the assumption that permeates the comparative literature on the subject is that whatever challenges judicialization may pose for the majoritarian principle of modern democracy, it is also a boon for human rights[10] and for minority representation.[11] In general, the more "advanced" a country's economy and political system, and the more connected it is to the norms of the international system, the more judicialized its regime seems to be, and often around a discourse of "rights." The increased judicialization of traditionally skeptical polities stems at least partly from the legalization of international relations and the domestic consequences of treaty commitments such as those related to the European Court of Human Rights.[12] Even in the absence of such treaty commitments, the international system does drive judicialization to an extent because of the degree to which "the rule of law" is seen as a prerequisite for trade relations and foreign direct investment.[13]

In these ways, judicialization is treated as almost an inevitable consequence of democratization and conformity to Western (now international) norms: judicial power and advancement of democracy seem to go together. For instance, Neal Tate argues that "In Afro-Asia, outside India, it may be that only in the Philippines is the judicialization of politics a significant, current political development" because only the Philippines is democratic.[14] Christopher Larkins bemoans the lack of judicialization in Argentina and sees this fact as indicative of the fact that Argentina's delegative democracy falls short of democratic norms.[15] Judicialization is an almost wished upon development for "developing" democracies and nondemocracies.

We may be inclined to agree that judicialization in an authoritarian setting is an advancement for such regimes. Before the "Arab Spring," Tamir Moustafa had demonstrated the beneficial aspects of the judicialization in Mubarak's Egypt.[16] The bravura of the Pakistani Supreme Court under military rule is also not so distant in memory: it was that court's argument—that the authority of the court continues even when the written constitution is suspended by a coup—which forced Musharraf to pledge a return to democracy within a three-year time frame (which he lived up to, however reluctantly). However, the existence of such positive examples of judicialization in an authoritarian context does not automatically indicate that judicialization is always a boon for democracy, but merely suggests that it is at times a much needed check on excesses of authoritarian and majoritarian rule.

However, that is only half of the picture. Judiciaries can also be troublingly anti-democratic even when such checks are not clearly warranted. For instance, in a number of influential articles and a book, Ran Hirschl has argued that the judicialization trend around the world is not at all about constitutionalization of civil rights but better explained as an attempt for "hegemonic preservation":

> When their hegemony is increasingly challenged in ma-
> joritarian decision-making arenas, powerful elites and
> their political representatives may deliberately initiate and
> support a constitutionalization of rights in order to trans-
> fer power to supreme courts, where they assume, based
> primarily on the courts' record of adjudication and on the
> justices' ideological preferences, that their policy prefer-
> ences will be less contested.[17]

Hirschl goes on to demonstrate this pattern with references to several democracies around the world such as Israel, New Zealand, the
Republic of South Africa and Canada. If Hirschl is right, judicialization is on the rise around the world not as an aid of democracy
but as an obstacle to mass participation. As democracies around the
world have become more inclusive and more representative, elites
who used to control the state through legislative means have to resort
to using the courts in order to maintain their power and impose their
worldview.

It is interesting to note, however, that such elites are not always
motivated by economic or self-interested reasons (alone), but often
act or justify their actions in the name of what they believe are higher
principles. For instance, in Israel, the Constitutional Revolution in
1992 and the accompanying expansion of judicial review was initiated by the secular, mostly Ashkenazi bourgeoisie, who felt increasingly threatened by the growing influence of peripheral and religious
interests and worried about what that influence will mean for the
fundamental character of the Israeli state in the future. Through judicialization, they have been able to ensure that the country stays true
to their vision of a secular, Zionist, Western democracy. Given the
fragmentation of Israeli politics and the great demographic changes
the country is undergoing, this is an outcome that is no longer guaranteed through electoral politics and will become less likely in the
future. The Turkish Constitutional Court, supported by the secular
Turkish elite, played a similar role until recently against the perceived
threat of the Islamization of the Turkish republic, dissolving twenty-
five political parties in twenty-six years for anti-secular and seces-
sionist activities, and upholding the headscarf ban by interpreting the
secularism principle to be of such a high order to trump the individual freedom to observe one's religion.

Justifications of Judicialization

Judging from such examples, it may be tempting to believe that hegemonic preservation is itself good for democracy as a lesser of two evils because it protects the state from interests that are not as committed to basic democratic values. Usually this argument is made (and is found convincing) when judicialization goes against the interests of what are seen as un-"modern" segments of society (more on that in a moment). For now, let us note that this is not so different from how judicialization is often justified in so-called established democracies. The argument is that too much mass involvement is itself corrosive to democratic institutions and controverts democratic values to impose anti-democratic measures (often on minorities). It is believed that the legal elite may justifiably stand in the way of such a tragic but likely outcome in modern representative democratic systems. In fact, this argument is familiar to us from Tocqueville's *Democracy in America*, among other places. In *Democracy in America*, after his warnings about the possibility of the tyranny of the majority turning democracy into despotism,[18] Tocqueville pointed out that only two things stood in the way of such an outcome: lack of administrative centralization and American lawyers. Tocqueville then argued that lawyers in the United States, owing both to their training and education, had a taste for rituals and rules, and were a calm, rule-oriented elite standing in opposition to the whims and passions of the majority.

Similar anti-majoritarian justifications have been advanced throughout American history about the Supreme Court's exercise of judicial review. In what is considered the traditional era of the American Supreme Court (until the end of the nineteenth century), judicial power was first exercised through the assertion of judicial review in *Marbury vs. Madison* (1803) and later in service of building a strong central government.[19] During the property rights era (roughly the first quarter of the twentieth century), the Court struck down legislation that it believed to be in conflict with the spirit of the Constitution—derived from "natural law"—understood especially to protect individual property rights and laissez-faire economic principles. This type of activism was later replaced by the Court's deference to "universal" human rights and enforcement of civil rights. In American politics, how one views each of these periods in the history of the Supreme Court usually depends on where one's personal views fall on the political spectrum; Republicans are more likely to remember the property rights era fondly and Democrats tend to favor judicial activism when it is committed in defense of civil liberties. However, what these positions have in common is the belief in "the assertion that the Constitution or [natural law or] the universal human rights tradition contains a set of knowable rights and that judicial review is supposed to defend those rights from the infringement by the majority."[20] Similar defenses are being used now in the European context as well.[21]

Essentially, the principal way judicialization is justified in modern democracies is by appeal to some set of higher principles the consideration of which should override utilitarian[22] considerations. What those higher principles are supposed to be varies with the person making the argument. Three potential candidates for justifying the subordination of the will of the majority in Western democracies are appeals to (1) the sanctity of the constitution, (2) natural law, and (3) universal human rights.[23]

Deference to Higher Principles

In practice, the defense of judicialization often takes an elitist or, at the very least, an anti-majoritarian character.[24] For example, within the American context, the sanctity of the constitution is often rooted not in the manner it was ratified but in the identity of its authors. According to this view, the crafters of constitutions have some special quality that makes them wiser about the needs of the populace than the populace itself does at any given time.[25] That special quality may be their status as founders of state, their past heroism, their education, their commitment to the long-term view of state affairs and/or freedom from political bias. It may even be argued that it is the job of crafting the constitution that elevates these men; because no legislation in a representative democracy really represents the will of the majority, it is better to defer to the crafters' wisdom (as understood through judicial review) than to let the majority always decide. This argument places its faith in the foresight of constitutional crafters over the actions of present-day politicians.[26]

A similar reasoning holds the constitution to be special because it already exists and it has been followed in the past. Revering the constitution in this manner may bring to mind what Weber called legitimacy based on traditional authority, "a belief in the legitimacy of what has always existed." The same argument could also be made by invoking Burke;[27] it could be argued that having a particular constitution already in place (or any traditional institution) to constrain politics is a healthy check on the revolutionary impulses of the masses, especially as they are exploited by those who claim to speak in the name of the masses. Neither frame really amounts to a demonstration that the constitution embodies higher principles, and perhaps because of their explicit anti-democratic bent, such arguments are less popular today.[28]

What this discussion demonstrates is that it is difficult to use the constitution as the sole justification for judicialization without invoking even higher principles. In most established democracies, the constitution itself is held to be legitimate to the degree[29] that it is in accord with such higher principles. In any case, arguments about the sanctity of the constitution do not travel well, even in the Western world. These arguments are rather limited to the unique aspects of the American experience (such as the "Founding Fathers" discourse). If judicialization is to be justified from a global perspective, some higher principle rooted in natural law or universal rights seems to be a more promising candidate.

The idea of the existence of natural laws more binding than man's law was first advanced by the social contract theorists of the early modern era such as Thomas Hobbes and John Locke, who argued that through rational reflection about man's nature, one could discern the natural, inalienable rights of men.[30] This reasoning was intended to replace the need for explicitly invoking God as a justification for political decisions. While that particular method of arriving at a justification for the inalienable rights of men through consideration of human nature has been brought into question, first by eighteenth-century theorists such as Rousseau and Hume who were more interested in social convention, then by nineteenth-century theorists such as Hegel and Marx who were more interested in the teleological movements of history, the idea that human beings have inalienable rights was the consensus that emerged from the Enlightenment.

Nowadays, most people in most Western societies (to begin with) do hold certain rights to be inalienable and they do not think this belief needs justification. Especially dogmatic[31] is the belief that all people are by nature equal and that they should be treated as such by their respective states.[32] The belief that each human being is no better or worse than another human being is certainly what is behind the commonly accepted wisdom (at least in the West) that democracy is the best type of government. Democracy is often justified not only as the regime type that best protects "human rights" (as this phrase is generally understood), but also on the ground that the ability to self-determine is often considered to be one of the most inalienable of rights. By allowing citizens to rule themselves, democracy guarantees this most basic of rights.

Expansive judicial review is frequently justified in current debates by an appeal to the same seemingly evident principles about equality, respect and human rights. What seems like congruity on its face is actually a bitter tension: the introduction of judicial review into a democracy inevitably puts two types of rights in conflict. If we have the right to self-determine, and the majoritarian voting principles of democratic regimes are the best way we have found to exercise that right, why should the majority not be able to vote to give up or restrict rights? How do we know that there are universal, inalienable, non-negotiable rights that need to be protected, even against the democratic will of the people?

As we know, there are several ways a belief in universal rights can be justified. One is by invoking God(s). It can be argued that God(s) made people a certain way and gave them certain rights, and God(s) created the universe, so the rules she or he or they made apply everywhere universally. The problem with *deux ex machina* explanations is that they are only convincing to the choir. Furthermore, religious and quasi-religious justifications do not pass muster as rational legitimation, which is what is required in modernity of "good" political regimes.

A second way, as discussed earlier, is by replacing the idea of God with nature. In this reasoning, there is something generalizable about human nature, for example, reason, or the ability to suffer, from which higher principles about equality and other rights can be derived. We have rights because they are essential prerequisites for expressing our humanness. Space does not permit me to go into a detailed discussion of the various natural rights doctrines, but it should suffice to say that such justifications do not travel very well outside of the European context and therefore are not particularly germane to the present discussion. Leaving aside the incongruity of using reason or pain to draw boundaries about humanness and our actual practice, there is also the possibility that such beliefs about the essence of humanity are culturally and historically contingent, and therefore not particularly compelling as universal eternal principles.

Judicialization in Comparative Perspective

However the justifications may fare in the Western context; all such justifications discussed earlier for judicialization and deference to higher principles run into greater difficulty the moment they are scrutinized from a comparative perspective. For instance, while the Judeo-Christian tradition has moved to the point that one could plausibly make an argument, without encountering much resistance, that God made people equal, not every religion shares this belief. The belief in the inferiority of women is widespread across different religions (some more than others) and some religions reserve equal treatment only for their members. Many people around the world think that universal declarations about human nature (especially those based in individual reason) amount to Judeo-Christian morality in another guise. For example, many Muslim countries have criticized the Universal Declaration of Human Rights on such grounds and have gone so far as to advocate an alternative version, that is, the Cairo Declaration on Human Rights in Islam.[33]

Even if the argument about the universality of human nature is conceded, it is not clear what rights one is guaranteed just by being human. Even in Western society consensus on higher principles is limited—there are a few people who reject the secular articulation of higher principles in favor of what they believe to be the God-ordained vision of their world; there are many others who agree on the principle of equality but not much else. Some say that the fact that we are equal merely means we are equally protected from government intrusion; others think equality means that the government should make sure that the playground of life is not uneven. In other words, there is a great deal of disagreement over whether we deserve positive or negative rights, entitlements or protections. When we travel outside "the traditional West" the issue of higher principles becomes even thornier. Not all cultures elevate the individual to the same level. Other societies may hold different principles to be more important than majoritarianism: the Turkish Constitutional Court, for instance, throughout the twentieth century viewed secularism as *laicite* to be a principle of highest order for the survival of the state.

All of this is to say that even when higher principles are invoked, or precisely when they are invoked, there is a great deal of ambiguity. Ultimately, granting that judges have the right to parse through that ambiguity is to place a lot of faith in the objectivity of judges. This faith in the judges in the pro-judicialization camp is often combined with the belief that the majority cannot be trusted entirely. This may be because the majority rigs the system to perpetuate its interests,[34] or because it is emotional and not rational,[35] or because it is driven by short-term needs. Lawyers by contrast "think more clearly and are more dedicated to the commonweal than the rest of us."[36] The law, unlike majoritarian legislation, is supposed to be precise, neutral and rational.[37] The ontology of modernity values and legitimizes those traits more than any other.[38] In fact, as discussed earlier, the majoritarian principle of democracy itself is justified according to such a standard, but it is a mistake to assume that the demands of modernity and democracy always run in the same direction.[39] Democratization outside of the West brings that inherent tension to the fore.

I noted in the opening pages that elites outside of the West engage in hegemonic preservation through judicialization not only because their material interests are threatened by mass participation but because they often tend to believe that they are acting in the service of a higher principle. Unlike Western democracies, the higher principle at stake in non-Western states tends not to be equality or human rights, but rather some element seen as essential to a particular state's modern/national identity. In most of the world outside of the traditional West, state-building trajectories have often required a heavy hand, and were executed by a self-appointed elite that has very entrenched ideas about what the nation needs/stands for. If such a state-building trajectory is coupled with a strong outside pressure to conform to norms of representative democracy (or if the elites' self-understanding is such that being "civilized"/"modern," and so on requires such conformity), elites can devise a work-around by increasing judicial power at the expense of democratic politics.[40]

It is easy to criticize this kind of capture of the judiciary by elite interests because the stated goal deviates from the frequently invoked justifications in the West, but, as discussed earlier, the traditionally accepted appeals to higher principles in "established" democracies are no less problematic from a theoretical perspective. There is some-times an automatic tendency to assume that politics outside of the West is somehow more "political," if we take political to mean messy. There is often a belief that politics "over there" is more corrupt than it is here—this belief is partly explained by psychological biases that tend to pathologize others' motives and idealize one's own, and partly by the perceptual blind spots created by the various hierarchical cat-egorizations of the world we have internalized as a result of moder-nity.[41] If a country is labeled "developing" or "democratizing," it seems more natural that judicialization there must be more anti-democratic.[42] Yet there is no coherent *philosophical* perspective (at least as things stand today) to argue that judicialization that protects some set of universal rights is better (or less political) than judicial-ization that protects some other universal truth as it is perceived by an elite. Neither does that preclude us from looking for such a per-spective—to the contrary. We simply must stop assuming things are automatically better in the West and start thinking about substantive justifications for our evaluations (even if every now and then we may find that there are none).

Conclusion

What we are witnessing around the world is an ironic trend toward a convergence between "democracies" and "authoritarian regimes" on the matter of judicialization. On the one hand, as mass participa-tion increases, elites in established democracies and semi-democra-cies are driving judicialization, if and when they find that they can no longer control/predict electoral results, and often in the name of higher principles; on the other hand, authoritarian regimes intro-duce judicialization as a way of gaining legitimacy in a world that values the rule of law. We may be looking at a global future where the real division is not between juristocrats and democrats but rather between different types of juristocrats or self-appointed elites serv-ing a sacred principle of their choosing, which makes the search for a coherent position from which to judge judicial interventions even more urgent.

The argument gets even murkier when we try to distinguish between judicialized democracies and semi-democracies, on the one hand, and authoritarian regimes where an elite group puts limits on mass participation in the name of some higher principle, on the other. If majoritarian representation and electoral politics are being trumped by courts everywhere, for example, in Europe by invoking the language of rights, in the United States the constitution, in Israel core-values, in Thailand the royalty, and so on, what makes one kind of intrusion better than another? Is there a theoretical way to distinguish the judicialization of a democracy from modern participatory polities with elite vanguards that does not collapse into an ad hominem fallacy? More disturbingly, what makes these types of intrusions better than the intrusion of the Council of Guardians in Iran, which, also, claims to speak for higher principles (which, admittedly are not universal per se,[43] but held to be universally valid by the Iranian Council of Guardians)?

In other words, given current trends in "established" democracies, would we have to take Iran seriously as a democracy if the Council of Guardians started calling itself a Supreme Court? This is a question we must take seriously. By dividing the field into reified subcategories about so-called advanced democracies and developing democracies or the industrialized world and the developing world, not only do we sentence those in the latter category to a perpetual state of imperfection but we also shield countries in the first category from comparative scrutiny, which is ultimately damaging to the health of these democracies. Without reasoned justification, democracy and rights simply become meaningless labels of in-group superiority.

This is not to argue for a relativistic moral equivalency between established democracies, struggling democracies and nondemocracies, but to point out how the a priori affixing of labels affects our judgment of what is actually happening on the ground. There must be other ways of evaluating political processes that do not collapse into nineteenth-century schemas of civilization and barbarity. For instance, judicialization may be judged from a temporal and a comparative perspective. If judicialization allows the elite to give up some of its power through nonviolent means, then it arguably is preferable to alternatives. If it results in a better system than what was in place before, in terms of the life chances of the citizens, then it is better than alternatives.

Yet such a pragmatic evaluation is unlikely to satisfy those who are in search of more generalizable principles. One possible way of making a higher order distinction based on such principles is by looking at dispersion of power, as also observed by Tocqueville.

According to Tocqueville, what stood in the way of the tyranny of majority was not just judges but also the decentralization of power. This may be read as a more general warning that too much power in the hands of the same people is problematic regardless of what the regime calls itself, not from an absolutist sense, but because it tends to generate a stagnant polity.

As cynical as we may be about the elite push for judicialization, there are compelling arguments that judicial power is defensible to a degree as a check on other branches, and useful when the legislative branch is paralyzed for some reason. It may be especially needed where the administrative system is highly centralized and therefore prone to be easily controlled by whoever comes to power (as is the case in Turkey). Parliamentary systems already lack many of the checks and balances of presidential systems. In such systems there may be good reasons to worry about what will happen if all institutions of governance are captured by the same worldview. However, this is not such a rarity in world politics or even in democratic politics that it should be treated automatically as a crisis. Assuming that rules for recruitment are written in a neutral, rational, and inclusive way, and enforced impartially, temporary consolidation of power may not be particularly problematic. In that case, as the political situation changed, so would those in power. Systems that allow for this type of circulation are likely to be better than others. It could be argued that power tends to perpetuate power: once in power, some groups may not practice neutrality no matter what the rules say. This, however, points to a very important fact: what really distinguishes good regimes from bad regimes is not so much how institutions are crafted but how people understand the norms of behavior in everyday practice. In other words, the gap between balanced and unbalanced systems is one of nuance and not so much of substance. This suggests that even the most established systems are more vulnerable than they seem.

Finally, despite all warranted cynicism, there is something to be said for the binding effect of rules and laws that are often the basis of judicialization. Even the most politicized courts operate within the constraints of legal-rational authority, and that should count for something. Out of all possible types, legal-rational rules are most likely to create a normative environment of restraint and repetition, most of the time.[44] In an increasingly unpredictable world, that is no small feat.

Notes

1. I am grateful to the organizers of the 2010 Middlebury conference and editors of this volume for the very rewarding opportunity to reflect on some very interesting issues that are outside of my normal research agenda. I would also like to thank the two anonymous reviewers for their valuable comments. My greatest debt is and will always be to Professor Murray Dry, who was my undergraduate politics advisor and whose example inspired me to pursue a career in academia.
2. John Ferejohn, "Judicializing Politics, Politicizing Law."
3. Ran Hirschl, "The Political Origins of Judicial Empowerment Through Constitutionalization: Lessons from Four Constitutional Revolutions," 93–94; for possible exceptions, cf. Shapiro, 101–12; and Ferejohn, "Judicializing Politics," 41–68.
4. See, for example, Barry Holmström, 153–164; Jan Kate, Jan and Peter Koppen, 143–151; Christine Landfried, 113–124; Maurice Sunkin, 125–133; C. Neal Tate and Torbjörn Vallinder, eds.; Alec Stone Sweet; Carlo Guarneri and Patrizia Pederzoli; and Ran Hirschl, *Towards Juristocracy: The Origins and Consequences of the New Constitutionalism.*
5. This seems to be true even in countries such as United Kingdom and Sweden, where the judiciary has traditionally exercised power very narrowly; see Sunkin, *Judicialization in the UK*, 130; and Holmström, *Judicialization in Sweden*, 161.
6. Ran Hirschl, "Judicial Empowerment Through Constitutionalization," 91; and Leslie Friedman Goldstein, 611.
7. Notwithstanding the interesting but perfunctory (from an accumulative perspective) discussions of judicialization in a few non-European contexts; cf. Shannon Ishiyama Smithey and John Ishiyama, 719–742; Christopher Larkins, 423–442; and C. Neal Tate, "The Judicialization of Politics in the Philippines and Southeast Asia," 187–197.
8. For the first advancement of the argument, see Tamir Moustafa, 883–930.
9. For the most notable exceptions, cf. Ran Hirschl, "The Political Origins of Judicial Empowerment through Constitutionalization: Lessons from Israel's Constitutional Revolution," 315–335; Hirschl, "Judicial Empowerment through Constitutionalization"; and Hirschl, *Towards Juristocracy.*
10. Ronald Dworkin; François Furet and Mona Ozouf, eds.; and François Furet.
11. R. Kent Weaver and Brett Rockman, eds.; George Tsebelis, 289–325; Henry Abraham, 7–20; Jan-Erik Lane; Christian Davenport, 627–654; Alfred Stepan and Cindy Skach, 1–22; and Jon Elster and Rune Slagstad, eds.

12. See Goldstein et al., *From Democracy to Juristocracy*; and Holmström, "Judicialization in Sweden," 161.
13. In "Law Verses the State" Tamir Moustafa argues this is one of the reasons why the authoritarian government of Egypt has allowed a considerable degree of judicialization.
14. Tate, "Judicialization in the Philippines," 187.
15. Larkins, "Delegative Democracy in Argentina," 442.
16. Moustafa, "Law Verses the State," 883–930.
17. Hirschl, "Judicial Empowerment Through Constitutionalization," 103.
18. For example, "In the United States the omnipotence of the majority, which is favorable to the legal despotism of the legislature, likewise favors the arbitrary authority of the magistrate. The majority has absolute power both to make the laws and to watch over their execution; and as it has equal authority over those who are in power and the community at large, it considers public officers as its passive agents and readily confides to them the task of carrying out its de signs" (*Democracy in America*, bk. I, ch. 15).
19. Shapiro, "Juridicalization in the U.S.," 102.
20. Ibid., 110.
21. For an overview of how European polities were judicialized—the process often followed institutionalization of a rights regime (and was aided by the legal super-structure of the European Commission/Union), see for example, Sweet, *Governing with Judges.*
22. The best justification for the majoritarian principle may be found in the philosophical stance of Utilitarianism, which permeates most understandings of democracy today. Letting the majority decide a question is the most straightforward way to ensure the greatest happiness of the greatest number. For an overview of utilitarianism and the possible critiques against it, see J.J.C. Smart and Bernard Williams.
23. Interestingly, the argument that there should be no check on majoritarianism is rarely made. One possible candidate is Mancur Olson, who argued that a second invisible hand guides democratic politics just as it guides the market. According to this argument, majorities are made up of rational individuals, and since they are rational, they will realize that the self-interested thing to treat everyone in society, even the minorities, equally. Neo-Hegelians make a similar argument about the unsustainability of unequal relationships in the long run—they see the historical trend to be toward inclusivity and equal recognition, with or without checks on the majority. See *Power and Prosperity: Outgrowing Communist and Capitalist Dictatorships.*
24. As a side note, these higher principles themselves can be justified within a normative framework that is a generally deferent to

majoritarianism, but that type of argument is neither the frequent recourse of judicialization proponents nor found compelling when it is. For instance, it could be claimed that constitutions become legitimate through procedural demands based on extreme majoritarianism. In other words, constitutions trump the regular exercise of the will of the majority because they are difficult to ratify and ratification requires more than a simple plurality. Unfortunately, this argument is not particularly convincing because constitutions are also difficult to change whereas the populace inevitably changes over time—hence, Thomas Jefferson's suggestion that the American Constitution be rewritten every generation (nineteen years). While the argument for the extreme majoritarian legitimacy for the constitution may hold during the founding period, it is unlikely to be valid hundred years later. This problem may be solved through judicial review—but justifying judicial review by allusions to the changing populace would only beg the question of Jefferson's suggestion. Why not craft a new constitution or new amendments instead of empowering an elite not accountable to the populace? See Thomas Jefferson to James Madison, September 6, 1789, in the papers of Thomas Jefferson, University of Virginia Library.

25. At times (but not always) such appeals to authority end up crossing the threshold to logical fallacy.

26. Another psychological fallacy is the idealization of the distant past.

27. For example, "I shall only say here, in justice to that old-fashioned constitution under which we have long prospered, that our representation has been found perfectly adequate to all the purposes for which a representation of the people can be desired or devised. I defy the enemies of our constitution to show the contrary. . . . Something they must destroy, or they seem to exist for no purpose . . . it is with infinite caution that any man ought to venture upon pulling down an edifice which has answered in any tolerable degree for ages the common purposes of society" Edmund Burke, 49, 50, 53.

28. Although, maybe they should be: it may be that there is something positive about having a set of neutrally articulated rules that does not hinge on the philosophical essence of these rules. I return to this point in the conclusion.

29. This is not to say that they are not considered wholly illegitimate otherwise—but violations are much easier to justify if they are in accordance with what comes to be considered as higher principles. For instance, in the American context, it is the attempts to flaunt slavery laws that are remembered fondly and not the three-fifths clause of Article I.

30. The argument that one can see through their mind's eye the ordering principles of the universe dates back to Plato—modern theorists simply eliminated the requirement of a special mind as a prerequisite for such sight.

31. I say dogmatic not because of personal disagreement but to point to the received wisdom quality of this claim in modern society.

32. For example, "All human beings are born free and equal in dignity and rights. They are endowed with reason and conscience and should act towards one another in a spirit of brotherhood." United Nations, *Universal Declaration of Human Rights*, art.1, www.un.org/en/documents/udhr/index.shtml

33. See, for example, www1.umn.edu/humanrts/instree/cairodeclaration.html for the full text.

34. Shapiro calls this justification the "correcting the failures of democracy" rationale. "Juridicalization in the U.S., 110–111. See John Hart Ely.

35. See, for example, the discussion about Tocqueville above. Ferejohn also argues that that the framers feared abuses by the legislative branch most of all ("Judicializing Politics," 47).

36. Shapiro, "Juridicalization in the U.S.," 110.

37. Goldstein et al., *From Democracy to Juristocracy*, 387.

38. The idea that the people as a whole are not rational and are driven by short-term happiness is obviously as old as Plato—it is the belief that lawyers (as bureaucrats) can be the embodiment of rationality is the modern one.

39. In fact, it is telling that it is difficult to place democratic institutions in Weber's three-prong typology of authority. Legal-rational authority, closely associated with modernity, is the authority of the bureaucrat. See Martin E. Spencer, 129.

40. In addition to the previously discussed examples of Israel and Turkey, the recent constitutional changes in Thailand after the 2006 coup fit this pattern.

41. See Ayşe Zarakol, *After Defeat: How the East Learned to Live with the West*, chs. 1–2.

42. This perception is often shared by people who live in those countries—they buy into the same comparative mind-set. See Zarakol, *After Defeat*, introduction. This argument should not be construed as saying that judicialization outside of a Western context is not antidemocratic. It may or may not be—the challenge is only to the automatic assumption to always think that things are worse "over there."

43. I mean the discriminatory rules about women, and so on.

44. When they are abused, they lead to the worst type of extremism. See Zygmunt Bauman.

Bibliography

Abraham, Henry. "Reflections on the Contemporary Status of Our Civil Rights and Liberties and the Bill of Rights." *Journal of Law and Politics* 13 (1997): 7–20.

Bauman, Zygmunt. *Modernity and Holocaust.* Ithaca: Cornell University Press, 1989.

Burke, Edmund. *Reflections on the Revolution in France.* Edited by J.G.A. Pocock. Indianapolis: Hackett, 1987.

Davenport, Christian. "Constitutional Promises and Repressive Reality: A Cross-National Time-Series Investigation of Why Political and Civil Liberties Are Suppressed." *Journal of Politics* 58, no. 3 (1996): 627–654.

Dworkin, Ronald. *A Bill of Rights for Britain.* Ann Arbor: University of Michigan Press, 1990.

Elster, Jon, and Rune Slagstad, eds. *Constitutionalism and Democracy.* New York: Cambridge University Press, 1988.

Ely, John Hart. *Democracy and Distrust: A Theory of Judicial Review.* Cambridge, MA: Harvard University Press, 1980.

Ferejohn, John. "Judicializing Politics, Politicizing Law." *Law and Contemporary Problems* 65, no. 3 (2002): 41–68.

Furet, François. *The French Revolution: 1770–1814.* Translated by Antonia Nevill. Oxford: Blackwell, 1996.

Furet, François, and Mona Ozouf, eds. *A Critical Dictionary of the French Revolution.* Translated by Arthur Goldhammer. Cambridge, MA: Harvard University Press, 1989.

Goldstein, Judith, M. Kahler, R. Keohane, and A.M. Slaughter. "Introduction: Legalization and World Politics." *International Organization* 54, no. 3 (2000): 385–399.

Goldstein, Leslie Friedman. "From Democracy to Juristocracy." Review of *From Democracy to Juristocracy? The Power of Judges: A Comparative Study of Courts and Democracy.* By Carlo Guarneri and Patrizia Pederzoli. *Law & Society Review* 38, no. 3 (2004): 611–629.

Guarneri, Carlo, and Patrizia Pederzoli. *From Democracy to Juristocracy? The Power of Judges: A Comparative Study of Courts and Democracy.* Oxford: Oxford University Press, 2002.

Hirschl, Ran. "The Political Origins of Judicial Empowerment Through Constitutionalization: Lessons from Four Constitutional Revolutions." *Law & Social Inquiry* 25, no. 1 (2000): 91–149.

———. "The Political Origins of Judicial Empowerment through Constitutionalization: Lessons from Israel's Constitutional Revolution." *Comparative Politics* 33, no. 3 (2001): 315–335.

————. *Towards Juristocracy: The Origins and Consequences of the New Constitutionalism*. Cambridge, MA: Harvard University Press, 2004.

Holmström, Barry. "The Judicialization of Politics in Sweden." *International Political Science Review* 15, no. 2 (1994): 153–164.

Kate, Jan, and Peter Koppen. "Judicialization of Politics in the Netherlands: Towards a Form of Judicial Review." *International Political Science Review* 15, no. 2 (1994): 143–151.

Landfried, Christine. "The Judicialization of Politics in Germany." *International Political Science Review* 15, no. 2 (1994): 113–124.

Lane, Jan-Erik. *Constitutions and Political Theory*. New York: St. Martin's Press, 1996.

Larkins, Christopher. "The Judiciary and Delegative Democracy in Argentina." *Comparative Politics* 30, no. 4 (1998): 423–442.

Moustafa, Tamir. "Law Versus the State: The Judicialization of Politics in Egypt." *Law & Social Inquiry* 28, no. 4 (2003): 883–930.

Nietzsche, Friedrich. *Beyond Good and Evil*. Translated by Walter Kaufmann. New York: Vintage Books, 1989.

Olson, Mancur. *Power and Prosperity: Outgrowing Communist and Capitalist Dictatorships*. New York: Basic Books, 2000.

Shapiro, Martin. "Juridicalization of Politics in the United States." *International Political Science Review* 15, no. 2 (1994): 101–112.

Smart, J.J.C., and Bernard Williams. *Utilitarianism: For and Against*. Cambridge: Cambridge University Press, 1973.

Smithey, Shannon Ishiyama, and John Ishiyama. "Judicial Activism in Post-Communist Politics." *Law & Society Review* 36, no. 4 (2002): 719–742.

Spencer, Martin E. "Weber on Legitimate Norms and Authority." *The British Journal of Sociology* 21, no. 2 (1970): 123–134.

Stepan, Alfred, and Cindy Skach. "Constitutional Frameworks and Democratic Consolidation: Parliamentarianism Versus Presidentialism." *World Politics* 46, no. 1 (1993): 1–22.

Sunkin, Maurice. "Judicialization of Politics in the United Kingdom." *International Political Science Review* 15, no. 2 (1994): 125–133.

Sweet, Alec Stone. *Governing with Judges: Constitutional Politics in Europe*. Oxford: Oxford University Press, 2000.

Tate, C. Neal. "The Judicialization of Politics in the Philippines and Southeast Asia." *International Political Science Review* 15, no. 2 (1994): 187–197.

Tate, C. Neal, and Torbjörn Vallinder, eds. *The Global Expansion of Judicial Power*. New York: New York University Press, 1995.

Thucydides. *The History of the Peloponnesian War*. Translated by Rex Warner. Edited by M.I. Finley. New York: Penguin, 1972.

Tsebelis, George. "Decision-Making in Political Systems: Veto Players in Presidentialism, Parliamentarism, Multicameralism, and Multipartyism." *British Journal of Political Science* 25, no. 3 (1995): 289–325.

Weaver, R. Kent, and Brett Rockman, eds. *Do Institutions Matter? Government Capabilities in the United States and Abroad.* Washington, DC: Brookings Institution, 1993.

Zarakol, Ayşe. *After Defeat: How the East Learned to Live with the West.* Cambridge: Cambridge University Press, 2011.

Chapter 4

If There's a Right, Is There a Remedy?

The Federal Courts' Role in Remedying Constitutional Violations

Barbara Kritchevsky[1]

Introduction

The Supreme Court's decision in *Marbury v. Madison*,[2] most importantly, established the principle of judicial review.[3] The Court based the doctrine on its view of the role of the federal courts, explaining that it was "emphatically the province of the judicial department to say what the law is."[4] The premise of constitutional government was that the Constitution trumped a law that was in conflict with that document, making a law that violated the Constitution void.[5] The Constitution itself was a form of law that it was the courts' job to interpret.[6] It was the courts' obligation, then, to interpret the Constitution and statutory law to determine if the two types of law conflicted so that the statutory law must give way.[7]

The *Marbury* Court articulated the doctrine of judicial review in order to determine if it could remedy a loss of individual rights. The decision rested on the premise that courts should act to provide redress to a person who suffered a loss of a legal right,[8] making the determination that Marbury's rights were at stake a key predicate to the Court's decision.[9] After determining that Marbury had a right to the commission he sought,[10] the Court asked: "If he has a right, and that right has been violated, do the laws of this country afford him a remedy?"[11] The Court responded that "the very essence of civil liberty" rested on an individual's right to claim legal protection when he received an injury.[12] One of government's primary duties was to provide that protection.[13] The United States Government was a "government of laws, and not of men. It will certainly cease to deserve this high appellation if the laws furnish no remedy for the violation of a vested legal right."[14]

The *Marbury* opinion reflects the principle *ubi jus, ibi remedium*, that rights require remedies.[15] The idea that rights required remedies was well-accepted in the early days of the republic and led courts freely to imply remedies for violations of federal laws.[16] The United States Supreme Court's 1916 opinion in *Texas & Pacific Railway Company v. Rigsby*[17] illustrates the early-twentieth-century Court's adherence to this view. The *Rigsby* Court found that a railroad employee could sue his employer to recover for injuries attributable to the railroad's violation of a federal law regulating railroad safety.[18] The Court explained that disregard of the statute was a "wrongful act," and that the common law gave the person for whose benefit the statute was enacted a right to recover from the wrongdoer.[19] The Court explained that allowing the injured person to sue for damages, even absent a specific statutory remedy, was simply "an application of the maxim, *Ubi jus ibi remedium*."[20]

Cases such as *Rigsby* illustrate that the Supreme Court has long believed that the power to authorize remedies does not lie solely in Congress's hands; federal courts can act independently to provide a remedy to a person who suffers harm a statute aims to prevent. Statutes are not the only form of law. The *Marbury* Court recognized that the Constitution is also a type of law and that individuals have a right to seek redress for violations of legal rights.[21] The question that logically arises is whether courts may imply remedies for constitutional violations in the same way they do for statutory ones.

The Court has long exercised some forms of remedial power to protect individuals who are the victims of constitutional violations. It has allowed individuals to use the Constitution as a shield against the unconstitutional exercise of government power. Federal courts will not allow the government to convict a person by using evidence authorities obtain in violation of the Fourth or Fifth Amendments[22] and can prevent prosecution under an unconstitutional statute.[23]

Courts have also long acted to enjoin government actors from violating the Constitution.[24]

The courts' exercise of power to protect a person from unconstitutional exercises of authority uses the Constitution to shield individuals from harm. Do courts also have the power to provide redress if a person has suffered a violation of his constitutional rights? Can courts infer a damages remedy from the Constitution, allowing individuals to use the Constitution as a sword, or does the power to authorize relief in damages rest exclusively in Congress's hands? Congress has authorized a damages remedy against state officials who deprive an individual of constitutional rights.[25] But Congress has provided no similar remedy against federal officials. Can the federal courts provide the remedy?

The Court did exactly that in *Bivens v. Six Unknown Named Agents*,[26] allowing a private suit seeking damages from federal agents who violated the Fourth Amendment. The *Bivens* Court relied on *Marbury*,[27] the Court's power to infer private rights of action for statutory violations,[28] and its power to order injunctive relief.[29] It did so over dissents that accused the Court of violating separation of powers principles by exercising legislative power.[30] According to the dissents, only Congress could authorize such remedies.[31]

A majority of the Court now shares the concerns of the *Bivens* dissenters, that implying statutory rights of action threatens the separation of powers and fails to show proper deference to Congress.[32] The Court's recent jurisprudence frowns on implied statutory remedies, arguing that the Court overreaches and treads on Congress's role when it freely implies statutory remedies.[33] Members of the Court now argue that *Bivens* remedies represent a similarly overbroad view of judicial power. Justice Scalia, for instance, calls *Bivens* a remnant of the "heady days" of implied statutory rights of action.[34] A majority of the Court now demonstrates animosity to *Bivens* actions and refuses to apply *Bivens* beyond its strictest holding.[35]

The fundamental question is whether the same concerns arise when a court implies constitutional rights of action as when it implies statutory ones. Should the Court's unwillingness to imply statutory remedies lead to a similar unwillingness to imply a right to redress under the Constitution? I argue that it should not. Constitutional rights, unlike statutory rights, do not originate with Congress and are not subject to Congressional repeal. The courts should act to protect constitutional rights if Congress does not. The courts should also guarantee that all citizens can receive the same redress if they suffer violations of Constitutional rights, making state remedies inadequate redress for constitutional harms.[36]

The *Bivens* Case

The Supreme Court implied a private right of action under the Constitution in *Bivens*, allowing an individual to sue a federal officer who violated his constitutional rights for damages even in the absence of a statute authorizing such a remedy. The Court's decision stands against the background of 42 U.S.C. § 1983,[37] in which Congress provided that an individual who suffered a constitutional violation at the hands of a person acting under color of state law could sue for damages. The Court's decision in *Monroe v. Pape*[38] established section 1983's broad reach.

The Background: *Monroe v. Pape*

Thirteen Chicago police officers broke into James Monroe's home one early morning in 1958.[39] They routed Mr. Monroe's family from bed and made them stand naked in the living room.[40] They ransacked the home, emptying drawers and ripping mattress covers.[41] Police then took Mr. Monroe to the police station and held him for ten hours, interrogating him about a murder.[42] Police did not take Mr. Monroe before a magistrate or let him call his family or an attorney.[43] Police then released him without charge.[44]

Monroe sued the police and the City of Chicago under section 1983,[45] alleging that they violated his Fourth Amendment rights while acting "under color of the statutes, ordinances, regulations, customs and usages" of the city and state.[46] The defendants moved to dismiss, arguing that the fact that their actions violated the state's constitution and laws meant that they did not act "under color" of state law.[47] Defendants argued that Monroe should seek redress in state court.[48]

The Court rejected the defendants' argument, finding that Congress intended to provide redress for officials' abuse of their power.[49] The main reason Congress enacted § 1983 was to combat officials' failure to enforce state law. The Court said that it was "abundantly clear" that Congress passed the statute "to afford a federal right in federal courts because, by reason of prejudice, passion, neglect, intolerance or otherwise, state laws might not be enforced and the claims of citizens to the enjoyment of rights, privileges, and immunities guaranteed by the Fourteenth Amendment might be denied by the state agencies."[50] This federal remedy was supplemental to any remedies available under state law, making it irrelevant that the plaintiff could seek relief under state law.[51]

Section 1983 was not a new statute. It had been on the books since 1871, when Congress enacted it as part of a first wave of post–Civil War civil rights legislation.[52] The statute had little practical significance before *Monroe*, however.[53] *Monroe* made it clear that plaintiffs could sue state officials in federal court for damages without regard to the availability of state remedies.[54] The Constitution truly was a sword, not just a shield[55]—at least when a state official committed the constitutional violation.

There is no statutory analog to section 1983 that provides a remedy against federal officials. This void raised the question of whether a person who suffered a constitutional violation at the hands of federal officials could also bring a federal action for damages, or whether the victim was at the mercy of whatever remedies a state might provide. That was the question the Court addressed in *Bivens*.

Bivens: The Federal Analog

Webster Bivens was in much the same position as James Monroe. Federal Narcotics agents entered his apartment on the morning of November 26, 1965.[56] They manacled him in front of his wife and children and threatened the entire family with arrest.[57] Officers searched the entire apartment.[58] They then took Mr. Bivens to a federal courthouse, interrogated him, booked him, and subjected him to a strip search.[59] Mr. Bivens argued that the officers violated the Fourth Amendment.[60] Existing case law established that federal courts had jurisdiction over suits alleging that federal officers violated the Constitution, but the Supreme Court had reserved the question of whether the violation could give rise to a cause of action for damages.[61] The *Bivens* Court held that it did.[62]

Justice Brennan wrote for the Court. He first rejected the defendants' argument that Bivens's only remedy was "an action in tort, under state law, in the state courts," in which the Fourth Amendment would serve to limit the agents' defense that they were exercising federal power.[63] The Court said that the defendants' view rested on an unduly limited interpretation of the Fourth Amendment and ignored the fact that the agents exercised governmental power.[64] State law could neither authorize unconstitutional action nor limit federal authority.[65] The "inevitable consequence" of the determination that state law was irrelevant to the success of the federal claim was that the federal question was "not merely a possible defense to the state law action, but an independent claim both necessary and sufficient to make out the plaintiff's cause of action."[66]

The Court then said that it should not be surprising that an individual could obtain damages to compensate for injuries stemming from federal officials' violations of the Fourth Amendment.[67] Damages were the historic remedy for invasions of liberty interests.[68] The Court had recognized, for example, that damages could redress deprivations of the right to vote.[69] While the Fourth Amendment did not explicitly "provide for its enforcement by an award of money damages," it was settled that "where legal rights have been invaded, and a federal statute provides for a general right to sue for such invasion, federal courts may use any available remedy to make good the wrong done."[70]

The Court said that the question was not whether a damages award was necessary. Citing an implied statutory right of action case, the Court said that the question was "merely whether petitioner, if he can demonstrate an injury consequent upon the violation by federal agents of his Fourth Amendment rights, is entitled to redress his injury through a particular remedial mechanism normally available in the federal courts."[71] The Court continued, quoting *Marbury*: "The very essence of civil liberty certainly consists in the right of every individual to claim the protection of the laws, whenever he receives an injury."[72] The Court concluded that Bivens stated a cause of action under the Fourth Amendment and that he was "entitled to recover money damages for any injuries he has suffered as a result of the [federal] agents' violation of the Amendment."[73]

The Court did not ignore separation of powers concerns or Congress's potential role in creating remedies. It suggested that there were two situations, neither of which was present in *Bivens*, in which courts could not properly infer damages remedies. The Court stated that the case did not involve "special factors counseling hesitation in the absence of affirmative action by Congress," such as questions of federal fiscal policy.[74] The Court also explained that Congress had not addressed the remedial question. There was "no explicit congressional declaration that persons injured by a federal officer's violation of the Fourth Amendment may not recover money damages from the agents, but must instead be remitted to another remedy, equally effective in the view of Congress."[75]

Justice Harlan concurred in the judgment, explaining why he did not believe that the federal courts' power to grant a remedy depended on a statute creating a cause of action. There was no dispute that Bivens had a federally protected interest. The question was whether Congress had the exclusive constitutional power to authorize a damages remedy.[76] The statutory private right of action cases reflected the Court's determination that the decision to grant compensatory relief did not involve "policy considerations not susceptible of judicial discernment."[77] The fact that a constitutional right was at stake did not dictate a different result. It would be "at least anomalous" to say that the federal judiciary could use traditional remedies to implement statutory and common law policies but not constitutional ones.[78] More importantly, the Court had previously found that federal courts could grant equitable relief without Congressional authorization, showing that not only Congress could authorize remedies for constitutional violations.[79] If courts could issue injunctive relief without explicit authorization, they should similarly be able to grant remedies at law.

Justice Harlan explained that it was proper for the federal courts to ensure that victims of constitutional violations could obtain relief. The Framers intended the Bill of Rights "to vindicate the interests of the individual in the face of the popular will as expressed in legislative majorities."[80] The federal courts had a responsibility to assure that individuals could vindicate constitutional interests, such as those the Fourth Amendment protects.[81] Damages were the only remedies that could vindicate Bivens' rights. He advanced the sort of claim that would normally be compensable in damages and damages were the only possible remedy for someone in his position. "For people in Bivens' shoes, it is damages or nothing."[82]

The dissenting justices said that the *Bivens* Court erroneously usurped Congress's role. Chief Justice Burger argued that the Court would better preserve the values of separation of powers by recommending a solution to Congress, which had the power to legislate. Chief Justice Burger said that, "Legislation is the business of the

Congress, and it has the facilities and competence for that task—as we do not."[83] Justice Black also dissented, arguing the Court was exercising power "that the Constitution does not give" by creating a damages remedy.[84] Justice Black also argued that the Court should decline to create a remedy even if it had the constitutional power to do so. He feared that implying a damages remedy would unduly tax an already overburdened judicial system.[85]

The Aftermath of *Bivens*

Bivens covered a narrow category of cases. The Court held only that an individual who suffered a Fourth Amendment violation at the hands of a federal officer could sue that individual for damages.[86] The Court did not address whether the holding would apply more broadly. The Court also did not address the scope of the implicit exceptions the majority opinion recognized: that the Court would refrain from implying a remedy in the face of "special factors counseling hesitation"[87] and that the Court would defer to Congress when that body had created an alternative remedy.[88] The *Bivens* Court also did not address a number of other potential issues. It did not discuss whether *Bivens* claims would lie for violations of constitutional provisions other than the Fourth Amendment. It also did not discuss whether agencies or private parties acting under color of federal law were proper *Bivens* defendants.

The Short-Lived Expansion of *Bivens*

The Court has expanded the narrow holding of *Bivens* in only two cases. The Court applied *Bivens* to a claim under the equal protection component of the Fifth Amendment in *Davis v. Passman*,[89] allowing Shirley Davis to sue Congressman Otto Passman for sex discrimination. The Court said that it assumed that the courts could enforce justiciable constitutional rights.[90] If those rights are not to become merely precatory, individuals who allege a violation of their constitutional rights and "have no effective means other than the judiciary to enforce those rights," must be able "to invoke the existing jurisdiction of the courts for the protection of their justiciable constitutional rights."[91] The Court noted that it had previously implied a cause of action directly under the equal protection component of the

Fifth Amendment.[92] The Court next determined that relief in damages was an appropriate form of relief, relying on *Bivens*. For Davis, as for Bivens, it was "damages or nothing."[93]

The Court again found *Bivens* applicable in *Carlson v. Green*,[94] allowing plaintiffs to sue federal prison officials for violating their son's Eighth Amendment rights by allegedly denying him medical care out of racial prejudice. The Court allowed the case to go forward even though the plaintiffs could have sued the United States under the Federal Tort Claims Act (FTCA).[95]

The Court said that neither of the limitations the Court set forth in *Bivens* applied. There were no special factors counseling hesitation because the defendants did not have "independent status in our constitutional scheme" and qualified immunity would guard against over-deterrence.[96] The availability of a remedy against the United States did not preclude a *Bivens* action against the culpable officials because there was no explicit Congressional declaration that injured persons would have to pursue a different remedy.[97] Nothing in the FTCA or its legislative history indicated that Congress intended to preclude *Bivens* claims.[98] The Court noted that the ability to recover damages from individual defendants would aid deterrence.[99] The Court also explained that a *Bivens* remedy would be more effective than one under the FTCA. Punitive damages were not available under the FTCA but would be available in a *Bivens* action; jury trials were not available in FTCA actions, unlike in *Bivens* claims; and the FTCA allowed only claims that the plaintiff could pursue under state law.[100] These factors favored allowing a *Bivens* claim.

Davis and *Carlson* suggested a broad reach for *Bivens*. The Court said that one reason the statutory remedy was not the equivalent of relief under *Bivens* was the fact that FTCA claims depended on state law. The Court also expanded the *Bivens* remedy to constitutional claims that did not stem from the Fourth Amendment. *Carlson* explicitly rejected the idea that the existence of a federal statute that could provide some measure of redress precluded the application of *Bivens*. Going further, the Court suggested that the fact that a *Bivens* action would provide more relief than an alternative remedy favored allowing a *Bivens* action. Any sense that the Court would be receptive to further expansion of *Bivens* was, however, short-lived. The Court's later cases narrowed *Bivens* dramatically.

How the Court Has Narrowed Bivens

The Court has sharply restricted the *Bivens* cause of action in the years since *Carlson*. The Court has broadened the concept of special factors counseling hesitation, shown an increased willingness to assume that federal statutory activity in an area precludes *Bivens* actions, and has held that *Bivens* actions lie only against individual defendants. Most recently, it has restricted the constitutional claims actionable under *Bivens*.

Expanding the Bivens Exceptions

The Court's first approach to narrowing *Bivens* was to expand the idea of "special factors" that precluded a remedy. The Court first took this approach in *Chappell v. Wallace*,[101] in which it refused to let Navy enlisted men bring a *Bivens* action against their superiors.[102] The Court said that "[t]he unique disciplinary structure of the military" and "Congress's activity in the field" constituted "special factors" precluding such a remedy.[103] The Court relied on *Chappell* in *United States v. Stanley*.[104] In that case, the Court refused to allow a serviceman given LSD in an army experiment to bring a *Bivens* action because the injuries arose out of activities incident to military service.[105] This expansion of the "special factors" concept has been influential in the circuits. The Second Circuit, for example, relied on the idea of "special factors counseling hesitation" in refusing to allow an alien to pursue a *Bivens* action against the government officials who were allegedly responsible for his extraordinary rendition to Syria, where he endured torture.[106]

Other cases demonstrate a greater willingness to determine that Congressional action in an area shows that Congress did not intend to allow *Bivens* actions. The Court now freely finds that Congressional action in an area precludes *Bivens* claims even when there is no explicit Congressional declaration to that effect.[107] The first major case in this vein was *Bush v. Lucas*,[108] in which the Court refused to allow an aerospace engineer to bring a *Bivens* action seeking damages after he had obtained nonmonetary relief for defamation and retaliatory demotion from the Civil Service Commission's Appeals Review Board.[109] The Court considered "special factors counseling hesitation" and the existing remedial scheme. In this matter of "federal personnel policy," it would be inappropriate to augment Congress's "elaborate remedial system" with a new judicial remedy.[110]

The Court followed *Bush* with *Schweiker v. Chilicky*,[111] which it found indistinguishable from *Bush*. In *Chilicky*, the Court ruled that claimants whose social security benefits were terminated during disability reviews but were later restored could not sue the Secretary of Health and Human Services for damages.[112] The Court found that the existence of statutory mechanisms giving meaningful remedies against the United States, even if those remedies did not provide complete relief, were special factors indicating that the Court should defer to Congress and not create a *Bivens* remedy.[113]

As in the "special factors" area, the lower courts interpret the Supreme Court decisions dealing with alternate remedies broadly and refuse to authorize *Bivens* actions when there are alternative remedial schemes, even if there is no explicit Congressional statement that alternate remedies should prevail and even if damages are not available. In *Western Radio Services v. United States Forest Service*,[114] for example, the Ninth Circuit refused to allow a *Bivens* action challenging forest service officials' refusal to stop noncompliance with a site plan, delaying action on plaintiff's application to install antennae.[115] The court said that the fact that the plaintiff could raise a claim under the Administrative Procedure Act provided adequate relief.[116] Similarly, a Second Circuit decision found that a plaintiff could not bring a First Amendment *Bivens* claim against an IRS agent challenging a retaliatory audit decision.[117] The court said that the comprehensive statutory scheme allowing taxpayers to challenge IRS actions and their ability to bring civil claims against the government precluded *Bivens* relief.[118]

Limiting the Class of Defendants

The Court has made it clear that *Bivens* claims only lie against individuals. *Bivens* claims do not lie against federal agencies. The Court reached that conclusion in *Federal Deposit Insurance Corporation v. Meyer*,[119] emphasizing the *Bivens* decision's focus on individual deterrence. The Court said that the logic of *Bivens*, which looked to deterring individual wrongdoing, did not support extending the remedy to suits against agencies.[120] The purpose of *Bivens* was to deter the officer,[121] and part of the reason for creating the *Bivens* remedy was the unavailability of a claim against the Government.[122] The Court also relied on the special factors analysis, saying that the potential financial burden on the United States was a factor counseling hesitation.[123] The Court concluded that it was up to Congress to determine whether to expand governmental liability so significantly.[124]

The Court relied on *Meyer* and refused to interpret *Bivens* to allow suits against private entities acting under color of federal law in *Correctional Services Corporation v. Malesko*.[125] The Court emphasized that it had consistently refused to extend *Bivens* liability "to any new context or category of defendants" in the years since its decision in *Carlson*.[126] The Court said that the purpose of *Bivens* was to deter individual federal officers from violating the Constitution. "*Meyer* made clear that the threat of litigation and liability will adequately deter federal officers for *Bivens* purposes no matter that they may enjoy qualified immunity, are indemnified by the employing agency or entity, or are acting pursuant to an entity's policy."[127] The Court said that *Meyer* also made clear that the *Bivens* Court did not intend to deter individual wrongdoing through the threat of a suit against an individual's employer.[128] The Court feared that the availability of entity liability would undermine individual deterrence because plaintiffs would focus their efforts on suing corporate defendants, not individual wrongdoers.[129]

The Court did note that claimants such as Malesko did not lack effective remedies. Malesko had full access to remedial mechanisms that the Bureau of Prisons established.[130] More importantly, the Court looked to state law as a source of relief and said that Malesko could avail himself of tort remedies.[131] The *Malesko* dissent strongly criticized the majority's inquiry into state law and conclusion that the availability of tort remedies was relevant to the *Bivens* analysis.[132] The dissent argued that reliance on tort law would undermine uniformity and said that "the Court's reliance on state tort law will jeopardize the protection of the full scope of federal constitutional rights."[133]

The *Malesko* dissent said that the driving force behind the majority opinion and its limitations on relief was a disagreement with *Bivens* itself.[134] The dissent argued that the Court should not allow its hostility to *Bivens* to control. One reason for adhering to *Bivens* was stare decisis, another was Congress's implicit approval of the doctrine.[135] "Congress has effectively ratified the *Bivens* remedy; surely Congress has never sought to abolish it."[136]

Recasting the Bivens Claim

The Court's most recent response to *Bivens* has been to recast the inquiry into whether to allow a *Bivens* claim. The Court altered its standard approach to *Bivens* actions in *Wilkie v. Robbins*,[137] suggesting that factors other than the limits in *Bivens* itself could factor into the determination of whether relief was available.

Robbins, a ranch owner, filed a *Bivens* action alleging that federal officers violated his Fourth and Fifth Amendment rights by engaging in a campaign of harassment and intimidation in an effort to force him to grant an easement.[138] The Court said that the first question it faced was "whether to devise a new *Bivens* damages action for retaliating against the exercise of ownership rights, in addition to the discrete administrative and judicial remedies available to a landowner like Robbins in dealing with the Government's employees."[139] The Court said that the determination involved a two-step approach. First, the Court asks if "any alternative, existing process for protecting the interest amounts to a convincing reason for the Judicial Branch to refrain from providing a new and freestanding remedy in damages."[140] Second, even absent an alternative process for protecting the interest, the court should determine whether it "was appropriate for a common-law tribunal," looking to special factors counseling hesitation, to authorize a "new kind of federal litigation."[141]

The *Wilkie* Court found that relief was inappropriate under its two-step approach. On the first point, the Court said that Robbins had "an administrative, and ultimately a judicial, process for vindicating virtually all of his complaints."[142] The law did not plainly show that a *Bivens* action should not be available, but it also did not give an "intuitively meritorious case for recognizing a new constitutional cause of action."[143] On the second point, the Court said the case called "for weighing reasons for and against the creation of a new cause of action, the way common law judges have always done."[144] While Robbins had other remedies, none would address all components of the alleged harassment. While the proposed *Bivens* action could provide a single remedy, it would also be difficult to define a workable cause of action. The Government had the right to ask for an easement, and recognizing a claim for overreaching "would invite claims in every sphere of legitimate governmental action affecting property interests."[145] Ultimately, the Court said that Congress was better situated to evaluate "the impact of a new species of litigation" and tailor any remedy to the problem.[146]

Justices Thomas and Scalia concurred in *Wilkie*, arguing against any extension of *Bivens* and its progeny.[147] They said that they would not extend *Bivens* to the facts in *Wilkie* even if the case's reasoning applied. *Bivens*, according to the concurrence, was outdated and a product of the Court's overstepping its boundaries to create a cause of action when it lacked authority to do so.[148] Justices Ginsburg and Stevens dissented in part. The dissenting justices explained that the Court did not find that an administrative scheme such as that at issue in *Bush* or *Chilicky* precluded the claim.[149] The dissenters said that the Court instead relied on "a special factor counseling hesitation quite unlike any we have recognized before," the fear of an onslaught of lawsuits.[150] The Court had rejected that sort of concern before, and should have done so here.[151]

The *Wilkie* Court's refusal to recognize a *Bivens* action for a constitutional violation increased uncertainty about whether all constitutional violations are actionable under *Bivens*. The Court assumed that First Amendment claims were actionable in *Ashcroft v. Iqbal*,[152] a *Bivens* action brought by a Pakistani Muslim arrested and subjected to restrictive confinement in the aftermath of the September 11 attacks. He claimed that his treatment was attributable in part to religious discrimination.[153] The Court, quoting *Wilkie*, noted that it had been reluctant to extend *Bivens* to new contexts or defendants "[b]ecause implied causes of action are disfavored."[154] The Court noted that *Bush v. Lucas* had refused to extend *Bivens* to a First Amendment claim.[155] The Court then assumed that the First Amendment claim was actionable because the defendants "do not press this argument."[156] These cases call into question whether all constitutional claims are now actionable under *Bivens*.[157]

Much of the debate on the reach of *Bivens* involves separation-of-powers concerns regarding the roles of Congress and the courts. The dispute focuses first on whether the Court can imply a cause of action under the Constitution or whether only Congress has that power. Assuming the courts can imply a cause of action, the subsidiary question is how much deference courts should give Congressional action in a field. Should courts stay their hand whenever there is a legislative program that can grant some relief or only when Congress explicitly precludes an implied right? While the Court has not totally repudiated its original determination that courts can imply private rights of action, its recent cases show increasing deference to any Congressional action and a willingness to assume that any available remedy precludes *Bivens* relief.

The Role of State Remedies

It is clear that the availability of federal remedies can preclude a *Bivens* claim. The current question is the extent to which the availability of state remedies has the same effect. This issue was in the spotlight in *Malesko*. The *Malesko* majority opinion considered the availability of tort remedies in refusing to allow a claim against a private correctional institution.[158] The dissenting justices argued that state remedies were irrelevant. They said that reliance on state tort law would undermine uniformity and "jeopardize the protection of the full scope of federal constitutional rights."[159]

A strong majority of the Court held that the availability of state remedies was relevant to the availability of a *Bivens* action in *Minneci v. Pollard*,[160] finding that the availability of state tort remedies precluded a prisoner from bringing a *Bivens* action against employees of a privately run federal prison.[161] The reach of *Minneci* is, however, far from clear. The Court considered the legal context in great detail and specifically stated that it was leaving "different cases and different state laws to another day."[162] It remains to be seen if the Court's willingness explicitly to hold that state remedies can preclude *Bivens* actions outweighs its careful discussion of the remedies available in that case.[163]

The Background

The *Minneci* Court granted certiorari to resolve a circuit split on the question of whether individuals incarcerated in privately run prisons could bring *Bivens* actions against prison employees who violated their constitutional rights.[164] The majority view was that a *Bivens* remedy was not available. The Tenth Circuit relied heavily on *Malesko* in reaching that conclusion in *Peoples v. Corrections Corporation of American Detention Centers*,[165] finding that *Bivens* actions were unavailable when the plaintiff could pursue other state or federal claims. The court noted a tension between *Carlson*[166] and *Malesko*, but determined that the more recent decision should control. "*Malesko* indicates that a *Bivens* claim should not be implied unless the plaintiff has no other means of redress or unless he is seeking an otherwise nonexistent cause of action against the individual defendant."[167]

The Fourth and Eleventh Circuits reached the same conclusion. The Eleventh Circuit, in *Alba v. Montford*,[168] held that *Bivens* claims were unavailable against private prison employees because the plaintiff had alternative remedies under state law.[169] The court relied on *Malesko*, which it said rejected the argument that a *Bivens* remedy should be implied because there was no other way to challenge a deprivation in *federal* court.[170] The Fourth Circuit took the same approach in *Holly v. Scott*.[171] The court found that the fact that the plaintiff had "alternative—and arguably superior—causes of action against defendants under the state law of negligence" was a "special factor counseling hesitation" that precluded bringing a *Bivens* action against employees of a privately operated prison.[172]

The Ninth Circuit broke with the other circuits in its post-*Wilkie* decision in *Pollard v. GEO Group, Inc.*,[173] allowing a prisoner to bring a *Bivens* action alleging that employees of a private corporation that contracted with the Bureau of Prisons to run a correctional facility violated his Eighth Amendment rights.[174] Expressly disagreeing with the Fourth and Eleventh Circuits (and noting that the vacated Tenth Circuit decision lacked precedential value), the court found that the defendant employees acted under color of federal law for purposes of *Bivens* liability and that availability of a state tort remedy did not foreclose a *Bivens* action.[175]

The *Pollard* court applied the *Wilkie* approach, finding first that the availability of a state law remedy did not counsel against allowing a *Bivens* cause of action.[176] It said that only congressionally crafted remedies could have such a preclusive effect.[177] The court explained that the availability of alternative remedies was relevant to the *Bivens* inquiry "because the judicially created *Bivens* remedy should yield to congressional prerogatives under basic separation of powers principles."[178] Allowing state tort law to preclude a *Bivens* action would mean that uniform rules would not govern federal officials.[179] The court then considered "special factors counseling hesitation" and weighed reasons for and against allowing the claim. It found that claims were feasible and would not undermine the purpose of deterring individual officers from violating the Constitution.[180]

Minneci v. Pollard

The Supreme Court reversed the Ninth Circuit in a short, 8–1, decision. The Court also began its analysis by discussing *Wilkie v. Robbins*,[181] which it said set standards that "seek to reflect and to reconcile the Court's reasoning set forth in earlier cases."[182] It then reviewed its earlier *Bivens* cases[183] and concluded that *Wilkie* "fairly summarize[d]" the considerations underlying those decisions.[184] Saying that it was applying the *Wilkie* approach, the Court concluded that Pollard could not bring a *Bivens* claim "primarily because Pollard's Eighth Amendment claim focuses upon a kind of conduct that typically falls within the scope of traditional tort law."[185] In the case of privately employed defendants, tort law provided "an 'alternative, existing process' capable of protecting the constitutional interests at stake."[186] The existence of that alternative was a convincing reasoning not to provide a new damages remedy.[187]

The Court's explanation of its decision took the form of refuting Pollard's arguments for recognizing a *Bivens* action. The Court first rejected the argument that its decision in *Carlson v. Green*[188] governed. *Carlson* was different because the plaintiff there sought damages from a government employee.[189] The potential availability of an adequate, alternative remedy was dramatically different in the two cases. Prisoners ordinarily cannot bring tort actions against federal employees, but they ordinarily can bring such actions against employees of a private firm.[190]

The Court next rejected the related argument that only federal remedies were relevant in determining if alternative remedies were available.[191] That argument failed for the reasons it did in *Malesko*. "State tort law, after all, can help to deter constitutional violations as well as to provide compensation to a violation's victim."[192]

The Court then rejected the argument that state tort law did not provide remedies that were adequate to protect the interests at stake.[193] The Court explained that Pollard sought compensation for physical and emotional harm resulting from the sort of action that tort law generally forbids.[194] California law provided redress for this sort of harm, and California courts had specifically applied the law in claims against jailers, including private prison operators.[195]

The relevant tort law, as far as the Court could tell, was the same in every state.[196] State tort law might allow a less generous recovery than would a *Bivens* action, but that was not grounds for finding the law inadequate.[197] State law and *Bivens* remedies did not have to be perfectly congruent.[198] The question was whether, "in general, state tort law remedies provide roughly similar incentives for potential defendants while also providing roughly similar compensation to victims."[199] The Court was convinced that the answer, in this case, was yes.[200]

The Court, lastly, responded to Pollard's argument that there could be Eighth Amendment claims that state tort law did not cover by saying he did not convincingly show that there were such cases.[201] The Court noted that it could not be certain that the law would remain static, but the present law was clear enough to leave those questions for another day.[202] The possibility of a different future case was not grounds for reaching a different conclusion here.[203]

The Court concluded by restating its holding. It could not imply a *Bivens* action in the case of a federal prisoner who sought damages from privately employed employees at a privately operated prison "where the conduct allegedly amounts to a violation of the Eighth Amendment, and where that conduct is of a kind that typically falls within the scope of traditional state tort law."[204] In those cases, the prisoner must seek a remedy under state tort law.[205]

Justice Ginsburg was the lone dissenter. She noted that Pollard would have had a federal remedy for the Eighth Amendment violations he alleged if he were incarcerated in a state prison or a facility that the federal government operated, and said that she would not deny that same avenue of relief to a person who a federal contract placed in a privately operated prison.[206] "I would hold his injuries, sustained while serving a federal sentence, 'compensable according to uniform rules of federal law.'"[207]

Conclusion

The Court has continually restricted the *Bivens* cause of action over the last thirty years. It has found that virtually any Congressional action in an area precludes *Bivens* relief,[208] and has now held that state-law remedies can have the same effect.[209] It has refused to extend the class of defendants amenable to suit under *Bivens*.[210] The Court's refusal to extend *Bivens*, and its consideration of state remedies in determining if a *Bivens* action is available, are unfortunate. Justice Scalia may be right that *Bivens* actions came into existence in the days when courts freely implied statutory rights of action,[211] but the Court's current antipathy to implied statutory remedies should not extend to implied constitutional remedies and lead it to restrict *Bivens* claims.

The Court should not equate implied constitutional and statutory causes of action. Congress creates statutory rights and it is reasonable to expect it to provide for private remedies when it intends for individuals to protect the right through private actions. Congress enacts statutes and its intent on whether to allow a private remedy is determinative.[212] Congress does not create constitutional rights and its intent does not govern the meaning of the Constitution.[213] Courts should not refrain from using appropriate remedial tools to ensure that individuals can receive redress when they suffer a deprivation of their constitutional rights.

There is another error in equating *Bivens* actions with implied statutory remedies. Doing so suggests that the roots of *Bivens* lie solely in statutory cases and ignores the *Bivens* decision's roots in cases implying equitable relief for constitutional violations and designing remedies such as the exclusionary rule to enforce constitutional dictates.[214] Justice Harlan's concurrence in *Bivens* expressly drew on cases allowing injunctive relief against federal officials in the absence of Congressional action.[215] As Justice Harlan explained, the power to award damages was a logical outgrowth of any power to imply remedies because of the courts' inherent power to tailor relief to the harm.[216] Injunctive relief cannot redress all harms.[217] As Justice Harlan recognized in *Bivens*, and the Court reiterated in *Davis v. Passman*, sometimes damages are the only meaningful remedy.[218]

The failure to emphasize the link between *Bivens* actions and cases awarding injunctive relief increases the likelihood that the Court's current animosity to *Bivens* will lead the Court to chip away at the case's underpinnings. The Court could become increasingly reluctant to use other remedies, such as injunctions, to address constitutional violations. If a court cannot imply a damages remedy, the next logical step could be to restrict other forms of relief.

A refusal to equate *Bivens* actions with implied statutory claims does not mean that the Court should not consider whether there are factors that really do counsel hesitation before judicial intervention. It is possible that some cases could truly implicate national security concerns or risk undue interference with the executive branch.[219] In considering the need for hesitation, however, courts should recognize that there are other doctrines that address many such concerns. Doctrines such as individual immunities, for example, address the potential disruption of damages suits and the danger of overdeterrence.[220]

The recognition that *Bivens* actions have roots in courts' inherent remedial powers also does not forget that separation-of-powers concerns are present when the Court uses a power that Congress could also exercise or suggest that Congressional action in a field is irrelevant. The Court should defer to express statutory remedial schemes. It should, however, adhere to its statement in *Bivens* and stay its hand only when there is an "explicit congressional declaration that persons injured by a federal officer's violation of the Fourth Amendment may not recover money damages from the agents, but must instead be remitted to another remedy, equally effective in the view of Congress."[221] The declaration should be explicit and there should be a deliberate judgment that alternative remedies are equally effective.

This approach does not ignore legitimate legislative prerogatives. It instead recognizes that Constitutional rights are not subject to legislative repeal; the Bill of Rights is counter-majoritarian.[222] Just as Congress cannot repeal the Bill of Rights or insist on enforcement of an unconstitutional statute, it should not be able to undermine the effectiveness of constitutional guarantees by failing to enact remedial schemes or by acting to undermine the effectiveness of existing remedial schemes.

This concern is not fanciful, as the Prison Litigation Reform Act (PLRA)[223] illustrates. Congress demonstrated its animosity to certain constitutional rights and to individuals who are especially likely to bring civil rights claims in enacting the PLRA, which has the effect of preventing victims of constitutional violations from recovering damages.[224] The Court should extend *Bivens* to allow courts to provide damages remedies for state officials' constitutional violations that statutes such as the PLRA insulate from redress.

While the courts should consider Congressional action in determining if *Bivens* actions are appropriate, the availability of state law remedies should not lead courts to refrain from recognizing *Bivens* actions. The Court reached the wrong decision when it held to the contrary in *Minneci*.[225] Allowing state remedies to control constitutional remedies can lead to inconsistent enforcement of constitutional protections.[226] Just as significantly, it ignores the fact that the Constitution and state tort law protect different interests.[227] By allowing a tort remedy to provide redress for a constitutional right, the *Minneci* Court retreated from the idea that constitutional rights have a unique value. The *Bivens* Court recognized this, as did the early cases it cited recognizing that damages could be an appropriate means for redressing a deprivation of the right to vote.[228] The Court should have reaffirmed that view in *Minneci*.

Constitutional law has evolved since the days of *Marbury* and the belief that the existence of a right requires a remedy. But federal courts should adhere to *Marbury*'s recognition of constitutional supremacy and the *Bivens* Court's recognition that courts can design the relief necessary to redress a constitutional violation. Part of the federal courts' role in a constitutional democracy is to enforce the Constitution, even when the political branches might prefer that certain constitutional rights go unenforced.

Notes

1. I offer special thanks to my research assistants, Madeline Bertasi and Jacob Hubbell. Writing this makes me fully aware of how indebted I am to Murray Dry, who first introduced me to these topics and whose influence has been with me at every step of my teaching career.
2. *Marbury v. Madison*, 5 U.S. 137 (1803).
3. See *Dictionary of American History*, 2nd ed., ed. James Truslow Adams and R.V. Coleman, 6:156 (calling *Marbury* "the most important decision in Supreme Court history because it established the doctrine of judicial review and that the courts had the ultimate power to interpret the Constitution").
4. 5 U.S. 137 (1803), 177.
5. Ibid.
6. Ibid.
7. Ibid., 178.
8. Ibid.
9. The underlying question in *Marbury* was whether William Marbury had a right to a commission as a justice of the peace for the District of Columbia. President Adams had appointed Marbury in the waning hours of his presidential term (ibid., 137). The commission was signed and sealed, but had not been delivered when the Jefferson administration took office (ibid.). The incoming administration decided

to disregard the appointments for which commissions had not been delivered (ibid.). Marbury and others in his position went to the Supreme Court, seeking a writ of mandamus to compel Jefferson's Secretary of State, James Madison, to deliver the commissions (ibid.). The Court ultimately determined that it did not have the power to hear the case as an exercise of original jurisdiction (ibid., 180).

10.   Ibid., 162.
11.   Ibid.
12.   Ibid., 163.
13.   Ibid.
14.   Ibid.
15.   The phrase "*ubi jus, ibi remedium*" means "where there is a right, there is a remedy" (*Kiyemba v. Obama*, 555 F.3d 1022, 1027 [D.C. Cir. 2009]). See generally Tracy A. Thomas, "Ubi Jus, Ibi Remedium: The Fundamental Right to a Remedy Under Due Process," *San Diego Law Review* 41 (2004), 1233.
16.   See John E. Noyes, 164–168 (explaining that courts in the early 1900s had a more expansive view of judicial power than do current courts and emphasizing the importance of the "where there is a right, there is a remedy" approach to courts of the era).
17.   *Texas & Pacific Railway Company v. Rigsby*, 241 U.S. 33 (1916).
18.   The law was the Federal Safety Appliance Act, Act of March 2, 1893 cpt. 196, § 8, 27 Stat. 531.
19.   241 U.S. 33 (1916), 39.
20.   Ibid., 39–40 (citing William Blackstone, *Commentaries*, 3:51,* 123*).
21.   5 U.S. 137 (1803), 156.
22.   *Mapp v. Ohio*, 367 U.S. 643 (1961) (establishing the exclusionary rule, which prevents government from relying on evidence seized in violation of the Fourth Amendment to obtain a conviction); *Rochin v. California*, 342 U.S. 165 (1952) (finding that officers violated the Due Process Clause when they obtained evidence by involuntarily pumping an arrestee's stomach, precluding use of that evidence at trial); *Bram v. United States*, 168 U.S. 532 (1897) (excluding evidence authorities obtained in violation of the Fifth Amendment).
23.   See *Poulos v. State of New Hampshire*, 345 U.S. 395 (1953); *Ex parte Nielsen*, 131 U.S. 178 (1889); see also *Steffel v. Thompson*, 415 U.S. 452 (1974) (recognizing right to seek pre-enforcement relief against an unconstitutional prosecution).
24.   See *Bolling v. Sharpe*, 347 U.S. 497 (1955) (holding that equitable relief should be available to individuals denied admission into the District of Columbia's segregated schools); *Ex parte Young*, 209 U.S. 123 (1908) (authorizing injunctive relief against a state official); *United States v. Lee*, 106 U.S. 196 (1882) (allowing an ejectment action against

federal officers to enforce the Fifth Amendment Takings Clause). See generally Alfred Hill, "Constitutional Remedies," 1109; Al Katz, 1.

25. 42 U.S.C. § 1983 (2012); see below, note 45 (quoting the statute).
26. *Bivens v. Six Unknown Named Agents*, 403 U.S. 388 (1971). For a detailed discussion of *Bivens*, see next section.
27. 403 U.S. 388 (1971), 397.
28. Ibid., 406; see above, text accompanying notes 15–19.
29. 403 U.S. 388 (1971), 410; see above, text accompanying notes 22–23.
30. 403 U.S. 388 (1971), 411–412 (Burger, C.J., dissenting); ibid., 428 (Black, J., dissenting).
31. See dissents cited above, note 29 and below, text accompanying notes 82–84.
32. See cases cited below; Michael P. Robotti, 2, 7 (noting that the *Bivens* dissents had a "profound influence on the Court's future").
33. See *Alexander v. Sandoval*, 532 U.S. 275 (2001), 286–287 (saying that private rights to enforce federal law must originate with Congress); *Transamerica Mortg. Advisors, Inc. v. Lewis*, 444 U.S. 11 (1979), 15–16 (saying that the ultimate question is whether Congress intended to create a private remedy); see also *California v. Sierra Club*, 451 U.S. 287 (1981), 292–297; Thomas A. Lambert, 1155, 1228–1232.
34. *Corr. Servs. Corp. v. Malesko*, 534 U.S. 61 (2001), 75 (Scalia, J., concurring).
35. See next sections.
36. The Court still upholds *Bivens* in form, but increasingly finds that it does not apply when other remedies, including state-law remedies, are available. See sections below.
37. 42 U.S.C. § 1983 (2012); see below, note 45.
38. 365 U.S. 167 (1961).
39. Ibid., 169.
40. Ibid.
41. Ibid.
42. Ibid.
43. Ibid.
44. Ibid.
45. Ibid.
46. 365 U.S. 167 (1961), 169.
47. Ibid., 170.
48. Ibid. The City of Chicago also argued that it was not a proper defendant because municipalities were not "persons" amendable to suit under the statute (ibid., 187). The Court accepted that argument (ibid., 187–188), but overruled that aspect of the opinion in *Monell v. N.Y.C. Dep't of Soc. Servs.*, 436 U.S. 658 (1978).
49. 365 U.S. 167 (1961), 180.

50. Ibid.
51. Ibid., 183.
52. P.L. 96–170. For discussion of the historical background, see *D.C. v. Carter*, 409 U.S. 418 (1973), 425–456.
53. Litigants rarely invoked section 1983 in the years before *Monroe*. Individuals brought only twenty-one suits under the statute in the years between 1871 and 1920. Comment, "The Civil Rights Act: Emergence of an Adequate Federal Civil Remedy?," 26 *Indiana Law Journal* 361 (1951), 363. In 1960, the year before the Court decided *Monroe*, plaintiffs filed only 300 federal suits under all the civil rights acts. Admin. Off. of the U.S. Courts, 1960 Ann. Rep. of the Director 232.
54. 365 U.S. 167 (1961), 187. The increase in the number of suits was staggering. The Administrative Office data for fiscal 2009 report 33,761 nonprisoner "civil rights" actions and 24,908 prisoner prison conditions and civil rights petitions. Admin. Off. of the U.S. Courts, 2009 Ann. Rep. of the Director.
55. This analogy comes from Marshall S. Shapo, 324.
56. 403 U.S. 388 (1971), 389.
57. Ibid.
58. Ibid.
59. Ibid.
60. Ibid.
61. *Bell v. Hood*, 327 U.S. 678 (1946), 685.
62. 403 U.S. 388 (1971), 397.
63. Ibid., 390.
64. Ibid., 391–392.
65. Ibid., 395.
66. Ibid.
67. Ibid.
68. Ibid., 396.
69. Ibid. (citing cases including *Nixon v. Herndon*, 273 U.S. 536 [1927], and *Swafford v. Templeton*, 185 U.S. 487 [1902]).
70. Ibid. (citing *Bell*, 327 U.S. 678 [1946], 684).
71. Ibid., 397 (citing *J.I. Case Co. v. Borak*, 377 U.S. 426 [1964], 433).
72. Ibid., 397 (quoting *Marbury*, 5 U.S. 137 [1803], 163).
73. Ibid.
74. Ibid., 396.
75. Ibid., 397.
76. Ibid., 401–402 (Harlan, J., concurring).
77. Ibid., 402 (citing *J.I. Case Co. v. Borak*, 377 U.S. 426 [1964]; *Tunstall v. Bhd. of Locomotive Firemen & Eng'rs*, 323 U.S. 210 [1944]).
78. Ibid., 403.

79. Ibid., 404 (noting that the presumed availability of equitable relief "appears entirely to negate the contention that the status of an interest as constitutionally protected divests federal courts of the power to grant damages absent express congressional authorization").

80. Ibid., 407.

81. Ibid.

82. Ibid., 410.

83. Ibid., 412 (Burger, C.J., dissenting).

84. Ibid., 428 (Black, J., dissenting).

85. Noting that the "courts of the United States as well as those of the States are choked with lawsuits," Justice Black argued that legislators might wish to respond to the growing number of frivolous claims by devoting "judicial resources to other problems of a more serious nature" (ibid.).

86. See 534 U.S. 61 (2001), 75 (Scalia, J., concurring).

87. *Bivens*, 403 U.S. 388 (1971), 396.

88. Ibid., 397. The Court suggested that Congress must have explicitly created an alternative remedy and that the other remedy must be "equally effective in the view of Congress" (ibid.).

89. 442 U.S. 228 (1979).

90. Ibid., 244.

91. Ibid., 242.

92. Ibid. (citing *Bolling v. Sharpe*, 347 U.S. 497 [1954] [the District of Columbia school segregation case]).

93. Ibid., 245. The Court did not find that either of the potential exceptions to *Bivens* was present. There were no special factors counseling hesitation and there was no explicit Congressional declaration that persons in Davis's position could not recover money damages (ibid., 246). The Court stated that any special factors counseling hesitation were coextensive with the protections of the Speech or Debate Clause (ibid.).

94. 446 U.S. 14 (1980).

95. 28 U.S.C. §§ 1291, 1346, 2671–2680 (2012). Congress enacted FTCA in 1948. June 25, 1948 c. 646, 62 stat. 982.

96. 446 U.S. 14 (1980), 19; see below, note 219 (discussing qualified immunity).

97. 446 U.S. 14 (1980), 19.

98. Ibid.

99. Ibid., 21.

100. Ibid., 22–23.

101. 462 U.S. 296 (1983).

102. Ibid., 305.

103. Ibid., 304.

104. 483 U.S. 669 (1987).
105. Ibid., 681.
106. *Arar v. Ashcroft*, 585 F.3d 559 (2d Cir. 2009) (en banc); but compare *Vance v. Rumsfield*, 653 F.3d 591 (7th Cir. 2011) (finding that U.S. citizens who allegedly underwent torture at the hands of U.S. military personnel in Iraq could bring a *Bivens* claim against the former Secretary of Defense); see 80 U.S.L.W. 204 (Aug. 16, 2011). See generally George D. Brown, 841. The Ninth Circuit recently relied on *Arar* in another context, finding that *Bivens* did not provide aliens not lawfully in the United States a remedy to sue federal agents for damages for wrongful detention pending deportation: *Mirmehdi v. United States*, 662 F.3d 1073 (9th Cir. 2011).
107. *Bivens* appeared to require an explicit Congressional declaration to preclude a *Bivens* damages claim. See above, text accompanying note 74.
108. 462 U.S. 367 (1983).
109. Ibid., 390.
110. Ibid., 388–389.
111. 487 U.S. 412 (1988).
112. Ibid., 429.
113. Ibid., 426–427. Most recently, in *Hui v. Castaneda*, 559 U.S. 799 (2010), the Court unanimously found that a prisoner could not bring *Bivens* action against United States Public Health Service employees for medical malpractice because the Federal Torts Claim Act provided that its remedy would be exclusive in such suits (ibid., 806). The Court said that *Carlson* was not relevant because the defendants in that case did not raise a similar claim of immunity (ibid., 807). This case is different from *Bush* and *Schweiker* because the Court in *Hui* found that Congress explicitly intended to preclude *Bivens* claims.
114. 578 F.3d 1116 (9th Cir. 2009).
115. Ibid., 1119.
116. Ibid., 1123 (citing 5 U.S.C. § 704).
117. *Hudson Valley Black Press v. IRS*, 409 F.3d 106 (2d Cir. 2005).
118. Ibid., 108.
119. 510 U.S. 471 (1994).
120. Ibid., 486.
121. Ibid.
122. Ibid., 485.
123. Ibid., 486.
124. Ibid.
125. 534 U.S. 61 (2001).
126. Ibid., 68.
127. Ibid., 70.

128. Ibid.
129. Ibid., 71.
130. Ibid., 70.
131. Ibid., 73–74.
132. Ibid., 76 (Stevens, J., dissenting).
133. Ibid., 80. The dissent explained that not all constitutional violations had parallel tort causes of action. Idem.
134. Ibid.
135. Ibid., 83.
136. Ibid.
137. 551 U.S. 537 (2007).
138. Ibid., 543. Robbins alleged that the United States, which failed to record an easement a former owner of Robbins's property had granted it, demanded that Robbins grant the easement (ibid., 542). When Robbins refused, government officials allegedly trespassed on Robbins's land and sought to investigate Robbins for trespass or permit violations (ibid.). As part of their alleged campaign of intimidation, defendants threatened Robbins with the cancellation of a reciprocal maintenance right-of-way and later cancelled the right-of-way (ibid., 544). Defendants also cancelled Robbins' use permit allowing cattle grazing and charged him with trespass (ibid., 545). Defendants refused to repair damage to the only public road that reached Robbins's land and fined Robbins for trespassing when he decided to repair the damage himself (ibid.). Defendants allegedly continued to harass Robbins after he filed suit, denying him permission to renew his use permit, videotaping him, and threatening to impound his cattle (ibid., 546–547). Robbins and defendants entered a settlement agreement, but it fell apart when defendants instituted formal trespass proceedings against Robbins (ibid., 547).
139. Ibid., 549.
140. Ibid., 550.
141. Ibid.
142. Ibid., 553 (noting that Robbins could seek a civil damages remedy for trespass, contest the administrative charges and obtain judicial review, bring a state law action for malicious prosecution, and pursue criminal charges).
143. Ibid., 554.
144. Ibid.
145. Ibid., 561.
146. Ibid., 562.
147. Ibid., 568 (Thomas, J., concurring).
148. Ibid.
149. Ibid., 575–576 (Ginsburg, J., dissenting in part).

150. Ibid., 577.
151. Ibid. See Natalie Banta, 119; Heather J. Hanna and Alan G. Harding, 193; Laurence H. Tribe, 23.
152. *Ashcroft v. Iqbal*, 556 U.S. 662 (2009).
153. Ibid., 666.
154. Ibid., 675.
155. Ibid. The *Bush v. Lucas* Court declined to grant relief because Congress provided remedies for the alleged violation, not because the claim came under the First Amendment. See *Bush v. Lucas*, 462 U.S. 367 (1983), 378.
156. 556 U.S. 662 (2009), 675.
157. See David Baltmanis and James E. Pfander, 117 (arguing that federal courts should presume that a well-pleaded complaint alleging a violation of an individual's constitutional rights should give rise to an action under *Bivens*).
158. *Malesko*, 534 U.S. 61 (2001), 73–74.
159. Ibid., 80 (Stevens, J., dissenting).
160. 132 S. Ct. 617 (2012).
161. Ibid., 620, 626.
162. Ibid.
163. See below, text accompanying notes 192–199 and note 225.
164. 132 S. Ct. 617, at 621. The *Minneci* majority did not address a background issue that also split the lower courts. A *Bivens* action would be available only if the private prison employees acted under color of federal law, because only then would their actions violate the Constitution. The Fourth Circuit raised this issue in *Holly v. Scott*, 434 F.3d 287 (4th Cir. 2006), finding as a "special factor counseling hesitation" that precluded a *Bivens* action against employees of a privately operated prison that the private employee's actions were not "fairly attributable" to the federal government (ibid., 295). The Ninth Circuit expressly disagreed with this conclusion. *Pollard v. GEO Group, Inc.*, 607 F.3d 583 (9th Cir. 2010), 588, *rev'd sub nom. Minneci v. Pollard*, 132 S Ct. 617 (2012). Justice Ginsburg noted in her *Minneci* dissent that the Ninth Circuit found that the employees acted under color of federal law and the employees did not ask the Supreme Court to review that issue. 132 S. Ct. 617, at 627 n.*
It is not surprising that the petitioners in *Minneci* did not seek review of the under color issue. The Ninth Circuit reached the correct conclusion, even though the question is technically open (see *Richardson v. McKnight*, 521 U.S. 399 [1997] [refusing to decide whether private prison employees acted under color of state law]). The Supreme Court in *Malesko* stated that employees of a privately run prison would be proper defendants in a section 1983 action (*Malesko*, 534 U.S. 61

[2001], 77). Numerous lower court decisions reach that conclusion. See, e.g., *Street v. Corrections Corp. of Am.*, 102 F.3d 810 (6th Cir. 1996); *Blumel v. Mylander*, 919 F. Supp. 423 (M.D. Fla. 1996). While the section 1983 cases look at whether the entity acted under color of state law, state action precedent is relevant to determining whether conduct occurs under color of federal law. See, for example, *S.F. Arts & Athletics v. United States Olympic Co.*, 483 U.S. 522 (1987) (using state action precedent to determine whether an entity acting under authority from the federal government was engaged in governmental action).

165. 422 F.3d 1090 (10th Cir. 2005).

166. *Carlson v. Green*, 446 U.S. 14 (1980); see above, text accompanying notes 93–99.

167. *Peoples*, 422 F.3d at 1103. The Tenth Circuit, sitting en banc, vacated the *Peoples* decision but split evenly on the question of whether a *Bivens* action was available. The split decision reinstated the district court opinion dismissing the claim. *Peoples v. Corr. Corp. Am. Det. Ctrs.*, 449 F.3d 1097 (10th Cir. 2006) (en banc).
Judge Ebel dissented in *Peoples*. He said that only a constitutional cause of action could preclude a *Bivens* claim. "*Bivens*, after all, is a remedy implied for a *constitutional* violation. A state tort cause of action (not predicated on a constitutional violation) is not an adequate alternative remedy for a constitutional violation)." 422 F.3d 1109 (Ebel, J., dissenting). He criticized the majority for treating all claims for damages as "fungible units" (ibid.). If a tort claim against individual officers did not preclude a *Bivens* remedy in *Carlson*, it should be insufficient in other cases (ibid.).

168. 517 F.3d 1249, 1254 (11th Cir. 2008).

169. Ibid. The court assumed that federal prison employees acted under color of federal law (ibid.).

170. Ibid.

171. 434 F.3d 287, 295 (4th Cir. 2006).

172. Ibid. The other special factor was a belief that the employees' actions were not attributable to the federal government. See above, note 163. For discussion of these cases, see Lumen N. Mulligan, 685; John F. Pries, 723; Matthew W. Tikonoff, 981.

173. 607 F.3d 583 (9th Cir. 2010), *rev'd sub nom. Minneci v. Pollard*, 132 S. Ct. 617 (2012).

174. Ibid., 585. The Supreme Court opinion discussed the facts in detail. Pollard was a prisoner at a federally run federal facility that the private company Wackenhut Corrections Corporation operated. 132 S. Ct. 617, at 620. He sued various employees, alleging that they violated the Eighth Amendment by providing inadequate medical care for injuries resulting from a slip and fall (ibid.). He said that guards made

him dress in a manner that caused excruciating pain, made him wear arm restraints that caused pain, failed to comply with medical instructions, failed adequately to provide for meals or hygiene, provided insufficient medication, and forced him to work before his injuries were healed (ibid., 620–621).

175. 607 F.3d at 593.
176. Ibid., 595.
177. Ibid.
178. Ibid., 596.
179. Ibid., 597.
180. Ibid., 508–602.
181. 551 U.S. 537 (2007); discussed above at text accompanying notes 136–150.
182. 132 S. Ct. 617, at 621.
183. Ibid., 621–623.
184. Ibid., 623.
185. Ibid.
186. Ibid. (quoting *Wilkie*, 551 U.S. at 550).
187. Ibid.
188. 446 U.S. 14 (1980), discussed above at text accompanying notes 93–99.
189. 132 S. Ct. 617, at 623.
190. Ibid. The Court explained that it had rejected a similar argument in *Malesko*. See above, text accompanying notes 124–135 (discussing *Malesko*).
191. 132 S. Ct. 617, at 624.
192. Ibid.
193. Ibid.
194. Ibid., 625
195. Ibid.
196. Ibid.
197. Ibid. The Court gave the examples of damage caps, disallowance of damages for emotional harm, and procedural burdens such as expert administrative panels in malpractice cases (ibid.).
198. Ibid. The Court explained that the differences could cut both ways. *Bivens* plaintiffs could face burdens that state tort plaintiffs did not encounter. For example, negligence could not give rise to an Eighth Amendment violation and *respondeat superior* did not apply in *Bivens* claims (ibid.).
199. Ibid.
200. Ibid.
201. Ibid.
202. Ibid., 626

203. Ibid.
204. Ibid.
205. Ibid. Justice Scalia wrote a brief concurrence, joined by Justice Thomas, that restated his argument from *Malesko* that *Bivens* was a "relic" of the days when the court freely implied remedies (ibid., Scalia, J., concurring). He argued that the Court should abandon that approach as a constitutional matter, like it had in statutory cases, because Congress could presumably not repudiate the implied remedy (ibid.). He said that the Court should limit *Bivens*, *Davis*, and *Carlson* to the precise circumstances they involved. Ibid.; see above, text accompanying note 34 (quoting Justice Scalia's opinion in *Malesko*).
206. 2012 WL 43511, at 626–627 (Ginsburg, J., dissenting).
207. Ibid., 627 (quoting *Bivens*, 403 U.S. at 409 [Harlan, J., concurring]). Justice Ginsburg added that there was a stronger case for providing Pollard a federal remedy than there had been in *Malesko*. The core concern of *Bivens*, individual deterrence, was not at issue in that case. Here, however, the suit raised *Bivens*'s core concern: Pollard's suit seeking damages from "directly from individual officers would have precisely the deterrent effect the Court found absent in *Malesko*" (ibid.).
208. See above, text accompanying notes 106–112.
209. See above, text accompanying notes 130, 180–204.
210. See above, text accompanying notes 118–128.
211. *Malesko*, 534 U.S. 61 (2001), 75 (Scalia, J., concurring).
212. *Alexander v. Sandoval*, 532 U.S. 275 (2001), 286; see above, text accompanying notes 31–32.
213. That is the core point of *Marbury v. Madison*, which explained that the Constitution was a species of law and that it was the courts' job to say what the law was. See above, text accompanying notes 1–13.
    Justice Scalia argues that the Court should not imply remedies for constitutional violations because Congress, presumably, could not undo the remedy. *Minneci*, 132 S. Ct. 617, at 626 (Scalia, J., concurring). That argument is unconvincing. Congress should not be able to undo remedies for constitutional violations because allowing it to do so would allow Congress to prevent redress for politically disfavored rights. The counter-majoritarian nature of constitutional guarantees should lead courts to protect constitutional remedies from legislative attempts to weaken them.
214. See above, I.D.
215. *Bivens*, 403 U.S. 388 (1971), 400 (Harlan, J., concurring).
216. Ibid., 400–402; see also above, text accompanying notes 76–81 (discussing Justice Harlan's opinion).

217. See *Davis*, 442 U.S. 228 (1979), 245 (noting that injunctive relief would not help Davis).

218. Ibid.; *Bivens*, 403 U.S. 388, 410 (Harlan, J., concurring).

219. See *Arar v. Ashcroft*, 585 F.3d 559 (2nd Cir. 2009) (en banc); discussed earlier, text accompanying note 105.

220. Qualified immunity exists to encourage the "vigorous exercise of official authority." *Butz v. Economou*, 438 U.S. 478 (1978), 506. The doctrine not only protects officials against having to pay damages, but rests on the assumption that defendants will not have to proceed to trial on insubstantial claims. *Harlow v. Fitzgerald*, 457 U.S. 800 (1982), 814. The *Harlow* Court said that qualified immunity looks at the objective reasonableness of an official's conduct to prevent an individual from having to face trial or broad-reaching discovery based on bare allegations of malice (ibid., 817–818).

221. *Bivens*, 403 U.S. 388 (1971), 397.

222. The Court explicitly made this point in *Bivens* (ibid., 407).

223. Prison Litigation Reform Act of 1995, 110 Stat. 1321–1371, as amended, 42 U.S.C. § 1997e et seq.

224. One provision of the PLRA, for example, provides that a prisoner cannot recover damages for emotional distress in the absence of a physical injury. 42 U.S.C. § 1997e(e) (2012). This provision prevents damages recovery for conduct that violates the Eighth Amendment but does not cause physical harm. For example, it is doubtful that the prisoner plaintiff in *Helling v. McKinney*, 509 U.S. 25 (1993), who alleged an Eighth Amendment violation from exposure to environmental tobacco smoke, could now recover damages if he established a constitutional violation because he only alleged a risk of harm. The PLRA does not only preclude damages in Eighth Amendment cases. Most circuits interpret it to apply even to First Amendment cases. See *Royal v. Kautzky*, 375 F.3d 720 (8th Cir. 2004) (holding that the PLRA applies to First Amendment claims); *Thompson v. Carter*, 284 F.3d 411 (2d Cir. 2002) (saying that the PLRA applies to all constitutional claims). The fact that the circuits have somewhat ameliorated the harshness of the PLRA by allowing nominal damages and injunctive and declaratory relief, see, for example, *Allah v. Al-hafeez*, 226 F.3d 247 (3d Cir. 2000), does not eliminate the problem. Nominal damages and injunctive or declaratory relief do not compensate for loss and punitive damages are difficult to obtain. See *Smith v. Wade*, 461 U.S. 30 (1983) (saying that punitive damages are only available if the conduct was outrageous).

225. See earlier section.

226. See *Pollard*, 607 F.3d at 597, *rev'd sub nom. Minneci v. Pollard*, 132 S. Ct. 617 (2012).

It is difficult to tell how far the *Minneci* decision will go toward undermining protection for constitutional rights. The Court did, at least,
ensure that a tort remedy was available to Pollard and stated that its
decision to defer to state remedies might be different if a different
constitutional right or different state remedial system were at issue.
132 S. Ct. 617, at 625. It did require that state remedies be "roughly"
equivalent to those available in a *Bivens* action. Idem. There is, however, a real danger, given the Court's antagonism to *Bivens*, that it will
retreat from those caveats, just as it did from the *Bivens* Court's statement that alternative congressional remedies had to be "explicit" and
"equally effective in the view of Congress." *Bivens*, 403 U.S. 388 (1971),
397.
227. *Bivens*, 403 U.S. 388 (1971), 391–395.
228. See above, text accompanying note 68.

Bibliography

Adams, James Truslow and R.V. Coleman, eds. *Dictionary of American
History*, 2nd ed., rev. New York: Scribner, 1961.
Baltmanis, David, and James E. Pfander. "Rethinking Bivens: Legitimacy and
Constitutional Adjudication." *Georgetown Law Journal* 98 (2009).
Banta, Natalie. "Death by a Thousand Cuts or Hard Bargaining?: How the
Court's Indecision in Wilkie v. Robbins Improperly Eviscerates the Bivens
Action." *Brigham Young University Journal of Public Law* 23 (2008).
Brown, George D. "Counter-Counter-Terrorism via Lawsuit—The Bivens
Impasse." *Southern California Law Review* 82 (2009).
"Comment: The Civil Rights Act: Emergence of an Adequate Federal Civil
Remedy?" *Indiana Law Journal* 26 (1951).
Hanna, Heather J., and Alan G. Harding. Comment: "Ubi Jus Ibi
Remedium—For the Violation of Every Right, There Must be a Remedy:
The Supreme Court's Refusal to use the Bivens Remedy in Wilkie v.
Robbins." *Wyoming Law Review* 8 (2008).
Hill, Alfred. "Constitutional Remedies." *Columbia Law Review* 69 (1969).
Katz, Al. "The Jurisprudence of Remedies: Constitutional Legality and the
Law of Torts in Bell v. Hood." *University of Pennsylvania Law Review*
117 (1968).
Lambert, Thomas A. "The Case Against Private Disparate Impact Suits."
Georgia Law Review 34 (2000).
Mulligan, Lumen N. "Why Bivens Won't Die: The Legacy of Peoples v. CCA
Detention Centers." *Denver University Law Review* 83 (2006).
Noyes, John E. "Implied Rights of Action and the Use and Misuse of
Precedent." *University of Cincinnati Law Review* 56 (1987).

Pries, John F. "Alternative Remedies in Constitutional Torts." *Connecticut Law Review* 40 (2008).

Robotti, Michael P. "Separation of Powers and the Exercise of Concurrent Constitutional Authority in the Bivens Context." *Connecticut Public Interest Law Journal* 8 (2009).

Shapo, Marshall S. "Constitutional Tort: Monroe v. Pape, and the Frontier Beyond." *Northwestern University Law Review* 60 (1960).

Thomas, Tracy A. "Ubi Jus, Ibi Remedium: The Fundamental Right to a Remedy Under Due Process." *San Diego Law Review* 41 (2004).

Tikonoff, Matthew W. Note: "A Final Frontier in Prisoner Litigation: Does Bivens Extend to Employees of Private Prisons Who Violate the Constitution?" *Suffolk University Law Review* 40 (2007).

Tribe, Laurence H. "Death by a Thousand Cuts: Constitutional Wrongs without Remedies After Wilkie v. Robbins." *Cato Supreme Court Review* 2006–07 (2007).

Part II

Law and Executive Authority

Chapter 5

The Necessary and the Good in Lincoln's Wartime Reconstruction Policy

Sean Mattie

Throughout his political career, Abraham Lincoln exalted the goodness of self-government and exhorted his fellow citizens to aim high for it, using language of elegant and moving simplicity.[1] Yet Lincoln was no simple dogmatist about liberty, nor did he urge it upon the country with idealistic immoderation. As a human good to be sought in or through politics, liberty requires that there be first— or most urgently—law and order, and thus a force powerful enough to meet this need. The good of self-government depends for its possibility on the necessity of *government*.[2] However, the balance between the good of liberty and the need for security (or government) is delicate, especially in political life's unavoidable contingency and susceptibility to passions. Citizens and statesmen may come to see politics and policy principles as reduced to *either* the high or optimal end of freedom *or* the low yet pressing end of peace and submission. Lincoln succinctly framed this difficult dilemma through the question, "Must a government, of necessity, be too *strong* for the liberties of its own people, or too *weak* to maintain its own existence?"[3]

Lincoln raised his question not abstractly, but rather in a dire crisis in the country and the Constitution. In 1860–1861, parties in several states carried the idea of self-government to the extreme of disunion. In his inaugural address, before the armed attack on Fort Sumter but after secession resolutions in seven states, Lincoln argued emphatically for union against disintegration. He highlighted on the Constitution's provisions for individual and political liberty while observing the necessary limits on those goods. It protects fundamental rights from political reassignment, while also providing a representative, majority-rule political process to set policy and settle disputes on all other public matters. However, citizens must accept that not every object of their choosing—for example, slavery in the federal territories—is constitutionally guaranteed, just as those in the minority on a vote need to comply with its result.[4] This argument failed on its intended audience, for whom self-government entailed secession and who enforced that view by besieging and seizing Fort Sumter. As Lincoln declared, the "assailants of the Government" began the conflict of arms, forcing on the country the alternatives of "immediate dissolution, or blood." As president, he argued, he could not legitimately accept or effect the former option.[5] "No choice was left," then, but to "call out the war power of the Government" to put down the rebellion—to "resist force, employed for its destruction, by force for its preservation."[6] In the war for the Union, the need to seize, hold, and exploit the advantage over rebel arms led not only to the mightiest exercise of the national armed forces to date (and ever on American soil), but also to some of the most forceful and discretionary (and, in some cases, extralegal) executive actions in American history.[7]

Although he viewed supremacy over the rebellion as necessary to the Union, Lincoln sought to avoid elevating necessity—that is, whatever means were militarily effective—into an exclusive ruling principle. To Lincoln, the Union to be preserved was the *good* regime under the Constitution, which he described as the "form, and substance of government, whose leading object is, to elevate the condition of men—to lift artificial weights from all shoulders—to clear the path of laudable pursuit for all." He expected that in serving this good in the harsh conditions of rebellion, the national government would "from necessity . . . [yield] to partial, and temporary departures." Policy, especially war policy, cannot be as fixed and formal as moral principle. Yet, precisely because he recognized the moral importance of constitutional form, Lincoln distinguished departures from it *as* departures, confined in extent and duration. Concern for this form influenced Lincoln's entire effort to preserve the Union against the insurrection—especially the process to restore or reconstruct popular, Unionist governments in secession-plagued states. With a few notable exceptions,[8] scholars on reconstruction have generally focused on the period after Lincoln's death and the end of the Civil War, giving scant attention to Lincoln's policy and thought, overlooking Lincoln's organized effort to restore local self-government in the midst of—and as a way to defeat—insurrection.[9]

This chapter aims to remedy that. Drawing on Lincoln's speeches, proclamations, and correspondence, and focusing on political events in Louisiana, it discusses Lincoln's policy of wartime reconstruction as it illustrates his insight about the necessary and the good in American politics. The first section observes the initial course of reconstruction during 1861–1863, focusing on Louisiana. The chapter's second section examines Lincoln's Declaration of Amnesty and Reconstruction of December 8, 1863, as his formal statement of his policy of political restoration. The third section discusses the course of reconstruction in 1864–1865, when local political reorganization proceeded more cohesively and quickly but Congress' doubts about the "republican form" of the Unionist governments and their claim to representation in the national government necessarily slowed reconstruction. The chapter's fourth section examines Lincoln's April 1865 national address about reconstructed Louisiana, defending the success thus far in the difficult path to restoring the state to its "proper practical relation to the Union." This speech illustrates Lincoln's support for the good of political liberty, even though limited in extent or time by particular circumstances. For the rest of the Union to reject the pro-Union results of Louisiana's state elections as imperfectly popular or free would necessarily disable progress toward local self-government. Moralistic intolerance of necessary compromises would, in truth, and ironically, keep Louisiana under the rule of necessity (i.e., military occupation). Lincoln's case for the partial good as a necessary condition for accomplishing any greater good in politics revisited and put a finer point on his argument throughout reconstruction about the relation and distinction between the necessary and the good.

Early Attempts at Reconstruction: Louisiana, 1862–1863

Military success in southern Louisiana in 1862 presented Lincoln with not only an important material advantage in the war against the rebellion, but a prime opportunity to promote reconstruction. In late spring 1862, the Union Navy drove rebel arms from New Orleans, which allowed Army General Benjamin Butler's troops to enter and occupy the city, a necessary condition for reconstruction. Butler placed Colonel George Shepley in command of New Orleans, and in June, Lincoln appointed Shepley military governor. The next necessary step was identifying or distinguishing the friends of the Union, and this proved difficult. Upon taking the city in May, Union troops faced open contempt from the many rebel sympathizers there, and Butler responded with harsh police regulations on public conduct, and an order that all residents subscribe to a Union loyalty oath. Even with those residents who came out publicly for the Union by summer 1862, many did so primarily on narrow grounds of self-interest. For example, Cuthbert Bullitt wrote Lincoln to complain not only about Butler's regulations, but also other federal restrictions on rights to trade and to property, including slaves. At the outbreak of hostilities, Lincoln ordered a blockade, which Congress later endorsed in a statute empowering him to render illegal any "commercial intercourse" with anyone in rebel-overrun areas. Congress in March 1862 also legislated that the Army could not return those slaves who had sought sanctuary in the Union army, and the following July it passed the second Confiscation Act, which made all property of rebels subject to military seizure and use, and court condemnation.[10]

Lincoln acknowledged these extraordinary constraints on residents' rights frustrated local sympathy and support for the Union cause, a condition for reconstruction. He defended such harshness not as ordinary policy, or as punitive measures, but as "military necessity." In particular, he argued that "what is done, and omitted" about slaves derives from the Union army's need "to have men and money," which it could not meet if "we keep from, or drive from, our lines, slaves coming to them." However, "military necessity" need not always or altogether rule in Louisiana. Lincoln argued that the people of Louisiana could avert military rule by removing the cause of war. For persons to reclaim the goods of civil and political rights in the Union, they must do their civic "duty" to suppress the rebellion, by either directly helping or at the very least "[permitting] the [national] government to do it" without interference. What Lincoln most desired was for "the people of Louisiana" themselves, acting in "good faith," to "reinaugurate the national authority" by setting up a state government consistent with the Constitution; in this way, they would serve their own good as well as the Union's. The Union army, he pledged, would provide the necessary "protection" during such a process, and would be "withdrawn"—that is, the exigency of military *rule* removed—as soon as "the State government can dispense with it."[11]

By the end of summer several thousand persons in New Orleans declared loyalty to the Union (and thus were able to retain their property), but none had *acted politically*; no group had assembled or asserted themselves as the authoritative "people of Louisiana." Although the military command in New Orleans assumed direction of civil administration, it had not attempted to organize any persons toward responsible civic action. Secretary of War Stanton had sent Shepley instructions to "re-establish the authority of the Federal Government over the State of Louisiana and [protect the people]" until they can reestablish a "civil government consistent with the Constitution of the United States." However, Stanton's instructions did not provide any further guidance; rather they left it to Shepley's "sound discretion" to "adopt such measures as circumstances may demand." Though he was Lincoln's appointee, Shepley saw no urgency or necessity about restoring civilian rule, interpreting his office as concerned only with public order and administration.[12] As Unionist civilians' deliberation and choice was necessary to Lincolnian reconstruction, their inaction during the summer slowed the policy, despite Lincoln's wishes.

In October, Lincoln received a propitious sign of civilian public spiritedness: a telegram from New Orleans resident John Bouligny that he and other friendly persons in the city wished to have "peace again upon the old terms of the constitution of the United States" and to "manifest that desire by elections," particularly for members of Congress. Lincoln requested Butler and Shepley, "in all available ways," to give such persons "a chance to express their wishes at these elections." This was a task beyond simple protection against "secession interference," and it particularly illustrated Lincoln's comprehension of the complexity of restoring popular government under law, amid the exigencies of insurrection. For reconstruction to be useful in preserving the Union and discrediting the insurrection, loyalists in rebel-overrun states must be prompt in acting and appearing as the legitimate, loyal government of the state. One opportunity was an election for two New Orleans seats in the U.S. House that had been left empty by secession. Loyalists voting on these before the end of 1862 would empower and legitimize the Union political-military cause in Louisiana and nationally. However, state law did not call for any election before January 1863, nor would the "regular election officers" be available or reliable.[13] In this failure of Louisiana law to enable popular expression, Lincoln turned, in necessity, to the military government there.

Unified by orders, and governing by command, the military regime in New Orleans could better effect "the expression of the largest number of people possible" in the election, Lincoln believed. There were, though, necessary conditions for this expression of popular will, so that its form would be legitimate and its results compatible with Union safety. Election administrators must distinguish and admit only "respectable" citizens as voters and candidates, such persons as personally declare or demonstrate support for the Union and Constitution (though Lincoln had not yet proclaimed a sufficient test or proof). However, such loyal persons must be also local, Lincoln added. Even if more convenient for reconstruction, to import "Northern men" or "federal officers" would be "understood (and perhaps really so)" as election "at the point of the bayonet," a situation that Lincoln judged "disgusting and outrageous." For the sake of responsible citizenship, it would be "all the better" for the locals to resolve not only on candidates but also on "a day and a way" for the election. However, if they "stand idle not seeming to know what to do," the governor was to "fix these things for them by proclamation." If practical disorganization tangled political organization, "these knots must be cut," Lincoln instructed Shepley.[14] On November 14, 1862, Shepley announced an election for each of the two congressional districts, to be held three weeks later. On December 3, eight thousand Unionists turned out to elect local politicians Benjamin Flanders and Michael Hahn. In a rare opportunity, Hahn spoke on the House floor, attesting to the safety and legitimacy of the election. Henry Dawes, the chair of the House Committee on Elections, concurred, declaring that the electors in the districts conformed "in letter and in spirit" to "the minutest up to the most important requisition of the statutes of Louisiana . . . the constitution of the State . . . [and] of the nation." The "single exception" arose from a situation not "in their power"—the practical need for the military governor to call for the election. On February 17, 1863, the House voted to seat Flanders and Hahn for the remainder of the Thirty-Seventh Congress.[15]

For reconstruction to proceed from this success, a Unionist body politic for the state, not only New Orleans, was necessary.

Lincoln held that a civilian governor and a popular legislature could relieve the Union military of local administration and policing, while the Union political cause could grow (and the secession cause would be weakened) by two more loyal senators selected by a legitimate state government. However, Unionists statewide disagreed on the proper form of proceeding, and, implicitly, on the common good. On June 6, 1863, Hahn wrote Lincoln of this division. One segment that called itself the Free State General Committee and that Hahn described as "the more radical or free-soil" men favored a convention to amend the state constitution against slavery and toward greater political equality and freedom. However, another segment, organized as the Executive Central Committee and favoring "slavery," was "strongly opposed" to amendment, and wished to maintain the 1852 constitution (which, Hahn declared, "unjustly" advantaged rural parishes in the state legislature over the more populous New Orleans). Earlier that month, Thomas Cottman had written Lincoln on behalf of the latter faction ("the Planters" of Louisiana) to pledge allegiance in return for recognition by the national government of "all the rights of the State, as they existed prior" to secession; Cottman also requested that Lincoln order an election in November for all state and federal officers.[16]

In the need for clarity, Lincoln had to address which form of proceeding (and, implicitly, which segment of the Unionists) was better or more useful for advancing and not slowing reconstruction, without dividing or alienating Unionists by decisively endorsing one side or one political agenda over the other. The situation also forced upon Lincoln questions not only of procedure but also of substance: what state laws, even what state constitution, might or should be up for election? Replying to Cottman and cognizant of Hahn's report, Lincoln held that the desire of "a respectable portion of the Louisiana people" to amend the state constitution first was a "sufficient" cause to defer executive recognition of any constitution, however much another portion of the people desired it. Although Lincoln believed it necessary to distinguish between friends and enemies of the Union, he thought it neither necessary nor good to draw lines *among* Unionists, or to intervene to favor one group over another. Expressing his confidence in "people of Louisiana," without identifying it with any particular segment of it, Lincoln refrained from ordering a convention or election for amending or replacing the 1852 constitution. This, he argued, did not necessarily preclude any election. The people "shall not lack opportunity of a fair election for both Federal and State officers," certainly not "by want of anything within [his] power to give them." Military protection of Unionists was simply and always necessary, whereas executive intervention in state politics was neither necessary nor good. Moreover, a state government established without large popular consent, yet claiming authority to relieve the military administration there, would be problematic. Questions of its legitimacy would confound the transition of power, disturb security and civil administration, and overall "embarrass" wartime reconstruction.[17]

Establishing a statewide Unionist populace toward the next election was also contingent on another kind of agreement: particular responsibility for enrolling persons. Lincoln viewed his delegation of power (and self-restraint) as both necessary and proper in the process of restoring popular politics, so he looked to Military Governor Shepley to initiate the process. Shepley, in turn, commissioned Thomas J. Durant, the provisional attorney general and a leading member of the Free State General Committee, to compile a statewide registry of voters to prepare for a constitutional convention later in the year. Durant and his assistants "applied a rigid test of past loyalty" that was not ordered by Lincoln, Banks, or Shepley, and that "many conservatives could not or would not take."[18] Furthermore, although Durant was attorney general, he had no force at his command, and so, practically, he could not communicate with "a large portion of the state," as he wrote in an October 1 letter informing Lincoln that registration had stalled. Durant added that he thought that Union forces should have "undisturbed control of a considerable territory" before the "commencement of a registration." For two months, Durant had not communicated these concerns to Shepley, or to Lincoln, while Shepley had assumed that Durant was proceeding with the registry and therefore refrained from calling any election. As a consequence, "nothing had been done," as Benjamin Flanders informed Lincoln. Such disorganization and delay squandered the political momentum for reconstruction that the prior congressional election imparted.

This situation disappointed Lincoln "bitterly," prompting him to restate his concern for timeliness. In a November letter to Banks, Lincoln urged him, Shepley, Durant, and other Unionists to "lose no more time" in organizing elections. He judged that "more territory," or a larger military advantage, in the state, was not a necessary condition before attempting a broader vote. With reconstruction stalled and the war dragging on, it was not possible to assemble the whole Unionist population in the state. Lincoln instead sought the good that was possible and indeed already existed by then: a "tangible nucleus" of Unionists, which "the remainder of the State may rally around as fast as it can," and which he as president "can at once recognize and sustain as the true State government."[19] In his Proclamation of Amnesty and Reconstruction, issued in December 1863, Lincoln would restate this fundamental practical notion.

Formal Policy: The Proclamation of December 8, 1863

Lincoln believed that by December 1863, "the elements for resumption" of Unionist governments in several states seemed "ready for action, but remained inactive," due to the lack of a "rallying point" or "plan of action." In his Proclamation of Amnesty and Reconstruction, issued December 8, Lincoln sought to provide the plan, formally declaring the conditions he considered necessary and good for restoring loyal citizenship and popular government. The proclamation's preamble clarified the connection between amnesty and reconstruction. In the rebellion, the "loyal State governments of several States" had been "for a long time subverted" and "many persons have committed and are now guilty of treason against the United States."[20] This later pronouncement was obvious and yet astounding in its implications. The Second Confiscation Act declared death as the punishment for treason.[21] As the Act legislated that judicial process would establish guilt and apply the sentence, the president's "finding" of mass guilt also suggested not only broad prosecutions but also extralegal or extraconstitutional punishment. To Lincoln, though, the prospect of actual departures from such form were remote, and they were invoked only as a means to make the true end of his proclamation more effective. His point in declaring mass treason was to call to rebels' minds the goods they stood to lose that they could secure by returning to loyal citizenship in the Union.[22] Lincoln expected that the loyalty oath he proposed in the proclamation would be sufficiently effective in "[separating] the opposing elements"—those against the rebuilding of Union governments—"from the sound." He also considered the oath "sufficiently liberal" to the person who takes it, requiring only "sworn recantation of his former unsoundness."[23] For the good of the Union, its policies must distinguish and strengthen "the element within a State, favorable to republican government, in the Union" against "an opposite and hostile element external to, or even within the State."[24]

As part of Lincoln's offer or policy, he would secure the exercise of political privileges as well as civil rights to life and liberty. Those who took the oath were to "reinaugurate loyal . . . governments within and for their States." Lincoln conceived of this reinauguration as *restoration* of the body politic, a conservative stance, as reflected in Lincoln's condition that "the election law of the State existing immediately before the so-called act of secession" would govern voter qualifications. However, Lincoln also comprehended that exigencies of the war affected the good of relying on standing law, which, if applied simply as in antebellum politics, would enfranchise even those who opposed the Union. Thus, the proclamation set a new condition for legitimacy in the political process, one that modified traditional majority rule. Lincoln declared that he as executive would protect governments established by an electorate numbering at least "one tenth . . . of the votes cast in such State" in the presidential election of 1860.[25] In the rebellion's disturbance of both civil life and public sentiment, Lincoln recognized that simply waiting on the antebellum electorate was neither possible, nor timely, nor good for reconstruction. Still, as he acknowledged in his First Inaugural, minority rule is "wholly inadmissible . . . as a permanent arrangement"—that is, inconsistent with the *form* of American government.[26] Lincoln proposed a 10 percent electorate not to impose oligarchy onto American politics, but as a necessary and temporary political *minimum* to enable a loyal core of legal voters to assert political responsibility, establish legitimate government, and— crucial to Lincoln's *dynamic* view of reconstruction—draw other local persons to them, growing the citizenry toward that of normal popular government. As Louisiana already demonstrated, Unionists observed majority rule among themselves in making public decisions.

Pardon and political privileges also depended on compliance with laws and executive proclamations on emancipation, which Lincoln incorporated into his loyalty oath. This necessary condition reflected his long and careful reflection about whether and how freedom became an indispensable means in the struggle for the Union. Lincoln had always believed in individual liberty as a moral end, a permanent or formal good. Slavery was, thus, an evil, always or inherently; "if slavery is not wrong, then nothing is wrong," Lincoln held.[27] However, as he recognized, the Constitution granted the national government no power to interfere with the right to slavery as legislated by particular states. In his Inaugural Address, he reiterated this institutional limitation as he did his own disinclination to interfere with slavery, in regular politics or in peacetime. However, the extraordinary circumstances of rebellion, occurring in states with slavery, raised the question of whether and how the national government's war power reached the institution. In 1861 and 1862, Congress legislated, as articles of war, that slaves of rebels were lawful prize, subject to capture, and, as "captives of war," free from bondage; furthermore, it declared, the President may employ former slaves and other "persons of African descent" as he may "deem necessary and proper for the suppression of this rebellion."[28] Waiting until the crucial Union victory at Antietam in September 1862, Lincoln proclaimed emancipation as a military policy in all rebel areas, beginning the following January; the final Emancipation Proclamation, on January 1, 1863, also announced the policy of enlisting former slaves and other blacks into the Union army.

To Lincoln, emancipation was not the "paramount object" of the war, but was rather an instrument that he would use as (and only as) it served the paramount object, preserving the Union. "What I do about slavery, and the colored race," he declared to antislavery activist Horace Greeley, "I do because I believe it helps to save the Union," and whatever Lincoln refrained from doing reflected his judgment that such restraint would "help to save the Union." He added, "I shall do *less* whenever I shall believe what I am doing hurts the cause, and I shall do *more* whenever I shall believe doing more will help the cause."[29] Emancipation was contingent and instrumental, but therefore also possible and valuable. Furthermore, the value of military emancipation would increase as it became more closely identified with—that is, more necessary to—the Union cause. By August 1863, Lincoln already viewed military emancipation and the accompanying "use of colored troops" as "the heaviest blow yet dealt to the rebellion," adding that at least one military victory "could not have been achieved when it was, but for the aid of black soldiers." In his December message to Congress, Lincoln observed that this policy continued to benefit the Union, and he urged that the Union maintain the freedom of the former slaves as both a practical and a moral imperative. To allow or even to suggest that freed slaves might be returned to bondage during or after the war would be not only "to relinquish a lever of power" but to commit "a cruel and an astounding breach of faith." Lincoln argued that the former slaves risked their lives for the Union and would continue to do so only on "a pledge" from the Union to protect their freedom.[30] To abandon these friends of the Union (as to neglect loyal Unionists in the rebel states) would be both unjust and impolitic.

Once the formal good of emancipation became practically necessary to the Union, Lincoln seized on it. However forceful and far-reaching his policy, he still considered it vital to proceed as much as possible by the rule of law and to respect the states' legislative power. As slavery existed there by organic law, it would be best for the people in the states to effect permanent abolition by removing it themselves. Insofar as wartime reconstruction addressed the reorganization of government (and organic law), Lincoln saw fit to make compliance with emancipation a condition for persons who would claim such political privileges. Lincoln trusted that such citizens would recognize the connection between free government and individual freedom, and that friends of the Union would observe justice among themselves.[31] He also considered it both good and necessary for local citizens, rather than the national government, to have political latitude about the complex and difficult aftermath of slavery. Lincoln acknowledged that military liberation had caused a "total revolution of labor" in the states that it affected, and this inevitably brought "confusion and destitution" to "all classes" there. He held that in the complex conditions of abolition and its aftermath, local citizens could best comprehend the variables of policy, especially in providing for the education and welfare of a "laboring, landless and homeless" class of persons. Although he reserved the power of the national government "to prevent [any] abuse," Lincoln emphasized that he would accept "any reasonable temporary arrangement" for public provision and public order.[32] For states destabilized by, first, insurrection and then emancipation, the practical good of a free and civil society was thoroughly contingent on local social conditions and local public opinion. Therefore, the national executive must refrain from imposing any political form on social and economic policy there, and must restrict himself to the uniform duty of protecting Unionists and the free governments they establish.

The Proclamation Policy in Practice:
Louisiana, 1864–1865

Local Political Organization and Action

Lincoln's proclamation provided direction and energy to Unionist public action in Louisiana (as well as Arkansas and Tennessee).[33] General Banks cheered Lincoln's offer of pardon, declaring that it could not fail to produce "great national results" and that "many classes of people in the South" would accept its offer of "escape."[34] He also considered the antislavery emphasis in Lincoln's plan feasible. Although much of Louisiana was exempt from the Emancipation Proclamation, many Unionists in Louisiana, even those of "the strongest southern sympathies," believed it "practicable" to restore the state government with "absolute extinction of slavery at the start." However, the exact mode of restoring the government—for example, the next action that Unionists must or ought to take—remained controversial, reflecting the disagreement and partisanship that still existed among Unionists in Louisiana. As in 1863, the planter or rural faction favored maintaining the 1852 constitution (and their preponderance in the legislature) and simply electing state and federal offices, while the radical (or New Orleans–based) segment viewed constitutional revision (to abolish slavery as well as planter overrepresentation) as primary, with elections for offices following only after. Cognizant of this disagreement and its confounding effect on reconstruction, Lincoln "distinctly" instructed Banks to be "master of all," settling these political differences to give the Union "a free-state re-organization of Louisiana, in the shortest possible time."[35]

Banks' practical understanding of his charge emerged as he determined the next stage of Unionist political organization. At a January 8, 1864, meeting in New Orleans, a gathering of Unionists endorsed the Free State General Committee recommendation for Governor Shepley to call a popular election for a constitutional convention, which would then define the state government. Banks, however, believed that this mode would not "promise results so speedy or certain" for reconstruction. In his estimation, "the election of delegates [could not] be called before March," the convention "could not sit before April," and as it would "scarcely occupy less than two months," the constitution "could hardly be submitted to the People . . . before July."[36] Rejecting the Free State proposal, Banks set February 22 for the election of governor and other state officials, and the first week in April for delegates to a constitutional convention. Voters would be qualified according to Lincoln's proclamation and to "the Constitution and Laws of Louisiana," except regarding slavery, which existed there only statutorily.[37] In countermanding the state's slavery laws, Banks did not intend to signal or effect abolition in the state. Rather, he declared them inoperative due to what he saw as a double necessity at that time: "No law for the enforcement of the rights of master over the slave could be executed by citizens or by State officers without a disturbance of the public peace"; military enforcement of slavery "was forbidden by order of Congress."[38] Suspending state slavery laws also kept public opinion focused on the decision about officers, and not directly (or not yet) on slavery.

As Banks argued in a letter to Lincoln, an indirect approach to the good of abolition was necessary for its ultimate popular approval in Louisiana. To pose the question of slavery directly to voters would expose the institution to the "chances of election," possibly sustaining it. Furthermore, the people's "self-respect" would be appeased if they were not required to vote—and thus display the division of Unionist opinion—on slavery. Instead, Banks urged, "offer [the people] a Government without slavery," as the delegates drafting a new constitution would likely do, and the people "will gladly accept it as a necessity resulting from the war."[39] Banks' electoral program provoked Durant and other radicals to protest to Congress and the president about military usurpation of "the whole question of civil reorganization."[40] Faced with another challenge to wartime reconstruction and another strain on the fragile Unionist body politic in Louisiana, Lincoln had to decide on Banks' policy. Trusting that Banks' action would enable more than disable loyal, popular politics in Louisiana, Lincoln approved, instructing him to "frame orders, and fix times and places ... according to [his] own judgment."[41]

The February election was the first test of Lincoln's formal reconstruction policy, and his first informal guidance of the process through his delegation to Banks. The turnout was 11,411, nearly one-fourth (not merely one-tenth) of the 1860 electorate.[42] Michael Hahn, the moderate former congressman whose views of reconstruction mirrored Lincoln's, was elected governor over two other candidates, and took office March 2. In his inaugural address, Hahn declared the restoration of state government but also admitted that "for the moment" civil government "must necessarily harmonize with military administration," though he promised that commanders "will interfere but little with individual action."[43] On March 13, Lincoln wrote to Hahn to congratulate and recognize him as "the first free-state Governor of Louisiana." Two days later, Lincoln invested Hahn with "the powers exercised hitherto by the Military Governor of Louisiana."[44] This latter statement addressed an issue that Lincoln left ambiguous in the December 8 proclamation: the status of military governors in the stages of reconstruction. Lincoln's transfer of power to Hahn signaled the return of civilian rule over public administration, which he considered good as well as useful in advancing reconstruction.

The next stage of political reorganization in the state was the constitutional convention that met in New Orleans from April to July. At the recommendation of Hahn, who opposed the plantation oligarchy in Louisiana, Banks determined the basis of representation without regard to number of slaves, who had formerly been counted. Offended, the conservative planter Unionists decided to send no delegates, and thus only moderates and radicals composed the convention. They could and did agree on freedom, and quickly and overwhelmingly voted to write emancipation, without compensation, into the draft constitution. However, education or provision for former slaves deeply divided the delegates. Black enfranchisement was even more controversial at the convention. Hahn advocated it strongly, with intelligence and armed service as the necessary qualifications. Lincoln had privately suggested this proposition to Hahn.[45] Lincoln considered the black soldier a solid friend of the Union, and so granting suffrage would do good (or be a just reward) and advantage the Union politically. If enfranchisement were extended (yet limited) to an outstanding class of black persons, then the proposition might be more agreeable to public opinion in the state, which Lincoln considered necessary to reconstruction at all phases. The convention ultimately declined to provide black suffrage, though it did ban slavery and authorize the legislature to extend the vote, on the conditions that Hahn and Lincoln favored. The charter also revised the basis of representation in the legislature, so as no longer to favor plantation parishes.[46] Hahn and Banks supported the constitution, as did Lincoln, who considered it "excellent" and "better for the poor black man than we have in Illinois."[47] On September 5, voters approved the constitution 6,836 to 1,566.[48] They also selected representatives to the state legislature and members for three of the five congressional districts into which the new constitution divided the state. Soon after the new state legislature convened in New Orleans on October 3, it selected R. King Cutler and Charles Smith for the Senate. On October 31, the body passed an act enabling it to appoint seven presidential electors and on November 8, 1864, it selected electors declaring for Lincoln.[49] The following February, Governor Hahn officially received the Thirteenth Amendment proposed by Congress and referred it to the legislature, which passed it nearly unanimously.[50] As we see in the next section, Lincoln viewed such civic action as good by being necessary to further political restoration of the state in the Union.

Besides enabling elections and public decisions, actual governance also tested how good or how effective was the Unionist regime. Dissension among Unionists about offices and patronage vexed the Hahn administration and prompted another call to Lincoln to intervene politically. Radicals like Benjamin Flanders not only disdained the new constitution as insufficiently liberal, especially on black education and enfranchisement, but also sought to defeat it politically. Flanders and several other radicals had offices in U.S. Treasury Department in the state, and after the September 5 election, Hahn wrote Lincoln of their obstructionism and asked him to make good on his implicit promise to remove them. Lincoln declined, as he saw a greater good, or more pressing need, in keeping peace between moderates and radicals not only in New Orleans but also in the Republican Party, which faced an uphill struggle in the imminent 1864 election.[51]

The Hahn administration also confronted resistance from the military regime, and again Lincoln had to reconcile differences among the Union's necessary friends. After the September election, Lincoln assigned Banks to confer with Congress, replacing him with Major General Stephen Hurlbut. Appalled by what he considered corruption in civil appointments and management of public finances, Hurlbut assumed power over both. For support, Hurlbut wrote General Edward Canby, newly in charge of the Trans-Mississippi West, declaring the "present civil government of Louisiana" to be "an experiment liable to be cut short at any time by military orders"; until the state (and its government) be approved by Congress, it remained "wholly within ... martial law." Canby emphatically agreed. Hahn, in turn, protested to Lincoln about "the most barefaced and unnecessary attempts made to crush out a State government ... formed to aid the country and the administration."[52] The Hurlbut-Canby exchange, originally private, came to Lincoln's notice, and corroborated Hahn's account of the crisis. Confronting this "bitter military opposition to the new State Government of Louisiana," Lincoln again had to bring order to confused, conflicting elements that threatened to defeat and discredit reconstruction, or to undermine the military command still necessary to security in the state.

On November 14, Lincoln wrote Hurlbut, endorsing the new civil government as crucial for the future of the state and the Union. "A very fair proportion of the people of Louisiana" inaugurated a new state government and made a new state constitution. Reiterating a fundamental theme of his reconstruction policy, Lincoln declared that such citizenry and civic institutions formed a "nucleus around which to build" a people and state more loyal, more self-governing, and sooner able to resume its "position" in the Union. Lincoln judged that, at that moment, an overreaching commander—more than the rebellion—threatened to dismantle the new civil government, and he instructed Hurlbut about restraints on his power. However, his rhetoric was indirect, and he defined civil-military relations in such a way as not to alienate the general or simply deny the need for some rule by command. "In the condition of things at New Orleans," he declared, "the military must not be thwarted by the civil authority." In matters of "military necessity"—conditions or actions that affect security in the state—"the commanding general" must prevail, as "master." Furthermore, Lincoln asserted, the commander is also "judge" of the need for his rule in a situation. Still, however much it demanded and authorized discretion and force, "military necessity" was a finite notion *politically*, limited by the good of popular government under law. If a commander used force when not strictly necessary, he would necessarily undermine civil rule. Although Lincoln declared Hurlbut "judge and master" in any disputes bearing on security, he also advised Hurlbut to examine his own judgment and actions, as Lincoln would. Any purpose to "transcend all military necessity ... [to] crush out the civil government," would "not be overlooked," Lincoln warned.[53]

Lincoln reiterated this argument in a letter to Canby. He affirmed that nothing must "take precedence of the military, while the necessity for the military remains." Lincoln assuaged the general by endorsing Canby's disdain for cronyism. "There is no worthy object in getting up a piece of machinery merely to pay salaries, and give political consideration to certain men," he admitted. However, Lincoln believed that this contemptible political situation—to the extent that it existed—did not authorize military intervention, and would be corrected by civil authorities, in time. Indeed, Lincoln's view of progress—his principle of the good as what is possible at the time, and as the basis for accomplishing a greater good—deeply informed his protection of the state government, however imperfect its inauguration. To Lincoln, it was a "worthy object" to "again get Louisiana into proper practical relations with the nation," and, he added, "we can never finish this, if we never begin it."[54]

Confronting Congressional Limitations

In 1864–1865, the Unionist government of Louisiana faced an even larger test when it came before Congress' judgment. In his Proclamation of Amnesty and Reconstruction, Lincoln acknowledged that the restoration of any state government would not be complete or succeed without the consent of Congress, a condition that rendered a complex process even more so. The Constitution establishes Congress as separate in its composition, powers, and will from the president. Each chamber of Congress decides independently of the other, particularly on its members; though the states elect them, Congress determines their final qualifications. The Constitution also places the duty and power to conduct the official count of presidential electors chosen by the states. Through its free judgment on these subjects, as well as by its basic power to legislate, Congress—that is, the Thirty-eighth Congress, meeting in two sessions in 1864–1865 evaluated Lincoln's wartime reconstruction policy, in its parts and as a whole. In doing so, Congress directly challenged Lincoln's judgments about what must and what ought to be done to restore the Union.

Congress addressed reconstruction as a whole through the Wade-Davis Bill, which set necessary conditions for the legitimacy of any government in rebel-overrun states.[55] The bill spoke to the same basic aspects as Lincoln's program: citizen loyalty; civil administration; and the process for establishing a state government that the United States would recognize. However, the bill's policy on each contrasted with Lincoln's in its premise and details. Fundamentally, Wade-Davis presumed (but did not provide the necessary means for) suppression of "the military resistance to the United States" in a state; similarly, the bill took for granted the people's "return to obedience" to the Constitution and laws. A "provisional governor," appointed by the president and subject (as military governors had not been) to the Senate's advice and consent, would oversee both civil administration and the process of restoring popular government in the state. Reconstruction would begin with a general enrollment and specific qualifications for citizenship. The electorate would consist only of those "white, male citizens of the United States" who would swear loyalty in the form Congress had legislated in 1862, an oath stricter than Lincoln's.[56] Furthermore, as a condition for exercising any political privileges, these persons must be the majority of all persons in the state.

In contrast to the political flexibility that Lincoln considered necessary to the good and the success of reconstruction, the Wade-Davis Bill set a single procedure for all states. The electorate must first choose delegates to a convention to redraw the state constitution, which must formally repudiate the Confederate war debt, disqualify Confederate officers from voting and holding office, and abolish slavery. If the convention did not legislate these conditions, the provisional governor was to dissolve it; if the electorate did not approve a constitution with those provisions, such a constitution would be void. Only after a sufficient constitution approved by the sufficient electorate, and following express congressional endorsement, would the state return to self-government and to representation in Congress and the Electoral College. Until the state constitution abolished slavery, the bill itself would make those held as slaves "forever free."[57]

Henry Winter Davis offered the most detailed and fundamental argument for the bill, in a speech on the House floor March 22. As Lincoln had, Davis cited Article IV, Section 4 of the Constitution to authorize the bill. This section, he asserted, "not merely confers the power" but also "imposes . . . the duty" to "accomplish the result" of republican government, that is, to guarantee that it "shall exist" in each state. To accomplish this end, the national government had "a plenary, supreme, unlimited political jurisdiction, paramount over courts, subject only to the judgment of the people." This power extends to everything "necessary and proper to make the guarantee effectual." It includes the right to say "what is and what is not . . . inconsistent with republican government," and, accordingly, to "insist upon" any conditions for "the permanent supremacy of republican government" and "the permanent and enduring peace of the country." In contrast to Lincoln's stance, Davis' argument illustrates the basic position that reconstruction *must* have the uniform structure of *law*, to be both legitimate and secure. To "accomplish the result" of "republican" government where (in Congress' view) hostility and anarchy so thoroughly ruled, Congress must set rigid conditions, as for loyalty, the size of the electorate, and emancipation. The "great fundamental principle of American government," Davis declared, was "legislation shall guide every political change," especially "the tottering footsteps of those who seek to restore governments which are disorganized and broken down."[58] Without this formulaic (and centralized) approach, political restoration necessarily fails, he argued.

Congress presented Lincoln with the Wade-Davis Bill on July 4, 1864, the end of its first session. That day, the radical congressmen Charles Sumner, Zachariah Chandler, and George Boutwell visited Lincoln to advocate personally for his prompt signature. After Lincoln doubted Congress's authority to prohibit slavery, Chandler replied, "It is no more than you have done yourself," alluding to the Emancipation Proclamation and its reinforcement by the Proclamation of Amnesty and Reconstruction. Lincoln returned that he as president may do things "in an emergency" and "on military grounds" that Congress cannot do as civil policy for peacetime. Speaking privately to his cabinet, Lincoln added that Congress' claim of plenary power over states in insurrection implied that those states were essentially "no longer in the Union." To Lincoln, it was "unnecessary" to force this "merely metaphysical" question into policy debates. Successful policy depended on political consensus, and such an abstract, overly formal question about the Union, while its civil peace was uncertain, would necessarily produce "confusion," "disturbance," and "violent quarrel" among its friends.[59]

Lincoln allowed the bill to expire by withholding his signature, as Congress went out of session. On July 8, he issued a proclamation on the bill that elaborated on his private comments and served as his broadest, most public statement on reconstruction since the previous December. He declared that he was not prepared to affirm "a constitutional competency in Congress to abolish slavery in the states." Lincoln did not imply that the president instead had this grant of power; he defended the Emancipation Proclamation as a war measure and he publicly admitted the possibility that the Supreme Court might alter or invalidate it, especially if the rebellion was suppressed.[60] Thus Lincoln urged adoption of a constitutional amendment, which the Senate had already passed, as the necessary and sufficient condition to make abolition legitimate, national, and permanent as civil policy. On the bill's procedure for reconstruction, Lincoln declared that he was not prepared to be "inflexibly committed" to a "single plan" for restoring state governments. As Lincoln's reconstruction policy had emphasized local citizenship, and as opinions varied among citizens as to the best political process for reconstruction, Lincoln saw fit not to impose a uniform structure on that process, except for such necessary conditions as Union loyalty. Under the national government's self-restraint in local politics, "free-state constitutions and governments [had] already [been] adopted and installed," as in Louisiana. Endorsing the Wade-Davis Bill's orders for reconstruction would necessarily "set aside" and nullify such political success, thereby "repelling and discouraging the loyal citizens who have set up the same" as to "further effort." Sounding a note of reconciliation, Lincoln praised the bill's reconstruction plan as "one" (among others possible) that would be "proper" for the loyal people of any state "choosing to adopt it."[61] This element of choice, and thus contingency, in Lincoln's construction of the bill reflected his acknowledgment of conditions that were both necessary and good for reconstruction. As Davis and others illustrated, the bill intended precisely to remove contingency (and thereby, Lincoln would say, the judgment of local Unionists).

Congress also addressed reconstruction as it existed, by evaluating particular congressional delegations. Each chamber held that its ultimate decision reflected "the effect which [it] is disposed to give to the efforts to reorganize a state government." On February 11 and 17, 1865, the House Committee on Elections issued a report and recommendations that the three representatives-elect from Louisiana were entitled to seats. However, the whole House voted to table the report, and took no action.[62] On February 18, the Senate Judiciary Committee reported to that chamber that Louisiana's two claimants were "duly elected Senators by the legislature" that convened there in October. However, the Committee recommended that before King and Cutler be seated, Congress pass a resolution recognizing the Louisiana government inaugurated according to the April convention as "legitimate" and "entitled to the guarantee and all other rights of a State" under the U.S. Constitution.[63]

During debate on the resolution, several senators doubted that the necessary conditions existed to authorize a state government; that is, they denied that any rebel-affected state had a *people* that was *loyal, free,* and *whole.* Some argued that the population in Louisiana officially—and thus actually—was still in insurrection, having been described as such by Lincoln himself in an August 1861 proclamation.[64] Unless or until the President or Congress declared that the whole people of Louisiana had returned to loyalty, Congress should not consider any political action as authoritative; a "nucleus" with the potential to attract others was not acceptable, even temporarily.[65] Other senators asserted that the insurrection imposed such duress that no persons could be considered politically free. Democratic Senator Lazarus Powell argued that General Banks' active role in organizing the elections in February and April 1864 demonstrated that "the people of Louisiana" did not form the new government "of their own volition . . . unawed and uninfluenced by the military power"; instead, "the military was in it from the beginning to the end." Republican Senator Jacob Howard concurred that Louisiana was governed superficially by civilians loyal to the Union, but really by "the fear of the bayonet . . . inspired solely by the President of the United States as Commander in Chief of the Army and Navy." To Howard, such a "hybrid, unnatural government," formally governed by a "privileged one sixth part" of the people was not only contrary to the "republican form of government" but also unstable ("a bubble, especially if unsustained by military power"). Republican Benjamin Wade likewise argued that Lincoln's plan for reconstruction was not merely inconsistent with the republican form of government, but "the most contentious, the most anarchical, the most dangerous proposition . . . ever put forth for the government of a free people." Wade viewed one-tenth as the maximum, not the minimum, of Unionists possible in an insurrection state, and as such "would be annihilated by the nine-tenths," who, he presumed, would remain committed to insurrection.[66] Thus, Wade implied, local popular politics was—and would remain—neither possible nor good in any state any part of which had been in insurrection at any time.[67]

Like Henry Winter Davis, Wade interpreted the terms of the Article IV, Section 4 simply, formulaically, even absolutely. A state is not "in the Union" unless or until its entire territory and people be at peace and submit to the Constitution, all at once. Similarly, a state has a "republican form" only if an overwhelming and loyal majority constitute its citizenry, and has a "government" only if those citizens decide and govern their affairs certainly and completely, that is, without external influence, assistance, or interruption. This strict view of the Constitution's "guarantee" provision obscures the tension (and relation) between force and freedom—of the necessary and the good—in the provision itself. This connection seems to counsel compromise and discretion in its enforcement—for example, in balancing Union power and state power, and military and civilian responsibilities. On February 27, Congress voted to postpone consideration of the Louisiana legitimacy bill until the next session in December, a decision that reflected its disagreement with Lincoln about not only the principle of reconstruction but also how principle applies to political particulars.[68]

The Partial Good and the Conditions for Progress

Issued several days after the decisive surrender at Appomattox, Lincoln's public address on April 11, 1865, was arguably his most important for reconstruction. It was his final statement on the policy, though not by his intention or choice; on the contrary, the speech announced his rededication (and called for greater public dedication) to the unfinished work of restoring the Union. It became his last statement when, three days later, John Wilkes Booth assassinated Lincoln. Abruptly deprived of its guiding mind by accident and force, Lincolnian reconstruction was left uncertain, both in its results and its continuance. Though its end was abrupt and senseless, one can assess the policy's meaning by noticing the argument about the partial good and progress that Lincoln made in that address. He began by observing that because of the successful military defense of the Union, political restoration of the Union pressed "more closely" on the public mind. However, good the restoration of peace, the fight for the Union continued in the "new and unprecedented" task of reuniting and restoring political privileges to citizens and states formerly under rebellion. In the wake of the disruption and destruction of civil war, a law or a form of proceeding would seem to have been a necessary condition for political reorganization. To Lincoln, though, the "great peculiarities" that existed in each state, before and especially after the war, necessarily limited any attempt to discover or devise a formula. Any "exclusive . . . inflexible plan" prescribing "details and collaterals" of reconstruction would, in the flux of circumstances, only become "a new entanglement." The country "must simply begin with, and mould from, disorganized and discordant elements." As the material of reconstruction was in disarray, so also were Unionists divided over the "mode, manner, and means," that is, the form of policy.[69]

Lincoln acknowledged these formal limits on reconstruction—or the limits that reconstruction placed upon governing by forms—to address another contingency of reconstruction: public opinion. He understood that public sentiment or judgment would make the success of reconstruction in Louisiana and elsewhere possible or impossible.[70] As political restoration could not (and did not) proceed simply or completely according to some higher form, public opinion ought not simply to condemn it for its formal imperfections. To Lincoln, this did not mean disregarding political forms or standards such as the Constitution. The political community is based on common, standing principles, which "may, and must, be inflexible." The community's particular deliberation and decisions begin from and return to these principles. Lincoln believed, though, that citizens should not conceive of the common good overly formally, in abstraction from the particulars and variables of human circumstances. Such a view of morality would overlook or squander the particular and partial goods that are possible in those circumstances, or would demand that circumstances become immediately and permanently fixed into a form. The result would be political failure, either anarchy or tyranny. If rulers are to govern by forms, or forms are to rule in politics, they ought to comprehend the necessities and contingencies of practical life. One such condition of moral reform is the individual's desire to rule himself, and to consent to being ruled by others (either persons or laws). Lincoln recognized that consent restricts but also tempers the rule of forms in politics; thus consent is both necessary and good in politics.[71] The propositions or political forms that Lincoln employed in reconstruction (e.g., in the December 8 proclamation) reflected his judgment of the principles and policies on which Unionists would agree, and act. He sought to avoid "pernicious abstractions" that were "practically immaterial" and "good for nothing at all," with "no effect other than the mischievous one of dividing our friends."[72] Thus, he framed the aim of reconstruction as restoring a rebel-overrun state to "its proper practical relation with the Union," a formulation flexible enough to include a broad range of Unionists across the country (and in Congress) and a broad range of policies across time and place.

Indeed, this view of the practical good as the formal good reconciled with both the necessary and the contingent underlay Lincoln's argument about Louisiana. The "question" for the country was whether the state and its people could be brought into the Union "sooner" by "sustaining" or by "discarding" the new government— *not* whether that government was "quite all that is desirable." If the rest of the country, fixating on the Louisiana regime's formal defects as popular government,[73] were to "reject, and spurn" the work of Unionists there as not even *conditionally* legitimate, this would do the "utmost" to "disorganize and disperse" them as *citizens* and as friends of the Union. This would necessarily have a "discouraging and paralyzing" effect on their efforts to help themselves *and* the rest of the nation. Simple dismissal of wartime reconstruction would signal the country's indifference and contempt about a shared good and political community—ironically, the very attitude of secession and insurrection.[74] However, if the country could "recognize and sustain" the Unionist government there, the "converse of all this"—progress—is not only possible but also inevitable:

> We encourage the hearts, and nerve the arms of the twelve thousand to adhere to their work, and argue for it, and proselyte for it, and fight for it, and feed it, and grow it, and ripen it to a complete success.[75]

To Lincoln, success in reconstruction, as in war, depended on present decisions that solidified prior victories and enabled advance to subsequent ones. Henceforth, each particular decision by the Union (e.g., by Congress) about Louisiana would necessarily either advance or set back the good accomplished to date by Unionists there. If the country did not support the ongoing restoration of government by local civilians, that project would stumble and fall, and some centralized or military rule would necessarily take its place; in this way, the country's judgment on Louisiana would necessarily affect the political form of the Union. Lincoln believed that the greater good of Union under the Constitution was necessarily built from, and maintained by, particular actions or partial goods accomplished over time.[76] To Lincoln, this political precept applied especially to evaluating reconstruction amid the chaos caused by civil war. Progress is possible if, and only if, the country comprehended the good this way. One might add that only in this way is politics possible. If the country views the good only through or as a form—complete, unchanging, and absolute— then it necessarily discounts the partial goods that are possible, and on which citizens can agree and act. One fundamental lesson that Lincoln's wartime reconstruction teaches is that if moral reform in politics insists too rigidly on formal perfection, then the good it seeks becomes *actually* impossible;[77] citizens cannot *proceed* to it, through ongoing, successive exercises of common reflection and choice. In seeking to eliminate contingency, rule by forms would exaggerate, ironically, the rule the rule of accident and force—as the conflicted course of reconstruction after Lincoln unfortunately demonstrated.

Notes

1. Consider, for example, his statement in the Peoria Address in 1854: "What I do say is, that no man is good enough to govern another man, *without that other's consent*. [T]his is the leading principle—the sheet anchor of American republicanism." In the Gettysburg Address, Lincoln framed political liberty famously as "government of the people, by the people, for the people" and lauded it as the Union cause in the Civil War. *Collected Works of Abraham Lincoln*, ed. Roy P. Basler, 2:266; 7:19.

2. As an illustration of this principle, Lincoln in the 1850s argued for the *government* to return to *enforcing* the *prohibition* on slavery in the federal territories north and west of Missouri, as it had since the Missouri Compromise legislation of 1820. Lincoln viewed the enforcement of such policy (and the repeal of the Kansas-Nebraska Act) as a necessary means, in the crisis of slavery expansion, to promote liberty. His public rhetoric did not consist of only moral exhortations not to take slaves.

3. *Collected Works*, 4:426.

4. Ibid., 4:267–269.

5. Lincoln asserted that his constitutional duty was to administer the present Government as it came to his hands and to transmit it unimpaired by him to his successor. He denied that he had any authority to fix terms for the separation of the States. *Collected Works*, 4:270.

6. Ibid., 4:426.

7. See Larry Arnhart, 121–131; Robert K Faulkner; Mark Neely Jr.; Herman Belz, *Reconstructing the Union: Theory and Policy During the Civil War* ; and Sean Mattie, 77–111.

8. Cf. Belz, *Reconstructing the Union*; and William C. Harris.

9. Although Allen Guelzo addresses reconstruction only incidentally, he characterizes Lincoln's prudence or sagacity aptly: "[It can] take in the whole of a situation at once and know almost automatically how to

proceed. It prefers incremental progress to categorical solutions, and fosters that progress through the offering of motives rather than expecting to change dispositions. Yet, unlike moderation, it has a sense of purposeful motion and declines to be paralyzed by a preoccupation with process, even while it remains aware that there is no goal so easily attained or so fully attained that it rationalizes dispensing with process altogether." *Lincoln's Emancipation Proclamation: The End of Slavery in America*, 3–4; see also William A. Dunning; Michael Perman; David H. Donald; and Eric Foner.

10. *The Statutes at Large, Treaties, and Proclamations of the United States of America from December 5, 1859 to March 3, 1863*, ed. George P. Sanger, 362, 257, 354, 589–592.

11. *Collected Works*, 3:325–326.

12. Harris, *With Charity for All*, 73. As New Orleans resident (and eventual congressman and state governor) Michael Hahn reported to Congress February 17, 1863, "Governor Shepley appoints all our judges and justices of the peace, and all other officers of a civil character whose appointments devolve[d] on the (civil) Governor." Congress, *Congressional Globe*, 37th Cong., 3d sess., 1863, 1031.

13. *Collected Works*, 5:462.

14. Ibid., 5:504–505.

15. *Statues, Treaties, and Proclamations*, 1031–1032.

16. *Collected Works*, 6:289.

17. Ibid., 6:288–289.

18. Harris, *With Charity for All*, 118.

19. *Collected Works*, 7:2.

20. Ibid., 7:1–2.

21. *Statues, Treaties, and Proclamations*, 589–590.

22. The oath reads, "I, ---, do solemnly swear, in presence of Almighty God, that I will henceforth faithfully support, protect and defend the Constitution of the United States, and the union of the States thereunder; and that I will, in like manner, abide by and faithfully support all acts of Congress passed during the existing rebellion with reference to slaves, so long and so far as not repealed, modified or held void by Congress, or by decision of the Supreme Court; and that I will, in like manner, abide by and faithfully support all proclamations of the President made during the existing rebellion having reference to slaves, so long and so far as not modified or declared void by decision of the Supreme Court. So help me God."

23. Lincoln comprehended that any test of citizenship, even or especially in the tension of a civil war, must avoid extremity, to be both good and possible. Loyal citizenship, as a theory, might demand that has someone "swear he has [never] done wrong" against the community.

Such severity, Lincoln believed, "rejects the Christian principle of for-giveness on terms of repentance." For Lincoln, it was "enough if the man does no wrong hereafter" (*Collected Works*, 7:169).

24. Ibid., 7:51–54.

25. Ibid., 7:55.

26. Ibid., 4:268.

27. Ibid., 7:281. On the subject of equality in inalienable rights, Lincoln declared, "[T]he negro is ... entitled to all the natural rights enumer-ated in the Declaration of Independence, the right to life, liberty and the pursuit of happiness.. . .[I]n the right to eat the bread, without leave of anybody else, which his own hand earns, he is my equal and the equal of Judge Douglas, and the equal of every living man" (ibid., 3:16). About the principle of government by consent of the governed, Lincoln held, "[T]he relation of masters and slaves is, PRO TANTO, a total violation of this principle. The master not only governs the slave without his consent; but he governs him by a set of rules altogether different from those which he prescribes for himself" (ibid., 2:266).

28. *Statues, Treaties, and Proclamations*, 589–592.

29. *Collected Works*, 5:388–389. In this vein, it is important to note Lin-coln's reasoning in countermanding two orders of emancipation is-sued by Union generals prior to the Emancipation Proclamation. In August 1861, General John C. Frémont, acting without Lincoln's knowledge or consent, proclaimed the permanent freedom, by martial law, of slaves of rebels in Missouri. Lincoln countered that military au-thority could not "fix [slaves'] permanent future condition," this mat-ter being "purely political" and to be settled "according to laws made by law-makers." On the same grounds, Lincoln overruled General David Hunter's May 19, 1862, proclamation, while leaving open the possibility that the president may judge emancipation "a necessity in-dispensable" to suppressing the insurrection (ibid., 4:531–532, 5:222).

30. Ibid., 7:51.

31. In his letter to James Conkling defending the Emancipation Procla-mation, Lincoln argued that black soldiers in the Union army fight to prove the proposition "that, among free men, there can be no success-ful appeal from the ballot to the bullet; and that they who take such appeal are sure to lose their case, and pay the cost" (ibid., 6:410). By framing the common Union cause this way, Lincoln suggests a basic likeness, in freedom, among all friends of the Union, black or white. In this way, the beleaguered Unionist in a rebel-overrun state could also see his effort to reestablish civil government reflected in the work of the black soldier—an important insight that connects law with uni-versal freedom.

32. *Collected Works*, 7:51.

33. For reconstruction history in Arkansas and Tennessee after the Proclamation, see Harris, *With Charity for All*, 197–228.
34. For a historical study of Lincoln's policy of general pardon and its results, see Jonathan Truman Dorris, 53–64.
35. *Collected Works*, 7:124, 90.
36. *Collected Works*, 7:125.
37. Amos E. Simpson and Vaughan Baker, 234.
38. Senate, *Miscellaneous Documents 2 and 9*, 38th Cong., 2d sess., 1865, 2.
39. *Collected Works*, 7:124
40. Belz, *Reconstructing the Union*, 192.
41. *Collected Works*, 7:124–125.
42. Harris, *With Charity for All*, 179.
43. Ibid., 179–181.
44. *Collected Works*, 7:243, 248.
45. In the March 13 letter to Hahn, Lincoln suggested that as local Unionists met to "define the elective franchise," they might consider "whether some of the colored people may not be let in," that is, "the very intelligent, and especially those who have fought gallantly in our ranks." To Lincoln, whites in Louisiana might agree to extend political privileges to these persons sooner than they would for all blacks in the state. Such an extension, though limited, would be both just (or good) and useful, Lincoln judged. It would help "in some trying time to come" to "keep the jewel of liberty within the family of freedom"—that is, to maintain emancipation politically against subsequent attempts to repeal it (ibid., 7:243).
    However, as he only privately suggested it to Hahn, Lincoln acknowledged that, however good and useful in itself, black enfranchisement was controversial among Unionists in Louisiana, and contingent on their consent.
46. The article on enfranchisement by the legislature granted it "power to extend the suffrage by laws to such persons, citizens of the United States, as by military service, by taxation to support the government, or by intellectual fitness may be deemed entitled thereto"; see also Simpson and Baker, "Michael Hahn: Steady Patriot," 243–244.
47. *Collected Works*, 8:107.
48. Harris, *With Charity for All*, 190.
49. Senate, *Miscellaneous Documents*, 2.
50. State Department, *Documentary History of the Constitution of the United States of America, 1786–1870*, 573–574.
51. Harris, *With Charity for All*, 191.
52. Ibid., 191, 194. Canby wrote that "all attempts at civil government, within the territory declared to be in insurrection, are the creation of military power, and, of course, subject to military revision and control."

53. *Collected Works*, 8:107.

54. Ibid., 8:164.

55. H.R. 244 was the work of the House Committee on Rebellious States, formed at the start of the 38th Congress, both to consider Lincoln's Proclamation of Amnesty and Reconstruction and to consider *legislation* "necessary and proper" to carry into execution the constitutional duty to "guarantee a republican form of government to the States in which the governments recognized by the United States have been abrogated or overthrown" (Congress, *Congressional Globe* [1863], 33).

56. Section 4 of H.R. 244 would require of a prospective voter that he solemnly swear that, inter alia, "I have never voluntarily borne arms against the United States since I have been a citizen thereof . . . I have voluntarily given no aid, countenance, counsel or encouragement to persons engaged in armed hostility to the United States [and] . . . I have not yielded a voluntary support to any pretended government, authority, power, or constitution within the United States hostile or inimical thereto." The resolution here cites the Act of July 2 (*Statues, Treaties, and Proclamations*, 502). Although in his public reservations about H.R. 244, Lincoln did not refer to the oath's demands, we can infer his opposition to its severity from his statement (noted above) that "an oath which requires a man to swear he has not done wrong . . . rejects the Christian principle of forgiveness on terms of repentance. "It is enough" for the individual and the community "if the man does no wrong hereafter." *Collected Works of Lincoln*, 7:169.

57. See Henry Steele Commager, ed., 437–439.

58. Congress, *Congressional Globe*, 38th Cong., 2d sess., 1865, app. 81–84. Davis asserted that Lincoln's policy "proposes no guardianship of the United States . . . no guarantee of law to watch over the organization of . . . government."

59. See John J. Nicolay and John Hay, 120–121.

60. In his Proclamation of Amnesty and Reconstruction, the loyalty oath stipulated support for "all proclamations of the President made during the existing rebellion having reference to slaves," but only "so long and so far as not modified or declared void by decision of the Supreme Court." *Collected Works*, 7:54.

61. Ibid., 7:433–434.

62. Congress, *Congressional Globe* (1865), 755–756, 870

63. House. *Report of Committee of Elections*, 38th Cong., 2d sess., 1865, 2.

64. *Collected Works*, 4:487.

65. Congress, *Congressional Globe* (1865), 535–536, 551–2, 554–555.

66. Ibid., 535–536, 551–552, 554–555, 1063, 1094.

67. For example, liberal Republican senator Charles Sumner, in an argument against seating the senators elected by the Arkansas government

restored according to Lincoln's plan, declared, "[T]he genius of our Government [is] that the *majority* should rule. A majority is the natural base of a republic." (Congress [1864], 2897).

Conservative Democrat senator John Carlile viewed the Lincoln plan and its Arkansas results similarly, arguing that no government "set up within any of the States of this Union by less than one fourth of the inhabitants of that State, less than one fourth of the constitutional voters in that state, is a government republican in form" (Congress, *Congressional Globe* [1865], 3366).

68. See George S. Taft, ed., 249–251.
69. *Collected Works*, 8:401.
70. Cf. Lincoln's observation in his Senate campaign against Stephen Douglas, "In this and like communities, public sentiment is everything. With public sentiment, nothing can fail; without it nothing can succeed" (ibid., 3:27).
71. Lincoln also recognized that false abstractions can become the objects of political attachment, and thereby corrupt and ruin the community. To Lincoln, both Stephen Douglas's amoral "popular sovereignty" and the "ingenious sophism" of secession as "lawful and peaceful" distorted the character of self-government in the United States. Each doctrine could be and was framed simply and categorically by its advocates, which Lincoln would consider further evidence that formality or generality is insufficient for moral soundness.
72. *Collected Works*, 8:403. One can argue that Lincoln understood even "friends" and "enemies" to be practically flexible or contingent, in that he tried to persuade or induce rebels to convert to loyal citizens. See, for example, the perorations in his First and Second Inaugural addresses, and his offer of general pardon.
73. Lincoln acknowledged in the address that the "amount of constituency" on which the government rested would be "more satisfactory to all" if it contained "fifty, thirty, or even twenty thousand" instead of its present twelve thousand. Additionally, the regime's failure to enfranchise black persons rendered it "unsatisfactory" to some. Lincoln himself publicly recommended the reform that he had privately suggested to Michael Hahn, suffrage for "the very intelligent [and] . . . those who serve our cause as soldiers."

    Still, Lincoln hailed that in the "heretofore slave-state of Louisiana," twelve thousand Unionists had legislated freedom for the state as well as for the nation, by unanimously approving the Thirteenth Amendment, thereby demonstrating their commitment to "the very things" and "nearly all the things" that the whole Union wanted (ibid., 8:403–404).
74. "We in effect say to the white men 'You are worthless, or worse—we will neither help you, nor be helped by you.' To the blacks we say 'This

cup of liberty which these, your old masters, hold to your lips, we will dash from you, and leave you to the chances of gathering the spilled and scattered contents in some vague and undefined when, where, and how'" (ibid., 8:404).

75. Lincoln added that the good of black enfranchisement would come sooner by "saving the already advanced steps toward it"—emancipation and public education—than by "running backward over them" (ibid., 8:404).

76. In this vein, Lincoln's case for recognizing and completing the work thus begun in wartime reconstruction recalls his argument about the tie between the past, present, and future—or ancestors, the living generation, and future generations—in the Gettysburg Address. Whether the "new nation, conceived in liberty and dedicated to the proposition that all men are created equal" will "long endure" depends on "our fathers" bringing it forth, and on "the brave men, living and dead" struggling for it when it was tested by war. But these actions, though necessary, were not sufficient; the prior generations' efforts would become "in vain" if "the living" were not also equally dedicated to progress in "the unfinished work" that those before "so nobly advanced": a "new birth of freedom," both individual and political. As with any political good, time makes that work contingent, though possible.

77. Lincoln argued similarly about true and false reasoning regarding individual moral reform. Consider, for example, his Temperance Address of 1842, in which he declared, "Another error, as it seems to me, into which the old reformers fell, was, the position that all habitual drunkards were utterly incorrigible, and therefore, must be turned adrift and damned without remedy, in order that the grace of temperance might abound to the temperate *then*, and to all mankind some hundred years *thereafter*. There is in this something so repugnant to humanity, so uncharitable, so cold-blooded and feelingless that it never did nor ever can enlist the enthusiasm of a popular cause" (*Collected Works*, 1:275).

Bibliography

Arnhart, Larry. "The 'God-Like Prince': John Locke, Executive Prerogative, and the American Presidency." *Presidential Studies Quarterly* 9 (1970): 121–131.

Belz, Herman. *Reconstructing the Union: Theory and Policy During the Civil War*. Ithaca, NY: Cornell University Press, 1969.

———. *Abraham Lincoln, Constitutionalism, and Equal Rights in the Civil War Era*. New York: Fordham University Press, 1998.

Commager, Henry Steele, ed. *Documents of American History*. 5th ed., vol. 1. New York: Appleton-Century-Crofts, 1949.

Donald, David H. *The Politics of Reconstruction, 1863–1867*. Cambridge, MA: Harvard University Press, 1984.

Dorris, Jonathan Truman. *Pardon and Amnesty under Johnson and Lincoln: The Restoration of the Confederates to Their Rights and Privileges, 1861–1898*. Westport: Greenwood Press, 1977.

Dunning, William A. *Reconstruction, Political and Economic, 1865–1877*. New York: Harper & Brothers, 1907.

Faulkner, Robert K. "Lincoln and the Constitution." In *The Revival of Constitutionalism*. Edited by James Muller. Lincoln: University of Nebraska Press, 1988.

Guelzo, Allen C. *Lincoln's Emancipation Proclamation: The End of Slavery in America*. New York: Simon and Schuster, 2004.

Foner, Eric. *Reconstruction: America's Unfinished Revolution, 1863–1877*. New York: Harper, 2002.

Hamilton, Alexander, James Madison, and John Jay. *The Federalist Papers*. Edited by Clinton Rossiter. New York: Mentor Books, 1999.

Harris, William C. *With Charity for All: Lincoln and the Restoration of the Union*. Lexington: University of Kentucky Press, 1997.

Lincoln, Abraham. *Collected Works of Abraham Lincoln*. Edited by Roy P. Basler. 8 vols. New Brunswick: Rutgers University Press, 1953–1955.

Mattie, Sean. "Prerogative and the Rule of Law in John Locke and the Lincoln Presidency." *The Review of Politics* 67 (2005): 77–111.

Neely Jr., Mark. *The Fate of Liberty: Abraham Lincoln and Civil Liberties*. New York: Oxford University Press, 1991.

Nicolay, John J., and John Hay. *Abraham Lincoln: A History*. Vol. 9. New York: The Century Co, 1914.

Perman, Michael. *Reunion without Compromise: The South and Reconstruction, 1865–1868*. New York: St. Martin's Press, 1963.

Simpson, Amos E., and Vaughan Baker. "Michael Hahn: Steady Patriot." *Louisiana History* 13 (1972): 229–252.

Taft, George S., ed. *Compilation of Senate Election Cases from 1789–1885*. Washington, DC: Government Printing Office, 1885.

United States. *Statutes at Large, Treaties, and Proclamations*. Edited by George P. Sanger. Vol. 12. Boston: Little, Brown, 1863.

U.S. Congress. *Congressional Globe*. 46 vols. Washington, DC, 1834–1873.

———. House of Representatives. *Report of Committee of Elections*. 38th Cong., 2d sess., 1865.

———. Senate. *Miscellaneous Documents 2 and 9*. 38th Cong., 2nd sess., 1865.

U.S. State Department. *Documentary History of the Constitution of the United States of America, 1786–1870*. Vol. 2. Washington, DC, 1894.

Chapter 6

Progress, Return, and the Constitution

C. Kevin Marshall

This section of the volume honoring Professor Dry, on "Law and Executive Authority," necessarily turns the mind to the bitter disputes over the claimed authority and the conduct of the president in prosecuting the variously named war that began, or at least was recognized, on September 11, 2001. I offer a blend of scholarly and professional reflections on some principles and authorities we should consider in these debates, drawing on my experience in the Department of Justice during the George W. Bush administration, including as deputy assistant attorney general in the Office of Legal Counsel, and also drawing on the liberal education that began with my courses at Middlebury College.

Following Congress's swift authorization of the use of force against those entities that carried out or aided the attacks of September 11, or harbored the attackers, President Bush on his own initiative (and in at least one case arguably contrary to existing statutes) pursued a series of policies to prevent another attack on the United States and to locate and neutralize those entities' members. The primary objects of scholarly and political wrath have been the indefinite detention of suspected terrorists as "enemy combatants"—primarily aliens held abroad, many at the Guantanamo Bay Naval Base in Cuba; the interrogation of those detainees, particularly the CIA's "enhanced" interrogation of certain "high-value" detainees abroad; and, the National Security Agency's interception of communications into and out of the United States by persons the executive considered to be linked to al Qaeda or related terrorist organizations.

More than a decade later, and under a new president, these issues and debates are very much alive. The need for thoughtful debate continues. And whatever one's political persuasion, the president's claim of a power to scoop up an American citizen in Chicago's O'Hare airport and detain him indefinitely, without criminal charges or a suspension of the writ of *habeas corpus*—as in the case of Jose Padilla—should at least make one sit up. More generally, as Congress's authorization fades in the mirror, the prospect of an *indefinite* war, against *worldwide* foes, *vaguely* defined, gives pause even to those who, in the name of securing the country, might accept, for a period, an executive power akin to the dictator of the Roman Republic.

In considering these questions, however, another feature of the decade since 2001 came to mind—the tendency of persons on the left wing of the political spectrum, including the current president (and his first secretary of state), to self-identify as "progressives," rather than "liberals." The features are related, as, during the last administration, the "progressives" led the charge against President Bush's war policies. Indeed, the war over the war seems to have accelerated this rebranding of the left. I wondered what this second feature of the early twenty-first century might offer for thinking about the first feature, our unresolved and heated debates about a continuing war and the legitimate, constitutional scope of executive power.

Puzzling over this led me to one of Professor Dry's own sources of inspiration. For one cannot celebrate Murray Dry's legacy without remembering that he is part of the legacy of his professor, Leo Strauss. While attending law school at Strauss's, and Dry's, University of Chicago, I picked up a collection of Strauss's essays and found myself enthralled by "Progress or Return?" Addressing the Hillel House at Chicago in the 1950s, Strauss pondered another problem—the "problem" of "progress" in the modern West.[1]

Strauss argued that "[t]he contemporary crisis of Western civilization may be said to be identical with the climactic crisis of the idea of progress." By the "idea of progress" he meant three interrelated propositions: (1) that "the development of human thought as a whole is a progressive development"; (2) that "[t]here is a fundamental and necessary parallelism between intellectual and social progress," and "no assignable limits" to either; and (3) that "[o]nce mankind has reached a certain stage of development, there exists a solid floor beneath which man can no longer sink." The second proposition had collapsed because, with an astronomical increase of scientific knowledge and technological prowess, there had been "no corresponding increase in wisdom and goodness," but rather a loss of confidence in any ability to distinguish between good and evil; thus, one instead employs "the distinction between progressives and reactionaries" and speaks of the unfolding of "history." And the third proposition, of a "solid floor," had been beaten down by the miseries of World War I, Communism, and Nazism, all suggesting regress, toward "barbarization," rather than progress. (Even the progressives had come to speak only of "change.") Finally, the shaking of the second and third propositions threatened to topple the first, fundamental one, of overall progressive development.

This crisis, Strauss observed, naturally prompts one to ask whether, instead of hoping in history and progress, one should consider the need for a "return" to some earlier view of the world. He argued that the West offered two alternatives—biblical, and classical Greek—and that, even though they were ultimately irreconcilable, the West's vitality flowed from their eternal debate.

Perhaps a similar approach may bear fruit in considering the contemporary crisis of executive power. Self-described progressives voiced grave concerns over the war policies that President Bush instituted. It is therefore natural to ask what the "Progressive" legacy in the United States, loosely covering the first half of the twentieth century and especially the first two decades, can offer for understanding, and constraining, executive power. If the Progressive legacy should prove to be a "problem" itself, as I conclude it is in the first section— given that the original Progressives were great advocates of aggressive, even unilateral, executive power—then we would have grounds for looking beyond today's progressives for sound guidance about executive power. Following Strauss's approach, the question of a return arises. Return to what? I suggest, in the remainder, a return to the political philosophy of John Locke, Montesquieu, and the American Founders, which informed the Constitution and its presidency, which prevailed in the United States for more than a century thereafter, and which (it is easy to forget) the Progressives spurned. The Founder's Constitution offers an executive who is muscular— but not simply and unqualifiedly so—and thus offers to the person concerned with executive power tools for restraint and accountability that the Progressive legacy cannot.

Progressivism and Executive Power

We can consider Progressivism and executive authority from three perspectives: On the level of theory, and then in two broad areas of application: war, our issue of the day; and domestic policy, keeping an eye out for "home-front" issues. From each perspective, the view is the same: a disposition and tendency toward expansive executive authority, and a lack of tools with which to check that expansion.

The State and Executive Power

To get to the general Progressive idea of expansive executive authority, it helps to begin with the Progressive idea of the state. We can see this through the views and actions of Woodrow Wilson, Herbert Croly (among other public intellectuals), and Franklin Delano Roosevelt.

Woodrow Wilson. Not only was Woodrow Wilson's presidency the most explicitly Progressive of the Progressive Era (Teddy Roosevelt's Progressivism peaked after he left office in 1909, and particularly as he ran against Wilson in 1912 as the nominee of the Progressive Party), but Wilson also was an academic, spelling out his Progressive ideas years before he could apply them.

Wilson caricatured the Founders' view of government and constitutionalism as Newtonian. He preferred Darwin. Wilson asserted in *Constitutional Government in the United States* (1908) that "[g]overnment is not a machine, but a living thing." He reiterated this on the campaign trail in 1912: "[L]iving political constitutions must be Darwinian in structure and in practice. Society is a living organism and must obey the laws of Life. . . . it must develop." He accordingly sought for Progressives "permission—in an era when 'development,' 'evolution,' is the scientific word—to interpret the Constitution according to the Darwinian principle."[2]

Wilson did not have in mind the incremental and random development of which Darwin had preached concerning the natural world. Nor even the cautious reform of Edmund Burke, done with reverence toward the past and humility toward the prospect of unintended consequences. Rather, the "Darwinian principle" meant a society *directed* by the state, which in turn meant a more powerful state—for developing organisms grow.

Wilson admired Hegel, and wrote that the essence of Progressivism was for the individual to "marry his interests to the state." The state would need authority if it was to embody society and "history" for a people, and for that authority to develop, the state should not be constrained. Thus, again on the campaign trail in 1912, Wilson rejected a key tenet of Jefferson as a principle "which no longer can obtain in the practical politics of America. You know that it was Jefferson who said that the best government is that which does as little governing as possible. . . . But that time has passed." He mocked "Fourth of July sentiments" and "non-sense . . . about the inalienable rights of the individual," and considered the checks and balances of the Constitution to have "proven mischievous." Earlier he had explained in his essay *Socialism and Democracy* (1887) that democracy rested on "the absolute right of the *community* to determine its own destiny *and that of its members.*" He added: "Limits of wisdom and convenience to the public control there may be: limits of principle there are, upon strict analysis, none."

Were the state to competently lead the people into the developing progressive future, it would itself need an adequate leader. A "living organism" needs a head and a brain. Wilson accordingly wrote that the Progressive goal was "to make self-government among us a straightforward thing of simple method, single, unstinted power, and clear responsibility." He could not "imagine power as a thing negative and not positive." One historian has explained that, "[i]f any trait bubbles up in all one reads about Wilson, it is this: he loved, craved, and in a sense glorified power."[3]

Wilson's initial preference, stated in *Congressional Government* in 1885, was for the British parliamentary model, with an unwritten, malleable constitution and a government under the sway of the leader of the parliamentary majority party. For America, however, he came to transfer his hopes to the presidency, particularly after seeing what Teddy Roosevelt did with the office. In *Leaders of Men* in 1890, he wrote, "Men are as clay in the hands of the consummate leader." And in *Constitutional Government in the United States,* written at the end of Roosevelt's administration, he wrote that "[t]he President is at liberty, both in law and in conscience, to be as big a man as he can. His capacity will set the limit."

Wilson also admired Otto von Bismarck, who as the "Iron Chancellor" of Germany in the last third of the 1800s developed many of the planks of the modern welfare state (a term he may have coined). It was a top-down and executive-driven system. Indeed, Bismarck's reforms aimed to forestall democratic reform.

Wilson praised Bismarck's system in his essay "The Study of Administration" (1886) as "admirable" and "the most studied and nearly perfected" in the world.

Herbert Croly and Other Public Intellectuals. A political philosophy similar to Wilson's was popularized by Herbert Croly, whose *The Promise of American Life* in 1909 captured the nation and helped to spur (or justify) Roosevelt's bid to return to the White House and replace his party's incumbent (Taft). Croly went on, during the Wilson administration, to found and edit *The New Republic*—whose stated mission was "to explore and develop and apply the ideas which had been advertised by Theodore Roosevelt when he was the leader of the Progressive Party."[4]

In his book, Croly deplored the "chaotic individualism of our political and economic organization." In his view, the "individual has no meaning apart from the society in which his individuality has been formed." Jane Addams, who nominated Roosevelt for president at the 1912 convention of the Progressive Party, similarly said: "We must demand that the individual shall be willing to lose the sense of personal achievement, and shall be content to realize his activity only in connection to the activity of the many."

For some, the Progressive view of the state even made it effectively divine. Walter Rauschenbusch, a leading figure in the Social Gospel movement, wrote in *Christianity and the Social Crisis* in 1907 that the state should become "the medium through which the people shall co-operate in their search for the kingdom of God and its righteousness." Richard T. Ely, a leading economist at Johns Hopkins and then the University of Wisconsin, who influenced both Teddy Roosevelt and Wilson, wrote: "God works through the State in carrying out His purposes more universally than through any other institution." The state was "a mighty force in furthering God's kingdom and establishing righteous relations."

It was a short step from such sentiments to the idea that a person finds his "freedom" not in the absence of constraint and the security of his rights, but in conforming to the state, since it is the state that relieves him from want. This thought appears in full flower in Franklin Delano Roosevelt's call for a "second Bill of Rights" in 1944, built on the proposition that "[n]ecessitous men are not free men." He had co-opted the rhetoric of rights to mean government-granted entitlements.

Such views of the developing organism that is the state do not nourish fear of executive power. On the contrary, they require an active, powerful leader.

In the 1920s, *The New Republic* found such a person in Mussolini. In defending the magazine's position in 1927 (by which time "Progressivism," trounced in the 1920 election, was becoming "Liberalism"), Croly sought to define Progressivism: "If there are any abstract liberal principles, we do not know how to formulate them. Nor if they are formulated do we recognize their authority. *Liberalism, as we understand it, is an activity.*" There was thus much to be said for Mussolini: "Whatever the dangers of Fascism, it has at any rate substituted *movement* for stagnation, *purposive behavior* for drifting, and visions of [a] great future for collective pettiness and discouragement."

In *The Promise of American Life*, Croly had sought a "national reformer . . . in the guise of St. Michael, armed with a flaming sword and winged for flight." And in 1925 he asked: "Who will be the prophets and pilots of the Good Society?" Progressives, he explained, believed that a "better future would derive from the beneficent activities of *expert social engineers* who would bring to the service of social ideals all the technical resources which research could discover and ingenuity could devise."

This desire for a great leader of the progressive state, on the order of Mussolini, created the risk not just of a powerful executive but of a cult of personality, built on the action and experimentation of the great man and his experts. These seeds sprouted under Teddy Roosevelt and Wilson—by design under Wilson, as we will see.

Franklin Delano Roosevelt. The seeds flowered under FDR, who had served in the Wilson Administration, had been the Democratic nominee for vice president in 1920, and became the only president to serve more than two terms (although Teddy had tried). As he put it in his first inaugural address: "The people . . . have not failed. In their need they have asked for discipline and direction under leadership. They have made me the present instrument of their wishes. In that spirit I take it."

This claim was not delusional. The British ambassador reported to London: The "starved loyalties and repressed hero-worship of the country have found in him an outlet and a symbol." H.G. Wells in 1939 described FDR's approach as "personal government." FDR himself boasted to Congress in 1936: "We have built up new instruments of public power. In the hands of a people's government this power is wholesome and proper." A popular and populist executive was to be trusted, not feared.

FDR's "discipline and direction" were, famously, not in the pursuit of any particular goal; rather, FDR promised "bold, persistent experimentation" and advised: "Take a method and try it. If it fails, admit it frankly and try another. But above all, try something." Implicit in this proverb is the heart of Progressivism: activity, movement, and experimentation by the state, in the name of the whole community, under the authority of a great leader, and without constraint. As Harry Hopkins told New Deal supporters: "[W]e are not afraid of exploring anything within the law, and we have a lawyer who will declare anything you want to do legal."

FDR was no political philosopher, but he had absorbed the political philosophy of his day. And a modest view of executive authority was not among its tenets.

War Powers

In America, the Progressive mind worked itself out both abroad and domestically. Abroad, the Progressive Era also was the imperialist era. Other intellectual and political forces contributed to America's imperial moment, and, not all Progressives were imperialists; but there are important points of convergence between imperialism and Progressivism, and many Progressives were imperialists. For example, Wilson applauded the United States' annexation of Puerto Rico and the Philippines after the Spanish-American War, and Teddy Roosevelt eagerly fought in that war.

This American imperialist inclination partly emerged from, and harmonized with, the philosophy of Progressivism just delineated. As one historian put it: "[I]mperialism and progressivism flourished together because they were both expressions of the same philosophy of government, a tendency to judge any action not by the means employed but by the results achieved, a worship of *definitive action for action's sake*, . . . and an almost religious faith in the democratic mission of America."[5] As another put it: "[T]he belief that American power, guided by a secular and religious spirit of service, could remake foreign societies came as easily to the Progressives as trust-busting, prohibition of child labor, and regulation of interstate commerce, meatpacking, and drugs."[6]

Moreover, the Progressive presidents to a large degree pursued this imperialism *on their own authority*, without blessing from Congress, including unilaterally using the threat of war and acts of war to influence or bring down foreign governments. But this is no more surprising than the imperialism itself: if forms are unhealthy constraints on the action and growth of a living organism, and if state power is positive, then the details of how to authorize and conduct war are not of great moment. The action is the thing, and the executive is made for action.

The unilateral initiation of war was a new thing in the practice of executive power under the Constitution. Before the Progressive Era, as one military historian has put it: "A familiar pattern developed: A revolution takes place; violence breaks out; American merchants and diplomats feel threatened; U.S. warships appear offshore; landing parties patrol the city for several days; then they sail away."[7] Teddy Roosevelt and Wilson, however, set new records for foreign intervention, and although a revolution often provided the pretext, there was much less bother about tying the initiation and conduct of armed intervention to the need to protect Americans threatened abroad. Three examples particularly illustrate this.[8]

First, Roosevelt in 1903, without congressional authorization, severed Panama from Colombia, of which it had been a part since independence from Spain eighty years before. He chafed at Colombia's intransigence in ratifying a treaty to build the canal. When a revolt broke out in Panama (with the administration's advance knowledge and at least tacit encouragement), Roosevelt precluded the Colombian government from suppressing it, by landing marines in the primary Atlantic port city of Colon, also the terminus of the existing, American-built trans-Panama railroad. This invasion spurred the Colombian army to depart the isthmus rather than try to march to Panama City to suppress the revolution. Within a week, the United States Navy had placed nine warships off the Panama coast, precluding any Colombian recourse. There was not, as far as I know, even a claim that the Colombian army—the forces of the established government—posed any threat to Americans. The president soon thereafter recognized an independent Panama, which dutifully signed a generous treaty allowing the United States to build the canal. The *New York Times* painted United States conduct as "an act of sordid conquest." When Roosevelt asked his attorney general to develop a defense, Attorney General Philander Knox, reportedly responded:

"Oh, Mr. President, do not let so great an achievement suffer from any taint of legality."

Second, Wilson in the 1912 election had presented himself as less militantly nationalistic than Roosevelt, but in office not only continued but even expanded the interventions. For present purposes, the most significant of Wilson's many interventions was his first in Mexico, in 1914. In 1913, as part of the Mexican Revolution, General Victoriana Huerta overthrew and murdered the president and took power. Wilson refused to recognize his government—a break from the United States' tradition of recognizing a government regardless of how it took power. He then set about overthrowing Huerta. The accidental and brief arrest of some American sailors in Tampico in April 1914 (for which the Huerta government promptly apologized) provided a pretext for Wilson to seek authorization from Congress for the use of force, but only the House approved it. The Senate adjourned, yet Wilson went ahead: the navy occupied Veracruz on the Gulf Coast, Mexico's largest port, to block the delivery of supplies to the government. The government's loss of customs revenue from Veracruz contributed to its downfall in July 1914. The United States' occupation, which continued until November, prompted rioting across Latin America.

Third is Wilson's invasion of the Dominican Republic in 1916. Teddy Roosevelt had defused an incident with European governments over that country's debt, by having the United States oversee its customs operations, pursuant to a 1907 treaty. (Roosevelt implemented the treaty by executive fiat for two years before the Senate ratified it.) Wilson pressured the president to expand this relationship through a treaty that would make the Dominican Republic effectively a protectorate. The Dominican president's openness to this led in early 1916 to impeachment proceedings against him and a revolt led by his war minister. With no claim of protecting Americans (or even foreigners) of which I am aware, Wilson dispatched the marines from Haiti to prop up the president and oppose the war minister. Even though the president resigned rather than join this armed intervention, the marines still occupied Santo Domingo and other key points. Wilson imposed martial law, and the United States directly ruled throughout Wilson's administration.

President Harding, returning America to "normalcy" with more than 60 percent of the popular vote in 1920, ended this era of Progressive American imperialism. He started no new interventions and wound down Wilson's occupation of the Dominican Republic (albeit not the indirect control of Haiti that Wilson had initiated through a puppet regime and continued through a treaty; Hoover wound this down, and FDR ended it). Similarly, President Coolidge in 1925 withdrew from Nicaragua the small force of marines that had arrived in 1912 under Taft to protect Americans during a revolution and had lingered under Wilson, although the United States was drawn back the next year in response to a coup and civil war, staying until early 1933.

Coming to power that year, FDR touted his "Good Neighbor" policy of befriending whoever was in power. As a result, the occasions for further development of the Progressive idea of executive authority to unilaterally dominate the Americas were reduced under FDR.

But the difference was one of policy; FDR did not repudiate or otherwise question the *authority* for Wilson's presidentially directed imperialism—in which he had played no secret role, as Assistant Secretary of the Navy. In the 1920 campaign, in which FDR was the Democrats' nominee for vice president, Harding declared that he would not "empower an assistant secretary of the navy to draft a constitution for helpless neighbors in the West Indies and jam it down their throats at the point of a bayonet."

In the lead-up to World War II, however, FDR did twice employ bold executive action on the order of his ideological forebears— giving fifty destroyers to Britain in 1940 in exchange for military bases in the Western Hemisphere (whose boundary FDR nudged to include Iceland) and then the Lend-Lease policy in early 1941. The first was of dubious legality given Congress's neutrality statutes (enacted pursuant to its constitutional authority to supply the navy) plus FDR's use of an executive agreement rather than a treaty; that said, Attorney General Robert Jackson, in his judicious opinion trying to justify this, avoided broad claims of executive authority. Lend-Lease was authorized by Congress—which delegated to FDR vast authority to give materiel to any country whose defense he deemed vital to the defense of the United States.

The Home Front

The most remarkable aspect of Progressivism with regard to executive authority domestically was its militaristic sensibility. Frequent appeals to war rallied support for bold, decisive, and unconstrained governmental action—particularly executive action.

The Broad Outline. In the United States, one might trace this notion to William James, in his 1906 essay, "The Moral Equivalent of War," which echoes to this day in, for example, the "War on Drugs." James urged that "[m]artial values must be the enduring cement" of American society, and this required "surrender of private interest" and "obedience to command."

War was celebrated as a model for organizing domestic society and, because of the domestic upheaval it produced, as a catalyst for societal reorganization. Upon the outbreak of World War I, in Wilson's administration, John Dewey praised the "social possibilities of war" and celebrated the "immense impetus to reorganization afforded by this war." He added: "We shall have to lay by our good-natured individualism and march in step." Herbert Croly in the *New Republic*'s first editorial, two months after the war began in Europe, hoped that war would "bring with it a political and economic organization better able to redeem its obligations at home." Wilson declared himself an "advocate of peace, but there are some splendid things that come to a nation through the discipline of war."

Yet war requires "obedience to command," and thus to one's commander. Thus, a sensibility of "war" at home elevated not just government in general but the executive in particular.

Again, Mussolini provided a model. The *New York Times* in 1923 praised him as "a Latin [Teddy] Roosevelt who first acts and then inquires if it is legal. He has been of great service to Italy *at home*." Charles Beard in the *New Republic* gushed: "Beyond question, an amazing experiment is being made here, an experiment in reconciling individualism and socialism, politics and technology." He urged that "the harsh deeds and extravagant assertions that have accompanied the Fascist process" should not "obscure the potentialities and the lessons of the adventure—no, not adventure, but destiny riding without any saddle and bridle across the historic peninsula that bridges the world of antiquity and our modern world." Mussolini's high-handed executive authority was consistent with the "American gospel of action, action, action."

Later, in 1937, New Dealer Luther Gulick advocated reducing the typical bill in Congress to "*a declaration of war,* so that the essence of the program is in the gradual unfolding of the plan in actual administration" by the executive. Thus was the analogy complete, including to the vast, unchecked power of the executive that is necessary to the conduct of actual war.

The Wilson Administration. Under Wilson, the analogy was a particularly ready one, because World War I—even though the United
States participated only for eighteen months—was invoked to justify
an unprecedented superstructure of domestic regulation, either by
executive fiat or under statutes bestowing wide discretion on the
executive.

The examples are many: Wilson established a War Industries
Board, one of whose members, Grosvenor Clarkson, described it as
"an industrial dictatorship by force of necessity and common consent
which step by step at last encompassed the Nation and united it into a
coordinated and mobile whole." Its legacy, he explained, was "a story
of the conversion of a hundred million combatively individualistic
people into a vast cooperative effort in which the good of the unit was
sacrificed to the good of the whole." In addition, a Committee on
Public Information, which Wilson established with the encouragement of the *New Republic*'s Walter Lippmann and was run by journalist
George Creel, was "the West's first modern ministry for propaganda"
and intentionally fostered a "Wilson cult."[9] And Wilson did not just
impose wage and price controls but also, through the Food
Administration run by Herbert Hoover, recruited an army of a half-
million to fan out across the country, knocking on doors and
pressuring Americans to signs pledges and oaths of compliant conduct.

Finally, Congress passed an Espionage Act in 1917, expanded by
the "Sedition Act" of 1918, which delegated essentially limitless discretion to the Postmaster General to deny use of the mails to disfavored publications—as he zealously did. In enforcing these laws, the
Department of Justice "arrested tens of thousands without just cause,"
and "[i]t has been estimated that some 175,000 Americans were
arrested for failure to demonstrate their patriotism in one way or
another."[10] The Department of Justice also created a citizens' auxiliary, the American Protective League, of hundreds of thousands to
collect information on friends and neighbors. And the "Palmer
Raids"—arresting thousands of alien radicals under the immigration
laws—occurred more than a year after World War I had ended.

FDR. FDR from his perch in the Navy Department cheered this
on, particularly the Espionage and Sedition Acts. And in 1920 he ran
as a loyal Wilsonian.

When his own opportunity as president came, he drew on the
same Progressive war imagery for domestic politics. In his first inaugural address, discussing the Great Depression, he sought the "power

to *wage a war* against the emergency, as great as the power that would be given to me if we were in fact invaded by a foreign foe." And he "assume[d] unhesitatingly the *leadership of this great army* of our people dedicated to a disciplined attack upon our common problems" (emphases added).

The cornerstone of the early New Deal was the National Industrial Recovery Act, which embodied the Progressive sensibility—combining a broad delegation to the executive with militaristic means. Congress authorized the President to promulgate codes of fair competition, with no statutory limit. It thus, in a delegation akin to the effect of a simple declaration of war, handed over to him its power to regulate interstate commerce (which he in turn delegated to trade associations). This prompted the Supreme Court for only the second time in its history to strike down a law as an unconstitutional delegation, unanimously, in *Schechter Poultry Corp. v. United States* (1935). The first such ruling, the same year (*Panama Refining Co. v. Ryan*), also struck down a portion of the NIRA.

The NIRA was enforced by the National Recovery Administration (NRA), which modeled itself on Wilson's War Industries Board. The NRA's symbol was the Blue Eagle, whose claws held lightning bolts and a cogwheel. The government made a business's display of the Eagle a mark of loyal citizenship. As FDR explained: "*The FDR Years: On Roosevelt and His Legacy*, by William Edward Leuchtenburg, p. 60. (Columbia University Press, 1995)." The NRA also used militaristic rallies, including a parade for "The President's NRA Day" in September 1933 that was then the largest in New York City's history, with a quarter million people marching for ten hours. Indeed, the NRA's first leader was a former general, Hugh "Iron Pants" Johnson—who had been the military liaison to the War Industries Board and directed Wilson's draft.

FDR's Civilian Conservation Corps also openly employed a militaristic model for the 2.5 million men who passed through it. FDR, again, was open about this, and, again, the model was World War I: he compared the development of the CCC to "the mobilization carried on in 1917." The Speaker of the House elaborated: "*The FDR Years: On Roosevelt and His Legacy*, by William Edward Leuchtenburg, p. 56. (Columbia University Press, 1995)."

Two unprecedented executive actions on the home front during World War II also merit mention. First was a series of three orders in

1942—soon after Pearl Harbor—by military commanders regarding Japanese-Americans. In March, a proclamation imposed a curfew on "all persons of Japanese ancestry," including citizens, within a "military area" comprising the entire Pacific coast. In May, the military ordered all such persons, again including citizens, excluded from designated areas on the West Coast. Finally, some excluded persons were detained in "relocation centers" throughout the war. The Supreme Court upheld the curfew order unanimously in *Hirabayashi v. United States* (1943); upheld the exclusion order 6–3 in *Korematsu v. United States* (1944); and held the detention order unauthorized in *Ex parte Endo*, decided the same day as *Korematsu*, only on the narrow ground that neither Congress nor the president had authorized it. (The military had issued the first two orders pursuant to an executive order that Congress had ratified.)

Discussions of these orders in subsequent decades have tended to focus on the racial angle, but of more interest here is the question of executive authority. Notwithstanding the congressional ratification of the first two orders, it remains remarkable that the military could feel free to issue them absent imposition of martial law and given that (particularly as to the detention order) Congress had not suspended the writ of habeas corpus. (By contrast, the territorial governor of Hawaii imposed martial law and suspended the writ after Pearl Harbor.)

The second unprecedented executive action arose from the capture in June 1942 of eight German saboteurs who had landed, equipped with explosives, on beaches in New York and Florida. The President rushed them to a secret trial before military commissions, a course that the Supreme Court, in its own rushed decision in *Ex parte Quirin* (1942), upheld unanimously. All eight were convicted. One of the eight, and one of the six executed, was a U.S. citizen. As far as I am aware, it was the first time that a citizen had been held in a place where the civilian courts were open yet been tried (much less executed), outside that system, for making war on the United States. The Supreme Court had rejected such a course in *Ex parte Milligan* (1866), when it held unconstitutional the military trial of a citizen in Indiana during the Civil War. So *Quirin* had to reject (or reinterpret) a portion of *Milligan* to uphold FDR's executive action.

The Founding and Executive Power

It thus seems that, at least on the question of controlling executive power—both the aim to do so itself, and also the means—the Progressive mind comes up short. Its account of the state and the state's leader tends to produce an overweening, unchecked cult of personality. Abroad, in employing the armed forces, the Progressive executive roams freely. Domestically, he drums up a war mentality and multiplies delegations of power. The Progressive view of executive power produces a practical (and intellectual) crisis about which later liberals or progressives have complained as much as conservatives have. Taking our cue from Strauss, then, let us consider whether the political philosophy that produced the American Founding offers an alternative to which one might "return."

The State and Executive Power

The State. John Locke, Montesquieu, and the Founders of our Constitution have a different, more constrained view of executive power than the Progressives—because they have a different, more modest, view of government.

For present purposes, one could use the Declaration of Independence as a proxy for Locke's view of the state: Individuals have natural or divine (or both) rights to life, liberty, and property. Government is instituted, by their consent, to secure those rights. Moreover, although government is necessary for such security it also can abuse its power, destroying security, and thus government needs guards.

Montesquieu in *The Spirit of the Laws* (1748) similarly identifies security as the modest, yet elusive, goal of government—security from the weakness of a state of nature, and security against the internal and external wars that result once societies form.[11] The ultimate end is "political liberty," the liberty compatible with membership in society, which he defines as "that tranquility of spirit which comes from the opinion each one has of his security, and in order for him to have this liberty the government must be such that one citizen cannot fear another citizen." But this "is found only in moderate governments," and even then only "when power is not abused" (*Spirit of the Laws*, I.3; XI.3–6; see XII.2).

The Federalist shares the view of Locke and Montesquieu. James Madison in *Federalist 10* affirms as "the first object of government" the protection of the diverse "faculties of men, from which the rights of property originate." More broadly, the goal is "the preservation of liberty" (*Federalist 51*). Given human nature, however, good government requires a balance, as Madison famously explained in *Federalist 51*: "But what is government itself but the greatest of all reflections on human nature? If men were angels, no government would be necessary. If angels were to govern men, neither external nor internal controls on government would be necessary. In framing a government which is to be administered by men over men, the great difficulty lies in this: you must first enable the government to control the governed; and in the next place oblige it to control itself."

Executive Power in the State. Within this humbler, more cautious understanding of government, the executive emerges as one part, rather than the culmination. Among other things, this contributes to the guards, moderation, and controls that human nature requires.

Locke in his *Second Treatise of Government* (1690) initially distinguishes between legislative and executive power.[12] Because absolute rule by one person is "inconsistent with civil society," the legislative power must be lodged in a collective body. Yet the legislature should not always be in session: Legislators must live under their laws, and allowing the "same persons who have the power of making laws, to have also in their hands the power to execute them" could be "too great temptation to human frailty apt to grasp at power." And the laws will need a "perpetual execution." So "the legislative and executive power come often to be separated" (sections 88, 94, 143, and 144).

In addition, a commonwealth must act externally, in relation "to the rest of mankind," with whom its members remain "in the state of nature." Locke calls this power "federative," which includes power over "war and peace, leagues and alliances, and all the transactions, with all persons and communities without the commonwealth." More generally, the federative power involves "employ[ing] the force of the community . . . abroad to prevent or redress foreign injuries, and secure the community from inroads and invasions." This power also is "much less capable to be directed by antecedent, standing, positive laws than the executive; and so must necessarily be left to the prudence and wisdom of those whose hands it is in, to be managed for the public good." The federative power, moreover, is "always almost united" to the executive power, because both require "the force of the society for their exercise," and to put "the force of the public . . . under different commands" would tend "to cause disorder and ruin" (sections 131, 145–48).

Even domestically, the executive does not simply execute the laws. Some matters must "be left to" his "discretion," because the legislature is not "able to foresee, and provide, by laws, for all that may be useful to the community." This "prerogative" does not just involve acting in the absence of direction from the law, "till the legislative can conveniently be assembled." Indeed, "the laws themselves should in some case *give way* to the executive power, or rather to this fundamental law of nature and government, *viz.*, that as much as may be, *all* the members of the society are to be preserved." Locke at least implies, however, that the executive will be accountable for whether he exercises his prerogative in a way "conformable to the foundation and end of all laws, the public good" (sections 159 and 165).

By these indirect steps, Locke arrives at a regime in which the legislature with its laws, on the one hand, and the executive with his federative power and prerogative, on the other, are simultaneously supreme. In ordinary times the former (representing self-government) will likely predominate, and in extraordinary times the latter (representing self-preservation) likely will. But there will be room for debate as to the nature of the times, with the people as the ultimate arbiters. In this tension, Locke hopes to find a secure liberty (section 168).

Montesquieu expands on Locke's idea with a full-fledged doctrine of separation of powers, in the pursuit of a government that not only is in tension but also is moderate. Moderation is rare and delicate: "one must combine powers, regulate them, temper them, make them act; one must give one power a ballast, so to speak, to put it in a position to resist another; this is a masterpiece of legislation that chance rarely produces and prudence is rarely allowed to produce." Further, moderation is not even sufficient for political liberty, because "any man who has power is led to abuse it." So "power must check power by the arrangement of things" (V.14 and XI.4).

Thus, Montesquieu among other things carves out of Locke's executive/federative power "the power of judging," that is, the "executive power over the things depending on civil right," which consists of punishing crimes and judging disputes between individuals. He describes as "moderate" those kingdoms in which a prince holds both the legislative and executive powers but "leaves the exercise of the third power to his subjects." He warns that the power of judging could not be placed "worse" than if given to the executive—who should instead "establish judges" but not himself judge. Montesquieu's concern is particularly that the power of judging operates immediately on individuals, making it both a great source of possible tyranny and "terrible among men." Indeed, he primarily envisions the power of judging as best placed in juries, and avoids—at least in his most prominent account of judicial power within a constitution devoted to liberty—even mention of judicial officers actually established by the executive. He is particularly keen to minimize fear of a government's punishing its citizens for political purposes. Indeed, he mentions only "prerogatives," not Locke's general "prerogative" (XI.6 and XI.11).

Even while constraining the executive domestically by carving off the judicial power, Montesquieu recognizes the importance of the power that the executive retains (which includes "executing public resolutions" and "the general will")—but also the need for accountability. He praises monarchical government because, "as public business is led by one alone, execution is more prompt." Likewise, the executive power is "the part of the government that almost always needs immediate action," which is better done "by one than by many"; nor, accordingly, should the legislative power be able to hinder the exercise of executive power. Nonetheless, Montesquieu would have the legislature authorize the army and navy only "from year to year." And he endorses the legislature's ability to call to account the executive's "counselors," to provide "satisfaction" to the people for "injustices" (V.10 and XI.6).

Both Locke and Montesquieu ground their theories in the experience of the model government of their days for protecting liberty—England. William Blackstone in his *Commentaries on the Law of England* (authoritative in early America) returns the favor, drawing on both Locke and Montesquieu in expounding the English constitution of the 1760s. He, too, emphasizes the need for, and the need for limits on, executive power. After setting out in his opening chapter the three "absolute rights of individuals," familiar later to Americans from our Constitution—"personal security," "personal liberty," and "property"—Blackstone adds five "auxiliary subordinate rights of the subject." Through these, one in society may "secure" the "actual enjoyment" of the absolute rights. The first three auxiliary rights all constrain the executive: (1) Parliament, kept in "full vigour"; (2) "[t] he limitation of the king's prerogative, by bounds, so certain and notorious, that it is impossible he should either mistake or legally exceed them without the consent of the people"; and (3) the "right of every Englishman" to "apply to the courts of justice for redress of injuries"—courts that "proceed according to the old established forms of the common law," not at the king's whim.

The American Constitution builds on these foundations while further limiting the executive. Its achievement, as Alexander Hamilton spent eight essays of the *Federalist* explaining, was to reconcile "the genius of republican government" with the proposition that "[e] nergy in the executive is a leading character in the definition of good government" and, correspondingly, that a "feeble executive" makes for "a bad government." There was "hardly any part of the system which could have been attended with greater difficulty," he admits. This included the delicate question whether the "ingredients which constitute" an "energetic executive" could be combined with "a due dependence on the people, and a due responsibility" once a president was in power, thus yielding "*safety* in the republican sense" (*Federalist* 68 and 70, emphasis in original).

In pursuing this difficult task, the Constitution *subtracts* from the president powers that Blackstone and Montesquieu, and especially Locke, took for granted as the executive's. The American executive may not prorogue or adjourn the legislature (with a narrow exception), or adjust the lower house's representation, or appoint members of the upper house. He lacks an absolute veto. He himself is subject to removal by the legislature through impeachment. The judiciary is a fully separate branch, with judges' appointments being subject to Senate confirmation (rather than being unilateral) and their removal, through congressional impeachment, being entirely out of the executive's hands (rather than on his initiative). The president lacks the power to declare war or to authorize private wars via letters of marque and reprisal. He lacks the power to raise or regulate armies and navies. He cannot appoint executive officers, including military officers, without the consent of the Senate (or, as to lower-level officers, a law authorizing unilateral appointment). He cannot make a treaty without the consent of the Senate, and the practice of the first century was that some congressional consent was needed before he could abrogate a treaty. Further, the Constitution never mentions "prerogative";

it cryptically declares that "[t]he executive power shall be vested in a President," without defining the executive power—a source of dispute at least since Hamilton and Madison sparred in the Helvidius-Pacificus debate over President Washington's Neutrality Proclamation (1793).

Thus, the Founders recognized that executive power, like the state itself, was both necessary and dangerous; it must be powerful and capable, but limited. Their fear and trembling in threading this needle contrast with the Progressives' glorification of executive power. And this divergence emerges further as we consider the Founders' regime in action, both abroad and at home.

War Powers

The Founders offer a critical limitation on executive war power that the Progressives do not; indeed, the Progressives jettisoned it. The deep foundations of that limited but still powerful executive, in both American theory and practice before the Progressive Era, have been increasingly forgotten. Congress has the power, through the Declare War Clause, to determine the *initiation* of the use of the armed forces against a particular enemy. Congress decides who are sufficiently our enemies to warrant armed conflict, absent any immediate need for the president to repulse attacks. This limitation is all the more remarkable as departing from Locke, Montesquieu, and Blackstone.

The consensus on this view of the Constitution endured through the 1800s, even amid occasional dispute over its application (such as Jefferson's response to the attacks of the Barbary Pirates, and Madison's taking possession of West Florida).[13] For example, President Washington wrote the Governor of Georgia, who was concerned over attacks by Creek Indians, that "[t]he Constitution vests the power of declaring war with Congress; therefore no offensive expedition of importance can be undertaken until after they shall have deliberated on the subject, and authorized such a measure." (Washington considered some retaliatory operations warranted by Congress's approval of an establishment of troops to protect the frontier against the Creeks.[14]) St. George Tucker, the first commentator on the Constitution after its ratification, and a Jeffersonian, wrote: "The constitution of the United States, intrusts the important power of making war, not in the president, nor in the president and senate, but in congress: where the people by their immediate representatives deliberate upon the necessity of involving the nation in such a state of calamity." Joseph Story, the third great commentator, a justice on the Supreme Court, and effectively a Federalist, described the power to declare war as one of "authorizing . . . hostilities." John Pomeroy, a leading commentator after the Civil War, explained that hostilities might commence "either through a formal declaration made by Congress, or a belligerent attack made by a foreign government which the President must repel by force." Thomas Cooley, probably the leading commentator in the Gilded Age, said simply: "The power to declare war being confided to the legislature, [the president] has no power to originate it, but he may in advance of its declaration employ the army and navy to suppress insurrections or repel invasion."

The greatest test of this principle during the first century, the Mexican-American War, confirms it. Both Texas and Mexico claimed the area from the Nueces River south to the Rio Grande, although Texas had in that disputed area occupied only Corpus Christi, on the south bank of the Nueces. As American annexation of Texas loomed in 1845, Mexico moved an army to the south bank of the Rio Grande and spurned President Polk's emissary. Polk ordered the army to position itself between the rivers, once Congress approved annexation. General Zachary Taylor crossed the Nueces into Corpus Christi, and Mexico did nothing. Polk then ordered Taylor to the north bank of the Rio Grande; once there, Taylor trained his cannon on the Mexican town on the other side. This provoked an attack, and Polk ran to Congress for a declaration of war—which Congress provided.

The conduct of Polk, a Democrat, drew the unyielding opposition of the Whigs, including Abraham Lincoln. They objected that Polk had provoked the war, usurping Congress's authority. Who was right depended in part on factual questions regarding the land between the rivers, yet both sides agreed on the constitutional rule: Polk never claimed power to initiate a war, and at least honored the Constitution in the breach, by straining to justify his action in constitutional language and by seeking and obtaining a declaration before entering any land that was *indisputably* part of Mexico.[15]

Once a war was properly initiated, however, the president, as commander in chief of the armed forces, determined its course with the resources Congress provided. *The Federalist* (following Locke, Montesquieu, and Blackstone) described his power of "direction of war" as "the supreme command and direction of the military and naval forces, as first general and admiral of the Confederacy"

(*Federalist* 69 and 74). His command includes deciding on and carrying out campaigns and their incidental activities—such as identifying and attacking targets; detaining (if not killing) those found in enemy or contested territory who are fighting against us or supporting those who are; trying those detainees outside the judicial system for war crimes; interrogating detainees; and collecting intelligence on the enemy abroad. On the last of these, the Supreme Court sensibly explained in *Totten v. United States* (1876) that, during the Civil War, the President "was undoubtedly authorized . . . as commander-in-chief . . . to employ secret agents to enter the rebel lines and obtain information."

I am unaware of any serious effort in the first century to restrict the president's authority in *engaging* a constitutionally identified enemy. Some may point to the Quasi-War with France under the first President Adams. Congress, however, pursued limited hostilities not by regulating the president's direction of the armed forces in war, but by avoiding a declaration of war and employing its other enumerated powers—restricting foreign commerce and the means of enforcing commercial restrictions, granting letters of marque and reprisal, and regulating captures of French shipping.

Moreover, in this, the Founders and the (original) Progressives find themselves in rare accord. Yet the *conduct* of *congressionally approved* wars was the focus of modern-day Progressives' denunciation of President Bush as an imperial president. Thus, a return to the Founder's Constitution would allow them a more restrained president in war—but not in the way they claimed to want, on which they stand alone in the American political tradition.

The Home Front

Domestically, the prospect of a "return" likewise offers to the person concerned with executive power resources for constraining it that Progressivism cannot.

Delegation and Discretion. Initially, the view of the executive's domestic authority that emerges from the Founders avoids militarism and the resulting ambition to delegate power. The Constitution charges the President to "take care that the laws be faithfully executed," a primarily domestic duty and one that contemplates that "the laws" (unlike a declaration of war) will constrain him and enable assessment of whether his execution was faithful or unfaithful. Locke similarly declares that "[t]he legislative power cannot transfer the power of making laws to any other hands," which would be "to make legislators" rather than laws; the legislature, an agent of the people, lacks authority to transfer its agency (*Second Treatise*, section 141). Montesquieu, in turn, warns that "there is no liberty" if one fears "that the same monarch or senate that makes tyrannical laws will execute them tyrannically" or if the executive power may unilaterally raise public funds (*Spirit of the Laws*, XI.6).

Accordingly, the delegations in the first century under the Constitution tended to involve application of law to particular circumstances, and in a "federative" area, touching foreign intercourse. They did not involve power to promulgate a code for domestic conduct. The two primary Supreme Court cases involved Congress's authorizing the president to make findings that triggered particular consequences for foreign commerce—reviving an embargo (*The Brig Aurora* [1813]) or imposing a specified tariff schedule (*Field v. Clark* [1892]). Congress also delegated authority to make findings to call out the militia (the Constitution arguably contemplates such a delegation); to determine whether to call up an allotted number of troops for the army; and, to determine where to place post offices and establish additional post roads.

Even when executive discretion was needed, early Congresses granted it jealously. Congress primarily allowed only the president or his cabinet to exercise substantial discretion, most officers acting within strict and narrow limits. This was true even within the early Treasury Department, where it was hard to avoid discretion in collectors of customs and the comptroller. Secretary Hamilton pursued a system in which "little or nothing is left to the discretion of the officers of the revenue" and any necessary discretion was lodged "high in the official ranks."[16] Thus (and regardless of whether any workable constitutional nondelegation doctrine exists), the Founders' default, domestically, was to minimize delegations to and discretion by the executive branch—the opposite of the aggrandizing Progressive sensibility.

Accountability. In the areas in which the executive properly has domestic authority, the president, in the Founders' contemplation, controls the officers who execute the laws. With a temporary exception after the Civil War (which was a cause of President Andrew Johnson's impeachment), the uniform approach from the First Congress was that "principal officers"—essentially the first tier below the president—served at the pleasure of the president; and that all other officers ("inferior officers") were at least removable for insubordination. (Civil service reforms involved mere employees, not officers.) This changed in the Progressive Wilson Administration, under which the Federal Trade Commission was created, whose commissioners the President could remove only "for inefficiency, neglect of duty, or malfeasance in office," a restriction that the Supreme Court upheld during the FDR administration, in *Humphrey's Executor* (1935).

One might contend that such limiting of the president's removal power was "good" for constraining executive power. But although the *president's* power might be constrained, the *executive* power persists—just not under his control. And the less power is under the *president's* control, the less accountable it is to the *people.* (If even the president's control was a concern, the solution, in the Founders' view, was to minimize delegations and discretion, not to transfer broad power to another officer.) Thus, restricting the presidential removal power, in the Progressive name of removing "politics" from the administration of the laws and empowering "experts," paradoxically *increases* executive power, by multiplying unaccountable executive officers.

Recent events have confirmed the Founders' wisdom on this issue, which many once dismissed as anachronistic formalism. In *Morrison v. Olson* (1988), the Supreme Court upheld the independent-counsel law notwithstanding its restriction on presidential removal of the counsel (among other issues). Justice Scalia's lonely dissent relentlessly deployed the text, context, and history of the Constitution against an unchecked, uncontrolled executive power (in the form of an effectively independent prosecutor—the law's explicit aim). The travails of President Clinton a decade later, however, made Scalia seem a prophet (even though he had simply been looking back), and *Morrison* seemed a myopic product of its time. The Supreme Court's decision a decade after that, striking down a removal restriction imposed by the Sarbanes-Oxley law (*Free Enterprise Fund v. Public Company Accounting Oversight Board* (2010)), suggests that some are relearning the benefits of constitutional principles that provide ballast amid the fancies of each age.

Extra-Judicial Detention. A final "home-front" example is also the most on point for our contentious debates about executive power in the twenty-first century. That is whether the president can detain an

American citizen as an enemy combatant within the jurisdiction of a functioning civilian court—without charging him in that court or suspending the writ of habeas corpus. The Supreme Court in *Hamdi v. Rumsfeld* (2004) held that the president could do so, but that a citizen had a right to at least some due process (vaguely defined by the Court opinion). Much as in *Morrison*, a plurality employed an ad hoc balancing test. Nothing in that test compelled them to come down where they did, and nothing prevents them from "balancing" differently next time.

Justice Scalia, by contrast, answered the question with an emphatic no in *Hamdi*. He was able to do so because he drew on the rich history of the writ of habeas corpus and the prosecution of citizens for treason, stretching back into England in the 1600s and forward through Blackstone and other English commentators and cases; to a letter of Thomas Jefferson; to cases from the War of 1812; and, to the Civil War (including *Milligan*). From these sources, he identified a *uniform* practice of detaining citizens or subjects, whom the executive suspected of making war on their country, *only* by either (1) arresting them and charging them with treason or a similar crime or (2) detaining them without charge following a suspension of the writ of habeas corpus—which the Constitution contemplates "when in cases of rebellion or invasion the public safety may require it" and which was done during the Civil War. Drawing on this legacy, Scalia readily rejected the World War II ruling in *Ex parte Quirin* as flawed to the extent it involved an American citizen.

Admittedly, a return to the Founders may not always yield simple or complete answers. *Hamdi* shows this splendidly, as Justice Thomas took the polar opposite position to Scalia. Thomas, a fellow originalist in constitutional interpretation, emphasized the President's Commander in Chief power and Congress's authorization for the use of military force. However, a battle over executive power fought on this terrain remains more likely to overcome the prejudices of the day—as a constitution should—than one fought in the self-consciously evolving world of the Progressive mind, a mind at best indeterminate and unpredictable and at worst glorifying executive power. Thus, for example, Justice Thomas's opposing position could be tested: he relied heavily on *Quirin*, from World War II, and a 1909 Supreme Court decision authored by the Progressive Justice Holmes; he admitted that Scalia's much earlier American authority generally supported Scalia's rather than his own position; and he did not answer the English history on which Scalia relied. Thus, the delicate task of constraining executive authority while not debilitating it is best accomplished by drawing from the deep well that the Founding Fathers bequeathed to us, not by repeatedly digging our own.

Strauss reminds us in another essay, "Liberal Education and Mass Democracy," which Professor Dry assigned, that "wisdom cannot be separated from moderation."[17] And "wisdom requires unhesitating loyalty to a decent constitution and even to the cause of constitutionalism." As we consider the necessity yet danger of executive power in a republic, and compare "progress" with a "return" to the more-than-decent Constitution that we have inherited, we may find true progress in turning around, doubting our own and the age's wisdom a bit, and humbling ourselves to relearn an "unhesitating loyalty."

Notes

1. See Leo Strauss, "Progress or Return? The Contemporary Crisis in Western Civilization"; the essay is from portions of three lectures Strauss delivered, "The Mutual Influence of Philosophy and Theology," and then "Progress or Return?" in two parts.

2. Wilson, *The New Freedom* (1913); see *Woodrow Wilson: The Essential Political Writings*.

3. Walter McDougall, *Promised Land, Crusader State: The American Encounter with the World Since 1776* (New York: Houghton Mifflin, 1997),128.

4. Many of the sources discussed in this section are critically analyzed in *The Progressive Revolution in Politics and Political Science: Transforming the American Regime*, eds. John Marini and Ken Masugi (Lanham, MD: Rowman & Littlefield, 2005). The general source for quotations in this section from the Progressive Era is Jonah Goldberg, *Liberal Fascism* (New York: Doubleday 2007).

5. William Leuchtenburg, "Progressivism and Imperialism," 39, *Miss. Valley Hist. Rev.* 483, 500 (1952).

6. McDougall, *Promised Land,* 120.

7. Max Boot, *The Savage Wars of Peace: Small Wars and the Rise of American Power,* 60.

8. Sources for episodes from the presidencies of Teddy Roosevelt and Woodrow Wilson can be found in Sidney Milkis and Michael Nelson, *The American Presidency: Origins and Development, 1776–2007.* The accounts of these episodes also draw on Boot's *Savage Wars of Peace.*

9. Goldberg, *Liberal Fascism,* 109, 127.

10.   Ibid., 114, 117.
11.   Montesquieu, *The Spirit of the Laws*, especially books XI and XII.
12.   See John Locke, *An Essay Concerning the True Original, Extent, and End of Civil Government (the Second Treatise)*.
13.   See David Currie, *The Constitution in Congress: The Jeffersonians, 1801–1829*, 121–129, 191–195.
14.   See David Currie, *The Constitution in Congress: The Federalist Period, 1789–1801*, 81–84.
15.   See David Currie, *The Constitution in Congress: Descent into the Maelstrom, 1829–1861*, 102–110.
16.   See *Officers of the United States Within the Meaning of the Appointments Clause*, 18–19 (April 16, 2007), www.usdoj.gov/olc/ opinions. htm
17.   Leo Strauss, "Liberal Education and Mass Democracy."

Bibliography

Boot, Max. *The Savage Wars of Peace: Small Wars and the Rise of American Power*. New York: Basic Books, 2003.

Currie, David. *The Constitution in Congress: The Federalist Period, 1789–1801*. Chicago: University of Chicago Press, 1997.

———. *The Constitution in Congress: The Jeffersonians, 1801–1829*. Chicago: University of Chicago Press, 2001.

———. *The Constitution in Congress: Descent into the Maelstrom, 1829–1861*. Chicago: University of Chicago Press, 2005.

Goldberg, Jonah. *Liberal Fascism*. New York: Doubleday, 2007.

Leuchtenburg, William. "Progressivism and Imperialism." In *Miss. Valley Hist. Rev.*, 1952.

Locke, John. *An Essay Concerning the True Original, Extent, and End of Civil Government (the Second Treatise), in Two Treatises of Government*. Edited by Peter Laslett. Cambridge: Cambridge University Press, 1988 [1690].

Marini, John, and Ken Musagi, ed. *The Progressive Revolution in Politics and Political Science: Transforming the American Regime*. Lanham, MD: Rowman & Littlefield, 2005.

McDougall, Walter. *Promised Land, Crusader State: The American Encounter with the World Since 1776*. New York: Houghton Mifflin, 1997.

Milkis, Sidney, and Michael Nelson. *The American Presidency: Origins and Development, 1776–2007*. 5th ed. Thousand Oaks, CA: CQ Press.

Montesquieu. *The Spirit of the Laws*. Translated and edited by Anne Cohler et al. Cambridge: Cambridge University Press, 1989.

Officers of the United States Within the Meaning of the Appointments Clause,
available at www.usdoj.gov/olc/ opinions.htm

Strauss, Leo. "Liberal Education and Mass Democracy." In *Higher Education
and Modern Democracy: The Crisis of the Few and Many.* Edited by
Robert A. Goldwin. Chicago: Rand McNally, 1967.

————. "Progress or Return? The Contemporary Crisis in Western
Civilization." In *The Rebirth of Classical Political Rationalism: An
Introduction to the Thought of Leo Strauss.* Edited by Thomas Pangle.
Chicago: University of Chicago Press, 1989.

Wilson, Woodrow. *Woodrow Wilson: The Essential Political Writings.* Edited
by Ronald J. Pestritto, Lexington, KY: Lexington Books, 2005.

Chapter 7

Ideas Meet Institutions and the People Rise Up

Four Classic Ideas and the Strange Century of Health Reform

James A. Morone

A s Franklin Roosevelt contemplated the end of World War II, he cast around for another crusade to lead. With FDR, one can never be sure, but he seemed to alight on "cradle to grave" national health insurance (NHI). Roosevelt assigned his longtime aide, Sam Rosenman, with drafting a health plan and, more important, a political strategy with which to win it. By the time the plan was ready, Roosevelt had died. The Rosenman draft passed on to President Harry Truman. Truman seized the reform with a fervor that surprised his aides—he would later call his failure to win it the greatest regret of his life[1]—and from Truman it passed down through generations of Democrats—the last, elusive, social democratic bequest from FDR's White House.

Few ideas have been pursued as long and as doggedly—or opposed quite as ferociously—as national health care. In this chapter, I use the quest for NHI to reflect on just how ideas matter within the great grind of institutions, interests, and political time. I do this with five snapshots of NHI in the political process: the idea in the hands of Harry Truman, Lyndon Johnson, Bill and Hillary Clinton, George W. Bush, and Barack Obama.

My purpose is to explore just how ideas matter in politics—and how they do not. Along the way I suggest that four enduring ideas—each with a long provenance in American politics—helped shape the politics of health care from Truman to Obama.

Many contemporary political scientists will be skeptical of the enterprise, for they doubt that ideas have independent power; contemporary political science is apt to cast around for something more concrete—political institutions, money, interest groups.

In fact, they stand in very good company, for they unwittingly reflect Alexis de Tocqueville's mordant side: "I know no country in which, speaking generally, there is less independence of mind and true freedom of discussion than in America." What Tocqueville had in mind was the power—the tyranny—of majority opinion.[2] Tocqueville's traveling companion, Gustave de Beaumont, put the same thought even more pointedly. "If one is born to think he thinks; if he is born to make money, he does not think."[3]

There were antidotes in the American regime, but none so strong as the habit and mores of participation. John Stuart Mill—who credited Tocqueville and *Democracy* for one of the most "substantial changes of opinion" in his thinking[4]—drew out Tocqueville's answer most explicitly: a democratic culture had to argue. And with national health insurance, few issues have given twentieth- and twenty-first-century Americans more opportunity to do just that. My purpose in this chapter is to understand just how and when those arguments mattered.

Harry Truman: The Myth of Pluralism, the Power of Congress, and Two Big Ideas

The story of Truman's health reform generally reflects the pluralism that was so popular in the social science of the time. When Truman proposed the Roosevelt plan, the American Medical Association (the AMA) did something unprecedented: they hired a public relations firm to campaign against the legislation. And what a job Whitaker and Baxter did. They, in turn, hired thirty-seven assistants who found all kinds of creative ways to shout socialism in the middle of a red scare.[5]

The Barking Dogs Don't Count

The campaign's real brilliance lay not in its overheated warnings of impending doom—the well-documented, often repeated images

were over the top—but in its extraordinary organization of organizations. The public relations firm lined up hundreds of groups (by one
count, 1,829 of them) and scripted their indignation over socialized
medicine. The papers of Truman administration officials bulged with
letters from VFW posts and chambers of commerce, all worded sus-
piciously alike. The carefully coordinated letters, memorials, memos,
and petitions expressing outrage all flowed into Washington.[6]

The campaign's arguments filtered deep into the national discourse. We can trace their reach by following just one rhetorical
flourish as it rippled through the culture. Whitaker and Baxter published a document with a quote concocted from Lenin: "Socialized
medicine is the keystone to the arch of the socialist state." The
quote—as far as anyone has been able to tell, it was dreamed up by a
creative thinker at Whitaker and Baxter—sprang up in newspaper
editorials across the nation. Five years later, Truman's point person
on health reform, Oscar Ewing, received a report on NHI from the
New York Bar Association (he was a member) and there was the
quote, burrowed on page ten. The line, like many others from this
campaign, slipped into the American rhetorical ether, recycled from
generation to generation down to our present day. You can find it, for
example, in a recent president's letter in the (conservative) Association
of American Physicians and Surgeons publication, the *Medical
Sentinel*.[7]

The usual story of Truman's reform is that the great barrage of
money and propaganda mobilized the opposition and buried
national health insurance. It makes for a great pluralist tale full of
sound and fury. But this interpretation is mainly myth.

The truth is that all that lobbying did not matter much. Congress
was dominated by Southern Democratic barons who chaired the key
committees (and by a conservative coalition of Southern Democrats
and Republicans); they had no intention of passing national health
insurance. The committee chairs were perfectly explicit about their
disinterest. The House Ways and Means chair, Clarence Lea (D *and* R,
CA) did not even bother to schedule hearings. The chair of Senate
Finance was so hostile that the Democrats stripped the finance provision from the bill to avoid his committee. No matter, Senator Robert
Taft was ready for "the most socialistic measure Congress has ever
had before it." The media of the day—*Time, Newsweek, New York
Times*—all commented after the bill was proposed that no one
expected it to go anywhere.

The story about the AMA campaign is colorful as political theater. But the explanation for what happened to the Truman national health insurance plan is simpler: the institutional reality of a Congress, controlled by powerful committee chairs, had the power to stop the legislation. They never had any intention of letting the legislation go through to a Congress that never had near the votes to pass it.

One of the great culture stories about the United States is that it did not have comprehensive health reform because Americans don't like government. There is a lot of truth, as we'll see, to that view of the culture. But it cannot explain this social welfare exceptionalism. The design of our institutions explains why there is no national health insurance in America. If the United States had been playing by Parliamentary rules, it would have had an NHI program when Truman first proposed it, in 1945–1946, or when he featured it prominently in his long-shot reelection bid in 1948. The voters did not seem panicked by socialized medicine when they returned him to office by 2 million votes (4 percent). Electoral mandates are often exaggerated; many voters no doubt chose Truman despite his support for NHI (or with knowledge that Congress was not likely to pass it). Nonetheless, it was neither an anti-governmental American culture, nor the powerful health care lobby, that was the immediate obstacle. Rather, the institutional design of the American legislature defeated Truman.

Two Ideas

But that is not the end of the Truman legacy. The stillborn proposal produced two great ideas that echoed down through time.

First, the idea of *social insurance*. Truman was entirely maladroit about getting his legislation through Congress. But he found his voice during the campaign of 1948. His staff stopped typing speeches and just gave him what we now would call bullet points. And he pounded them in a high pitched staccato, waving his hands, and mixing his points freely with insults. A clear and simple idea emerged from the rhetoric. A just and modern society takes care of people when they are sick—even if those people are failures who "lack ambition," as Truman once put it. Health care was not a question of merit or of markets. It was something we owed one another as fellow citizens. We were all in it together—just as we had been during the great wars. The idea would live on. Truman grew increasingly intense about the subject in his long ex-presidency. Though he never came anywhere close to winning the legislation, he pushed his idea—social insurance, we're all in this health care boat together, a good society takes care of its sick people—throughout his life. And that idea stuck.

Socialism. The counterargument also stuck. It may not have shaped the political outcome at the time, but the intensity of the attack on Truman's plan—shouting socialism in a multitude of ways—also lived on. Here was a politics of wild exaggeration: national health insurance may or may not have been wise policy but it never had the power to deliver America to the Soviets. Nevertheless, the attack gave NHI opponents a political argument and a rhetoric by which to oppose shifting health care from private to public sector. Thus, what began as a political strategy designed to bury legislation grew into a powerful concept, a precept, a thought, an opinion. The opposition to national health insurance—often cast as socialism, leading to communism, itself—became an important American idea.

The recurring brief against socialized medicine is a fine illustration of the famous argument made by Louis Hartz. The early American experience, argued Hartz, shaped a ferocious, Lockean market liberalism that provoked a gut-deep aversion to socialism, redistribution, or expansions of government authority. Since there were no feudal restraints—Americans were born free, he misquoted Tocqueville, without having to become so—any man could make it on his own. Government would only undermine the market test of virtue. Even the American democrat quailed at the prospect of the redistribution of income that was in his self-interest. Hartz's theory has come in for a great deal of criticism over the years: it traces all American thought to a simple dubious cause; it entirely ignores the great American binaries—race, gender, and religion; it can't explain how and why government grew; and conservatives would add that it is not so irrational to argue that government redistribution and welfare provision pose issues of social and fiscal sustainability. To be sure, there are flaws in Hartz's story of America. But it beautifully fits the conservative reaction to the Truman health insurance proposal: cry socialism! What is more, it is uncannily predictive of the public reaction to health care proposals, right down to the hot town meetings and Tea Party rallies in the summer of 2009.[8]

In sum: two overarching ideas. Social insurance, and the idea that social insurance is socialism. In the Truman period, the ideas themselves were scarcely the cause of change. Just the reverse, it was the memory of the fight—filtered through the 1948 campaign—that gave the ideas a kind of totemic power for future generations.

Johnson and Mills: Medicare and the Myth of the Congressional Machine

The Congressional story, generally overlooked in the Truman years, in turn is oversold in the passage of Medicare in 1965. The usual explanation is simple: an electoral landslide tamed the Congressional process and made the legislation inevitable. What has been lost (or, until recently, buried) is the way that two canny leaders reframed the Medicare legislation. The social insurance idea reached its high tide after the 1964 election. But what would that mean in legislative terms? Here, it was not just Congressional process or horse trading. It was President Johnson's insatiable appetite for more and bigger legislation; and, later, his fear of overreaching.

The Usual Story

After President Kennedy's assassination, the Johnson administration and its congressional allies were extraordinarily successful— even breaking a long filibuster and winning the monumental civil rights bill of 1964. But they could not win Medicare. The Chairman of the Ways and Means Committee, Wilbur Mills (D-AK), remained opposed and bottled up the bill. Then came the 1964 Democratic landslide. Johnson won with 61 percent of the vote and carried huge liberal Democratic majorities into the House (295 Democrats to 140 Republicans) and Senate (68–32). Wilbur Mills bowed to the inevitable, switched sides, and led the Democrats to the victory he had long denied them.

The administration's Medicare proposal, whittled down after years of negotiation with Congress, amounted to nothing more than a hospital care bill for the elderly. In a packed hearing room, the usually ultra-cautious Mills took the administration's bill and linked it to two rival bills, tripling the size of the program. The new move extended Medicare to cover doctor's bills (now Medicare part B) and added health care for poor people (what we now call Medicaid). Taken by happy surprise, Johnson cheerfully acquiesced in Mills' coup, authorized the much larger budget, and watched the new and improved Medicare sail through Congress. In his autobiography, LBJ repeats this tale and adds that Wilbur became "a hero to the old folks."[9]

However, recently released White House tapes tell a very different story. Johnson was in on the plan from the very start, calling Mills again and again, beginning three weeks after he took office, to win Mills over to a bigger, better, Medicare. Johnson later said that he courted Mills more assiduously than he had Lady Bird. In one of their early conversations, Mills fretted that conservative Democrats (like himself) had long opposed Medicare and needed some cover for changing their vote. Suppose, said Mills, that he announced that the original proposal had been inadequate, suppose he combined all the rival health insurance proposals that were floating around Congress into one great package. "If you give me that bill, I'll underwrite it," responded Johnson, who then urged Chairman Mills to go ahead and add even more. As Mills warmed up, LBJ flattered him: "it will be the biggest thing you have ever done for the country." We will come in and "applaud you," he said. Mills would get all the credit. Lyndon Johnson repeatedly telephoned Mills, even stopping him as he walked on the floor of the House, and pushed him to expand Medicare, to make it bigger, to cover more programs. And then, when Mils did precisely that, President Johnson passed all the credit back to Congressman Mills.[10]

In the Senate, the administration grew cautious about the costs and squashed liberal efforts to add three features to Medicare: prescription drugs, long-term nursing care, and catastrophic coverage (for big bills and long hospital stays). Ironically, the politics of Medicare in subsequent decades would constantly feature efforts to win these three additions. Even more ironically, it would be Republicans who actually would win them: Reagan passing catastrophic coverage over the objection of almost his entire staff and cabinet (later repealed), and George W. Bush adding a prescription drugs benefit.

When Medicare passed in March 1965, President Johnson immediately decided to fly out to Independence, Missouri and sign the bill in front of Harry Truman. His staff fretted about connections to "socialized medicine," but Johnson was adamant. At the signing ceremony, LBJ credited Truman with creating the ideal: "It was really Harry Truman who planted the seeds of compassion and duty"—the essential social insurance vision. "Many men can make many proposals . . . but few . . . have the courage to stake reputation and position and the effort of a lifetime upon a cause when there are so few to share it."

Truman never got very far. But he kept an idea alive and it inspired the next generation. That idea needed a major institutional break—the 1964 landslide—or it is would not have won. But even the idea and the institutional alignment were not enough.

The passage of Medicare is a marvelous example of that old poli sci concept, policy formulation. The idea was in place. And the majority. But most politicians were willing to settle for the meager bill that had been shaped by the hostile (to Medicare) politics of the early 1960s. New Dealers and advocates of the Great Society must note that it took two canny leaders—Johnson and Mills—to adjust the proposal to the new politics. In doing that, they aligned the social insurance vision with the actual legislative proposal.

Liberal commentators look back wistfully on this moment: Why didn't Johnson go for the whole loaf and win national health insurance? It was the last chance. The idea—Harry Truman's lost reform—would linger on to inspire one Democrat after another. But the later legislative proposals themselves would take a whole new tack: neo-Progressive efficiency would replace New Deal social insurance.

The legacy of Medicare would add a complication to efforts to portray American politics and culture. Future efforts to expand NHI would set off the same overheated (Hartzian) rhetoric of socialism. At the same time, *pace* Hartz, Medicare joined social security as part of the third rail of American politics. Indeed, the left would eventually discover a marvelous new trope: the outraged talk radio show guest, furiously denouncing the government takeover of Medicare.

The American anti-government impulse appears to be alive and well in the twenty-first century. And yet the great programs that do pass—like Social Security and Medicare—remain so popular that politicians touch them at considerable peril. The real American culture is complicated, even paradoxical, with room for robust self-interest (don't touch my Medicare), robust government bashing (socialism!), and dreams of social insurance (the Democrats' perennial).

The Clintons and the Neo-Progressive Turn

In December 1978, the Democrats held a midterm party convention in Memphis. The highlight was a health care debate between Ted Kennedy, poised to challenge the Carter administration in the Democratic primaries, and Joseph Califano and Stuart Eizenstat, the administration's highest ranking health officials. It was a dramatic event, for the hall was full of Kennedy supporters roaring for him to run. The moderator was a thirty-two-year-old governor-elect named Bill Clinton. Clinton was thrilled, impressed by the electricity in this issue. He'd eventually learn the dangers.

The Clinton reform is the subject of much terrific analysis. Theda Skocpol, Jacob Hacker, Mark Peterson, Larry Jacobs, Robert Shapiro, and many others have elegantly analyzed the defeat. If the literature has a central theme, it is the one captured in Sven Steinmo and Jon Watts title: *It's The Institutions, Stupid.* A fragmented, federated, system with Congress at the legislative center is not one that can manage this kind of big reform. Clinton could not get it through Congress. Put LBJ aside and no one else could—or will—get it through Congress. The system is designed that way. Steinmo and Watts originally wrote the article before Clinton even submitted the reform.[11]

I won't repeat the excellent points that have been made. For our purposes, I focus on what the Clinton years meant for the great ideas that had driven the debate since Truman: social insurance, the cries of socialism, and a third idea that Clinton added to the mix.

Two Ideas Revisited

Clinton made plenty of mistakes. However, his speeches—though he gave them very late in the process—were artful and moving. He seized onto the language of social insurance with perfect pitch. First he recalled social security. "It is hard to believe there was once a time . . . when retirement was synonymous with poverty . . . and older Americans died in the streets. That's unthinkable today because over half a century ago, Americans had the courage . . . to create a social security system." And then the leap from one great social insurance reform to another. "Forty years from now our grandchildren will . . . find it unthinkable that there was a time in this country when hardworking families lost their homes, their savings, their businesses, lost everything simply because their children go sick or because they had to change jobs."[12]

However, the Clintons' actual proposal injected a rather different idea into the debate, one that had its own long, reformist legacy: the Progressive idea that there is a managerial solution to social problems. Good engineering could meet the problems of society. The Clintons signaled this solution during the presidential transition. They fired the old Washington hands who had been advising them on health care: traditional, backward looking, stuck in the mud, liberal thinking. Instead, they turned to an apolitical business consultant with an air of whiz kid (Ira Magaziner). They would use efficiency and markets—"managed competition"—to overhaul the system.

The result was a New Democratic pastiche: the language of social insurance would evoke Harry Truman and rouse the base. The classic Progressive vision—the same logic that prescribed an Interstate Commerce Commission to "mathematically determine" and impose just rates on the railroads that had been squeezing the American farmers—now would produce the health care solutions that no one had been smart enough to think of before.[13]

Clinton, had he moved fast, might have won a scaled-down version of his managed competition. At the time, some Republicans were drawn to the idea of a more efficient health care system—and wary of what seemed a popular groundswell for health care reform. Senator John Chafee, an old liberal Republican from Rhode Island, put together his own counterplan and got Senate Minority leader Robert Dole to sign on. The plan introduced Washington to an individual mandate, lately known as Obamacare. Senator Chafee described the progress of the Republican alternative as the Clintons frittered away their first year in office without submitting their legislation: Robert Dole, said Chafee, started by calling it "my plan" (during the Clinton honeymoon, when health reform seemed inevitable) then went to "the Chafee–Dole plan" (as the reform teetered) and, finally, to "that goddamn plan of Chafee's (as Republicans united against Clintoncare).[14]

On the other side, the Republicans eventually hit upon a strategy. Famously, they united in opposition and reverted to the rhetoric of socialist catastrophe that stretched right back to the Truman era. That strategy succeeded beyond anyone's dreams and a new era in Washington Politics was born: the ferocious opposition to health care—crying socialism—now spread to greet every Democratic proposal.

The Republicans, surging into the majority in 1994, developed a new health care strategy of their own. Anything smacking of the old Democratic social insurance model was still socialism if not worse. But they faced a problem with the popularity of the programs already in place—Medicare and, to their surprise, Medicaid. The Republican strategy that emerged was forcefully articulated by Newt Gingrich: take the old programs designed on the social welfare model (tax-based, government-administered) and turn them over to private competition. Privatizing the program would always be described as "modernization."[15]

In short, each side had a variation on their old idea: *Democrats* had the old social insurance idea and a new, complicated regulatory technique—with a base that valued one and a leadership that relied on the other. *Republicans* had their cry of socialism—and market competition for programs that were too popular to raze or oppose.

For all the partisan roaring, the parties actually shared a thin area of agreement: Democratic technique overlapped with Republican markets. An area of convergence in the Washington middle imagined a more efficient health care system in some mix of regulation and market. The managerial notions were despised by the base of each party, which would cling religiously to, reading left to right, the Democratic dream of social insurance and the Republican rejoinder that this was Lenin's Soviet dream haunting America, or more mildly, an undesired governmental intrusion into private markets.

Implications of Defeat

The biggest error of the Clinton experience, not often noted, lies in what came after. His autobiography, *My Life*, sums up his epilogue to health care reform. "I felt bad for Hillary and for Ira Magaziner." In retrospect, he wished he had tried welfare reform first. His reflections were all about strategy and blame. Where was the memory now of those "hardworking families who lost everything because their children got sick"? The fiery faith of July '93 had burned out entirely by November '94.

There is no shame in losing health reform. Clinton got much further than Truman ever had. But Truman never abandoned the idea. He kept it alive in a vibrant way. It was no coincidence that LBJ chose to honor him when he signed Medicare into law. Contrast Clinton. He walked away from the reform without a backward look—wishing quietly that he had taken on another issue—and permitted opponents to control the historical spin. Republicans had feared this reform might rejuvenate the Democratic connection to the middle class; ever since the reform collapsed, however—and to this day—everyone "knows" the Clinton plan would have been a disaster.

Except, perhaps, the private sector, which seized on managed competition and applied it up and down the health care system. As Clinton promised—to rounds of hooting—these devices yielded significant controls over medicine. And considerable cost savings. So much, in fact, that consumers angrily rebelled.

Truman and Clinton offer the flip sides of the same reform lesson: learn how to lose. Losing well inspires the next generation. Losing well means leaving a big idea behind to fight for, to rally around. The Clintons are tagged with a long list of mistakes. The way they walked away from their defeat was the most significant.

George W. Bush: Another Program to Privatize

During the 2000 election campaign, George W. Bush faced noisy calls for prescription drug coverage for the elderly. The issue did not fire up the Republican brain trust—much less its base. However, the issue would not go away and, eventually, the Bush administration decided to try and take health care away from the Democrats and remake it to Republican specifications. The new Medicare drug entitlement posed an opportunity to privatize—the administration always called it modernize—the program.

Medicare remained a great bastion of the old social insurance model. An enormous, tax-financed, government program that paid (single payer!) and regulated health care providers; the program beneficiaries were all in the same great insurance pool. The Republican idea was to use a new benefit to drag the system out of government and into markets. Let Medicare beneficiaries choose between competing plans and the state would pay part of the premium. The president put it, boldly, if in his own quirky way, in Harry Truman's hometown:

> Medicare is—they usually call it in the political lexicon, "Mediscare." See . . . someone takes your words and tries to . . . frighten people who rely on Medicare. . . . That doesn't deter me . . . Why shouldn't we say, let's give the seniors choices.[16]

Democrats were divided: they saw the assault on a cherished principle—the social insurance idea that all beneficiaries were in the same insurance pool and treated the same way—but at the same time they were eager for the new prescription drug benefit.

Once the Republicans recaptured the Senate in 2002, the administration moved swiftly to achieve the plan. Interviews with White House and Congressional staff reveal an unexpected picture: a detail-oriented President Bush chaired the White House planning meetings, came well-prepared (unlike his father, he had read the briefing books), spoke without notes, asked probing questions, and summed up (always on time) at the end of the hour.

The Bush administration approach was to set out broad principles and a budget, in consultation with Congressional leaders, and leave the Congressional process to Congress. Did it work? Bush got everything but what he wanted.

The original idea was simply to privatize Medicare and add prescription drugs as a sweetener. When that proved too difficult, the administration decided to dangle the prescription benefit as a carrot: it would offer drug benefits only to those beneficiaries who took their Medicare business to a private plan. Beneficiaries would get a choice: stick with the old dinosaur Medicare or switch to the new, modern competitive version and get drug benefits. This proved a step too far, even in a Republican Congress. In the end, the old Medicare remained intact.

All that remained of privatization were two attenuated moves to the market: an option to get the new drug benefit through private plans (that were more lavishly funded). And four demonstration projects that would, in the uncertain future (depending on which party controlled Congress), test out the original proposal for Medicare modernization.

The all-Republican conference committee had an extremely difficult time reconciling House and Senate bills. The House Republicans wanted competition—or, rather, modernization—injected into the old entitlement program. They sent angry delegations to the meeting (ignored); their point person, Bill Thomas, left in a huff (coaxed back); and in the end, they could only manage the two small concessions, a market option for the new benefit and demonstration projects. Despite Democratic fears (and dire predictions by some analysts), the old-fashioned social insurance Medicare program withstood the marketeers. Time will tell whether the Bush administration managed an opening wedge or a futile assault. Bush's achievement with the prescription drug plan—which, after all, expanded health coverage while coming in under the initial budget estimates— is an orphan in our polarized era. Democrats got the benefit expansion they sought but would not acknowledge its success; and many Republicans still find any health care reform anathema.

The Republicans have had an idea—privatize Medicare. It has never been terribly popular with either beneficiaries or with the public. However, it has become an intense faith in Republican Washington. The Gingrich House pursued it directly with little success while Clinton was in the White House. The Bush administration picked up the idea and tried to win it wrapped in a Democratic favorite—entitlement expansion. In the end, the Democrats got their benefit, the Republicans won a little privatization—and perhaps a frame for future Medicare reform. The Republican base, in turn, grew furious at the Bush administration for its mad entitlement (more government!) with its outlandish price tag ($400 billion over ten years, although the politics of that number would take another paper). By the 2006 midterm, the Democrats enjoyed their largest lead over the Republicans on the question, which party do you trust with health care—a whopping 31 percent spread in one *Washington Post*/ABC News poll.

Perhaps this is simply a story of incrementalism in the Congressional process. It is easier to add a benefit to an existing program than to introduce more far-reaching changes. However, it is interesting to note that the neo-liberal Republicans appeared to fall into the same trap as the neo-Progressive Clinton Democrats—they pursued a Washington idea quite at odds with the idea that fired up their party supporters.

Today, the Republicans are back with another try at their market ideal. Congressman Paul Ryan floated the latest effort to modernize (now described as saving) Medicare. This latest effort is likely to face the same stiff political winds as the past tries. Still, the idea has grown more familiar and perhaps, as many Republicans believe, its time is coming.

Obama Discovers the Enduring Appeal of Lockean Liberalism

The Obama administration and the Congressional Democrats managed the extraordinary by winning health care reform in 2010. After years of frustration, first the Republicans won a $400 billion package, then seven years later, the Democrats added their own $1 trillion reform (over ten years). But what exactly happened? What did they win? And why does neither party seem to be reaping political benefits from its breakthrough?

All we can do at this point is try a very rough first draft of history. But it may be that Barak Obama and the Democrats got caught in the same tension as the Clintons: the promise of social insurance (cheered on by the base) meets the technical wizardry of neo-Progressive thinking (with its wan hopes of attracting Republican support).

Obama's Progressive Turn

After a fitful start, Obama finally seemed to find the unabashed Truman rhetoric of social insurance. Speaking at a fund raiser in February 2010, for example, the president hushed the audience with the story of an uninsured Obama volunteer from St. Louis who was dying from breast cancer. "She insisted she is going to be buried in an Obama T-shirt," the president continued. "How can I say to her, 'You know what, we're giving up'? How can I say to her family, 'This is too hard'? How can Democrats on the Hill say, 'This is politically too risky'? How can Republicans on the Hill say, 'We're better off just blocking anything from happening?'"[17] Once again, the clarion call of the great social insurance principle. Invariably, the audiences responded, "yes we can."

However, what the administration actually won was more a neo-Progressive efficiency concoction than the social insurance program that the party faithful were cheering for. By one count, the final legislation contains 1,563 *Secretary Shalls*—that is, items that require rules from the implementing agencies. That's more than five times as many as those counted up for any prior health care reform. These regulations affect the nuts and bolts of the medical system. While observers imagined that the reform was largely focused on insurers, 974 (or 64 percent) of those called-for regulations focused on medical providers. The idea—buried in all those regulations—is to impose efficiencies on the health care system.

Was this result—not New Deal–style social insurance but Progressive Era managerial reform—inevitable? An inexorable result of the political process? Perhaps.

It may be no coincidence that the Obama administration so closely followed the Bush administration playbook. Like the Bush administration, which cut a deal with the pharmaceutical companies over prescription drugs, the Obama administration cut a deal with the insurance companies; both administrations moved to calm the politics of pluralism, of aroused interest groups. And, again like the Bush administration, the Obama team set out broad guidelines and left the details of the Congressional process to Congress. In any case, the politics of health care played out in two very different venues: in the labyrinths of Congress, and, in the raucous town meetings.

Think Institutions

Start with what happened in Congress. As the Obama effort wended its way through the legislature, the nation got a seminar in legislative politics and learned an unsavory lesson: Congress may just be the most complicated, exasperating, unwieldy legislative body in the industrial world. Consider the gauntlet this reform had to run. In the House, three different committees produced two quite different bills. Speaker of the House Nancy Pelosi (D-CA) then hammered them into a single bill through long negotiations with different coalitions—the conservative blue dogs, the progressive caucus, the black caucus, the Hispanic caucus, abortion opponents, and the list goes on. Then—after going to the rules committee to set the terms of the debate—she brought the legislation to the floor where it squeaked by 220–215.

Over on the Senate side, two committees produced two more bills. Majority leader Harry Reid (D-NV) then renegotiated the package, not with blocks but with individuals, searching for the magic 60 votes that shut off a filibuster. The Senate bill finally passed on December 24 and then went to conference where the substantial differences between the bills passed in House and Senate could be negotiated into still another bill—with, count 'em, three more filibuster opportunities on the Senate side. That conference committee would have been the *seventh* different health bill (produced by five committees, two chambers, and one conference). Then, just as the reform neared completion, a special election in Massachusetts yielded a Republican who had run on a striking platform: Stop this health reform. That, in turn, short-circuited the "direct" approach through conference and required fresh rounds of parliamentary maneuvering.

The sausage metaphor has been ubiquitous. But there is a more profound point: this is a uniquely tortured way to pass legislation. Political scientists have been dubbing the Congress—and especially the Senate—"the broken branch." According to one view, such a path from policy ideal, to bicameral legislative negotiation, to enacted law is just the kind of complexity that our constitutional framers intended, requiring compromises all the way. It seems more accurate to say, instead, that the legislative gauntlet through which the Affordable Care Act was forced to pass is far more arduous than anything the framers had in mind; among other things, they did not anticipate political parties, much less Senate filibusters.

Many observers have criticized the Obama administration for not sending a more robust plan to Congress. The criticism is naive about modern Congressional process. The crucial element lies not in the plan's details (which Congress will rewrite multiple times) but the clarity of its principles. And here there is a real question. Both Lyndon Johnson and George Bush deferred the legislative details but came in with a clear, strong bottom line. Johnson wanted a big Medicare package and he got it. Bush wanted to inject competitive principles into the program although he lost much of that in the Congressional process. Did Obama have a similar, clear set of principles? Or did he drift though the Congressional gauntlet?

It will be years before interviews, archives, and the actual consequences of the reform—if it is ever fully put in place—yield an answer to that question. However, it appears that many members of the administration—from the economists to the President himself—put considerable stock in the efficiencies and technical improvements that health services research seemed to promise. Although they were not as naive about it as the Clinton team, this group, too, put its faith in the cost savings of, say, information technology, electronic medical billing, and the lessons health services researchers can offer to clinicians.

Once again, the seductions of technique seemed to wink across the aisle. A small knot of Republicans, led by Charles Grassley (IA), negotiated long and hard—underscore long—with Senator Max Baucus, the Senate Finance chair. The subtext of their negotiations can be summarized like this: keep the social insurance out of this package (no public option, no Medicare buy-in, hide the entitlements in the tax spending and the existing programs) and a couple of us Republicans might just support it.

Passionate Ideas: Cry Socialism

Perhaps that framing robbed Obama of his eloquent voice. His speeches on health care descended into the political weeds. They baffled the Democratic faithful—who could not find the connection between all the dull details of good technique and the simple idea they espoused. Once again, there was a disconnect between two very different ideas. The Democratic party base was eager for some version of social insurance—even in a modified version: at least let people who wish to do so go into the Medicare program. The Washington Democrats, on the other hand, were seeking once again a Progressive-style managerial solution that might—just maybe—find common ground with some Republicans. It was not until there was no chance of Republican support that Obama found his voice—speaking in bold social insurance rhetoric over a package that had, in fact, been negotiated with the aim of winning Republican votes.

The most dramatic turn in the debate came in the long, hot summer of 2009—long before Obama started to call out to his base. Right-wing populists, self-styled Tea Party activists, roared into the health care policy discussion screaming their familiar slogan: "socialized medicine." This time, they managed a new rhetorical variation on the idea of Lenin and the Soviet state: this plan meant government-run death panels—a pungent, memorable, simple, and effective symbol of evil government. The administration never found a way to recapture public attention or offer a simple counter to the charges. Like Truman or Clinton before them, the Democrats tried denial (this is not socialized medicine, there are no death panels), backtracking (striking the counseling provisions in the house bill that had set off the media storm), and delving into the details (here is what is really in the bill). Once again—yet again—the opposition won the battle of popular perceptions.

In past debates, the opposition came from well-oiled (and financed) corporate lobbies like the physicians or the insurers. These activists also were well financed. However, it is a classic mistake to dismiss populist energy as misguided and manipulated—the standard response to populist movements from, say, the capitalists in 1896 or the segregationists in 1963. The furious outbursts in response to Obama's plan tapped a powerful idea that stretches back over time. They may have been well funded, but ordinary people responded with their veins bulging.

The health care debate has turned into a debate about what kind of nation the United States is. It is no coincidence that the most deeply felt issues of our time—race, immigration, welfare, the role of government, and abortion—all were roiled by health care reform. It was the issue of illegal immigration that moved Congressman Wilson to shout, "You lie!" as the president spoke before Congress; it was abortion that almost derailed the reform among then Democrats in the House. And, as always, there were plenty of claims that race was roiling at least some people on the right.

Perhaps every nation's health care system offers a snapshot of essential national characteristics, of the kind of community the nation aspires to be. It may be that health care in the United States raises the deepest communal question: Who are we?

The right-wing populism grew so hot that even Charles Grassley turned and pandered. "You have every right to fear. You shouldn't have counseling at the end of life. . . . We should not have a government program that determines if you're going to pull the plug on grandma."

Democrats in Washington, who thought they were prepared for the standard inflated rhetoric about socialism, were gobsmacked about death panels. Where was *this* coming from? We should ask the deeper question: Why were they surprised after seventy years? Death panels flow from a venerable national wellspring. It is the familiar, rightist fear about government's power growing too great, going too far. The same passionate idea that Louis Harz called irrational and Richard Hofstadter termed alternately "the anti-intellectual impulse" and "the paranoid style." Back in the 1950s, both understood it was powerful. Call it what it is: an enduring American idea.

Sixty years earlier, the American Medical Association hired a public relations firm that found a way to frame Democratic health care proposals: socialism. The framing was so successful because it reflected a long-standing American suspicion toward government. It is not, by any stretch, a universal American idea or the only passionate political stance. But it is powerful. Once health care reform had been framed as socialism, each effort drew that argument to the surface. By 2009—in an especially heated political moment marked by an African American president presiding over a terrible economy—the arguments burst out of the grassroots with a ferocity that matched anything that came before it.

Yes, institutions matter. Congress explains a great deal about the programs that the United States has—and doesn't have. But the power of simple ideas—like the faith in social insurance and the fear of an overly powerful state—pack a powerful wallop of their own. The latter wallop proved strong enough to frighten a would-be statesman like Senator Grassley right off his bipartisan perch. We may very well be facing the right-wing populists—and the latest recurrence of the cry against socialism—for a long time to come.

Ideas Matter, Too

Not many political arguments last sixty years. The health care debate, which traces back to Harry Truman's passionate embrace of social insurance, offers us a fine opportunity to watch how ideas work in politics, mixing with institutions, interests, and chance.

I've described four ideas. First, the social insurance notion of shared responsibility and a citizen's right to decent care; I am inevitably my brother's keeper, as Martin Luther King put it, because I am my brother's brother. For the Democratic left, this is the idea that animates health reform. Through the Johnson administration, it was the idea the Democrats put in play.

Second, the Hartzian idea: see health care reform and cry socialism. Come to think of it, Hartz and, for that matter Richard Hofstadter, would describe it as something deeper than an idea, more like a psychological condition, at least in its populist form: the United States is a nation committed to liberal markets that test the merits of individuals. Government action threatens the great liberal test—and the liberal nation itself. The idea of free health care is a profound—an existential—threat to American liberty.

This idea is easy to overlook. It began its life as a quite cynical public relations campaign. To the left, the idea itself seems bizarre; leftists are always shocked—they never learn—at the intensity with which it roars up during social insurance debates. However, it taps the one thing that Louis Hartz got right: a strange, quirky, often over-stated but nevertheless enduring dread of governmental power seen as unlimited, as going too far. The left underestimates it at its repeated peril.

Third, the Progressive faith in technique. There's a technical fix for the problems at hand. The signature move of the new Democrat: jettison the ambitious values of the social insurance model and find expert solutions that might stand beyond partisanship and politics. There is no Democratic or Republican way to pave a street, cried the original Progressives; let's work out a bipartisan solution to the health care mess, echo their intellectual heirs. In truth, there is a thin area of agreement where the B school wonks of the left and the right find common ground. The solutions are unstable, however, because the true believers in both parties despise them. In every generation, the Progressive impulse—fix the machinery—runs aground on the stubborn shoals of politics.

Finally, the neo-liberal solution of meeting social needs through private markets. Republicans turn to this idea when they feel political pressure to confer entitlements (as Reagan and Bush both did) or when they confront programs that are too popular to raze—most notably, Medicare and Social Security. Despite—or perhaps because of—the Democratic howls, these programs have, until now, been as difficult to privatize as they have been to retrench. Perhaps Democratic neo-Progressives in the White House (fretting over deficits) and Republican firebrands in Congress will find a way to finally vanquish (or modernize) these legacies of social insurance.

These are all old ideas, perfectly familiar a half century ago. They do not operate independently. I've tried to sketch the way institutional realities—Congress above all—often explain away what is attributed to ideas and culture. However, I've also tried to point to the opposite error: Pretending that ideas and the culture that sustains them do not matter. We can't understand what just happened to Obama and the Democrats—or to any of the administrations sketched here—without appreciating the power of these enduring ideas.

Notes

1. Harry Truman, *Memoirs*, 1:19.
2. Alexis de Tocqueville, *Democracy in America*, vol. I, pt. 2, ch. 7, pp. 254–255.
3. Gustave de Beaumont, 108.
4. John Stuart Mill, 149; for discussion, see James Morone, "John Stuart Mill and American Liberalism," forthcoming.
5. See Max Skidmore, *Medicare and the Rhetoric of Reconciliation* and Richard Harris, *A Sacred Trust* for examples of the rhetoric and symbols.
6. Details in David Blumenthal and James Morone, *The Heart of Power: Health and Politics in the Oval Office.*
7. Report of Committee on Federal Legislation, the NY Bar Association, The Papers of Oscar Ewing, Box 35; Ewing Papers, Truman Library. Lawrence Huntoon, "Universal Health Coverage—Call It Socialized Medicine," *Medical Sentinel* 5:4 (2000): 134–136.
8. Louis Hartz, *The Liberal Tradition in America: An Interpretation of American Political Thought Since the Revolution.* See the symposium on Hartz in *Studies in American Political Development* 19:2 (2005).
9. Lyndon B. Johnson, 215. For the classic analysis, updated for new information here, see Theodore R. Marmor.
10. See David Blumenthal and James Morone, "The Lessons of Success, Revising The Medicare Story," 2384–2389.
11. See Sven Steinmo and John Watts, "It's the Institutions, Stupid! Why Comprehensive National Health Care Always Fails In America."
12. William J. Clinton, "Address to a Joint Session of Congress on Health Care Reform," September 22, 1993, 13. On the Progressive tradition, see James Morone, *The Democratic Wish* ch. 3.
14. Blumenthal and Morone, *The Heart of Power*, 372.
15. See Jonathan Oberlander.
16. See George W. Bush, "Remarks at Truman High School, Independence, Missouri," August 21, 2001. 17. See Robert Pear and David M. Herszenhorn, A9.

Bibliography

Beaumont, Gustave de. *Marie: Or, Slavery in the United States.* Translated by Barbara Chapman. Baltimore: Johns Hopkins Press, 1999.
Blumenthal, David, and James Morone. *The Heart of Power: Health and Politics in the Oval Office.* Berkeley and Los Angeles: University of California Press, 2009.

————. "The Lessons of Success, Revising The Medicare Story." *New England Journal of Medicine* 359:22:22 (2009), 2384–2389.

Bush, George W. "Remarks at Truman High School, Independence, Missouri," August 21, 2001. Online by Gerhard Peters and John T. Woolley, *The American Presidency Project*. www.presidency.ucsb.edu/ws/?pid=62637

Clinton, William J. "Address to a Joint Session of Congress on Health Care Reform," September 22, 1993. Online by Gerhard Peters and John T. Woolley, *The American Presidency Project*. www.presidency.ucsb.edu/ws/?pid=47101

The Ewing Papers. Papers of Oscar Ewing, Truman Library.

Harris, Richard. *A Sacred Trust*. New York: New American Library, 1966.

Hartz, Louis. *The Liberal Tradition in America: An Interpretation of American Political Thought Since the Revolution*. New York: Harcourt, Brace and World, 1955.

Huntoon, Lawrence. "Universal Health Coverage – Call It Socialized Medicine." *Medical Sentinel* 5:4 (2000), 134–136.

Johnson, Lyndon B. *The Vantage Point: Perspective of the Presidency, 1963–1969*. New York: Holt, Rinehart and Winston, 1971.

Marmor, Theodore R. *The Politics of Medicare: Second Edition* (Hawthorne, NY: Aldine de Gruyter, 2001 [1970]).

Mill, John Stuart. *Autobiography*. New York: Penguin, 1990.

Morone, James. *The Democratic Wish*. New Haven, CT: Yale University Press, 1998.

————. "John Stuart Mill and American Liberalism." In *Liberty, Equity, and Paternalism: Public Health and the Legacy of John Stuart Mill*. Edited by Ron Bayer and Amy Fairchild (forthcoming).

Oberlander, Jonathan. *The Political Life of Medicare*. Chicago: University of Chicago Press, 2003.

Pear, Robert, and Herszenhorn, David M. "Democrats Ask, Can This Health Care Bill Be Saved?" *New York Times*. February, 6, 2010, A9.

Skidmore, Max. *Medicare and the Rhetoric of Responsibility*. Tuscaloosa: University of Alabama Press, 1970.

Steinmo, Sven and Watts, John. "It's the Institutions, Stupid! Why Comprehensive National Health Care Always Fails In America." *Journal of Health Politics, Policy and Law* 19:1 (1994).

Studies in American Political Development 19:2 (2005), 196–239.

Tocqueville, Alexis de. *Democracy in America*. Translated by George Lawrence. New York: Harper, 1998 [1835, 1840].

Truman, Harry. *Memoirs*. 2 vols. New York: Doubleday, 1955.

Part III

Liberal Education, Constitutionalism, and Philosophic Moderation

Chapter 8

The Polis, the State, and the Constitution

James R. Stoner Jr.

One of the most poignant exchanges in the history of American letters, at least from the point of view of a student of American politics, occurred between two former presidents, John Adams and Thomas Jefferson. Close political allies in their revolutionary youth, then bitter political enemies in their presidential years, Adams and Jefferson were reconciled in retirement and embarked on the project, as Adams put it, through letters of explaining themselves to one another before they passed from the earth. In the course of this correspondence, on July 5, 1814, Jefferson announced that he had found the leisure in retirement to work through the whole of Plato's *Republic* and was appalled by what he found: "the whimsies, the puerilities, and the unintelligible jargon of this work . . . such nonsense." Adams, who had studied the dialogues some years before, wholeheartedly agreed. In reading Plato, he wrote, "My disappointment was very great, my astonishment was greater, and my disgust shocking."[1]

Although it will be evident to readers of this collection of chapters that the range of political difference among Murray Dry's students is no less than that between Mr. Jefferson and Mr. Adams, we nevertheless could never share their experience—for Mr. Dry introduced us to Plato's *Republic* when we were barely past our teens, and his counterparts at other colleges and universities have done the same for their many students. Like Adams and Jefferson, modern students recognize immediately that the *Republic*'s argument is at odds with the principles of American politics, but in Mr. Dry we had the very same teacher who had explained to us the development of those principles—in the writing of the Constitution and in their being put to trial and refined by Abraham Lincoln in the crisis of the Civil War—now showing us how to understand Plato as he understood himself, that is, showing us how to read the *Republic* as though it might contain the key to truth about political things. The central teaching of the book in his account is that the life of the mind is the highest human life, the one that is intrinsically choice-worthy, not just any old "pursuit of happiness" but the one life that could satisfy those able to lead it. It is not a life available to all—one had a crushing feeling of inadequacy as, mentally, one compared one's own abilities with Socrates' list at the beginning of book VI of the capacities of the truly philosophic nature—and, even at the age of twenty, one can recognize that it is hardly a life in which most people had an interest in any event. In short, like Jefferson and Adams, modern students find some of Plato's notions disappointing or shocking—although the equality of the sexes in book V is surprisingly up-to-date—and probably find some things unintelligible. But reading the *Republic* with Mr. Dry left no one with the thought that it was nonsense or that its argument could be easily dismissed.

Now, there is no denying that the preeminence of Socrates' claim that the philosophic life is the best life governs every maxim of Plato's politics. Because rule requires wisdom, and because only philosophers are wholly wise, philosophers alone must be rulers. Spirited men could serve as their auxiliaries—indeed, must be their enforcers—while men and women of ordinary wants and needs are left to go about their business, though without authority or honor. Yes, Socrates makes clear in the *Republic* that the coincidence of philosophy and political power would be very rare and was not something to be engineered; who would engineer it, the philosophers not wanting to rule and the others not asking them to? Still, the picture of Plato's best regime makes all other political ideals seem imperfect if not mistaken. And if philosopher-kingship was of no practical use in politics except to critique and thus perhaps to moderate indignation or enthusiasm or cynicism, in the hands of an able teacher the life of philosophy comes across as a live possibility: "Perhaps in heaven," says Socrates at the end of book IX, "a pattern is laid up for the man who wants to see and found a city within himself on the basis of what he sees."[2]

Once one emerges from Plato's *Republic* thus understood, American politics, even in its noblest principles, cannot help but appear, if not second-rate, at least no longer self-evidently attractive. Exactly once in the debates of the federal convention is there anything like consideration of Plato's central theme. On Friday, July 13, in that Philadelphia summer of 1787, exasperated by Pierce Butler's demand for protection of slavery, Gouverneur Morris's warning that the eastern states not be overwhelmed by the rude west, and many others' insistence that the states retain their equal representation in Congress, James Wilson blurts out that he "could not agree that property was the sole or primary object of Government and society. The cultivation and improvement of the human mind was the most noble object."[3] Wilson gets his half of the Great Compromise a few days later, ensuring not property but numbers are the basis of representation in the House and more or less in the election of the president, but except for mid-August proposals to the Committee of Detail by James Madison and Charles Pinckney that the enumeration of powers include allowance for Congress to promote the advancement of useful knowledge by granting copyrights and patents, as well as to establish a national university, most of the convention's deliberations concerned the mechanics of institutional design, not the higher ends of human learning.[4] The city in speech in Plato's *Republic* mirrors the human soul, and to watch it unfold in the dialogue is to be shown something about what it means to be a human being, something about possibilities easily overlooked and about limitations readily forgotten. The Constitution in writing that emerges from the Framers' deliberations is also tripartite, but attention to the soul appears only in occasional discussions among its advocates of the need for character, especially in the executive; in caution about the dangers of avarice and ambition; and in constant attention to the strength of the interests of men. The plan is not to make a government that imitates a well-ordered soul, but to calibrate an instrument that holds passions and interests in balance. The *Republic* famously builds toward a showdown between the tyrant and the philosopher, between two kinds of soul governed by *eros* or longing for something beyond itself. The Constitution is evidently unerotic—unless you count its nod to "ourselves and our posterity" and its rejection of "corruption of the blood"—and when its original interpreter, Publius, speaks of love in *The Federalist*, it is obliquely as a cause of faction, to be cured by the extended sphere, that is, by spreading it thin.[5]

Thus far I have spoken of the excitement of reading Plato and may seem to have disparaged the work of the American Founders by contrast. But surely to do so would be grossly unfair. The American Founders, after all, were eminently practical men, as well as eminently ambitious ones. Gathering far from the centers of civilization over the course of a decade or so in a couple cities near a rude frontier, they imagined the project of reconfiguring human politics, establishing republican government as respectable among civilized men and women, allowing a continent of men to live in peace with one another, and unleashing human capacities hitherto repressed by fear and ignorance. Whatever the imperfections of their product—which they never doubted, in fact leaving Philadelphia in September 1787 with a document they all thought imperfect, because compromised—we can see clearly from our time that the government they established has met or exceeded even their astounding ambitions, becoming the most powerful polity since ancient Rome and redefining the terms of political discussion in the world at large. Plato, too, wrote a more practical book about politics, the *Laws*, and the city there outlined was decidedly less radical than either the city of the *Republic* or the American Constitution: men were to live on their own estates, which they held as property, women were not equal, wealthy families had slaves, commerce was limited, the city was small, and philosophy was not to rule in the open but had to hide itself.[6] Many of the men at Philadelphia—one thinks of Washington and Madison, for example—may have lived lives not so different from those that Plato's Athenian Stranger in the *Laws* recommends for the second-besters, cultivating the virtues of their families on moderate estates, accepting the service of slaves, and the like, but they nevertheless chose to implement a very different set of political principles and to look forward to a very different world.

Let me focus the contrast between the *Republic* and the Founding on three points. First, Plato's account of human nature, and so Socrates' city, is aristocratic; it supposes so radical an inequality among men that its fundamental myth describes the different classes as different substances—gold, silver, iron or bronze—and it assigns them radically different roles in the city's activity.[7] There is a paradox in comparing the city to the soul: although every soul has all three parts—the calculating, the spirited, and the desiring—in the city each class allows two of them to atrophy, for the rulers do all its thinking, the auxiliaries its fighting, and the moneymaking class gets all its ordinary pleasures (well almost all: it seems as though the rulers get the most sex, but it is not clear that they are allowed to enjoy it). Pushing the analogy of city and soul seems perverse if not unjust—can the moneymakers really not think? Should fighters not be allowed to enjoy the gentler pleasures? Don't the rulers have to fight?—but I suppose Plato's answer is the insight of the division of labor: Everybody thrives if those do most what they do best. Still, the liberal political philosophy implicit in the Declaration's "self-evident truth" that all are equal in their rights clearly emphasizes what people have in common as prior to what makes us different. Not all are equally clever, but each is wise enough to learn to discern his or her own interest, and at any rate each cares enough about his or her own happiness that superior wisdom is insufficient to counterbalance that superior's likely indifference to anyone other than her- or himself. Spiritedness, too, is universal, or can be taught well enough to all that they can stand up for their rights, as becomes free men and women. And how can anyone's enjoying good things make up for another's lack? (I used to think the very suggestion nonsensical, but observing modern celebrity culture, perhaps it is possible after all.)

My second point is that this fundamental difference on whether to accentuate the unequal or the equal in human nature when founding a city is the source of many further differences. If men are fundamentally equal, they have no natural rulers among them, so their relations must originate in consent: consent to be governed, on the one hand, and mutual consent (or contract) in all the varied relations of civil life. Their society, then, will be commercial rather than educational, emphasizing freedom more than virtue, fidelity to contract more than simple duty.[8] It will be large rather than small, not by accident but by design; in *Federalist* #10, Madison ingeniously explains how an extended republic better secures rights and the general prosperity than small republics do, and this feeds back upon itself, for free and prosperous republics will naturally expand. All of this, at any rate, is the self-understanding of the classical liberalism of the Founders; their practice, as is notorious, took some while to catch up with their theory, for it is no small irony that in Plato's *Republic* there is no class of slaves and the sexes are equal, while the end of slavery cost Americans a civil war and sexual egalitarianism remains unstable if not indeterminate even in our own day.

My third and most important point of contrast between Plato's polis and the Founders' Constitution concerns the character of education in the first and liberty of conscience in the second. Socrates proposes two distinct curricula: music and gymnastic for the auxiliaries, and geometry-harmonics-astronomy-dialectics for the philosophers.[9] While the latter curriculum forms the basis of the medieval quadrivium, it receives only a quick sketch after the image of the cave in book VII; much more attention is devoted to education in music or poetry, including a whole program of censorship to insure that poetry inculcates virtue and condemns vice. As in the *Apology of Socrates*, Plato's implicit critique of Athens is not for the Athenians' demand that citizens share in common worship and that they refrain from corrupting the young, but that they mistake what virtue is and portray the gods themselves as vicious. Like any polis, maybe even more so, Plato's *Republic* supposes that citizens can share in the life of the city only if they share a conception of justice, and the business of the philosopher-king seems to be above all to form or reform that conception. He is not said to lead men out of the cave, or at least not more than an able few, but it seems to be his role to refine and perfect the images, the right opinions, by which they live.

But American constitutionalism, by contrast, from the first days of independence, includes the principle of liberty of conscience. The polity has no authority or interest in establishing orthodoxy, which means literally "correct opinion," but leaves it to every individual or at least to lesser communities to discover the first principles by which to live. This, I think, is above all what the Founders meant when they wrote "Novus Ordo Seclorum" on the Great Seal: empires before had been able to tolerate religious diversity so long as the emperor's suzerainty is acknowledged, but republics and even mixed kingdoms were thought to depend on like-mindedness, *homonoia*, because after all citizens have to deliberate in common and judge one another's character when called on to vote. It is not that the Founders supposed Americans needed no thoughts in common—rather that thought was not such a thing as could be dictated and thus enforced by law. It is the nature of thought to seek the truth, in everyone some of the time, in some people all or almost all the time. What Americans can share is a commitment to the Constitution and, as they eventually realized, a commitment to some basic political principles that explain its precepts—a commitment, in other words, not only to the letter of the law but also to its reasons.[10] This is no mere overlapping consensus à la John Rawls;[11] the text of the Constitution and the institutions it establishes are chosen, and the constitutional principles are formed, by statesmanship and argument, sometimes even in the forge of common experience. Still the meaning of freedom of conscience, properly noted by Rawls, is that agreement cannot be demanded "all the way down" to first principles or ultimate beliefs. For example, there is nothing to prevent Protestant and Catholic, skeptic and Jew, Deist and Unitarian from agreeing that the federal legislative power belongs to Congress and judicial power to one Supreme Court and such lower courts as Congress constitutes. Likewise, even the principle that all men are equal can be variously grounded: by a Catholic in natural law, by an Evangelical in the Gospel, by a Hobbesian liberal in our vulnerability to one another, by an Aristotelian in the necessity of consent, and so forth. So long as one can pledge in good conscience to support the Constitution and its basic principles, one can be a good American, whatever one's more fundamental commitments.

Is the contrast between Platonic political philosophy and American political principles an artifact of the difference between theory and practice, between literature and law? One way to see is to compare the Platonic account to a very different version of political philosophy, in fact one that has been influential in the establishment of modern politics in general and perhaps even of American politics in particular. I have in mind the thought of Thomas Hobbes, recognized as a founder of the modern doctrine of sovereignty and so of the modern state, and considered by some to be a founder of modern liberalism, or at least of many of its characteristic ideas. His masterwork, *Leviathan*, nicely contrasts with the *Republic*; indeed, Hobbes himself suggests the comparison in the middle of his own book.[12] Hobbes was a relentless critic of Aristotle, but refers to Plato as "the best Philosopher of the Greeks," praising in particular his requiring as a prerequisite for philosophy the study of geometry, "the only Science that it hath pleased God hitherto to bestow on mankind."[13] Still, while Hobbes may have admired Plato for his insistence on precision in the use of speech and reason, his political philosophy differs in almost every respect: in its way of proceeding, in its account of the political problem and its solution, and in its understanding of human nature itself.

The *Republic* is a dialogue, and its characters—Socrates and several interlocutors—proceed dialectically, that is, by offering opinions and testing their truth: sometimes by reasoning out their

consequences to a contradiction or an otherwise repugnant conclusion, sometimes by drawing an image and comparing it to experience, sometimes by parsing distinctions and sorting things into
classes or types. Dialectics, as noted earlier, is praised as the apex of
the philosophers' education, and while not every movement in the
dialogue is dialectical—some are poetic, as, for example, when an
interlocutor interrupts—the poetry seems to reinforce the argument,
presenting a lively examination of what justice is and whether it is
good, ascending to first principles and elaborating their meaning for
human life. *Leviathan*, by contrast, begins its train of reasoning with
the author's introspection and his invitation to others to consider
whether their own observation and experience do not conform to
his, "For this kind of Doctrine, admitteth no other Demonstration."[14]
Reasoning, Hobbes explains, proceeds by defining general terms
unambiguously and then by drawing out their general consequences.
Science results when the consequences are many and the reasoning
sound, though the premises technically remain as arbitrary as individuals' self-interpretation. Socratic dialectics works back from
human opinion to the principles inherent in the nature of things;
Hobbesian science is a human construction that sets aside ordinary
opinion to reconstitute what men think based on their knowledge of
themselves and makes its case based on the consequences of such
insight for the achievement of the things people want.

The fundamental concept from which Hobbes constructs his doctrine of sovereignty and the state is "the condition of mere nature,"
that is, an account of what life would be like for individuals living in
each other's proximity without government.[15] Notoriously, this state
of nature is a state of war of all against all, conditioned by a rough
equality of men in their ability to threaten one another and triggered
by scarcity and competition, by anticipation of others' hostility, and
most ominously by the pride of those who insist that others acknowledge their imagined superiority. Hobbes finds no warrant in nature
for men to claim a right to rule their fellows; instead, nature supplies
a right to each to preserve his own life and to do whatever he has to
in that regard. Reason itself has no claim to rule, nor do the most
rational men, for,

> when men that think themselves wiser than all others,
> clamor and demand right Reason for judge; yet seek no
> more, but that things should be determined, by no other

mens reason but their own, it is as intolerable in the society of men, as it is in play after trump is turned, to use
for trump on every occasion, that suite whereof they have
most in their hand. For they do nothing els, that will have
every of their passions, as it comes to bear sway in them,
to be taken for right Reason, and that in their own controversies: bewraying their want of right Reason, by the
claym they lay to it.[16]

There is no philosopher-king in *Leviathan*, nor any class of wise men
who can justly claim a right to rule on the basis of their wisdom.
There are only imperfectly rational and continuously passionate
men.

Still, reasonable men, looking to preserve themselves, can
recognize—at least when someone like Hobbes points it out to
them—that the smartest thing they can do is lay down their right to
harm others if others will do the same, establishing a covenant among
themselves and agreeing on a referee to define and enforce its terms.
Hobbes calls this theorem a "law of nature" and calls the referee the
"sovereign," whose command henceforth becomes law and whose
sword keeps the peace. Much of the *Leviathan* is devoted to working
out the consequences of sovereign power—put briefly, sovereign
power must be absolute in scope, but its aim should be limited merely
to keeping the peace—and to refuting the many political opinions
that he thinks interfere with the exercise of sovereign authority and
thus plunge men back into a state of war. The question of the regime
has only instrumental importance, for Hobbes; any form of government, whether by one, few, or many, must necessarily designate a
single man or body of men to hold sovereign power, and anything in
the form that obstructs sovereignty is damaging to the end of government, which for every form is peace and protection.[17] According to
Hobbes, it matters much less who rules than that everyone agrees
who rules. Although sovereigns may vary in their prudence, no
advantage of wisdom at the top can replace the harm done by civil
war in the struggle to get to the top. Besides, Hobbes has confidence
enough in men's ability to seek enlightenment concerning their own
good not only to trust most men with their own affairs, but also to
trust that whoever is (or are) dealt responsibility for the public interest will find it in his (or their) own interest to ensure that public
peace and prosperity are pursued.

In his first widely disseminated version of his political theory, *De Cive*, Hobbes began as I just have with the state of nature, which he describes as an inference from the passions of men, verified by the experience of civil war.[18] In *Leviathan*, however, he goes into more detail about human nature, providing an anthropology to explain why "nature dissociates," why men "without a common Power to keep them all in awe" find themselves in "a warre, as is of every man, against every man."[19] Despite asserting that the universe is nothing except body,[20] Hobbes has little to say about the human body per se; rather, he describes men in terms of their sense, thought, speech, reason, and passions. All of these are in motion, not only part by part but taken together, so that human happiness or felicity "consisteth not in the repose of a mind satisfied," but in "a continuall progresse of the desire, from one object to another; the attaining of the former, being still but the way to the later."[21] Reason is not the master of this process but its servant or facilitator: "the Thoughts, are to the Desires, as Scouts, and Spies, to range abroad, and find the way to the things Desired."[22] In this account of man, Hobbes makes no mention of the soul; what unity there is comes only from the dependence of all the many thoughts and desires on the individual's not suffering death, which causes all to cease, and thus on the ultimately futile attempt "to assure for ever, the way of his future desire."

Still, the prospect of death, especially violent death at the hand of an enemy, seems to be sufficient in Hobbes to focus the mind, for the Hobbesian individual thinks principally if not continuously about his own good, or as came to be said a century later, his own interest. Partly this is because the human good is individualized in Hobbes's account. The passions of men are the same, he posits, but their objects differ from person to person, at least for the most part, the exception being life itself, which all humans desire; as he pungently elaborates, at least by nature, "private Appetite is the measure of Good, and Evill," a common measure coming only artificially, through the making of law.[23] Even law does not change the object of men's concern: "of the voluntary acts of every man," he writes "the object is some Good To Himselfe."[24] What about virtue? For Hobbes, moral philosophy consists in the laws of nature, that is, the precepts of reason that advise men how to be sociable with one another; virtue is a means to peace, not an end in itself or a key to felicity. Even though men reason alike when doing mathematics, in human affairs every man insists on thinking for himself, at least until he consents to another's direction or takes another's advice. Instituting a sovereign is the overriding moment of consent to let another define one's good, and it is granted only under the duress of universal war. On the whole, and so in matters that the sovereign leaves men free to decide for themselves—when a sovereign is unchallenged and rational, he will leave many things to private choice—it makes sense, Hobbes thinks, for men to make their own decisions or take counsel from those they choose: "A plain husband-man is more Prudent in affaires of his own house, then a Privy Counseller in the affaires of another man."[25] As for those whose passion of curiosity leads them to wonder about the causes of things, they should be free to do so if the sovereign finds their research no threat to social peace, though any science they develop must not be imposed by the scientists on the polity, only employed by the sovereign for "the benefit of mankind."[26]

The contrast between the *Republic* and the *Leviathan* should be obvious. Though both authors think political knowledge is possible and both apparently favor a sort of kingship—indeed, both seem to favor a sort of absolute kingship—they differ on the question of inequality and equality of minds, at least for practical purposes, and they differ on the size and character of the city, Hobbes allowing an indefinite expansion if men consent to a common sovereign and signaling approval of a progressively developing society if men can avoid the disputes that lead them to fight. On education, Plato and Hobbes agree that the ruler ought to exercise control over doctrine, though by different means and to different ends. Socrates in the *Republic* is concerned with the poetry that teaches the young what is noble, just, and good; let the ruling classes hear virtue praised and vice dishonored and they will learn to live by the former and eschew the latter. Hobbes's concern is only with doctrines that undermine civic peace, not private character, but in practice that might entail at least as meddlesome a supervision, for he thought the most constant threats to peace were classical literature and certain doctrines of the Christian church. Socrates' rulers were charged to monitor theology, for the poetry of the Greek world needed to be purged of tales of misdeeds of the pagan gods; Hobbes' sovereign, more worried about Aristotle than about Homer, was charged to monitor theology to insure that God's commands were never taken to contradict the sovereign's and to see that saints were never praised for breaking the law.

Does Hobbes's theory define American politics and thus clarify the aforementioned contrasts we saw between Plato's polis and the

American constitutional order? On the one hand, that would appear preposterous. Hobbes was not a constitutionalist: the whole point of the doctrine of sovereignty was to insist that a person or a body of people makes the law, not that law confines governmental power, and his insistence on the unity of the sovereign explicitly rejected the then-nascent doctrine of the separation of powers, which became central to American constitutionalism.[27] Moreover, Hobbes was not a republican: true, he explained his support for monarchy was based on probabilities rather than demonstration, and his theory of sovereignty makes room for a body of lawmakers comprised of the many or the few, but from his earliest writings he was a critic of oratorical display and democratic deliberation, seeing only the clash of ambitious men willing to upset public peace for personal glory.[28] Americans in the time of the founding and for many years thereafter claimed the common law as their own and made ample use of juries in the administration of justice, but Hobbes was an inveterate critic of common law, anchored as it was in lawyers' learning and popular custom rather than in sovereign command.[29] And Hobbes's reputed atheism, amply implied in *Leviathan* despite—an orthodox believer might say, because of—his devoting the longest section of the book to squaring its doctrine with the Bible, surely helps account for his absence from American colonial libraries and from most pamphlets or other publications from the Revolutionary and Constitution-making age.

On the other hand, Hobbes's successors in the tradition of modern political philosophy developed his basic principles—natural equality, government by consent, and sovereign power—in ways that made them more congenial to constitutionalists and republicans and maybe even to friends of common law. John Locke's liberalism took Hobbes's theory of the state of nature, the social contract, and sovereign power and modified each step to seem congenial to constitutionalism—and this while only slightly adjusting Hobbes's account of the human individual and the character of scientific knowledge.[30] Locke differed from Hobbes on one critical matter of political judgment—whether it was worse to risk civil war (as Hobbes thought) or absolute, arbitrary power (as Locke held)—and he thought he could confine the latter without precipitating the former by inventing a natural right to property whose protection would give government a measurable goal and by permitting religious toleration to those groups (not, by the way, the ones Hobbes most feared) whose tenets began with tolerating others, a prospect Hobbes himself had raised.

Likewise, Jean-Jacques Rousseau's *Social Contract* adopted Hobbes's theory of sovereignty as the origin of law, now turning it against kings in the name of the people, expanding the role of the state beyond what Hobbes imagined, and confining the role of religion at least as much as Hobbes intended, perhaps even more, insofar as Rousseau made the sovereign people themselves an object of reverence. If Locke met the constitutionalist objection to Hobbes, Rousseau met the republican or democratic one. And the reconciliation of Hobbesian sovereignty and common law appeared in Blackstone's *Commentaries*, immensely popular in America, though more for its preservation of common-law practice than for its echoes of Hobbesian sovereignty, which were generally ignored when not decried.[31]

Considering, then, not the influence of Hobbes alone but of the Hobbesian tradition thus defined, how liberal is American constitutionalism? From the vantage of the early twenty-first century, we are likely to exaggerate its importance at the Founding and to overlook the later choices in American political development that edged us closer to a Hobbesian state. Today Hobbes's account of the desiring self with its own definition of good and evil seems an apt description of the modern individual, and the chaotic social diversity that results is widely thought to require a strong if not an absolute state, sometimes by conservatives who fear the breakdown of social order, sometimes by liberals annoyed either by the wide inequalities endemic in a market economy or by the continued authority of religion in an enlightened age. At the time of the Founding, by contrast, the fruits of such liberalism were less apparent even if the seeds were already in the ground. To be sure, Locke's account of a right to revolution is drawn upon, sometimes verbatim, in the Declaration of Independence, but even then that document is significantly clearer than Locke ever was in anchoring natural rights in the law of the Creator, and Locke's latent hostility to the Bible is uncommon in the nineteenth-century American mainstream. As for Rousseau, one can find echoes in the early republic of his idea of the constitutive authority of a sovereign people and of his celebration of a founding legislator, but it is harder to find anyone eager to call for "total alienation" of all one's natural rights to the state, much less anyone who promoted a small community in the name of democracy rather than the "manifest destiny" of a large republic once the Anti-Federalists had gone down in defeat. In none of the philosophers of the modern state does one find the respect for religious or, for that matter, philosophic conscience that goes beyond mere toleration to full and equal citizenship, as Washington described it,[32] and thus a genuine openness to political development that can resist as well as embrace continuous modernization. And that brings us back to the question of the relation of the American constitutionalism to the Platonic tradition in philosophy.

My account of an American consensus on constitutional principles and practices—one that allows for the diversity that liberty of conscience on truly first principles encourages—suggests that certain commitments are indeed un-American in the sense that no one who holds them can honestly support the Constitution: Absolute monarchists, Nazis, Communists, violent jihadists, and since the Civil War, aristocratic slaveholders cannot honestly take the oath of citizenship, and there is no bigotry in recognizing this fact and seeing those who hold such beliefs as political enemies of constitutional government. To be sure, Americans have often been confident enough of the cogency of our constitutional tradition and of its overwhelming support among the people to allow advocates of such positions the toleration we accord to more ordinary political opponents. In Jefferson's words, "If there be any among us who would wish to dissolve this Union or to change its republican form, let them stand undisturbed as monuments of the safety with which error of opinion may be tolerated where reason is left free to combat it."[33] Still, it remains possible to distinguish friends and enemies even of our nonregimented regime, and it is easy enough to imagine circumstances—related, for example, to immigration policy or to war—where the distinction might be prudently drawn. Call this, perhaps, a Platonic moment in our politics, for the argument of the *Republic* never wholly abandons the distinction between friends and enemies in the discussion of justice with which, in the definition offered by Polemarchus, it practically began.[34]

Second, as I suggested earlier, the underlying reasons for the constitutional consensus are likely to be dynamic, as new groups immigrate at the invitation or with the acquiescence of older populations and as demographics shift, as education changes, as intellectual life varies and develops, as people win each other over by argument and dialectic, or win over the young, who are actively looking for truth by which to orient their lives. Socrates' city in the *Republic* is not dynamic, except in the account of political decay in books eight and nine, and in the *Laws* change is permitted only through the mediation of the Nocturnal Council and thus not openly, lest respect for law and authority be undermined. Platonic philosophy and American practice thus differ dramatically on the question of stability and change, but perhaps they share a political insight: if opposite consequences arise from opposite forms, the human capacities that are the cause might be the same.

In describing Americans as free by virtue of liberty of conscience from subscribing to a common civic creed or political religion, I am not saying that people can live well without deep reasons—rather that they must claim those reasons for themselves, not be required to utter them without belief. The boldness of America is to suppose that even ordinary people mean to live their lives in the light of the truth—not only their private lives, but their lives as citizens. The alternative is the Platonic world of noble lies, and we insist that we eschew them. We have the right to bear witness to our convictions (call them knowledge, call them faith) as we deliberate public policy, a right that tends toward civility in its exercise (if not compromise of forthrightness) when there is a need to persuade or to build a winning coalition, and perhaps that tends towards overstatement (another kind of untruth) by the desire to gain attention in a crowded and noisy world. Moreover, we have the right to translate our comprehensive beliefs ourselves in politics, without asking permission from professors or other authorities who monitor what is politically correct. The reward and the challenge of political liberty consist in thinking and speaking for oneself and accepting the consequences.

What does all this mean for the relation of Plato's *Republic* to the American Founding? As I tried to explain earlier, I am wary of too easy a synthesis, for example, to say that Americans, or their liberal political philosopher-teachers Hobbes and Locke, solved the problem of the relation of philosophy and the city that the *Republic* and the *Apology* might be said to have posed, allowing philosophers full freedom of speech alongside many other claimants, and allowing them to prove the superiority of their claims by the benefits they invent for human life. In the dialectic between the sects and the parties, does the search for truth get lost in political competition? Do our consciences relax too quickly because of our surfeit of choice? Can we really, without risk of corruption, take seriously a book like the *Republic* that calls into question the almost-first principles on which our constitutionalism rests? Can we prepare the most talented among the young for the responsibilities of citizenship and the call of statesmanship by cultivating a form of wisdom that transcends self-interest and ambition? If we can face these questions in practice, that is because Platonic political philosophy and American constitutionalism share the virtue of magnanimity, a heightened generosity or greatness of soul. Like any true virtue, it is no mere abstract pattern, but ought to be embodied in a real person and in the actions of an actual life. Magnanimity is said to be a virtue of great statesmen, but I think it is as well a virtue of great teachers, or at least a virtue that they teach, for they often deflect to others the honors that a magnanimous man is said to claim for himself. I do not doubt that the authors of the essays here collected would get into a big argument if we tried to identify a living magnanimous statesman, but we have seen and heard and felt that virtue in our great teacher and true friend.

Notes

1. Aletnative citation: Adams to Jefferson, July 16, 1814, DLC Jefferson Papers; printed in Lester J. Cappon, ed., *The Adams-Jefferson Letters*, 2:437.
2. Allan Bloom, trans., *The Republic of Plato*, 592b.
3. James Madison, *Notes of Debates in the Federal Convention of 1787*, 287.
4. Ibid., 477–478.
5. Alexander Hamilton, John Jay, James Madison, *The Federalist*, ed. George W. Carey and James McClellan, no. 10, p. 44.
6. Thomas Pangle, trans., *The Laws of Plato*.
7. *Republic*, book III, 414d ff.
8. On the contrast between the classical and the commercial republic, see Paul A. Rahe, *Republics Ancient and Modern: Classical Republicanism and the American Revolution*.
9. *Republic*, cf. books II and III with book VII.
10. On the role of Abraham Lincoln incorporating the principles of the Declaration of Independence into Americans' understanding of the Constitution, see Harry V. Jaffa, *Crisis of the House Divided: An Interpretation of the Issues in the Lincoln-Douglas Debates*.
11. See Rawls, *A Theory of Justice*, 340, and *Political Liberalism*, expanded ed., Lecture IV.
12. Thomas Hobbes, *Leviathan*, ch. 31, end.
13. Ibid., ch. 4, 46. Hobbes's admiration for Plato is noted in Leo Strauss, *The Political Philosophy of Thomas Hobbes: Its Basis and Its Genesis*, ch. 8.
14. *Leviathan*, intro.

15. Ibid., ch. 13.
16. Ibid., ch. 5.
17. Ibid., ch. 19.
18. Thomas Hobbes, *Man and Citizen.*
19. *Leviathan*, ch. 13.
20. Ibid., ch. 34, 46.
21. Ibid., ch. 11.
22. Ibid., ch. 8.
23. Ibid., ch. 15.
24. Ibid., ch. 14.
25. Ibid., ch. 8.
26. Ibid., ch. 5.
27. Cf. *Leviathan*, ch. 29, with *The Federalist*, no. 47–48.
28. Richard Schlatter, ed., *Hobbes's Thucydides.*
29. See *Leviathan*, ch. 15, 26; Thomas Hobbes, *A Dialogue between a Philosopher and a Student of the Common Laws of England.*
30. Scholars differ widely on the relation of Hobbes and Locke. I discuss the matter at greater length in my *Common Law and Liberal Theory: Coke, Hobbes, and the Origins of American Constitutionalism*, ch. 8.
31. See ibid., ch. 10. Also Paul O. Carrese, *The Cloaking of Power: Montesquieu, Blackstone, and the Rise of Judicial Activism.*
32. "Letter to the Hebrew Congregation in Newport," August 1790, in William B. Allen, ed., *George Washington: A Collection*, 548.
33. Thomas Jefferson, First Inaugural Address, in James D. Richardson, ed., *A Compilation of the Messages and Papers of the Presidents, 1789–1897*, 322–323.
34. See Leo Strauss, *The City and Man*, ch. 2.

Bibliography

Allen, William B., ed. *George Washington: A Collection*, Indianapolis: Liberty Fund, 1988.

Bloom, Allan, trans. *The Republic of Plato.* New York: Basic Books, 1968.

Cappon, Lester J., ed. *The Adams-Jefferson Letters.* 2 vols. Chapel Hill, 1957.

Carrese, Paul O. *The Cloaking of Power: Montesquieu, Blackstone, and the Rise of Judicial Activism.* Chicago: University of Chicago Press, 2003.

Hamilton, Alexander, John Jay, and James Madison. *The Federalist.* Edited by George W. Carey and James McClellan. Indianapolis: Liberty Fund, 2001.

Hobbes, Thomas. *A Dialogue between a Philosopher and a Student of the Common Laws of England.* Edited by Joseph Cropsey. Chicago: University of Chicago Press, 1971.

————. *Man and Citizen.* Edited by Bernard Gert, Indianapolis: Hackett, 1991; orig. 1642.

————. *Leviathan.* Cambridge: Cambridge University Press, 1996; orig. 1651.

Jaffa, Harry V. *Crisis of the House Divided: An Interpretation of the Issues in the Lincoln-Douglas Debates.* New York: Doubleday, 1959.

Madison, James. *Notes of Debates in the Federal Convention of 1787.* Edited by Adrienne Koch. Athens: Ohio University Press, 1985.

Pangle, Thomas, trans. *The Laws of Plato.* Chicago: University of Chicago Press, 1988.

Rahe, Paul A. *Republics Ancient and Modern: Classical Republicanism and the American Revolution.* Chapel Hill: University of North Carolina Press, 1992.

Rawls, John. *A Theory of Justice.* Cambridge, MA: Harvard University Press, 1971.

————. *Political Liberalism,* expanded ed. New York: Columbia University Press, 2005.

Richardson, James D., ed. *A Compilation of the Messages and Papers of the Presidents, 1789–1897.* Washington, DC: Government Printing Office, 1896, vol. 1.

Schlatter, Richard, ed. *Hobbes's Thucydides.* New Brunswick, NJ: Rutgers University Press, 1975.

Stoner Jr., James R. *Common Law and Liberal Theory: Coke, Hobbes, and the Origins of American Constitutionalism.* Lawrence: University of Kansas Press, 1992.

Chapter 9

Adam Smith's Invisible Hands

Peter Minowitz

I first read Adam Smith in a seminar co-taught by Murray Dry and Paul Nelson in 1976.[1, 2] Although attentive to the implications old texts can have for contemporary controversies, these unforgettable Middlebury teachers strove to understand every author "as he understood himself." Regarding Smith, their approach helped me appreciate how his pioneering efforts as an economist were rooted in philosophy, history, and other disciplines; they likewise illuminated the complexity of Smith's rhetoric and the fastidiousness of his prose. In the 225 years that have elapsed since Smith's death, alas, he has regularly been extolled or excoriated by commentators who fail to study him with sufficient care.

This chapter examines the invisible hand, Smith's most famous phrase, which came to symbolize the economic processes that help societies prosper in ways that individuals neither intend nor comprehend—and which continues to be marshaled in vituperative debates about the proper scope of economic regulation. My primary target is an article on Smith that appeared in an exalted academic venue, the *Journal of Political Economy*—via the pen of William D. Grampp, one of our nation's most venerable historians of economic thought.[3] If the invisible hand is too subtle for Grampp, perhaps we can be more forgiving of presidential candidate Mitt Romney's musings,[4] not to mention the accounts issued by contemporary journalists.[5]

Grampp poses the long-disputed question, "What Did Adam Smith Mean by the Invisible Hand?" and proceeds to answer it presumptuously. In trying to constrain the reach of Adam Smith's invisible hand, he offers this summary of what it is—and what it is not:

> [T]he invisible hand does have a consequence that is unintended, but the consequence is not a beneficial social order. It is a benefit that, while important, is of a lesser order. It is to contribute to the defense of the nation. It is nothing so complex and so grand as the social order or the price mechanism within it.[6]

Grampp merits approbation for his sensitivity to puzzles that are often neglected and for warning against the common tendency to "see" an invisible hand any time Smith argues against governmental regulation. Grampp imaginatively confronts some widely held views, wisely reminds us of Smith's departures from *laissez-faire*, and courageously accuses Smith of forgetfulness, inconsistency, implausibility, irrelevance, and other shortcomings. Unfortunately, Grampp also conveys oversimplifications, exaggerations, and distortions that represent a long backward step in Smith studies.[7]

To combat Grampp's iconoclastic agenda, I offer a detailed elaboration of Smith's three references to an invisible hand. After criticizing Grampp's attempt to narrow the grasp of the invisible hand within *An Inquiry into the Nature and Causes of the Wealth of Nations* (*WN*), I turn to his account of the invisible hand in Smith's other book, *The Theory of Moral Sentiments* (*TMS*).[8] Although Grampp's interpretation of this book errs palpably, it raises questions that can help us fathom the long-disputed tension between *Moral Sentiments* (1759), which extols God along with love and benevolence, and *Wealth of Nations* (1776), which expels God and emphasizes self-interest; this religious contrast mirrors the earlier book's more optimistic perspective on the poor and its more ambivalent evaluation of "riches and power." I conclude by addressing the posthumously published essay in which Smith attributes belief in invisible hands to superstitious "savages" and thus seems to impugn the appeals to an invisible hand in his own books. Although Grampp is wise to stress the inconsistencies, exaggerations, and enigmas that Smith bequeathed to his readers, some of Grampp's criticisms are glib, and he deserves blame for trivializing the invisible hand. The invisible hands, I maintain, not only illuminate the rhetorical strategies that helped Smith influence institutions and public policies; they also signal his commitment to promoting curiosity and inquiry.

"In Many Other Cases"

However tempting it is to regard the invisible hand as a metaphor/ simile for Smith's whole project, Grampp prudently focuses our attention on the precise context in which the invisible hand manifests itself. He concludes that the invisible hand does *not* have "a principal place" or even a "salient" one in *Wealth of Nations*.[9]

The key chapter—"Of Restraints upon the Importation from foreign Countries of such Goods as can be produced at Home" (IV.ii)— is the first of a series in Book IV that criticize mercantilist policies. Here are the three sentences that launched the invisible hand:

> As every individual . . . endeavours as much as he can both to employ his capital in the support of domestick industry, and so to direct that industry that its produce may be of the greatest value; every individual necessarily labours to render the annual revenue of the society as great as he can. He generally, indeed, neither intends to promote the publick interest, nor knows how much he is promoting it. By preferring the support of domestick to that of foreign industry, he intends only his own security; and by directing that industry in such a manner as its produce may be of the greatest value, he intends only his own gain, and he is in this, as in many other cases, led by an invisible hand to promote an end which was no part of his intention.[10]

For Grampp, the unintended public benefit that the invisible hand promotes is the *domestic* build-up of capital.[11] His abstract goes so far as to assert that Smith's invisible hand is "simply" the "inducement a merchant has to keep his capital at home, thereby increasing the domestic capital stock and enhancing military power."[12]

Earlier in the chapter, Smith laments that import restrictions create monopolies (for domestic producers) that channel a society's capital in suboptimal ways. The typical reader of *Wealth of Nations* understands Smith's point that a capital owner, by directing his industry "in such a manner as its produce may be of the greatest value . . . intends only his own gain." Grampp is right to observe that this chapter emphasizes the owner's incentives to deploy capital domestically. Smith states that, upon "equal or nearly equal profits," any wholesale merchant "naturally prefers the home-trade to the foreign trade of consumption, and the foreign trade of consumption to the carrying trade." Smith offers several plausible reasons in explaining the merchant's posture: among other things, the merchant can more easily know "the laws of the country from which he must seek redress" and "the character and situation" of the people he has to rely on.[13]

Grampp carefully summarizes nine ways that scholars have interpreted the invisible hand; he faults all of them for perceiving an invisible hand in other situations Smith describes whereby someone "intends only his own gain" but ends up producing benefit to others. For Grampp, by contrast, an invisible hand "guides a merchant only when circumstances induce him to keep his capital at home."[14] One prominent obstacle Grampp must confront is Smith's statement that an invisible hand operates "in many other cases" to promote an end that the relevant agent did not intend. Grampp's response is unpersuasive, not least because it is convoluted:

> Does the word "cases" mean there are transactions, other than placing capital in competitive domestic trade, that add to domestic wealth and to defense? Or does "cases" mean that transactions that place capital in domestic trade contribute to something other than defense, for example, to what he calls elsewhere the "greatness" of the nation? Or does the word have all three meanings?[15]

Let me offer a guess about what Grampp here envisions as the *three* "meanings" that "cases" can have: capital allocated to competitive domestic trade; other "transactions" that promote domestic wealth and defense; capital, allocated to competitive domestic trade, that contributes to national greatness or another public end (beyond national defense).

I credit Grampp for emphasizing the rhetorical weight Smith puts, in the build-up to the invisible hand, on fear of capital flight, but Grampp neglects three aspects of the chapter that inspire many readers to conceive the invisible hand more broadly. First, although the paragraph emphasizes the allocation of capital—an activity that some people, for example, "those who live by wages,"[16] are not equipped to undertake—the quoted section begins with two references to "every individual," including the remarkable claim that "every individual" (not just every merchant or investor) "necessarily labours to render the annual revenue of the society as great as he can." Second, the paragraph concludes with Smith stating, "I have never known much good done by those who affected to trade for the publick good."[17] If Grampp's interpretation were correct, the paragraph should instead conclude with Smith saying, "I have never known much good done by those who affected to trade to augment domestic capital and thereby promote national defense." By here questioning the accomplishments of individuals who claimed that they were trading to promote "the publick good" generally, Smith suggests that an invisible hand may operate to produce a *variety* of public benefits.[18] The conclusion of the paragraph establishes a contrast between the failure of merchants who intended to promote the common interest and the success of merchants who intended to promote only their own interests. Third, a few pages earlier the chapter seems to anticipate the invisible hand with a paragraph that ignores the distinction between domestic and foreign investment:

> Every individual is continually exerting himself to find out the most advantageous employment for whatever capital he can command. It is his own advantage, indeed, and not that of the society, which he has in view. But the study of his own advantage naturally, or rather necessarily leads him to prefer that employment which is most advantageous to the society.[19]

Smith does proceed to elaborate the two prongs that Grampp stresses: that "home" is "the center, if I may say so, round which the capitals of the inhabitants of every country are continually circulating, and towards which they are always tending";[20] and that in pursuit of profit the owner will seek to maximize the productivity of his capital.

In the paragraph that immediately follows the invisible hand, Smith provides another strongly worded claim that reinforces his commitment to economic liberty:

> What is the species of domestick industry which his capital can employ, and of which the produce is likely to be

of the greatest value, *every* individual, it is evident, can, in his local situation, judge *much* better than *any* statesman or lawgiver can do for him. The stateman [*sic*], who should attempt to direct private people in what manner they ought to employ their capitals, would not only load himself with a most unnecessary attention, but assume an authority which could safely be trusted, not only to no single person, but to no council or senate whatever, and which would nowhere be so dangerous as in the hands of a man who had folly and presumption enough to fancy himself fit to exercise it.[21]

Thus, even in the immediate context that Grampp emphasizes, Smith provides ample provocation for extending the application of the invisible hand. At several points, ironically, Grampp himself offers a ridiculously universalized statement, as if led by Smith's authorial hand to overuse the word "every" and thus exaggerate the scope of the invisible hand's benevolence. According to Grampp, Smith summons the invisible hand when describing a "condition . . . in which a man who intends to benefit only himself in a particular way may, in the act of procuring that benefit, produce a benefit of a different kind for *everyone* including himself."[22] Even confining our attention to the domestic front, it is difficult to specify a commercial transaction that would yield a benefit for a nation's entire population. Smith in IV.ii indeed uses a variety of terms in describing large groupings of people and praises what "every" *individual* can contribute by seeking profitable investments.[23] But the words "everyone" and "everybody" never appear. The chapter ends, moreover, with Smith lamenting that the "private interests of many individuals"—along with "the prejudices of the publick"—constitute an insuperable obstacle to "the freedom of trade" being fully "restored" (!) in Great Britain.[24]

Grampp speaks more carefully later when he states that the merchant who keeps his capital at home promotes the "interest of everyone" because "domestic wealth is a resource on which the nation can draw to defend itself."[25] The exaggeration remains— aren't there usually *some* inhabitants in a society whose "interests" are promoted when it is *less* able to defend itself?—but Grampp's emphasis on national defense can remind us of a more important point. Nations often wield their military strength to devastate *foreigners*.

"The Ordinary Revolutions of War and Government"

Although Grampp ignores the destructiveness of war when he re-peatedly invokes the benefit the invisible hand brings to "everyone," military considerations are (as noted earlier) central to his argument. He elaborates that the individual profiled in the invisible-hand para-graph would understand how keeping his capital at home boosts domestic employment and output. The consequence the capital-owner would *not* fathom is the possible augmentation of his nation's *power*.[26] How does Grampp make military power so important, given the absence of any reference to military affairs in the passages from *Wealth of Nations* we have examined?

One key premise is the claim, issued later in the invisible-hand chapter, that defense is "of much more importance than opulence";[27] Smith issues this claim while defending trade restrictions that pro-mote an industry "necessary for the defence of the country." Smith here defends the Navigation Act, which, although economically harmful, boosted the number of Britain's sailors and ships;[28] in his later chapter on government's expenses/duties (V.i), Smith empha-sizes that "the great expence of firearms gives an evident advantage to the nation which can best afford that expense"[29] and he laments the decay of "martial spirit" in commercial societies like Britain. To these passages (and others like them),[30] Grampp adds considerations he admits are only inferences. Apparently drawing on the invisible-hand paragraph's invocation of the capital owner's "security," Grampp infers that domestic capital is more "secure" than capital held abroad because it can more easily or reliably be marshaled to "support" defense (by funding military expenditures, one presumes).[31] But when Smith in his earlier chapter on "the natural progress of opu-lence" describes the differences in security among capital invested in land (highest), manufacturing (middle), and foreign commerce (lowest), his focus is on the situation of the *owner*, not the nation.[32]

Although Grampp may here go astray by confounding the nation's security with the merchant's, he is on much firmer ground when he invokes the grim conclusion of *Wealth of Nations*, Book III.[33] Smith here says that the capital "acquired to any country" via either manu-facturing or foreign commerce is a "very precarious and uncertain possession" until part of it has been "secured and realized in the culti-vation and improvement of its lands."[34] As Grampp highlights, Smith's focus here is on *national* security; Smith proceeds to remind his readers that a merchant "is not necessarily the citizen of any particular country" and to assert that "a very trifling disgust" will cause a merchant to move his capital (and the industry it supports) from "one country to another." The "ordinary revolutions of war and government easily dry up the sources of that wealth which arises from commerce only." Yet even the "more solid improvements of agriculture" can be destroyed, as happened during the fall of the Roman Empire, by "a century or two" of barbarian depredations. The development of firearms ameliorates this danger, but leaves others in its wake.[35]

I concede that it is easy to overlook some of the striking claims Smith makes on behalf of national-security issues, and that Grampp provides a major service by arguing for the connection between defense and the invisible hand. But if, as Grampp asserts, "the leading proposition of Smith's economic policy" is that "defense is more important than wealth,"[36] why didn't Smith title his book, *An Inquiry into the Nature and Causes of the Defence of Nations*? If his main focus had been on military power, why would Smith offer his knowledge to all "nations" indiscriminately? It is possible, albeit unlikely, that most nations could be well defended, but military power also includes offensive capabilities; and millions of people have believed that economic liberty as touted by Smith serves to benefit some nations at the expense of other nations. Smith concedes that although "the wealth of a neighbouring nation" is "certainly advantageous in trade," it is "dangerous in war and politicks."[37] In Book IV, Smith persistently attacks what he alleges are the zero-sum aspects of mercantilism—its agendas for imperialism and colonization (588, 613, 626–627), its obsession with self-sufficiency (435, 456–457, 458, 493, 538–539) and "the balance of trade" (431–432, 450, 488–489, 642), its appeals to "national prejudice" and "national animosity" (474, 475, 494, 495, 496, 503), and its premise that trading nations advance their "interest" by "beggaring all their neighbours" (493). His alternative is the "freedom of trade" (433, 464, 469, 580) that would allow many nations, if not all, collectively to advance "the accommodation and conveniency of the species" (30) and "the business of mankind" (592) via "the mutual communication of knowledge and of all sorts of improvements which an extensive commerce from all countries to all countries naturally, or rather necessarily, carries along with it" (627). He asserts, perhaps implausibly, that foreign trade is continually occupied in performing "great and important services" and providing "great benefit" to *all* of the participating countries.[38] He once even describes the typical smuggler as a man who "would have been in every respect, an excellent citizen, had not the laws of his country made that a crime which nature never meant to be so."[39]

Departing from Grampp, most scholars would locate "the leading proposition of Smith's economic policy" at the conclusion of Book IV. In here providing his most complete overview of the "system of natural liberty," Smith proclaims that "no human wisdom or knowledge could ever be sufficient" to provide the "sovereign" with the capability of "superintending the industry of private people" and "directing it towards the employments most suitable to the interest of the society."[40] For Grampp, Smith uses the invisible hand to discourage governments from trying to prevent merchants from investing their *capital* abroad. But Smith's reference here to "the industry of private people" should remind us that Smith also vigorously tried to discourage governments from "directing" the allocation of *labor*. The following passage is particularly vivid:

> The patrimony of a poor man lies in the strength and dexterity of his hands; and to hinder him from employing this strength and dexterity in what manner he thinks proper without injury to his neighbour, is a plain violation of this most sacred property. It is a manifest encroachment upon the just liberty both of the workman, and of those who might be disposed to employ him. . . . The affected anxiety of the law-giver lest they should employ an improper person, is evidently as impertinent as it is oppressive.[41]

According to Smith, the system of natural liberty would have a dramatic impact in harnessing "[t]he natural effort of *every* individual to better his own condition" (540), indeed, "the natural effort which *every* man is *continually* making to better his own condition" (674) [emphasis added]—not just the natural effort of merchants involved in foreign trade.

"The Economy of Greatness"

Although the invisible hand surfaces only once in *Wealth of Nations*, the book is pervaded by the prospect of an unseen agency—perhaps an unseen intelligence—that constructively channels the behavior of self-interested individuals and should deter political elites from being overly intrusive. In the aforementioned passages—and in countless others—Smith invokes *nature* as the principle or authority to which such leaders should defer.[42] To the hordes who condemn Smith for speaking of "natural" liberty—and especially for painting it in such an optimistic light—*The Theory of Moral Sentiments* might be even more objectionable because it portrays nature as exuding both power and benevolent purpose. *Moral Sentiments*, like *Wealth of Nations*, includes one reference to an invisible hand. Only in *Moral Sentiments*, however, does Smith attribute the invisible hand to Providence and speak frequently of nature's "wisdom," which he links with God. Only in this book does Smith invite the reader to imagine an invisible *hand* that fulfills the intentions of a superhuman being—and that shows particular care for the poor. Only in this book does Smith hint that people will be neither happy nor moral unless they believe in an afterlife, and only here does Smith ridicule "power and riches" as "trinkets of frivolous utility."[43] Grampp, alas, fails to convey these momentous contrasts between the two books—and he misreads the paragraph that presents the invisible hand.

In treating the *Moral Sentiments* invisible hand, Grampp does accurately recount the starting point. Smith is arguing that mankind has consistently survived and progressed despite pronounced inequality. A "proud and unfeeling landlord" may exult in his ownership of "extensive fields," but he cannot *eat* any more of the produce than can "the meanest peasant." Smith proceeds to argue that the soil "maintains at all times nearly that number of inhabitants which it is capable of maintaining." Shifting his attention from the landlord, Smith claims that "the rich" get to eat *better*, but not much *more*, than the poor eat;[44] despite their "natural selfishness and rapacity" and their "vain and insatiable desires," the rich end up sharing:

> They are led by an invisible hand to make nearly the same distribution of the necessaries of life which would have been made had the earth been divided into equal portions among all its inhabitants; and thus, without intending it, without knowing it, advance the interest of the society and afford means to the multiplication of the species.[45]

Grampp acknowledges key similarities between this invisible hand and the one in *Wealth of Nations*: each has a "favorable connotation," presumably because each "leads the selfish to help others and to help them without a cost to themselves."[46] He is right to challenge the plausibility of the *Moral Sentiments* version, but he ignores the disturbing lessons suggested by the surrounding material, and he goes embarrassingly astray in laying out the particulars.

When he attempts to specify the effects the invisible hand has on the rich, Grampp offers a fantasy:

> They imagine there is no limit to what they can enjoy and so order whole harvests to be brought to them. They then discover "the eye is larger than the belly" and must find something to do with what they cannot use themselves. And what is it? They give it to the poor. . . .[47]

For Grampp, this invisible hand thus differs from the *Wealth of Nations* hand because the relevant self-interest calls to mind "dumbbells who buy more than they can use and find themselves giving away much of it." The stupid landlords, furthermore, "never learn"—otherwise "there would be only one redistribution," after which "there would be no leftovers for the poor" and the invisible hand's work would be done.[48]

If Grampp had scrutinized merely the paragraph in which the invisible hand appears, he could have provided a far superior elaboration. Smith states clearly that the landlord distributes the surplus food to the people who *prepare* the food "he himself makes use of," to those who "fit up the palace" in which he dines, and to anyone else who provides or maintains "all the different baubles and trinkets, which are employed in the oeconomy of greatness."[49] Whether the relevant nonlandlords are workers, servants, serfs, slaves, offspring, or wives, the reader confronts an ongoing "oeconomy"—a word Smith rarely uses in *Moral Sentiments*—of *exchange*, not a one-time *gift* from a dim-witted landlord who initially thought he could consume the entire produce of his land. The reader also encounters an invisible hand that advances, via the "natural selfishness" of various individuals, "the interest of the society" and the propagation of the species—an invisible hand that harmonizes with most of the broad interpretations of *Wealth of Nations* that Grampp is criticizing.

As we have seen, Grampp lambastes *Moral Sentiments* partly because of his inference that the landlords are idiots who keep biting off more than they can chew and then disgorging the residue. Grampp and countless other readers, furthermore, are skeptical about Smith's claims that the distribution of "the necessaries of life" is "nearly" the same as it would have been if the earth were "divided into equal portions among all its inhabitants"—and that the soil *at all times* maintains "nearly that number of inhabitants which it is capable of maintaining." So let us dig deeper into the chronological foci of Smith's account.

The aforementioned remarks quoted and paraphrased are all in the present tense: the landlord "views" his large fields and the rich "select" the choicest produce, while the poor "derive" all that they need to subsist. The paragraph also begins in the present tense: "And it is well that nature imposes upon us in this manner."[50] To fathom *this* claim, however, we must address profound issues that Grampp's article ignores—and that Smith scholarship often depreciates.

Two paragraphs earlier in this short chapter (Part IV, chapter 1), Smith sketches the tragic fate of "[t]he poor man's son, whom heaven in its anger has visited with ambition." Abandoning the "real tranquility" that was "at all times in his power," the son endures a lifetime of study, toil, fatigue, worry, obsequiousness, and betrayal. As death approaches, he finally learns that wealth and greatness are "mere trinkets of frivolous utility, no more adapted for procuring ease of body or tranquillity of mind" than the tweezers-cases lugged around by "the lover of toys."[51] Smith now broadens his focus to explain why the palaces, gardens, equipage, and retinue of "the great" stir up universal longing. Despite their frivolity, such trinkets captivate us because "that love of distinction so natural to man" is readily augmented by our tendency to become infatuated by the potency of the *things* (tools, machines, and "systems") that help us gratify our wishes.[52] Smith then expands the lesson he drew from the parable of the poor man's son. When a person's vanity is eclipsed by "the languor of disease and the weariness of old age," or when he is compelled by "either spleen or disease to observe with attention his own situation," power and riches will finally appear to be "what they are," namely:

> Enormous and operose machines contrived to produce a few trifling conveniencies to the body, consisting of springs the most nice and delicate, which must be kept in order with the most anxious attention, and which in spite of all our care are ready every moment to burst into pieces, and to crush in their ruins their unfortunate possessor. . . .

They keep off the summer shower, not the winter storm, but leave him always as much, and sometimes more, exposed than before, to anxiety, to fear, and to sorrow; to diseases, to danger, and to death.[53]

It must be emphasized that the two quasi-synonymous pairs of general terms that Smith here impugns—*wealth and greatness* as "trinkets of frivolous utility," and *riches and power* as "operose machines" that perpetually threaten to destroy their "unfortunate possessor"—are precisely the pairs that *Wealth of Nations* deploys to identify the "object" or "purpose" of political economy.[54] And political economy is the scientific genre into which Smith places *Wealth of Nations.*[55] In light of these and other complexities, Grampp deserves praise for accentuating the evasions and enigmas that help define Smith's legacy.[56]

One cannot resolve the trinkets conundrum by assuming that Smith underwent an epiphany after 1759, when the first edition of *Moral Sentiments* appeared. At the start of a chapter (I.iii.3) added for this work's final edition in 1790, fourteen years after the publication of *Wealth of Nations*, Smith wrote that the disposition to admire wealth and greatness is "the great and most universal cause of the corruption of our moral sentiments."[57]

Smith's depiction of wealth and greatness as trinkets becomes even more complex in the paragraph that follows the one that ridicules the "[e]normous and operose machines" and that immediately precedes the paragraph on the invisible hand. Smith associates his denunciation of wealth and greatness with a "splenetic philosophy," familiar to everyone in times of "sickness or low spirits," that views things in an "abstract and philosophical light." But he proceeds to say that the same objects—when we view them from the more "complex" perspective that emerges in times of ease and prosperity—will appear "grand," "beautiful," and "noble," and hence as worthy of "all the toil and anxiety" we typically bestow upon them.[58] Smith has provided clues, but he never directly mediates between the two competing perspectives: sick/old/philosophical versus healthy/young/prosperous.

The invisible-hand paragraph opens in the present tense: "it is well that nature imposes upon us in this manner." Smith labels the above-described infatuation with systems and machines a "deception," but lauds it because it "rouses and keeps in continual motion the industry of mankind";[59] Smith here speaks about phenomena that are contemporaneous to him (as he does a few sentences later when he discusses the landlord's fields and the invisible hand that assists the poor). He proceeds immediately, however, to celebrate the deception as the spring of human *progress*:

> It is this which first prompted them to cultivate the ground, to build houses, to found cities and common-wealths, and to invent and improve all the sciences and arts, which ennoble and embellish human life; which have entirely changed the whole face of the globe, have turned the rude forests of nature into agreeable and fertile plains, and made the trackless and barren ocean a new fund of subsistence, and the great high road of communication to the different nations of the earth.[60]

After adding the claim that the earth "by these labours of mankind has been obliged to redouble her natural fertility, and to maintain a greater multitude of inhabitants,"[61] Smith presents the invisible-hand scenario about the "proud and unfeeling landlord."

Let me summarize. Our population has grown because "nature" tricked us into labor that transforms the earth, partly by multiplying the earth's "natural" fertility. The invisible hand serves to maintain "the multiplication of the species" in the face of widespread landless-ness. Under both scenarios, we advance collectively despite two types of moral shortcomings: the selfishness, rapacity, callousness, vanity, and pride that tarnish the economic elite (landlords and "the rich"); and the "natural" and widespread "love of distinction" that can prompt even "the poor man's son" to sacrifice tranquillity and happi-ness in the frivolous pursuit of "trinkets."[62] Nature wields its power and achieves its ends in complex if not paradoxical ways. Adam Smith grasps the two disparate perspectives on wealth and greatness: the "splenetic" negative perspective and the "complex" positive one. Unlike the rich, he cares for the poor; unlike most of us (including the poor man's son afflicted by ambition), he is never intoxicated by the "trinkets of frivolous utility."[63]

Smith's contribution is philosophical, one may infer, since he fathoms the paradoxical truths about how everything fits together. His contribution is also rhetorical. By arguing that we are "led"— certainly some of the time, perhaps most of the time—by an invisible hand to ends we did not intend to promote, Smith reminds us that we are supreme in neither comprehension nor power. At the conclusion of IV.i, however, Smith does smile on certain efforts to promote broad public benefits. It turns out that our "love of system"—our attraction to the "beauty of order, art and contrivance," the attraction that helps wealth and greatness seduce us—can fruitfully be manipulated to "implant public virtue in the breast of him who seems heedless of the interest of his country." To do this, you could proceed by describing "the great system" of public policy that helps feed, clothe, and house "the subjects of a well-governed state." After explaining "the connections and dependencies of its several parts . . . and their general subservience to the happiness of the society," you could "show how this system might be introduced" into the selfish man's country, describing the current "obstructions" and how they might be removed so that "the wheels of the machine of government" would "move with more harmony and smoothness."[64] From Smith's point of view, obviously, *Wealth of Nations* is well suited to "implant public virtue" along these lines. But this book also calls on the invisible hand, and many powerful arguments, to inoculate kings, princes, legislators, and statesmen from the "innumerable delusions" that would afflict anyone who sought to superintend the "industry of private people."[65]

A similar warning, which particularly seems to challenge Part IV's suggestions about using the "love of system" to bolster civic virtue, suffuses some passages in Part VI of *Moral Sentiments*, which Smith added for the 1790 edition. People "intoxicated by the imaginary beauty" of an "ideal system," Smith now warns, often succumb to "the madness of fanaticism."[66] The "man of system" who ignores "the great interests" or "strong prejudices" that may oppose his "ideal plan of government," furthermore, treats people as "the hand arranges the different pieces upon a chess-board" (note the impact of a *visible* hand). Such a man fails to recognize that "in the great chess-board of human society, every single piece has a principle of motion of its own, altogether different from that which the legislature might chuse (*sic*) to impress upon it."[67]

"A Few Lordly Masters"

By invoking an invisible hand to drive home human shortcomings in power, wisdom, and virtue, Part IV of *Moral Sentiments* communicates a lesson that most religions emphasize. And in the sentence after the one that describes the invisible hand, Smith incorporates a divine presence missing from *Wealth of Nations*. As he did in the preceding sentences, Smith reassures his readers about the fate of the masses deprived of land (and power):

> When Providence divided the earth among a few lord-
> ly masters, it neither forgot nor abandoned those who
> seemed to have been left out in the partition. . . . In what
> constitutes the real happiness of human life, they are in no
> respect inferior to those who would seem so much above
> them. In ease of body and peace of mind, all the different
> ranks of life are nearly upon a level, and the beggar, who
> suns himself by the side of the highway, possesses that se-
> curity which kings are fighting for.[68]

Although Smith in *Wealth of Nations* does offer a friendly comment on "the Deity" that ancient Greek physicists investigated as a "part" of "the great system of the universe"—and a disparaging comment on the superstitious recourse to "gods"—he never mentions God or Providence, and he portrays nature in a less exalted light.[69] His grimmer posture toward the cosmos corresponds to his harsher ac-counts of starvation and land ownership. Regarding starvation, the introduction laments the plight of primitive "nations" that subsist via hunting and fishing. Even though almost every able-bodied person works, these societies are so poor that they sometimes are forced to kill infants, old folks, and people "afflicted with lingering diseases"—or to abandon such individuals "to perish with hunger, or to be devoured by wild beasts." In "civilized and thriving nations," by contrast, "all are often abundantly supplied" despite the "great num-ber" of persons who consume lavishly but do not work.[70]

In *Moral Sentiments*, Smith lauds the invisible hand of Providence for ensuring, in all times and places, that the human "species" sur-vives and multiplies. *Wealth of Nations* proceeds in a far more empiri-cal fashion. Smith depicts both starvation and famine. As in *Moral Sentiments*, however, Smith does *not* place the blame on the monopo-lization of land ownership by "a few lordly masters."[71] Hunger and mortality plague hunting/fishing societies, despite their egalitarian economic arrangements—there simply is no property that "exceeds the value of two or three days labour" and the "[u]niversal poverty establishes . . . universal equality."[72] Circumstances improve as society advances "naturally" into the three subsequent "periods" or "states":

herding/pasturage, agriculture, and commerce (trade and manufacturing). But the torments of our origins recur even in the last two stages.[73]

In his most detailed discussion of food shortages, Smith focuses on the experience of Europe during recent centuries. He concedes that "dearths" have arisen from "real scarcity" caused sometimes by "the waste of war" but more often by "the fault of the seasons"; such scarcity can be ameliorated but not eliminated.[74] By blaming the seasons for dearths, Smith is blaming nature. Famine, on the other hand, "has never arisen from any other cause but the violence of government attempting, by improper means, to remedy the inconveniences of a dearth."[75] By tracing famines to abusive governments, Smith paves the way for nature's remedy—the "unlimited, unrestrained freedom of the corn trade"—which is also the "best palliative" of dearths.[76]

When he discusses subsistence and propagation in general terms, beyond the current situation in Europe, Smith likewise leaves us with questions about how nature and human institutions interact. One dilemma society confronts is that, as "[e]very species of animals naturally multiplies in proportion to the means of their subsistence,"[77] prosperity causes childhood mortality to decrease, which eventually causes wages to decrease. In a stationary economy, the "great body of the people" merely subsist; in a decaying economy they die off.[78] Smith suggests China as an example of the stationary state. It "has long been one of the richest, that is, one of the most fertile, best cultivated, most industrious, and most populous countries in the world"; yet centuries before Smith's time, it had "perhaps . . . acquired that full complement of riches which the nature of its laws and institutions permits it to acquire."[79] In *all* of its "great towns," tragically, children are "every night exposed in the street, or drowned like puppies in the water." Furthermore, for the hundreds (perhaps thousands) of underfed people in Canton who live on rivers and canals in fishing boats—and are "eager to fish up the nastiest garbage" thrown overboard from a European ship—a putrid cat carcass is "as welcome . . . as the most wholesome food to the people of other countries."[80] Do *these* landless beggars sun themselves on the banks of the river and enjoy "that security which Kings are fighting for"? Does the invisible hand of Providence bring them "ease of body and peace of mind"? Did Smith ever really believe that "all" of "the works of nature" were intended to promote "[t]he happiness of mankind" and to "guard against misery"?[81]

The evolution of society beyond the hunting stage also introduces threats to the economically *advantaged*. Smith describes, in stark terms, the plight of the owner of valuable property acquired by the "labour of many years": he is "at all times surrounded by unknown enemies . . . from whose injustice he can be protected only by the powerful arm of the civil magistrate."[82]

Reading aloud the *Moral Sentiments* passage extolling the "real happiness" enjoyed by the beggar cannot neutralize the dangers economic inequality poses. Only in *Wealth of Nations* does Smith provide detailed explanations of how sustenance can trickle down from wealthy owners of land and capital. Consider first the herding stage: a "Tartar chief, the increase of whose herds and flocks is sufficient to maintain a thousand men," cannot exchange his surplus "rude produce" for "any manufactured produce, any trinkets and baubles." He therefore employs the surplus by "maintaining a thousand men," who in exchange can provide only obedience; the chief's authority becomes "altogether despotical."[83]

In its early moments, the agricultural stage features shepherd-like political arrangements: the "sovereign or chief" is simply "the greatest landlord of the country." One example is "our German and Scythian ancestors when they first settled upon the ruins of the western empire."[84] Smith elaborates this earlier, in Book III, where he provides his most detailed discussion of the relationship between lords and their subordinates. A "great proprietor" in feudal Europe, lacking access to foreign commerce and "the finer manufactures," consumed his entire surplus in "rustick hospitality" that in effect purchased the allegiance of servants along with a "multitude of retainers and dependents."[85] The feudal proprietor thus resembles the shepherd chief.

According to *Moral Sentiments*, Providence "divided the earth among a few lordly masters." This description could not apply to the hunting stage, as presented by *Wealth of Nations*, for two reasons: there are no lordly masters who own the land, and widespread poverty inhibits "the multiplication of the species."[86] As we have seen, however, the description does apply to the herding stage—except that the "masters" here monopolize herds rather than fixed tracts of land.[87] And the description applies to feudal arrangements in Europe that more or less represent the agricultural stage. But when Smith describes the origins of feudalism, he offers a cynical explanation that invokes neither nature nor Providence: "the chiefs and principal leaders" of the conquering Germans and Scythians simply "acquired or

usurped to themselves the greater part of the lands of those countries."[88] For many years thereafter, "the open country" in Europe was
a "scene of violence, rapine, and disorder."[89]

Nature and convention also interact complexly in Smith's account
of primogeniture and entails, institutions that helped certain lordly
masters to maintain monopolistic patterns of land ownership in
Europe. Under feudal conditions, primogeniture and entails "might
not be unreasonable," because large estates supported political
authority in "those disorderly times." Sustained by family pride even
in Smith's day, however, primogeniture and entails remained major
obstacles to the subdivision and commercialization necessary for full
agricultural development.[90] Primogeniture and entails surely belong
among the "human institutions" that the preceding chapter blamed
for having "disturbed the natural course of things" in Europe[91] and
for having "inverted" what the chapter title (III.i) identifies as "the
natural progress of opulence."[92]

Smith's account in Book III of the demise of feudalism and the
emergence of commercial society draws on elements of both invisible
hands.[93] The power of the lords was "gradually" ended by "the silent
and insensible operation of foreign commerce and manufactures."
Whether or not a hand can be invisible, it can certainly be silent.
There are much stronger echoes, in any case. Once the lords had the
chance to purchase "frivolous and useless" items (e.g., diamond
buckles) that could be "all their own," they lost their disposition to
"share" their surplus, and thus "gradually bartered their whole power
and authority" for the sake of "the most childish, the meanest and the
most sordid of all vanities."[94] After completing the story by explaining how the lords similarly allowed their tenant *farmers* to become
independent, Smith observes that the "great proprietors" thus "sold
their birth-right, not like Esau for a mess of pottage in time of hunger
and necessity, but in the wantonness of plenty, for trinkets and baubles."[95] Smith speaks even more generally in the following, widely
cited passage:

> A revolution of the greatest importance to the publick
> happiness, was in this manner brought about by two dif-
> ferent orders of people, who had not the least intention
> to serve the publick. To gratify the most childish vanity
> was the sole motive of the great proprietors. The mer-
> chants and artificers, much less ridiculous, acted merely

from a view to their own interest, and in pursuit of their own pedlar principle of turning a penny wherever a penny was to be got. Neither of them had either knowledge or foresight of that great revolution which the folly of the one, and the industry of the other, was gradually bringing about.[96]

Grampp chides the scholars who see the invisible hand at work here, and is skeptical about whether we can specify the "relation" between the hand's two versions.[97] To me, there are obvious connections involving globalization, the monopolization of land, the contribution "trinkets and baubles" make in promoting public benefit via private vice, and the complex dialectics that infuse Smith's accounts of how nature shapes human morality, psychology, and institutions.[98]

Smith seems to define commercial society in the following terms: "[e]very man lives by exchanging, or becomes in some measure a merchant."[99] The fall of feudalism thus transformed rather than eliminated dependence. In modern Europe, each "tradesman or artificer derives his subsistence" from the employment of "a hundred or hundred thousand different customers"; though he is partly "obliged to them all," he is not "absolutely dependent" on any one;[100] in a "civilized" society, the division of labor renders *everyone* dependent on "the assistance and cooperation of many thousands."[101] Without intervention by government, furthermore, the division of labor threatens to annihilate the "intellectual, social, and martial virtues" among "the great body of the people."[102] Again, what became of the Providence that provides for the "real happiness" of the lowly?

Moral Sentiments does not employ the four-stages theory, although on several occasions it contrasts the harsh conditions of "savage" life with the ease of "civilized" circumstances.[103] In a section Smith added for the 1790 edition, he does offer a remarkable generalization that calls to mind passages from *Wealth of Nations* about modern Europe: in "commercial countries," the "authority of law is always perfectly sufficient to protect the meanest man in the state."[104]

Another dramatic echo of the invisible hand resonates in the subchapter of *Wealth of Nations* whose theme is religion. The medieval Church, Smith boldly suggests, was "the most formidable combination that ever was formed . . . against the liberty, reason, and happiness of mankind."[105] It controlled large tracts of land; like the lords, it gained political authority by distributing agricultural surpluses ("profuse hospitality" and "extensive charity"). Its power surpassed that of the lords for two reasons: its temporal force was accentuated by "spiritual weapons" and "the grossest delusions of superstition";[106] and it could act as "a sort of spiritual army, dispersed in different quarters," whose "movements and operations" were "directed by one head, and conducted upon one uniform plan."[107] This unprecedented "combination" eventually collapsed in the same way that the pernicious power of the barons did. Even though "all the wisdom and virtue of man" could never even have "shaken" it, nature—here, "the natural course of things"—again came to the rescue via the "gradual improvements of arts, manufactures, and commerce."[108] Contra Grampp, there are many reasons to think that Smith, in sketching the roots of modernity, incorporated some of the "many other cases" in which an invisible hand linked with commerce led a person to "promote" a beneficial "end which was no part of his intention."[109]

"Designing Power"

Readers of Smith encounter a third invisible hand—"the invisible hand of Jupiter"—in a posthumously published essay that Grampp expounds insightfully but briefly.[110] As we have seen, Smith sometimes presents sweeping claims that he himself may have regarded as exaggerations; in comparing *Wealth of Nations* and *Moral Sentiments*, I have suggested that Smith resorts to other types of rhetorical maneuvering (especially regarding the character of the agency or intelligence that the invisible hand embodies). The third manifestation of the invisible hand raises another set of questions about the relationship between Smith's two books, the way each of them blends science with rhetoric, and his posture toward religion. Smith bequeathed to the world a unique combination of lucid sentences and enigmatic books.[111]

Prior to 1759, when *Moral Sentiments* was published, Smith drafted three essays about "the principles which lead and direct philosophical enquiries."[112] The essay that is by far the longest addresses the history of astronomy. While discussing "the first ages of society," Smith contemptuously invokes the "the invisible hand of Jupiter" to illustrate the "pusillanimous superstition which ascribes almost every unexpected event, to the arbitrary will of some designing though invisible beings." Smith lists eclipses, thunder, lightning, comets, and meteors among the dazzling natural phenomena that people attributed to "intelligent, though invisible causes." People experienced *themselves* taking actions that altered the external world, and therefore imagined that a *divine* agency or "designing power" was responsible for the "irregular events" that surprised them. But even the primitive peoples who thought in such polytheistic terms—inhabiting a universe replete with gods, daemons, fairies, witches, and so on—did *not* perceive such entities acting to shape the "regular" phenomena of nature (e.g., the burning of fire and the falling of heavy bodies). Such events were part of "the ordinary course of things" that "went on of its own accord."[113]

In the short essay on the history of ancient physics, Smith likewise faults the superstitious primitives for positing "designing, though invisible" beings to explain "almost every unexpected event." As society progressed, fortunately, philosophy/science offered a superior vision (Smith equates philosophy and science), depicting the universe as "a complete machine . . . a coherent system, governed by general laws" that promote general ends: the preservation and prosperity of the system itself along with its various "species." Such a universe resembles the machines that human beings produce, and philosophers (e.g., Timaeus and Plato) introduced "the idea of a universal mind, of a God of all, who originally formed the whole, and who governs the whole by general laws, directed to the conservation and prosperity of the whole, without regard to that of any private individual."[114] By positing a God that created an orderly universe whose laws are friendly to "species," this theistic framework resembles the theology of *Moral Sentiments*, including Smith's Providential account of the invisible hand and his frequent appeals to nature's Author, Architect, Director, or Superintendent.[115]

Smith in *Wealth of Nations* nevertheless evicts God, however tempted he might have been to argue along the following lines: *human* rulers must avoid deploying the visible hand of the state too aggressively because there is a *divine* wisdom that "superintends" the universe and promotes the "interest" of groups (especially nations) despite the selfishness and other shortcomings of so many individuals. The non-human authority/standard that Smith does retain is nature, as manifested in his pitch for the "natural system of perfect liberty and justice" that would support the "natural progress of opulence," the "natural course of things," the "natural progress of things toward improvement," the "natural law of succession," the "natural

progress of law and government," the "natural effort of every individual to better his own condition," the "natural employments" of
industry and capital, the "natural division and distribution of labour,"
and so on.[116] As sketched earlier, Smith insists that no "human
wisdom" could equip "the sovereign" to superintend the industry of
private people.[117] Perhaps Smith abandoned theism in *Wealth of
Nations* partly because of the threat posed by human rulers who
restrict liberty while claiming access to some sort of divine wisdom.

Taken in isolation, however, the invisible hand of *Wealth of Nations*
suggests that Smith remained willing to appeal to a nonhuman intelligence that superintends the welfare of at least human "wholes" such
as societies (recall the philosopher's God that secures "the conservation and prosperity of the whole"). Smith in *Moral Sentiments* repeatedly invokes "the wisdom of nature," a phrase that highlights both
nature's intelligence and its capacity for "designing" (recall the distinction between the arbitrary "designing power" that superstitious
people project onto gods and the philosopher's God that "formed"
and "governs the whole").[118] But Smith mentions the wisdom of
nature only once in *Wealth of Nations*. When criticizing Physiocrats
who overestimate the importance of an "exact regimen of perfect liberty and justice," Smith likens the "political body" to the human body,
which contains "some unknown principle of preservation" that can
protect our health against flawed regimens; the "wisdom of nature"
can thus counteract "the folly and injustice of man."[119] By linking
nature's wisdom to the "principle of preservation" that protects *bodies*
(animal as well as human, one may infer), Smith signals another
departure from *Moral Sentiments*, where he presents a world that is
friendlier to human happiness, virtue, nobility, wisdom, love, benevolence, and tranquillity.

In Smith's two books, the invisible hand is *not* an entity that superstitious people imagine in trying to comprehend disorder and fright-
ening events; Smith formulates the phrase to help his
eighteenth-century (and beyond) readers see reassuring types of
societal *order*. Contra Grampp, the invisible hand does represent
something "so complex and so grand as the social order."[120]

Wealth of Nations innovates by depicting that order in totally secular terms. But by invoking an invisible hand that *leads* people (he
does not say that we are led "as if" by an invisible hand), Smith alludes
to divine action. He thus invites attentive readers to focus on the
book's treatment of religion, to notice the absence of God, and to

contemplate the viability of both atheistic (*WN*) and theistic (*TMS*) worldviews.[121] Only *Moral Sentiments* attributes an Author to nature, and some of the differences between the two books may signal that Smith has used "invisible" authorial skills to "lead" his readers, especially when he appeals to God or nature as *authorities*.[122]

Smith's essay on "the principles which lead and direct philosophical enquiries" incorporates rhetoric into its definition of science/philosophy. In a section that introduces his lengthy assessment of astronomy, Smith states that philosophy is "the science of the connecting principles of nature"; "by representing the invisible chains which bind together" the disjointed objects and events we encounter, philosophy tries to introduce order into the "chaos of jarring and discordant appearances," to restore the mind to "tranquility and composure."[123] Just as some readers of *Wealth of Nations* doubt the existence of an invisible hand that leads people to promote beneficial ends, some readers of the astronomy and physics essays may be led to doubt whether human beings can attain *knowledge* of invisible *chains* that allegedly unify the cosmos. Smith proceeds to describe the historical essays in the following terms: "Let us" examine the different philosophical systems "without regarding . . . their agreement or inconsistency with truth and reality." Smith will merely assess "how far each of them was fitted to sooth the imagination, and to render the theater of nature a more coherent, and therefore a more magnificent spectacle." This rhetorical dimension, he adds, is what determines whether the authors "succeeded in gaining reputation and renown"; no system could attain "general credit" unless its "connecting principles" were "familiar to all mankind."[124] After the long history of astronomy that culminates in effusive praise for the system of Isaac Newton, Smith concludes by apologizing, somewhat histrionically, for having ever implied that the "connecting principles" Newton presented were "the real chains which Nature makes use of to bind together her several operations."[125]

As a reformer confronting a variety of powerful prejudices and interests that would inspire opposition to the new system of political economy he offers to the world, Smith might have felt compelled to employ exaggeration, irony, and other tools of persuasion: "If the rod be bent too much one way, says the proverb, in order to make it straight you must bend it as much the other."[126] If "[a] philosopher is company to a philosopher only," a philosopher's books won't always broadcast all of the complexities and uncertainties that fill his or her mind.[127] In the 1790 edition of *Moral Sentiments*, Smith added praise of "the great wisdom of Socrates," the philosopher who remains renowned for identifying his wisdom with his *ignorance* concerning "the greatest things" and for proclaiming that "the unexamined life is not worth living."[128] In the *Astronomy* essay, furthermore, Smith emphasizes that human beings pursue philosophy "for its own sake," and that it began from "wonder" rather than from "any expectation of advantage from its discoveries."[129] Grampp may be wise in claiming that Smith's allegedly "obvious and simple system of natural liberty" is "neither simple nor systematic and is by no means meant for all markets."[130] But Grampp simply fails to appreciate how Smith's invocations of an invisible hand can lead a reader to *seek* wisdom— from God, nature, prophets, philosophers, or other sources. Centuries after Smith's death, we are still struggling to fathom a two-word phrase that stands out in a thousand-page book.

Notes

1. An earlier version of this essay was published online in *Econ Journal Watch* 1, no. 3 (December 2004): 381–412; it is reprinted here with the permission of this journal. I would like to thank Murray Dry, Dan Klein, William Sundstrom, and the late Joan Robins for their helpful assistance with the original version.

2. Smith later became the topic of my PhD thesis, a revised version of which was published as a book, *Profits, Priests, and Princes: Adam Smith's Emancipation of Economics from Politics and Religion*.

3. William D. Grampp, "What Did Adam Smith Mean by the Invisible Hand?," 441–465.

4. For criticism of Romney's comments on Smith, which invoked "the invisible hand of the market" to disparage "the heavy hand of government," see John Paul Rollert, "Sleight of the 'Invisible Hand,'" *New York Times*, October 21, 2012.

5. According to an article in the *New York Times*, Smith invoked the invisible hand to encapsulate the process whereby "the market omnisciently distributes goods and capital to maximize the benefits for all"; the article begins by arguing that the United States is shackled by the delusion that "the market is unfailingly wise." Peter S. Goodman, "The Free Market: A False Idol After All?" *New York Times*, December 30, 2007. In a similar spirit, James Buchan, writing in a Scottish newspaper, traced the invisible hand's prominence to "the rise of neo-conservative ideologies in the English-speaking

countries in the 1970s"; Buchan even asserts that the neo-conser-vative Adam Smith has "abolished" both history and morality. "The Fight for the Soul of Adam Smith," *Sunday Herald*, April 9, 2006. In his widely heralded book on Smith, Buchan denies that the invisible hand has "anything to do with free-market capitalism," 2. Another type of distortion is conveyed by Gus Tyler, who argues that *The Wealth of Nations* was intended to demonstrate God's benevolent will. "The Myth of Free Trade," *Dissent* (Spring 1988), 213. Writ-ing from the opposite end of the political spectrum, P.J. O'Rourke errs similarly, proclaiming that Smith (compared to both theism and deism) "believed in a more actively involved God" and that he "frequently depersonalized God by using the word *nature.*" See P.J. O'Rourke, 190–191.

6.   Grampp, "What Did Smith Mean?," 446.

7.   Grampp, who currently teaches at the University of Chicago, is pro-fessionally prominent in other important respects: there is a twen-ty-four-page chapter about him in *Historians of Economics and Eco-nomic Thought: The Construction of Disciplinary Memory*, eds. Steven G. Medema and Warren J. Samuels (Abingdon, Oxon: Routledge, 2001); Grampp's classic two-volume study, *Economic Liberalism*, is posted in the Online Library of Liberty; Grampp co-founded the His-tory of Economics Society and later served as its president. According to Google Scholar (in October 2014), his article on the invisible hand has been cited on 99 different occasions, and that is doubtless an un-dercount. The venue in which this article appeared, finally, is ranked in the top 2 percent of economics journals.

8.   For Smith's writings, I cite the Glasgow edition of the *Works and Correspondence of Adam Smith*, published by Oxford University Press (and later reprinted by Liberty Press).

9.   Grampp, "What Did Smith Mean?," 442.

10.   Adam Smith, *An Inquiry into the Nature and Causes of the Wealth of Nations*, 456.

11.   Grampp, "What Did Smith Mean?," 452.

12.   Ibid., 441.

13.   *Wealth of Nations*, 454.

14.   Ibid., 447.

15.   Grampp, "What Did Smith Mean?," 452.

16.   *Wealth of Nations*, 86, 266.

17.   Ibid., 456.

18.   When Smith, via the pronoun "I," makes himself conspicuous in his paragraph on an *invisible* hand—and when he invokes what he *knows* about consequences of which the immediate actors are *ignorant*—he encourages readers to pay special attention. It remains true that the

clause containing the invisible hand refers to "an end that was no part of his intention" without specifying that this end involves benefit to the *public*. This fact, however, supports the common view—that the invisible hand is a pivotal concept in *WN*—rather than Grampp's attempt to narrow the hand's grasp.

19. *Wealth of Nations*, 454.
20. Ibid., 455.
21. Ibid., 456 (emphasis added). Smith uses similar terminology later in Book IV when he states that "the law ought always to trust people with the care of their own interest, as in their local situations they must generally be able to judge better of it than the legislator can do" (ibid., 531). His main targets here, however, are laws that required farmers to sell their grain directly, without the intermediation of dealers; there's nothing about a merchant keeping his capital at home (Grampp, "What Did Smith Mean?," 447) and thus promoting national defense (ibid., 441, 443). Contra Grampp, it seems natural for the reader here to recall the invisible hand that Smith earlier invoked to discourage legislators from meddling.
22. Grampp, "What Did Smith Mean?," 443 (emphasis added).
23. In the previously discussed passage from *WN* IV.ii that anticipates the invisible hand, Smith himself exaggerates the public benefit that "every" investor brings. We read that every individual is continually striving to discern "the most advantageous" employment for his capital, and that his quest to promote his *own* advantage "necessarily" directs him to the employment that is "most advantageous" to the society (*Wealth of Nations*, 454). Let me suggest a dramatic contemporary counterexample. If a methamphetamine dealer earns a windfall by hatching brilliant new techniques for production and distribution, does his contribution to the proliferation of "crank" addicts constitute a major contribution to American society? On *WN*'s tendency to deploy terms such as advantageous, proper, improved, interest, greatness, and justice in a materialistic or "economistic" fashion, see Minowitz, *Profits, Priests, and Princes*, 15–17, 34, 37–39, 46.
24. *Wealth of Nations*, 471.
25. Ibid., 450.
26. Grampp, "What Did Smith Mean?," 454. I feel compelled to point out that *WN*'s invisible-hand paragraph refers only once to what the agent knows, but four times to what he intends—and once to his intention. Grampp similarly stumbles later when he implies that the invisible hand has only one unintended consequence, "to contribute to the defense of the nation" (ibid., 446). Even if the benefit to domestic employment is easy to know, that benefit is also unintended, and Smith does not value it merely as a prop to national defense. Smith's

emphasis in IV.ii on unintended consequences figures prominently in many of the nine interpretations Grampp attacks.

27. *Wealth of Nations*, 464–465.

28. Ibid., 463.

29. Ibid., 708.

30. Grampp usefully cites Smith's claim that "the great object of the political oeconomy of every country, is to encrease the riches and the power of that country" (*Wealth of Nations*, 372). Also crucial are Smith's statement that defense is "the first duty of the sovereign" (ibid., 689) and his incorporation of societal "greatness" (along with wealth) within "the great purpose" that every political economy "system" intends to promote (ibid., 687).

31. Grampp also hypothesizes that boosting domestic employment promotes national defense because workers abroad would be harder to summon for military service (Grampp, "What Did Smith Mean?," 453).

32. *Wealth of Nations*, 377–379. The capital of the landlord is "fixed in the improvement of his land" and "seems to be as well secured as the nature of human affairs can admit of" (ibid., 378); the "planter who cultivates his own land . . . is really a master, and *independent of all the world*" (emphasis added); the capital of the manufacturer, "being at all times within his view and command, is more secure than that of the foreign merchant" (ibid., 379).

33. Grampp, "What Did Smith Mean?," 459.

34. *Wealth of Nations*, 426.

35. See Peter Minowitz, "Invisible Hand, Invisible Death: Adam Smith on War and Socioeconomic Development," 305–315.

36. Grampp, "What Did Smith Mean?," 442.

37. *Wealth of Nations*, 494.

38. Ibid., 447.

39. Ibid., 898.

40. Ibid., 687–688.

41. Ibid., 138. Between two passages that tout the liberty of colonists "to manage their own affairs their own way" (ibid., 572, 584), Smith invokes "the most sacred rights of mankind" to condemn policies that prohibit "a great *people*" from "employing their stock and *industry* in the way that they judge most advantageous to themselves" (ibid., 582, emphasis added). Also relevant is his enthusiasm for "the free circulation of labour" (ibid., 135) and his criticism of institutions or policies that obstruct it: "exclusive corporations" (ibid., 146), apprenticeships (ibid., 151) and the Poor Laws (ibid., 152).

42. Friedrich Hayek and libertarians who highlight "spontaneous order" typically refrain from invoking any sort of non-human authority or intelligence. Hayek credits Smith (and other eighteenth-century

Scots) for showing that "an evident order which was not the product of a designing human intelligence need not therefore be ascribed to the design of a higher supernatural intelligence." Because "no human mind can comprehend all the knowledge which guides the actions of society," Hayek exhorts us to conceive of "an effective coordination of human activities without deliberate organization by a commanding intelligence"; such coordination often occurs via an "impersonal mechanism" such as a market. Friedrich Hayek, *The Constitution of Liberty*, 4, 59, 159. Emphasizing the limits on the knowledge a human individual can attain, Hayek (like Smith) encourages his readers to assume "an attitude of humility towards the impersonal and anonymous social processes by which individuals help to create things greater than they know." These "impersonal and anonymous" processes would include languages, markets, and a variety of laws and customs. Hayek, *Individualism and Economic Order*, 7, 8, 11, 15, 22, 32, 86–88. Hayek could complain that Smith's appeals to an invisible hand, "the wisdom of nature" (*Wealth of Nations*, 674), and so on, may encourage readers to mis-identify impersonal social processes as a superhuman intelligence that leads or directs us. Although *TMS* goes further with its frequent appeals to a superhuman *designer*, it anticipates Hayek by explaining how moral consciousness and conduct can emerge via the purely human interactions that create the "impartial spectator." For a penetrating discussion of Hayek in connection with Smith's invisible hand, see Emma Rothschild, 140–142, 145–153, 155.

43.   Adam Smith, *The Theory of Moral Sentiments*, 120–121, 131–132, 164; ibid., 181–182.

44.   However difficult it would have been for Smith to prove this thesis when he wrote, it would be harder for someone today to argue that the soil "maintains at all times nearly that number of inhabitants which it is capable of maintaining." Millions are obese, while millions are starving. In any case, Smith thrice in the invisible-hand paragraph places great weight upon the adverb "nearly." Cf. Anthony Brewer, 527–532.

45.   *Theory of Moral Sentiments*, 184–185.

46.   Grampp, "What Did Smith Mean?," 463.

47.   Ibid., 463.

48.   Ibid.

49.   *Theory of Moral Sentiments*, 184.

50.   Ibid., 183.

51.   Ibid., 181.

52.   Ibid., 182.

53.   Ibid., 182–183. Whereas Grampp imagines moronic landlords who never learn that the eye is larger than the belly (463), Smith chides the

"poor man's son"—and "our conduct" generally (ibid., 181)—for re-
peatedly forgetting that the "machines" that protect us from the summer shower are helpless against "the winter storm" (ibid., 181–183).
Smith also laments the loss in leisure, ease, and "careless security"
caused by our vanity-inspired quest for wealth and power at *TMS*,
50–51 (on vanity's contribution to the ubiquitous drive for "better-
ing our condition," compare these pages with *Wealth of Nations*, 190,
341–342, 869–870. In a recent book that devotes more than 300 pages
to the invisible hand—and that regularly protests how Smith has been
trumpeted by enthusiasts of laissez-faire—the late Warren Samuels
mentions neither the "summer shower" nor the "winter storm." See
Warren J. Samuels, Marianne F. Johnson, and William H. Perry.

54. *Wealth of Nations*, 372, 687. The latter passage—which asserts that
     every "system" of preference or restraint ends up subverting "the
     great purpose which it means to promote . . . the progress of the so-
     ciety toward real wealth and greatness"—does not mention political
     economy, but the term is strongly implied. The title of the relevant
     Book (IV) is "Of Systems of political Oeconomy," which highlights the
     mercantilist and agriculturalist (e.g., Physiocratic) approaches as the
     political economy "systems" marred by preferences and/or restraints
     (Smith introduces the "system of natural liberty" at the end of Book
     IV). On page 372, in any case, Smith proclaims that "the great object
     of the political oeconomy of every country, is to encrease the riches
     and power of that country."

55. When Smith speaks of "what is properly called" political economy, he
     uses language that specifies the subject matter of his world-renowned
     book: "the nature and causes of the wealth of nations" (*Wealth of
     Nations*, 678–679). *WN*'s title does *not* mention greatness or power,
     and its text spends relatively little time defining or discussing them.
     Another prominent definition likewise elevates wealth/riches above
     greatness/power: in the brief introduction to Book IV, Smith explains
     that political economy, "considered as a branch of the science of a
     statesman or legislator, proposes. . . . to enrich both the people and
     the sovereign" (428). The *Journal of Political Economy*, needless to say,
     depreciates greatness and power even more than Smith did.

56. Grampp, "What Did Smith Mean?," 442, 455, 462–464. As Grampp
     puts it, "[t]he effort to reconcile the diverse ideas is the greatest of the
     efforts a reader must make in order to understand the *Wealth of Na-
     tions*" (ibid., 460–461). In *Profits, Priests, and Princes*, I challenged the
     dominant trends in contemporary scholarship on Smith and strove
     to reopen the "Adam Smith Problem" posed by the contrasts between
     his two books. Buchan's recent volume has many virtues, but errs
     seriously when it contemptuously dismisses this "problem" as being

"unbiographical" (Buchan, *Authentic Adam Smith*, 22). In *How Adam Smith Can Change Your Life: An Unexpected Guide to Human Nature and Happiness*, a delightful mass-market book whose main mission is to convey the wisdom of *TMS*, Russ Roberts explores the "Problem" (218–220, 234) and highlights the delusory character of "trinkets" (91, 101–103). But he displays no awareness of *WN*'s claim that "wealth and greatness" are political economy's aims or of the religious contrasts between Smith's books. Despite his attention to the *TMS* invisible-hand, finally, he says nothing about "the winter storm." Individuals interested in the formidable complexity of Smith's writing and thinking should, at a minimum, consult the following books: Jerry Z. Muller, *Adam Smith in His Time and Ours: Designing the Decent*; Vivienne Brown, *Adam Smith's Discourse: Canonicity, Commerce, and Conscience*; and Charles L. Griswold Jr., *Adam Smith and the Virtues of Enlightenment*.

57. *Theory of Moral Sentiments*, 61. With little argument, Buchan maintains—implausibly—that Smith had soured on the prospects for wisdom and virtue because of the way he had experienced "courts and drawing-rooms" during the roughly thirteen years that elapsed between the publication of *WN* in 1776 and his final revising of *TMS* (Buchan, *Authentic Adam Smith*, 140). Smith was 53 when *WN* was published, and the original edition of *TMS* included memorable disparagements of wealth and greatness (*Theory of Moral Sentiments*, 45, 50–51, 53–54, 57). I would suggest, contra Buchan, that Smith added I.iii.1 (and comparable passages) to *TMS* in order to signal his awareness of certain horizons that *WN* tends to obscure.

58. *Theory of Moral Sentiments*,183.
59. Ibid., 183.
60. Ibid., 183–184.
61. Ibid., 184.
62. Ibid., 181–182.
63. Is this *TMS* chapter the work of a "tyro," as Grampp suggests ("What Did Smith Mean," 463), or the work of a sage? Seventy-three years before the *Journal of Political Economy* published Grampp's article, it published "Adam Smith and Laissez Faire," a pioneering article by Jacob Viner that was reprinted in his well-known book, *The Long View and the Short*. Although Viner skillfully displays the theological clash (and some related differences) between Smith's two books, he exaggerates both the optimism and the dogmatism in *TMS*. In faulting *TMS* for "absolutism" and "rigidity" (*The Long View*, 216), Viner ignores the complex dialectics of the trinkets puzzle. He likewise overstates the extent to which *TMS* posits "universal and perfect harmony" and presents an "unqualified doctrine of a harmonious order

of nature, under divine guidance" (ibid., 217, 220, 222–223). Viner overlooks mankind's continual vulnerability to "the winter storm," anxiety, fear, sorrow, disease, danger, and death (*Theory of Moral Sentiments*, 183). In addition, he overemphasizes the passages (ibid., 105, 166, 168) that identify the *happiness* and *perfection* of "the world" (and of its "species") as the purposes of Nature/God (*The Long View*, 217, 220, 229–230); and he ignores the passages that highlight individual preservation and species propagation (*Theory of Moral Sentiments*, 77, 87), humbler goods that resemble *WN*'s humbler articulation of "the wisdom of nature" (*Wealth of Nations*, 673–674). Like Grampp, finally, Viner is too quick to invoke Smith's alleged "absentmindedness" to explain inconsistencies (*The Long View*, 241). Anyone who savors the delicacy of Smith's prose and tracks the multitude of minute changes Smith made in revising his books has no reason to doubt his 1788 description of his approach as an author: "I am a slow a very slow workman, who do and undo everything I write at least a half a dozen of times" (Letter to Thomas Cadell, March 15, 1788).

64. *Theory of Moral Sentiments*, 185–186. Pierre Manent offers an intriguing elaboration: although the imagination in commercial society becomes entombed in artifacts and money and therefore "disappears as a glorious faculty," it assumes an even more vigorous role in "the mind of the spectator who observes commercial society from without" and sees it "as a grand machine." Pierre Manent, 99.

65. *Wealth of Nations*, 687.

66. *Theory of Moral Sentiments*, 232.

67. Ibid., 234.

68. Ibid., 185.

69. *Wealth of Nations*, 770; ibid., 767. Samuels, in *Erasing the Invisible Hand*, ignores the allegedly happy beggar—and *WN*'s erasure of God. It appears, moreover, that none of the distinguished contributors to *Adam Smith as Theologian* (New York: Routledge, 2011), a collection edited by Paul Oslington, has plowed carefully through *WN* and noticed how secular if not atheistic it is; despite their repeated assertions that Smith's teachings presuppose a providential God (pp. 5, 7, 10–11, 55, 71, 107, 108, 112, 117, 119), the contributors seem unaware that Smith's magnum opus mentions neither God nor Providence. For a critique of the invisible hand that suffers grievously from failing to notice *WN*'s atheistic ambiance, see Andy Denis, "The Invisible Hand of God in Adam Smith," 1–32.

70. *Wealth of Nations*, 10.

71. *Theory of Moral Sentiments*, 185.

72. *Wealth of Nations*, 709; ibid., 712.

73. The four-stages theory is infused by something like an invisible hand insofar as Smith says nothing to suggest that human leaders or visionaries have played a role in propelling society from one stage to the next (cf. ibid., 422 on the "great revolution" that brought down feudalism). Needless to say, none of the four stages involves human fulfillment of a *divine* plan.
74. Ibid., 526–527.
75. Ibid., 526.
76. Ibid., 527; cf. ibid., 538.
77. Ibid., 97.
78. Ibid., 86–8, 90–91, 97–99.
79. In the next chapter, Smith speaks more confidently: it is "probably" (not *perhaps*) the case that China had acquired all the riches it could, given "the nature of its laws and institutions" (ibid., 111). Smith proceeds to elaborate the toll exacted by those laws and institutions, particularly the obstacles to foreign commerce—and the vulnerability of the poor and of "owners of small capitals" to being "pillaged and plundered" by public officials (ibid., 111–112, 680–681).
80. Ibid., 89–90. One can only imagine the "[w]ant, famine, and mortality" that would afflict the beggars in a *shrinking* economy, "where the funds destined for the maintenance of labour were sensibly decaying." Smith suggests that this condition may obtain in some of Britain's colonies in India (ibid., 90–91), and later elaborates the pernicious policies of the East India Company (ibid., 635–641, 751–753).
81. *Theory of Moral Sentiments*, 166. Unlike Viner (and others), I am not prepared to belittle *TMS* as a juvenile work. Viner asserts that Smith, when he wrote this book, was a "purely speculative philosopher, reasoning from notions masquerading as self-evident verities" (*The Long View*, 230). Viner here overlooks the empirical components of *TMS*—for example, the way Smith uses "sympathy" and "the impartial spectator" to explain how moral standards and behavior emerge from widespread patterns of human interaction—many of which remain plausible. Regarding *WN*, however, Viner is wise to suggest that statements about natural harmony may be "obiter dicta, thrown in as supernumerary reinforcements of an argument already sufficiently fortified by more specific and immediate data" (ibid., 224). For a *Journal of Political Economy* article that does justice to *TMS* (and to Smith's philosophical essays), see Henry J. Bitterman, 487–520, 703–734. Particularly valuable are Bitterman's elaboration of the Newtonian aspects of Smith's approach (ibid., 497–504, 511–516, 717).
82. *Wealth of Nations*, 710.

83. Ibid., 712–713. Such a "little sovereign" ends up being supported by "a sort of little nobility": "Men of inferior wealth combine to defend those of superior wealth in the possession of their property, in order that men of superior wealth may combine to defend them in the possession of theirs" (ibid., 715).

84. Ibid., 717.

85. Ibid., 413–414.

86. *Theory of Moral Sentiments*, 184–185.

87. WN also refers to "the original state of things, which precedes both the appropriation of land and the accumulation of stock"; here a laborer is not required to share his produce with either "landlord or master" (*Wealth of Nations*, 82). The hunting/fishing stage seems to fit these criteria; in the second stage, the "chief" controls the herds and their produce; in the hunting stage, there is "little or no authority or subordination" (ibid., 712–713). When Smith states that the tiller of the soil usually has his maintenance "advanced to him from the stock of a master, the farmer who employs him," Smith seems to be describing the final two stages. Workers in "all arts and manufactures," similarly, typically need a "master" to advance them "the materials of their work, and their wages and maintenance till it be completed" (ibid., 83). The majority of human beings, except among hunting/fishing societies in which harsh poverty is universal, are thus subject to economic "masters," and Providence is not responsible.

88. Ibid., 381–382.

89. Ibid., 418.

90. Ibid., 382–386.

91. Ibid., 377–378.

92. On the prominence of family pride and inherited wealth in sustaining shepherd-stage authority generally, see ibid., 714, 421–422. Yet another important perspective on land-ownership patterns emerges in Smith's discussion of colonies, where he states that "[p]lenty of good land, and liberty to manage their own affairs their own way, seem to be the two great causes of the prosperity of all new colonies" (ibid., 572; cf. 566–567, 570, 572, 584).

93. Ibid., IV.ii and *Theory of Moral Sentiments*, IV.1.

94. *Wealth of Nations*, 418–419. In both books, Smith sometimes directs vicious criticism at the economically privileged. According to TMS, as we have seen, the landlord is "proud and unfeeling," while "the rich" are characterized by "natural selfishness and rapacity" and "vain and insatiable desires" (*Theory of Moral Sentiments*, 184). Smith speaks similarly during WN's discussion of the feudal lords who traded their authority for trinkets: "All for ourselves, and nothing for other people,

seems, in every age of the world, to have been the vile maxim of the masters of mankind" (*Wealth of Nations*, 418).

95. Ibid., 421. Recall how Smith simply *identified* "manufactured produce" with "trinkets and baubles" when explaining that a shepherd chieftain could only employ his surplus by "maintaining" a multitude of subordinates (ibid., 712); and recall the prominence of "baubles and trinkets" in the invisible-hand paragraph of *TMS* (*Theory of Moral Sentiments*, 184).

96. *Wealth of Nations*, 422.

97. Grampp, "What Did Smith Mean?," 464. Although Manent brilliantly uses what *TMS* says about "imagination" to challenge *WN*'s simplistic explanation of feudalism's demise (Manent, *City of Man*, 90–94), he (like Russ Roberts) fails to accommodate either the "winter storm" or the religious clash between the two books. According to Manent, in any case, a feudal lord would barter away his power and prestige "only when compelled to do so by the centralized royal power of the sovereign" (ibid., 97).

98. The two discussions, furthermore, are similarly located in their respective works: Book IV of *WN* and Part IV of *TMS* (*TMS* is divided into parts rather than books). The account of feudalism occupies the central book of *WN*, and is followed quickly by the invisible hand, which lies roughly in the middle of *WN*, page-wise. In *TMS*, similarly, the invisible hand appears in the central part. Cf. Daniel B. Klein and Brandon Lucas, 43–52.

99. *Wealth of Nations*, 37.

100. Ibid., 420.

101. Ibid., 22–23, 26.

102. Ibid., 781–782. Manent ignores this problem when he faults Smith for substituting "a linear progress" for Montesquieu's "complex dialectic" concerning the good effects of commerce (Manent, *City of Man*, 86). He goes further astray when he maintains that "the spirit of commerce so ruled Smith that it could not but incite him to equate it with human nature" (ibid., 96).

103. In *TMS*'s most sustained discussion of the differences between primitive and civilized societies (Part V, chapter 2), Smith condemns the infanticide practiced by "the polite and civilized Athenians" (*Theory of Moral Sentiments*, 210). Although *WN*'s introduction eschews condemnation and portrays infanticide among hunting/fishing nations as a regrettable necessity (*Wealth of Nations*, 10), *TMS* here—as elsewhere—conveys higher standards, saying only that infanticide is "undoubtedly more pardonable" in the "rudest and lowest" stage (*Theory of Moral Sentiments*, 210).

104. Ibid., 223.

105. *Wealth of Nations*, 802–803.
106. Recall how mercantilism drew on both public "prejudices" and private "interests" in sustaining itself (ibid., 471). Smith likewise links prejudices and interest in explaining his famous assertion equating the "laws concerning religion" with the "laws concerning corn" (ibid., 539).
107. Ibid., 800–803.
108. Ibid., 803.
109. Ibid., 456.
110. Grampp, "What Did Smith Mean?," 461–462.
111. Smith freely deploys understatement as well as overstatement. I've been emphasizing his exaggerations, but the equivocations, insinuations, and qualifications (e.g., the ubiquitous "perhaps") may be more prevalent. Cf. Viner, *The Long View*, 222–223 on *WN*'s recourse to phrases such as majority, frequently, "in most cases," and "in general."
112. Smith never published these essays, but he exempted them from the arrangement he eventually made to have his papers burned upon his death.
113. See Adam Smith, "The Principles Which Lead and Direct Philosophical Enquiries; Illustrated by the History of Astronomy," 48–50. For Smith, "nature" seems to mean the way something operates "of its own accord" (*Wealth of Nations*, 372, 458, 523), without the intrusion of human violence, plan, constraint, artifice, or custom (ibid., 28–29, 248, 265, 372, 489, 870).
114. Adam Smith, "The Principles Which Lead and Direct Philosophical Enquiries; Illustrated by the History of the Ancient Physics," 112–114.
115. *Theory of Moral Sentiments*, 77, 93, 105, 128, 166, 169, 236, 289, 292. Smith links each of the three invisible hands to a broad pattern of socioeconomic development. Like *TMS*, the philosophical essays rely on a general contrast between savage and civilized society rather than on the four-stages theory of *WN*. The "notions" of the weak and fearful savage are "guided altogether by wild nature and passion" (*History of Astronomy*, 49); philosophy/science only emerges in civilized society, where "law has established order and security, and subsistence ceases to be precarious"; "cheerfulness" and the consciousness of strength/security counteract the superstitious impulse to imagine "invisible beings"; with greater leisure, individuals who are "disengaged from the ordinary affairs of life" can be particularly observant (ibid., 50); and opulence allows for the "evident distinction of ranks" that tames "confusion and misrule" (ibid., 51).
116. *Wealth of Nations*, 606.
117. Ibid., 687–168.

118. For the 1790 edition of *TMS*, Smith added a passage that evokes the spirit of *WN*. Consistent with the spirit of *TMS*, however, this passage still elevates a creator (above nature) who thinks, judges, arranges, and directs in order to promote the welfare of the whole: the "wisdom which contrived the system of human affections, as well as that of every other part of nature, seems to have judged that the interest of the great society of mankind would be best promoted by directing the principal attention of each individual to that particular portion of it, which was most within the sphere both of his abilities and his understanding" (*Theory of Moral Sentiments*, 229).

119. *Wealth of Nations*, 673–674.

120. Grampp, "What Did Smith Mean?," 446.

121. One can also approach the religious clash between *WN* and *TMS* by recalling the elusive dialectic *TMS* presents (in its invisible-hand chapter) between the "philosophical" view that condemns wealth/ greatness and the "complex" view that celebrates them. The complex view emerges when "our imagination" leads us to confuse the "real satisfaction" that wealth/riches and greatness/power provide with "the order, the regular and harmonious movement of the system, the machine or oeconomy" by which that satisfaction is produced (*Theory of Moral Sentiments*, 183). By highlighting our proclivity to become intoxicated by machines, Smith's "philosophical" critique of wealth and greatness might even prompt us to question the theism Smith celebrates in his essays (and in *TMS*); the theistic philosophers, analogizing from the unity and order of the machines that human beings create, portrayed the universe as "a complete machine" (*History of Ancient Physics*, 113–114). Let me suggest one more conundrum. Insofar as Smith equates machines with "systems" (*Theory of Moral Sentiments*, 183; *History of Astronomy*, 66; *History of Ancient Physics*, 113) his "philosophical" critique of trinkets also poses a challenge to his own endeavors in formulating "systems" of political economy, moral philosophy, and jurisprudence (*Theory of Moral Sentiments*, 233–234, 265, 313–314, 340–342; *Wealth of Nations*, 233, 606, 679, 687, 768–769, 780–781, 794). On the other hand, intellectual systems that resemble machines would presumably excel in precision, cohesion, reliability, and efficacy. Given the high standards that Smith thus set for himself, finally, perhaps Grampp (and other scholars) should work harder before concluding that Smith was a sloppy thinker or writer.

122. The invisible hand can also remind us that, like our primitive ancestors, we are still prone to attribute agency to nonhuman powers that render us perplexed and puny.

123. *History of Astronomy*, 45–46.

124. Ibid., 46. The astronomy essay includes another remark that one can apply to the invisible hands of *WN* and *TMS*: in approaching a "strange" subject, Smith says, a writer could draw an analogy from a "familiar" subject, creating not just "a few ingenious similitudes" but a "great hinge upon which every thing turned" (ibid., 47).

125. Ibid., 105. If Smith in the 1750s was hesitant to claim that Newton had revealed the real but invisible *chains* that would "bind together" the movements of the planets, did Smith in 1776 believe that he himself had revealed a real but invisible *hand* that "led" lords, merchants, and others unwittingly to advance the "interest of the society," the "multiplication of the species" (*Theory of Moral Sentiments*, 185), "the publick interest" (*Wealth of Nations*, 456) and the wealth of nations?

126. Ibid., 664

127. *Theory of Moral Sentiments*, 34.

128. Ibid., 251; Plato, *Apology of Socrates*, 22d, 38a.

129. *History of Astronomy*, 51.

130. *Wealth of Nations*, 687; Grampp, "What Did Smith Mean?," 442.

Bibliography

Bitterman, Henry J. "Adam Smith's Empiricism and the Law of Nature, Parts I and II." *Journal of Political Economy* 48 (1940): 487–520, 703–734.

Brewer, Anthony. "On the Other (Invisible) Hand. . . ." *History of Political Economy* 41, no. 3 (2009).

Brown, Vivienne. *Adam Smith's Discourse: Canonicity, Commerce, and Conscience.* London: Routledge, 1994.

Buchan, James. *The Authentic Adam Smith: His Life and Ideas.* New York: Norton, 2006.

Denis, Andy. "The Invisible Hand of God in Adam Smith." *Research in the History of Economic Thought and Methodology* 23A (2005).

Grampp, William D. "What Did Adam Smith Mean by the Invisible Hand?" *Journal of Political Economy* 108, no. 3 (2000): 441–465.

Griswold Jr., Charles L. *Adam Smith and the Virtues of Enlightenment.* Cambridge: Cambridge University Press, 1999.

Hayek, Friedrich A. *Individualism and Economic Order.* Chicago: Henry Regnery, 1948.

———. *The Constitution of Liberty.* Chicago: University of Chicago Press, 1959.

Klein, Daniel B., and Brandon Lucas. "In a Word or Two, Placed in the Middle: The Invisible Hand in Smith's Tomes." *Economic Affairs* 31, no. 1 (March 2011).

Manent, Pierre. *The City of Man*. Translated by Marc A. Lepain. Princeton, NJ: Princeton University Press, 2008.

Minowitz, Peter. "Invisible Hand, Invisible Death: Adam Smith on War and Socioeconomic Development." *Journal of Political and Military Sociology* 17, no. 2 (1989): 305–315.

———. *Profits, Priests, and Princes: Adam Smith's Emancipation of Economics from Politics and Religion*. Stanford, CA: Stanford University Press, 1993.

Muller, Jerry Z. *Adam Smith in His Time and Ours: Designing the Decent Society*. New York: Free Press, 1993.

O'Rourke, P.J. *On The Wealth of Nations*. New York: Atlantic Monthly Press, 2007.

Roberts, Russ. *How Adam Smith Can Change Your Life: An Unexpected Guide to Human Nature and Happiness*. New York: Portfolio/Penguin, 2014.

Rothschild, Emma. *Economic Sentiments: Adam Smith, Condorcet, and the Enlightenment*. Cambridge, MA: Harvard University Press, 2001.

Samuels, Warren J., Marianne F. Johnson, and William H. Perry. *Erasing the Invisible Hand: Essays on an Elusive and Misused Concept in Economics*. New York: Cambridge University Press, 2011.

Smith, Adam. *An Inquiry into the Nature and Causes of the Wealth of Nations*. 2 vols. Edited by R.H. Campbell, A.S. Skinner, and W.B. Todd. Oxford: Oxford University Press, 1976.

———. *The Theory of Moral Sentiments*. Edited by A.L. Macfie and D.D. Raphael. Oxford: Oxford University Press, 1976.

———. "The Principles Which Lead and Direct Philosophical Enquiries; Illustrated by the History of Astronomy." In *Essays on Philosophical Subjects*. Edited by W.P.D. Wightman and J.C. Bryce, 31–105. Oxford: Oxford University Press, 1980.

———. "The Principles Which Lead and Direct Philosophical Enquiries; Illustrated by the History of the Ancient Physics." In *Essays on Philosophical Subjects*. Edited by W.P.D. Wightman and J.C. Bryce, 31–105. Oxford: Oxford University Press, 1980.

Viner, Jacob. *The Long View and the Short*. New York: Free Press, 1958.

Chapter 10

The Founders and the Conditions of Popular Political Deliberation

David R. Upham

At the conclusion of *Civil Peace and the Quest for Truth*, Professor Murray Dry writes that the American Founders' "constitutional and legal doctrines" had established two essential conditions for the "quest for truth": "freedom and security."[1] He notes, however, that any quest for truth, any inquiry, whether speculative or practical, requires "one more condition, Socratic moderation."[2] According to Professor Dry, then, inquiry requires that the inquirers enjoy freedom, security, and virtue; and while freedom and security have been furnished by modernity, it is ancient political thought that provides the best guide to virtue, especially that critical virtue of moderation.

It is the purpose of this chapter to inquire into a topic that is supplemental and subordinate to Professor Dry's conclusions. As the title of the chapter suggests, the inquiry considers conditions of one sort of inquiry: deliberation, and more specifically, political deliberation by the people. Moreover, this chapter focuses only on modern political thinkers, and only one subset thereof, the American Founders.

This chapter proceeds from at least four assumptions. First, political *deliberation* by human beings is a good thing; it is good that human beings discuss how they are to be governed. Second, at least to some extent, political deliberation by and among a self-governing people, and not only the few, is a good thing. Third, good popular deliberation is contingent—dependent on certain conditions not always prevailing in the course of human events. Fourth, the American

Founders have something instructive to say about how to foster these conditions.

The focus in this chapter is primarily on the teaching of a subset of the Founders: the participants in the constitutional ratification debates in New York. This focus seems appropriate in light of three considerations. First, these participants considered their deliberations as one of the most important instances of popular deliberation in all of history. The Anti-Federalist Brutus, for instance, identified his audience—the "Citizens of the State of New York," who were "called upon to investigate and decide . . . [t]he most important question that was ever proposed . . . to the decision of any people under heaven."[3] Similarly, in the opening paragraph of the *Federalist*, Hamilton, writing as Publius, told his audience—the People of the State of New York—that they were "called upon to deliberate on a new Constitution."[4] He cautioned that the American people's election would "decide the important question, whether societies of men are really capable or not of establishing good government by reflection and choice, or whether they are forever destined to depend for their political constitutions by accident and force."[5] The American people's deliberation and decision might prove critical to the future ability of any people, whether Americans or others, to establish free government by free deliberation and decision. Thus a wrong decision could be "considered as the general misfortune of mankind."[6] In a similar vein, James Wilson of Pennsylvania even claimed that the Constitution's ratification represented the greatest act of popular deliberation and decision . . . *ever*: "A people, free and enlightened, establishing . . . a system of government, which they have previously considered, examined, and approved! [This] spectacle . . . is the most dignified one that has yet appeared on our globe."[7]

To be sure, it is customary for political rhetoricians to ascribe great, if not singular, importance to their own times. For instance, every presidential election in recent time has been described as the "most important" election of the speaker's lifetime, if not all American history.[8] But given the enduring and worldwide significance of the Constitution of 1787, perhaps the Founders were at least partly justified in this ascription.

Second, there appears to be a general (if not unanimous) consensus among subsequent commentators that the ratification debates in New York occasioned the most thoughtful and interesting commentary on the proposed Constitution. As Professor Dry has noted, the

New York Anti-Federalists Brutus and Federal Farmer were "the ablest and most influential" opponents of the Constitution.[9] And Publius has long enjoyed nearly universal respect. In fact, our Supreme Court has held that the *Federalist* is "justly supposed to be entitled to great respect in expounding the constitution."[10] The *Federalist*'s "great authority" derives from its "intrinsic merit" as well as "the part two of its authors performed in framing the constitution."[11]

Third, the particular occasion for this essay suggests the propriety of focusing on the New York ratification debates. Professor Dry played a significant role in republishing the works of the Anti-Federalists and thus making them more easily accessible to contemporary readers.[12] Moreover, at the time of the debates, the college where he has taught for more than forty years was then located on land that remained a (disputed) part of the State of New York.[13]

As we see, the New York Federalists and Anti-Federalists have much to tell us about the conditions for popular deliberation. By word and example, they taught the importance of what one might call the intellectual virtues of candor, confidence, and knowledge, especially knowledge of history. At the same time, however, these Founders taught that good deliberation requires attention to the subrational or nonrational aspects of human nature—and hence besides intellectual virtues, popular deliberation requires attention to certain material conditions, including security and freedom, as well as the virtue of moderation in speech.

The Intellectual Virtues of Popular Deliberation

Confidence in the Inquiry

Although much of the ratification debate addressed fear—the dangers of adopting, or not adopting, the proposed Constitution—a contemporary reader of these debates might be struck by the optimism or confidence of the interlocutors. In part, these writers displayed a remarkable degree of faith both in the *inquiry* and in the *inquirers*.

Unlike many contemporary jurists, the Anti-Federalists and Federalists concurred that the goal of political deliberation was genuine truth, and more specifically, practical truth—truth as to what ought to be done. According to the Federal Farmer, the good citizen ought "coolly to state facts, and deliberately to avow the truth."[14]

Brutus similarly endeavored to "evince the truth" of his position, unhesitatingly spoke of "truth confirmed by the unerring experience of ages,"[15] and his aspiration to "lead the minds of the people to a wise and prudent determination."[16] And in his opening letter, Cato pledged to the "citizens of the state of New York" that he would "make such observations, on this new constitution, as will . . . be justified by reason and truth."[17]

For his part, in the first Federalist, Publius unblushingly proclaimed the purpose of his political inquiry to be the "discovery of truth," and urged his readers to make a decision free from "any impressions other than those which may result from the evidence of truth."[18] Later, he offered a brief epistemology in which he identified "truth" as the object of political as well as mathematical inquiry.[19] Political inquiry, he wrote, has the complementary purpose of refuting "error."[20]

More famously, the authors of the Declaration of Independence had asserted unblushingly the existence of practical political truth. Among the "harmonizing sentiments of the day"[21] that Jefferson had penned was the affirmation of certain purportedly "self-evident" political "truths."[22]

Contemporary theorists are much less confident that ethical or political judgments can be either true or false. Such "value judgments" are not genuine "judgments" at all. As Professor Dry has pointed out, modern jurists have seemingly endorsed the dichotomy between facts and values. Most notably, while the Founders' consensus affirmed self-evident truths, contemporary judges are generally on "common ground" in affirming the possibility of "false statements of fact" but denying there is any "such thing as a false idea."[23]

But the Founders believed that political inquiry not only led to truth, but that such truth was harmonious with, and depended on, the truth to be apprehended by other inquiry. Philosophical inquiry informed political decisions. As Harry Jaffa has pointed out, for the Founders, "the task of political philosophy [was] to articulate the principles of political right, and therefore to teach the teachers of legislators, of citizens, and of statesmen the principles in virtue of which political power becomes political authority."[24]

For some Founders, religious inquiry was similarly friendly to political inquiry. The Federalist James Wilson, for instance, concluded that the study of religion was in harmony with the study of law. Indeed, the two inquiries *overlapped* to the extent that religious inquiry both relied, in part, on reason (along with the "moral sense") unassisted by revelation:

> The law eternal, the law celestial, and the law divine, as they are disclosed by that revelation, which has brought life and immortality to light, are the more peculiar objects of the profession of divinity.

> The law of nature, the law of nations, and the municipal law form the objects of the profession of law.

> . . . Far from being rivals or enemies, religion and law are twin sisters, friends, and mutual assistants. Indeed, these two sciences run into each other. The divine law, *as discovered by reason and the moral sense*, forms an essential part of both.[25]

For some of the Founders, then, both Athens and Jerusalem had *much* to do with Philadelphia.

At the same time, however, the leading writers in the New York ratification debates shied away from religious authority even while liberally citing philosophers, especially Montesquieu.[26] Even when occasionally cited, Scripture typically provided not authoritative revelation but political history that taught cautionary lessons.[27] The reason for this silence is unclear. Perhaps some participants disbelieved in such purported revelation. Others, perhaps, concluded that such religious authority was not sufficiently relevant to their political deliberations. Still others may have concluded that even if biblical authority was both authoritative and politically relevant, its overt invocation may have undermined those deliberations by aggravating passions unfriendly to reason. That is, the silence may have reflected as much the Founders' moderation as their skepticism.

Confidence in the Deliberating People

The Founders placed confidence not only in the political inquiry, but also in the popular inquirers. Both Federalists and Anti-Federalists emphasized the *people*'s ability to deliberate on, as well as decide, political questions. The people, according to Brutus, could and should "investigate" the ratification question in the hope of "a wise and prudent determination."[28] Similarly, Publius called for the people's "sedate and candid consideration"[29] of the proposed Constitution, and explained that the "republican principle demands that the *deliberate* sense of the community should govern."[30]

Frequently, the Founders' faith in the people signaled a faith in humanity in general. Although more known for a sober (if not pessimistic) account of human nature, the *Federalist* equally reflects a considerable faith in the capacity of human societies to deliberate, decide, and otherwise govern themselves: "There is a portion of virtue and honor among mankind which may be a reasonable foundation of confidence."[31] Indeed, the republican theory of government "presupposes the existence of these qualities in a higher degree than any other [theory]."[32]

At times, Publius indicated that this confidence had been demonstrated; it was justified by "experience."[33] At other times, however, this confidence appeared not as a conclusion, but as both first principle and aspiration, a quasi-religious faith and hope. He spoke of "that honorable determination which animates every votary of freedom to rest all our political experiments on the capacity of mankind for self-government."[34]

This faith, this hope, was to be confirmed and vindicated in the American Republic; that is, the American people would provide the test case for humanity's capacity for self-government. Publius sounded this theme at the beginning of the *Federalist*. He told the "People of the State of New York," "you are called upon to deliberate on a new Constitution," and that it belonged to them, and indeed, the whole "people of this county," to "decide the important question, whether societies of men are really capable or not of establishing good government by reflection and choice."[35] It was, he said, the Americans' responsibility to "vindicate the honor of the human race."[36]

Yet more frequently, both Anti-Federalists and Federalists showed confidence not in humanity generally, but in human nature as developed under the civil and religious traditions of the American people. The Federal Farmer praised the American people specifically as "virtuous and friendly to good government, to the protection of liberty and property";[37] they "in general have a high sense of freedom, they are high spirited, though capable of deliberate measures . . . intelligent, discerning, and well informed."[38] Less reservedly, Cato proclaimed that the American people had "given to the world astonishing evidence of [their] greatness."[39] In identifying the source of the people's virtue, Federal Farmer focused on the Anglo-American constitutional tradition. Across the several states, the people concurred in supporting certain "fundamental and unalienable rights," for the people had "derived all these rights from one common source, the British systems; and having in the formation of their state constitutions, discovered that their ideas relative to these rights are very similar."[40]

Publius likewise praised the American people as particularly "intelligent and well-informed," who would only "seldom adopt and steadily persevere for many years in an erroneous opinion respecting their interests."[41] He suggested a variety of local factors that prepared the American people for popular self-government:

> Providence has been pleased to give this one connected country to one united people—a people descended from the same ancestors, speaking the same language, professing the same religion, attached to the same principles of government, very similar in their manners and customs, and who, by their joint counsels, arms, and efforts, fighting side by side throughout a long and bloody war, have nobly established general liberty and independence.[42]

For Publius and the other Founders, the American people were emphatically a "good people."[43]

Candor in Speech

This confidence in the (American) people suggested a related virtue—candor or frankness. Good citizens have nothing to hide, and no truths to hide from. Accordingly, the American Founders celebrated open and frank discussion. Most famously, the Founders invoked candor in the Declaration of Independence. As an introduction to their lengthy indictment against King George III, they declared, "Let facts be submitted to a candid World."[44]

Candor was likewise summoned during the New York ratification debates. Cato, for instance, urged the people to "reflect on" the proposed constitution "with candour."[45] Federal Farmer likewise could "discern but one rational mode" of considering the proposed Constitution—"to examine it with freedom and candour."[46] John Jay, writing as "A Citizen of New York," likewise exhorted his readers to "[r]eceive this Address with the same candor with which it is written."[47] And under the penname Publius, Jay asked New Yorkers to remember that the proposed Constitution is "neither recommended to *blind* appropriation nor to *blind* reprobation, but to that sedate and candid consideration which the magnitude and importance of the subject demand."[48]

Sometimes the speakers accused their opponents of lacking candor. The Federal Farmer alleged that the Federalists "do not attempt manfully to defend the defective parts [of the proposal], but to cover them with a mysterious veil."[49] Their proffered arguments "do more honor to their ingenuity, than to their candor and firmness."[50] He, on the other hand, would proceed, "so far as I am able, with candor and fairness."[51] So, for instance, although opposing ratification, he conceded there were "many good things in the proposed system."[52]

Conversely, Publius, in implicit reproach to the posture of indecision taken by the Federal Farmer,[53] announced that he would "affect not reserves which I do not feel. I will not amuse you with an appearance of deliberation when I have decided. I *frankly* acknowledge to you my convictions, and I will freely lay before you the reasons on which they are founded. The consciousness of good intentions *disdains ambiguity*. . . . My arguments will be *open* to all, and may be judged of by all."[54]

Primacy of Knowledge Gained from Experience

According to the participants in the New York ratification debate, the deliberators required not merely the virtue of candor, but also knowledge. The relevant knowledge was partly intuitive. Most famously, the Founders proclaimed certain "self-evident truths." For his part, Cato argued that "intuitive truth" and "intuitive reason" would reject the proposed Constitution.[55] With greater precision, Publius defined certain political truths as "self-evident": certain "primary truths, or "first principles" that "contain an internal evidence which, antecedent to all reflection or combination, commands the assent of mind," and upon which principles, "all subsequent reasonings must depend."[56] One such principle was "that the means ought to be proportioned to the end" or stated otherwise, that authority should be proportionate to responsibility.[57]

As a general rule, however, both Publius and his adversaries emphasized the knowledge that comes from *experience*. Again and again, these men identified experience as the chief source of political knowledge. According to the New York Anti-Federalists, experience "has taught mankind,"[58] "has proved,"[59] has "established,"[60] "has shewn,"[61] "prove[s],"[62] is (or at least can be) "unerring,"[63] and confirms "truth."[64] Experience is "the surest guide in political researches"[65] and therefore "ought to teach" the people.[66] Publius was even more laudatory. He composed a virtual litany of praises: Experience "assures us,"[67] "has instructed us,"[68] "has taught us,"[69] "has taught mankind,"[70] "will forever admonish,"[71] has "wrought a deep and solemn conviction in the public mind."[72] Experience, not fear of the Lord, is the "parent of wisdom"[73] and the very "oracle of truth."[74] Experience, therefore, is "the guide that ought always to be followed whenever it can be found."[75]

How does one have this experience? Personal experience can be a harsh but effective tutor. The saying is, "Good judgment comes from experience, and experience—well, that comes from poor judgment."[76] And at times, the people's experience of their own poor judgment is the *only* way a citizenry can learn important lessons. Publius explained, for instance, that it was only by Americans' experience of "national humiliation"[77] under the Articles of Confederation that the people had come to learn "the great and radical error which on actual trial has discovered itself."[78] The "great and radical" error was the conferral of governmental responsibility on Congress without the coercive authority requisite to enforcement.[79] This defect had, he said, been wholly overlooked by those who had framed, deliberated upon, and adopted the Articles.[80]

Yet at the same time, vicarious experience can also provide such lessons. The "poor judgment" that need not always be one's own. And at the school of vicarious experience, tuition is much lower, and the curriculum less exacting, as Publius noted: "The history of Great Britain is the one with which we are in general the best acquainted, and it gives us many useful lessons. We may profit by their experience without paying the price which it cost them."[81]

Consequently, both Federalists and Anti-Federalists agreed that knowledge of ancient and modern political history was critical to good deliberation. For Publius, of particular value were the lessons to be drawn from the histories of republics and confederacies, both "ancient and modern."[82] Armed with such knowledge, the Americans had already, in their "[state] constitutions" made "valuable improvements . . . on the popular models, both ancient and modern";[83] and continued attention to this history would show the necessity of an energetic central government.[84]

Similarly, the Federalist Noah Webster, writing from New York under the pen name "Citizen of America," declared, "[e]xperience is the best instructor—it is better than a thousand theories."[85] This experience can be acquired through reading "[t]he history of every government on earth."[86] He praised his fellow Americans, for in the formation of their state constitutions, "the wisdom of all ages is collected—the legislators of antiquity are consulted—as well as the opinions and interests of the millions who are concerned. In short, it is *an empire of reason*."[87]

The Anti-Federalists likewise saw in ancient and modern history important lessons—but these lessons counseled against ratification. Cincinnatus, for instance, argued that history should alert the people to the dangers of the Constitution, whose proponents "betray so little knowledge of ancient and modern history, as not to know, that some of the freest republics in the world, never kept up a standing army in time of peace!"[88] History, the Anti-Federalists insisted, is "worthy of the most careful attention of every lover of freedom."[89]

The importance of experience, whether personal or vicarious, is reflected in the Founders' design for both the Constitution and the whole American polity. Most notably, the Framers' appreciation of personal experience motivated their design of the presidential and senatorial offices. According to Publius, the lengthy terms of office for Senators and the President, as well as their indefinite personal re-eligibility, allowed the people to enjoy the benefits of accumulated personal experience.[90] The Anti-Federalists did not dispute the value of accumulated experience, but believed the benefits were outweighed by the risk that such personal capacity could lead to both a dangerous accumulation of personal power and the simultaneous dissipation of personal attachment to their constituents: "Men six years in office absolutely contract callous habits, and cease, in too great a degree, to feel their dependence, and for the condition of their constituents."[91]

Moreover, the Founders demonstrated the value of vicarious experience, learned principally from history, in their educational reforms. Several of the Founders prioritized history in their models for popular education. Noah Webster wrote that "every child in America should be acquainted with his own country. . . . As soon as he opens his lips, he should rehearse the history of his own country; he should lisp the praise of liberty, and of those illustrious heroes and statesmen who have wrought a revolution in her favor."[92] Accordingly, the "primary" schoolbook should include "the history of the late revolution, and of the most remarkable characters and events that distinguished it, and a compendium of the principles of the federal and provincial governments."[93] In a similar vein, Jefferson proposed that students in the primary grades read history: "The reading in the first stage, where [the people] will receive their whole education, is proposed to be chiefly historical. History, by apprising them of the past will enable them to judge of the future; it will avail them of the experience of other times and other nations; it will qualify them as judges of the actions and designs of men; it will enable them to know ambition under every disguise it may assume; and knowing it, to defeat its views."[94]

As Professor Dry has indicated, this reliance on history requires the sort of history pioneered by Thucydides: "if [my history] is judged worthy by those inquirers who desire an exact knowledge of the past as an aid to the understanding of the future, which in the course of human things must resemble if it does not reflect it, I shall be content."[95] This approach depends on the belief in a common human nature, transcending space and time, by which human beings can learn from others' prior experience.

At the same time, despite their heavy reliance on history, the Founders rejected a blind veneration of the past. They prided themselves as innovators who could learn from, but not be bound by, the past. Cato, for instance, declared that "in principles of politics, as well as in religious faith, every man ought to think for himself."[96] Similarly, Publius celebrated "the glory of the people of America," namely, "whilst they have paid a decent regard to the opinions of former times and other nations, they have not suffered a blind veneration for antiquity, for custom, or for names, to overrule the suggestions of their own good sense, the knowledge of their own situation, and the lessons of their own experience."[97] Accordingly, the Americans' revolution and their establishment of the state constitutions, as well as their ratification of the Constitution, would be innovations with enduring and worldwide significance:

> To this manly spirit, posterity will be indebted for the possession, and the world for the example, of the numerous innovations displayed on the American theatre, in favor of private rights and public happiness. Had no important

step been taken by the leaders of the Revolution for which a precedent could not be discovered, no government established of which an exact model did not present itself, the people of the United States might, at this moment have been numbered among the melancholy victims of misguided councils, must at best have been laboring under the weight of some of those forms which have crushed the liberties of the rest of mankind. Happily for America, happily, we trust, for the whole human race, they pursued a new and more noble course. They accomplished a revolution which has no parallel in the annals of human society. They reared the fabrics of governments which have no model on the face of the globe.[98]

Indeed, this innovation would rely on not only counter-antiquarian spiritedness but also scientific progress: the "great improvement" in the "science of politics."[99]

The "Equipment" (or the Physical Conditions) of Popular Deliberation

Popular deliberation requires more than intellectual virtues. The deliberators are not simple spirits; they are stubbornly bodily. And while the speakers' bodies facilitate deliberation—for the bodies provide the power of communication—this embodiment poses grave challenges as well.

The Restraints of Embodiment

One problem is that bodies impose restraints of space, time, and speech. In at least two respects, the participants in the New York ratification debate showed keen awareness of these limitations. First, the Founders understood that a people cannot deliberate together if they cannot understand one another. Accordingly, Publius highlighted the value of the people's common language. This common language was a critical indication that Americans could and should retain a political union: Americans are "one united people," in part because they speak "the same language."[100] More famously, the Federalist, and sometime New Yorker, Noah Webster, sought to reform and standardize the

American language in the interest of national political unity: "[A] *national language is a band of national union*. Every engine should be employed to render the people of this country *national*; to call their attachments home to their own country; and to inspire them with the pride of national character."[101] Cato, however, feared that the proposed Constitution would actually undermine this linguistic unity. The concentration of power in the central government would foster a federal "court" in the nation's capital: "The language and manners of this court will be what distinguishes them from the rest of the community, not what assimilates them to it."[102] A strong central and national government would not represent the existing community, but give rise to a separate and adverse community, with its own peculiar language and mores.

Second, the limitations of space and time require attention to the number of participants requisite to good deliberation. Thus, in designing the mode of selecting the president, the Founders sought to ensure an appropriate number of deliberators; size was seemingly one of the "conditions favorable to deliberation."[103] On the one hand, too many participants undermined rational discourse. One of the arguments for the Electoral College was that the immediate decision should be made by individuals who could meet in groups small enough to allow for effective discussion and decision.[104] According to the Framers' initial apportionment, the number of deliberators at each meeting of the Electoral College was to range from three to twelve.[105] According to Publius, such a "*small* number of persons, selected by the fellow-citizens from the general mass, will be most likely to possess the information and discernment requisite to so complicated an investigation."[106] The Anti-Federalists generally accepted this mode of selecting the President.[107]

On the other hand, the design of the Electoral College suggested that good deliberation required a minimum, as well as a maximum, number of deliberators. Each meeting of the Electoral College was to have at least three members. The Framers could well, for example, have assigned each state a number of electors equal to that state's representation in the House, and thereby established meetings of one or two electors in the smallest states. This mode would have reflected the Socratic model of philosophic inquiry, where one person might contemplate, or two persons engage in dialogue. But in choosing three as a minimum, the Founders suggested that more participants were needed for political deliberation. Conversely, and perhaps not coincidentally, the largest electoral meetings were to include a number equal or similar to the twelve customarily prescribed for petit juries, which likewise deliberated in order to judge particular individuals.

Yet the Founders' approach to *legislative*, as opposed to *electoral* or *judicial* deliberation, involved a very different scale. The Founders believed that legislative deliberation required a much larger number of persons. So under the Articles of Confederation, each state was required, at state expense, to send at least two delegates (even though each state could cast only one vote).[108] The result was that Congress included at least twenty-six members. Under the Constitution, Congress would likewise have a minimum size; the national legislature was to consist in two houses where the deliberators and deciders would consist of at least twenty-six senators and sixty-five representatives, based on the initial number of states and their allocated representatives.[109] Requiring two, rather than one, senator per state was probably motivated by this concern; the Framers could have readily mandated one senator per state, leaving the initial Senate with thirteen members, or roughly as large as a petit jury or a meeting of the Electoral College. These two legislative chambers were thus to include far more deliberators than the number found in the thirteen "chambers" of the Electoral College (but far fewer than found in our current Congress).

At the same time, the Founders concurred that a legislature should not be too large. In this regard, Publius remarked not only that "a certain number at least seems to be necessary to secure the benefits of free consultation and discussion, and to guard against too easy a combination for improper purposes,"[110] but also that "the number ought at most to be kept within a certain limit, in order to avoid the confusion and intemperance of a multitude."[111] The drafters of the Articles of Confederation had, perhaps for this reason, limited the size of state delegations to seven,[112] thus establishing a legislature with at most ninety-one deliberators (absent the admission of a fourteenth state). The Constitution also mandated a maximum number by requiring that "the Number of Representatives shall not exceed one for every thirty Thousand."[113]

Unlike the design of the Electoral College, the size of Congress occasioned significant debate. Federal Farmer believed that the proposed legislature was too small and would thus foster corruption—the legislators would easily be bribed or "form juntoes."[114] He favored a legislature significantly larger than the one proposed, arguing that an assembly could have well over a hundred members without becoming a "tumultuous mob."[115] Cato likewise objected that the proposed number was "too few to resist the influence of corruption."[116]

Still, as to the general principle, the Anti-Federalists largely agreed that good legislative deliberation required both a maximum and a minimum number of participants. The Anti-Federalists' more fundamental objection was that a national legislature could never be both small enough for effective deliberation and large enough to adequately represent the nation. A body that sufficiently represented the diverse interests of the national people would be enormous: "Perhaps, nothing could be more disjointed, unwieldy and incompetent to doing business with harmony and dispatch, than a federal house of representatives properly numerous for the great objects of taxation, et cetera collected from the several states."[117]

Therefore, the critical disagreement between Publius and his adversaries concerned not the precise numerosity necessary for deliberation, whether electoral or legislative. Rather, the interlocutors differed as to whether the Union was so large and so diverse that no common national legislature could include a representation small enough for good deliberation but large enough for just exercise of the nationwide powers to tax, to raise a standing army, and so on. The Anti-Federalists feared that the effort to establish such a legislature would not *represent* the nation's diversity, but perniciously add to this diversity by creating a new, distinct, and dangerously powerful minority community with its own language, opinions, and interests. To adopt the language of Publius, the Anti-Federalists feared that the effort to establish a large, politically centralized republic would create a governing minority faction, actuated by impulses of passions and interest and opinion adverse to the people at large.

The Dangers of Embodiment and the Necessity of Freedom of Speech

The deliberators' own bodies pose not only restraints, but also dangers. The embodied deliberators are vulnerable to physical violence, or the threat thereof, which can hinder or entirely cut off all deliberation. A single act of violence can destroy the individual's powers of communication, or even his very life. Even the threat of such violence can be sufficient to frighten most individuals from speaking.

Moreover, such threats engender not only fear, but other passions, such as anger, outrage, and even hatred, that likewise prevent or otherwise hinder rational discourse. To quote Publius, "When once the sword is drawn, the passions of men observe no bounds of moderation."[118]

The deliberators must, then, enjoy a freedom to communicate. This freedom requires that their bodies be secure against physical threats and violence, whether private or public. In other words, good deliberation requires good government—a government strong enough to protect the citizens against private violence but controlled enough not to be destructive to their security.[119] The government must use its coercion to facilitate free deliberation, not stifle it. As Professor Dry has written, "collective deliberation requires freedom of speech";[120] and attention to this freedom was consistent with a broader goal of modern liberal politics: "an expansion of the sphere of persuasion and a contraction of the sphere of coercion."[121] In a similar vein, the Federal Farmer proclaimed, "[o]ur true object is to give full efficacy to one principle, to *arm persuasion* on every side, and to render force as little necessary as possible."[122]

The Founders' attention to this condition of popular deliberation was the primary (but not exclusive) motive for their efforts to "arm persuasion" by guaranteeing to the citizenry the freedoms of communication. This primacy is indicated by two interesting features of the Founders' speech about the freedoms of speech. First, the Founders frequently reserved this constitutional guaranty to members of the political community—to citizens, and not all persons. To cite one example, the New York ratifying convention's proposed bill of rights would have secured each "person" due process rights, but only "the people" would enjoy "the right peaceably to assemble together to consult for their common good."[123] For the Founders, the usual meaning of "the people" was not "the inhabitants," but "the citizens." As Chief Justice John Jay (once known as Publius) later remarked, each citizen is a member of "the people":

> [A]t the revolution, the sovereignty devolved on the people; and they are the sovereigns of the country, but they are sovereigns without subjects (unless the African slaves among us may be so called) and have none to govern but themselves: the citizens of America are equal as fellow citizens, and as joint tenants in the sovereignty.[124]

His colleague, Justice James Wilson, similarly defined "the people" as "the citizens" and identified freedom of speech as a privilege of citizenship rather than a right of humanity.[125] Three decades later, the delegates at New York's constitutional convention of 1821, which included such Federalist alumni as James Kent and Rufus King,[126] likewise guaranteed the freedoms of speech and press only to each "citizen," while securing other rights, such as religious freedom and due-process rights, to all persons.[127]

The eventual First Amendment, however, obscured this distinction between citizens and persons. The text suggested that the freedoms of speech and press were as comprehensively secured as the free exercise of religion; no beneficiary was identified in the Free Speech, the Free Press, or the Free Exercise Clauses.[128] But here too only "the people" enjoyed the communicative freedoms of assembly and petition.[129] Madison's initial proposal was more specific, and would have extended all communication rights to the people alone. Two of his amendments would have provided the following: "The people shall not be deprived or abridged of their right to speak, to write, or to publish their sentiments; and the freedom of the press, as one of the great bulwarks of liberty, shall be inviolable";[130] and "The people shall not be restrained from peaceably assembling and consulting for their common good, nor from applying to the legislature . . . for redress of their grievances."[131]

A second way in which the Founders indicated the centrality of political deliberation to free speech, is that they most frequently explained the freedoms of communication in terms of popular collective sovereignty rather than personal autonomy. The New York Anti-Federalists, for instance, championed the freedom of the press as critical to the popular information and coordination requisite for deliberation and decision. Cincinnatus, for instance, called freedom of the press "the sacred palladium of public liberty" for without it, "all useful knowledge on the conduct of government would be withheld from the people."[132] According to Federal Farmer, "[a] free press is the channel of communication as to mercantile and public affairs; by means of it the people in large countries ascertain each others sentiments; are enabled to unite, and become formidable to those rulers who adopt improper measures."[133]

Although the Federalists in New York had little to say about these freedoms during the ratification debates,[134] their subsequent comments indicated their concurrence that free speech was primarily a political right of the sovereign citizenry. Most notably, Madison (who had impersonated a New Yorker as Publius) would identify the freedoms of speech and press as the "right of freely examining public characters and measures, and of free communication among the people thereon."[135] His fellow Republican and Virginian, St. George Tucker, would likewise explain that while the First Amendment's religion clauses protected rights of the "human mind" and "human reason," the Amendment's speech and press clauses vindicated "the great fundamental principle of the American governments that the people are sovereign and those who administer the government their agents and servants," and thus the people have the right "to enquire into, censure, approve, punish, or reward their agents."[136] Madison's fellow Federalist, the Pennsylvanian James Wilson, likewise defined the freedoms of communication as the right of the "*citizen* under a free government . . . to think, to speak, to write, to print, and to publish freely, but with decency and truth, concerning publick men, publick bodies, and publick measures."[137] Wilson sharply contrasted this right of citizenship with the rights of aliens.[138]

To a certain extent, however, the Founders identified freedom of speech as a nonpolitical human right rather than a political popular right. At times, Madison would explain the freedom of speech as both a public right of the citizen and a private right of the human being. The dual purpose was likewise indicated by New York's revised Constitution of 1821. Although extending the constitutional freedoms of speech and press only to "citizens," these freedoms concerned "all subjects" and not just political matters.[139]

Still, as a general rule, the Founders identified freedom of speech as a privilege of citizenship. Our distance from the Founders in this respect is revealed in two prominent features of our speech about the freedom of speech. First, the noncitizen's equal right to free speech, in its fullest extent, is now accepted without controversy. Justice Frankfurter seems to have been the last Supreme Court justice to raise any objection in this regard. In 1941, in a dissenting opinion, he (along with three of his colleagues) noted that free speech, as incorporated via the Fourteenth Amendment, might not extend to aliens (or corporations, for that matter):

> To say that the protection of freedom of speech of the First Amendment is absorbed by the Fourteenth does not say enough. Which one of the various limitations upon state

power introduced by the Fourteenth Amendment absorbs the First? Some provisions of the Fourteenth Amendment apply only to citizens and one of the petitioners here is an alien; some of its provisions apply only to natural persons, and another petitioner here is a corporation.[140]

Four years later, however, a unanimous Supreme Court flatly declared, "[f]reedom of speech and of press is accorded aliens residing in this country."[141] Today, our disputes presuppose the full and equal speech rights of aliens; rather we debate the speech rights of corporations and other artificial persons—regardless of whether aliens have effective ownership and control over these entities.[142]

Second, our frequent use of the expression "freedom of expression" obscures the popular-deliberative function of free speech. Expression is an individual, not communal act. A hermit can express himself, but a citizen must do more—he must communicate. Accordingly, before the twentieth century, authorities rarely used the phrase "freedom of expression" to designate the people's freedoms of communication.[143] The Supreme Court never did so. It was Justice Brandeis, in his dissent in the 1921 case, *United States ex rel. Milwaukee Social Democratic Publishing Co. v. Burleson*,[144] who seemingly introduced this quasi-neologism into the Supreme Court's lexicon.[145] Four years later, a court majority used the phrase "free expression,"[146] but it was not until the 1940s that the Court used these terms with much frequency.[147] The widespread use of this term signaled the marginalization of popular deliberation in favor of autonomous expression. For the Founders, however, the paradigmatic free speaker had been the republican citizen, not the esoteric philosopher, still less the perennially misunderstood artist.

The Moral Virtues Necessary for Good Deliberation

Disordered Passions and Deliberation

Besides the intellectual and physical conditions of deliberation, a third set of conditions must be attended to. Human beings are not simply intellects with bodies attached. Rather, they have such other subrational features as passions, emotions, and so on. And according to the Founders, these other features can cause great obstacles to good popular deliberation, and, more broadly, good popular self-government.

In New York, both Anti-Federalists and Federalists identified *passions* as adverse to good deliberation. Brutus's purpose was "to lead the minds of the people to a wise and prudent determination" by appealing to the "candid and dispassionate part of the community."[148] Cato decried those persons who, motivated by their own "resentments and little interests," sought to "influence [the people's] passions."[149] He disavowed any effort "to rouse your passions," but instead promised to "assist you in cool and deliberate discussion . . . to urge you to behave like sensible freemen."[150] Federal Farmer likewise recommended that the ratifying conventions consider the Constitution "coolly and deliberately"; indeed, they should "examine coolly over every article, clause, and word in the system proposed."[151] Publius likewise warned against "passions and prejudices little favorable to the discovery of truth."[152] Like his adversaries, Publius believed that "the cool and deliberate sense of the community ought [to prevail], in all governments," and accordingly the people should avoid the "tyranny of their own passions."[153] Stated otherwise, "it is the reason, alone, of the public, that ought to control and regulate the government. The passions ought to be controlled and regulated by the government."[154]

But dispelling anti-deliberative passions is easier said than done. Such passions are endemic. Federal Farmer explained, even "honest men" will not act impartially "when the interest of themselves or friends is concerned."[155] Indeed, it so common to be "*natural*," that men, motivated by interest or opinion, will "wish to hasten the adoption of a measure, to tell us now is the crisis—now is the critical moment to be seized . . . and to *shut the door* against free enquiry."[156]

Publius elaborated this sober account of human nature. Anti-rational passions and interests (which he sometimes identified as a species of "passion," but sometimes distinguished from passions)[157] were "sown into the nature of man."[158] Human beings, he said, were commonly moved by "impulses" arising from property interests or passionate attachment to opinions, whether religions, political, or otherwise.[159] Publius saw in these natural impulses a common source of the people's injustice and irrationality: "the passions of men will not conform to the dictates of reason and justice without constraint."[160] The "considerations of peace and justice" had proved no match for the unrestrained "impulse of any immediate interest or [other] passion."[161] Such passions, especially those arising from "immediate interest," had a "persuasive voice"[162] that "certainly bias judgment."[163]

The passions arising from economic interests seemed particularly unfriendly to sound deliberation: "the mild voice of reason . . . is but too often drowned before public bodies as well as individuals, by the clamors of an impatient avidity for immediate and immoderate gain."[164] Yet even in the absence of economic interest, self-love frequently renders human beings deaf to the voice of moral reason: raw "pride . . . naturally disposes them to justify all their actions and opposes their acknowledging, correcting, or repairing their errors or offenses."[165]

Recommended Veils

The Founding generation endeavored to counteract these destructive passions in many different ways, both in public and in private. To even sketch these efforts is far beyond both the scope of this essay and the capacity of this author. Still, we can identify a few of these efforts, especially those most proximate to deliberation itself.

First, the participants in the New York Ratification debate preached and practiced moderation in speech—even at the expense of candor. As noted earlier, the Founders ascribed great importance to candor in deliberation. Candor would seem to require "speaking one's mine," "telling it like it is," and "keeping it real." Candor tears off veils.[166] But such blunt speech can hinder, not facilitate, rational deliberation and decision. This difficulty arguably arises not only from the passions, but also from the deficiency of the human intellect. The intellect cannot at once see the whole "like it is"; rather, the mind apprehends only very limited particulars. The necessary focus on particulars aggravates the passions, which, in turn, can further both narrow and cloud the focus. When people get mad, they don't think straight; *in ira, stupiditas.*

Because of these limits of human nature, certain questions are "delicate."[167] And to give candid answers to these questions—"coolly to state facts, and deliberately to avow the truth"—can be "painful," as the Federal Farmer explained.[168] To mitigate this difficulty, Publius, by word and example, recommended a measure of circumlocution and veiling. One of these recommendations was to refrain from specifying political malefactors. For instance, in discussing the obstacles to ratification of the Articles of Confederation, he conspicuously refrained from singling out any state for blame. So while he expressly identified "New Jersey" as the one state that had offered an important amendment, he declined to name that "[o]ne State" that "persisted for several years in refusing her concurrence, although the enemy remained the whole period at our gates, or rather in the very bowels of our country."[169] That unnamed state (Maryland), he said, had ultimately concurred only under duress: simply from "the fear of being chargeable with protracting the public calamities, and endangering the event of the contest. Every candid reader will make the proper reflections on these important facts."[170] Similarly, Publius refused to name any state (e.g., Rhode Island) that might reject the Constitution but whose "*multiplied and important infractions*" of the Articles had forced the abandonment of the Articles.[171]

Publius' most elaborate discussion of rhetorical veils occurred in his treatment of the conflict between the Constitution's Article VII and the Articles of Confederation. He explained that by allowing just nine states to secede from the existing Confederation, this provision posed "[t]wo questions of a very delicate nature."[172] The first of these questions was whether the solemn promises of the Articles of Confederation, including the unanimity rule of the Thirteenth Article, could be rightly breached by such non-unanimous abrogation of the Articles: "On what principle the Confederation . . . can be superseded without the unanimous consent of the parties to it?"[173] In answering this question, Publius pointed to the revolutionary principles of the Declaration of Independence, which superseded the Articles, as well as the prior breach of the Articles by the nonratifying state, which nullified any reciprocal obligation.[174] Publius added that there had once been a "time when it was incumbent on us all to veil the[se] ideas," but that "[t]he scene is now changed," so a more candid discussion was appropriate.[175]

The second question was, "What relation is to subsist between the nine or more States ratifying the Constitution, and the remaining few who do not become parties to it?"[176] Unlike the first question, this question still required a veiled response: "the flattering prospect of [the question] being merely hypothetical forbids an overcurious discussion of it. It is one of those cases which must be left to provide for itself."[177] Publius then added the following obscure, not-too-curious, comments:

In general, it may be observed, that although no political relation can subsist between the assenting and dissenting States, yet the moral relations will remain uncancelled. The claims of justice, both on one side and on the other, will be in force, and must be fulfilled; the rights of humanity must in all cases be duly and mutually respected; whilst considerations of a common interest, and, above all, the remembrance of the endearing scenes which are past, and the anticipation of a speedy triumph over the obstacles to reunion, will, it is hoped, not urge in vain MODERATION on one side, and PRUDENCE on the other.[178]

Publius here did not identify which side—the assenting states or the dissenting states—should practice moderation and prudence, respectively. Moreover, he did not identify the political action (or nonaction) with respect to which moderation or prudence was appropriate.

Here Publius was probably circumlocuting around the prospect of civil war. By rejecting the Constitution, the dissenting states would become foreign states bordering the newly formed Union. Their citizens would thus become aliens to their former fellow Americans. These alien neighboring powers might threaten the national security of the United States, for as Publius had extensively elaborated, there would be a constant threat of war.[179] Indeed, the very "transcendent law" of self-preservation that justified the breach of the Articles might similarly justify the armed conquest of the dissenting states.

To avoid this danger and this necessity, the Union would need moderation. Without moderation, the Union might precipitously announce this crisis and openly plan for eventual invasion. Such premature belligerence would make peaceful reunion impossible, for when "the sword is once drawn, the passions of men observe no bounds of moderation."[180] Conversely, without *prudence*, the dissenting states might prematurely disavow reunion and seek instead either alliance or union with European powers to the detriment of the Union's vital interests.[181] And with this probable assistance,[182] the dissenting states might successfully resist forcible reunion.

Publius' manner of identifying and addressing these two "delicate" questions indicated a few general rules: First, citizens should generally veil the prospect of any radical political change, however necessary, until that change truly becomes necessary. Second, such veiling is especially appropriate where this radical change might involve war.

Therefore, a self-governing, deliberating people should not generally deliberate on, or even contemplate, that community's dissolution or other revolutionary change, especially if such change involves a reversion to the state of war. Candid, overly curious reflections on these topics foster not popular deliberation, but such anti-deliberative passions as pride, distrust, and fear.

Compulsory Veils

For the most part, the Founders merely recommended veils. But to a significant, though limited extent, many of the Founders favored legal restrictions on speech. One reason for these restrictions, it seems, was to shield the community against noxious language that would threaten the very conditions of genuine popular deliberation. Good popular speech might require that certain utterances be unfree.

To cite one example, largely foreign to contemporary sensibilities, many of the New York Federalists favored the enforcement of anti-blasphemy laws. One of the defenders of such laws was James Kent, who in 1788 was a young friend to Hamilton and supporter of the proposed Constitution.[183] Two decades later, as New York's chancellor, he upheld as constitutional a conviction for the common law offense of anti-Christian blasphemy. He explained that prohibiting blasphemous speech served two purposes: to protect individuals against offense and to preserve public morals: "Nothing could be more offensive to the virtuous part of the community, or more injurious to the tender morals of the young, than to declare such profanity lawful."[184] Kent thus suggested that both of these harms undermined the very community that made good deliberation possible.

Kent took pains to argue that the enforcement of such laws did not violate the fundamental principles of nonestablishment, free speech, and limited government. He insisted that such laws did not reflect "any religious establishment."[185] Rather, such "reviling is still an offence, because it tends to corrupt the morals of the people, and to destroy good order" and thus such reviling affects "the essential interests of civil society."[186] But was not the selective prohibition of anti-Christian blasphemy an establishment of Christianity? Kent answered that the law simply reflected the fact that because the predominant religion of the community was Christianity, such speech was far more harmful to the community.[187] Further, Kent made clear that this law did not operate as a heckler's veto. The government had the burden to prove, beyond a reasonable doubt, not simply that the words were offensive to the community, not simply that the words were uttered "in the presence and hearing of divers good and Christian people"— that is, the people likely to take offense, but also that the speaker acted with the *mens rea* of willful *malice*: "these words were uttered in a wanton manner, and, as they evidently import, with a wicked and malicious disposition, and not in a serious discussion upon any controverted point in religion."[188] What was critical, then, was not merely the interpretation of the offended hearer, but the offensive intent of the speaker. Finally, as Kent indicated, the restriction was not draconian, for the punishment was a fine and three-months imprisonment[189]—a severe sanction by contemporary American standards, but lighter than penalties often imposed in many medieval, modern, and contemporary theocracies.

One should not, however, overstate the significance of the few reported cases concerning anti-blasphemy, or anti-sedition prosecutions. As a general rule, the Founding generation, in both word and practice, favored a very limited government that, for reasons of prudence, justice, or otherwise, rarely engaged in coercing individuals to be moderate in speech.[190] The evidence, especially from the New York ratification debates, suggests the principal means relied on were example and exhortation. In other words, moderation in speech was generally pursued with moderation.

Charity in Speech—Where Kindness and Truth Meet

The tension between candor and moderation corresponds to the gap between kindness and truth. Kindness and truth, like justice and peace, do not easily meet. But if there is a place where the interests of both candor and moderation can flourish, where truth and kindness can meet, good deliberation may depend on taking full advantage of such convergence.

There are, perhaps, at least two such points of convergence—that is, where candor is moderate: first, where the speaker candidly criticizes himself, and second, where the speaker candidly acknowledges (or presumes) that opponents speak from intelligence and good will. By word and example, the opposing speakers in the New York ratification debates taught the importance of such candor. Most famously,

Publius provided an extensive example and recommendation in the opening number of the Federalist Papers:

> I am well aware that it would be disingenuous to resolve indiscriminately the opposition of any set of men (merely because their situations might subject them to suspicion) into interested or ambitious views. *Candor* will oblige us to admit that even such men may be actuated by upright intentions; and it cannot be doubted that much of the opposition which has made its appearance, or may hereafter make its appearance, will spring from sources, blameless at least, if not respectable—the honest errors of minds led astray by preconceived jealousies and fears. So numerous indeed and so powerful are the causes which serve to give a false bias to the judgment, that we, upon many occasions, see wise and good men on the wrong as well as on the right side of questions of the first magnitude to society. This circumstance, if duly attended to, would furnish a lesson of *moderation* to those who are ever so much persuaded of their being in the right in any controversy. And a further reason for caution, in this respect, might be drawn from the reflection that we are not always sure that those who advocate the truth are influenced by purer principles than their antagonists. Ambition, avarice, personal animosity, party opposition, and many other motives not more laudable than these, are apt to operate as well upon those who support as those who oppose the right side of a question.[191]

Candor here leads to moderation. A candid self-assessment will lead a speaker to avow the limitations of his own intelligence and virtue. Conversely, a candid assessment of one's opponents will often compel the acknowledgement of their intelligence and good intentions.

The Anti-Federalists, too, at times, showed an awareness of this principle. Federal Farmer, in particular, frequently made prominent concessions to the motives and views of the Federalists. He insisted that the people should not "unreasonably suspect men of falsehood."[192] He acknowledged that the proponents of the Constitution were "honest men"[193] who had "just cause" to be uneasy about the present Confederation.[194] Indeed, he acknowledged not only the decency of (some) of the Federalists' motives, but also the qualities of the proposed Constitution: there were, he said, "many good things in the proposed system."[195] Further, even while decrying the absence of a bill of rights, he did not accuse Federalists of *intending* to undermine these rights; rather, he proposed that his generation constitutionally secure them for future generations. Federal Farmer conceded that "we are not disposed to differ much, at present, about religion; but when we are making a constitution . . . for ages and millions yet unborn, why not establish the free exercise of religion, as a part of the national compact?"[196] More generally, he tempered any suspicion of the system with the observation that "good men will generally govern well with almost any constitution," but that "in laying the foundation of the social order," the people should not "unnecessarily leave a door open to improper regulations."[197]

Still, it would be a parody to suggest that the debates were conducted with the utmost cordiality. Both Federalists and Anti-Federalists indulged in personal attacks.[198] Moreover, there was significant principled disagreement as to the value of distrust to popular government. The Federal Farmer, for instance, celebrated "that perpetual jealousy respecting liberty so absolutely necessary in all free states."[199] Cato was much more emphatic: although "placing a reasonable confidence" in leaders, he quoted with approval Demosthenes' claim that "[d]istrust" is the "common bulwark with which men of prudence are naturally provided" and "the guard and security of all people, particularly of free states."[200] This distrust—this suspicion—is a priority of statesmanship in a free society: there is "no other way of [avoiding enslavement], than by establishing principles of distrust in your constituents, and cultivating the sentiment among yourselves."[201] Eternal suspicion, and not mere vigilance, was the price of freedom.

Publius, however, largely rejected such distrust as unfriendly to republican government. While conceding that "[j]eolousy is the usual concomitant of violent love, and the noble enthusiasm of liberty is apt to be infected with a narrow and illiberal distrust,"[202] distrust tended to undermine both the intellectual virtues and the moderation critical to popular deliberation. While "[c]aution and investigation are a necessary armor against error and imposition, . . . this untractableness . . . may degenerate into obstinacy, perverseness, and disingenuity."[203] Indeed, such "jealousy," when indulged so as to *presume* unjust purposes, can cripple both the reason and the will. With reference to the "supposition of usurpation"—that is, that federal legislators and officers will intend to violate their oaths and usurp authority not granted—Publius made remarks that could apply to any conspiracy theory:

> The moment we launch into conjectures about the usurpations of the federal government, we get into an unfathomable abyss, and fairly put ourselves out of the reach of all reasoning. Imagination may range at pleasure till it gets bewildered amidst the labyrinths of an enchanted castle, and knows not on which side to turn to extricate itself from the perplexities into which it has so rashly adventured. Whatever may be the limits or modifications of the powers of the Union, it is easy to imagine an endless train of possible dangers; and by indulging an excess of jealousy and timidity, we may bring ourselves to a state of *absolute scepticism and irresolution.*[204]

Apart from its effects on the individual citizens, distrust could destroy the people's sense of fellowship. Critical to popular self-government was a "benevolent and philosophic spirit" that would promote "policy, utility, and justice."[205] But a posture of distrust created a self-fulfilling prophecy: "Distrust naturally creates distrust."[206] Accordingly, Publius remarked that "by nothing is good will and kind conduct more speedily changed than by invidious jealousies and uncandid imputations, whether express or implied."[207] By "uncandid imputations" Publius probably meant unfounded accusations or suspicions that other citizens act from ignorance or bad will. Such imputations violated the rule of both candor and moderation. Here falsehood and unkindness meet, and a political community disintegrates.

In some sense, the Founders' disagreement as to interpersonal trust was ad hoc; the different opinion simply reflected the contingent issue at hand. The issue was whether to ratify a radical change in government proposed by a handful of men who secretly drafted a plan that violated the express charge given to them by Congress—to merely revise the Articles.[208] Under this circumstance, it was natural for proponents to preach hope and trust, and for opponents to counsel caution and distrust.

But in another sense, the disagreement may have reflected a more fundamental, enduring dispute as to human nature—a dispute reflected in the competing constitutional models. Whereas Publius favored a large republic, in the confidence that its size would frustrate faction but not destroy unity, the Anti-Federalists suggested that an increase in population and territorial extent weakened the bonds available only in local, smaller governments. Localism was so strong, in fact, that in a large republic, a strong central government would foster a new community in the nation's capital, where legislators and officials would be attached not to their purported constituents, but to a new small republic that would rule over the smaller communities of the nation.[209]

Publius showed more faith in the durability of human goodness—even among congressmen. "Duty, gratitude, interest, ambition itself are the cords by which they will be bound to fidelity and sympathy with the great mass."[210] By these same means "on which every State government in the Union relies,"[211] national legislators would remain faithful to their constituents. For professed republicans to say otherwise, Publius asserted, was to impeach the very principle of republicanism: such nametag republicans "pretend to be champions for the right and the capacity of the people to choose their own rulers, yet maintain that they will prefer those only who will immediately and infallibly betray the trust committed to them."[212]

Conclusion

Still, despite their substantial disagreements, the Federalists and Anti-Federalists proceeded from a broad agreement as to human nature and thus the conditions of popular political deliberation. They agreed that a deliberating, self-governing people required the intellectual virtues of candor and knowledge, especially historical knowledge, the moral virtue of moderation, the common language and institutions in which to deliberate effectively, and general peace and bodily security. Indeed, in large measure the distance between the Federalists and Anti-Federalists was small compared with their distance from us. Our republic seems based on a somewhat different conception of human nature. Whether the new anthropology is more accurate, more hospitable to good deliberation, and more favorable to the endurance of our republic, is a question to which experience, in the coming decades, may provide an answer.

Notes

1. Murray Dry, *Civil Peace and the Quest for Truth*, 288.
2. Ibid., Professor Dry refers to the conditions "to pursue the rational life, in our practical affairs and our other inquiries as well."
3. Brutus, in *The Complete Anti-Federalist*, ed. Herbert Storing, 2.9.1–2.9.2. All references to the text are to volume, chapter, and paragraph number, as assigned by Storing.
4. Alexander Hamilton, "Federalist No. 1," 27. All subsequent references are to this edition. Elsewhere in that number, Publius referred to the "plan offered to our deliberation" (ibid.).
5. Ibid. Elsewhere, Publius used the more Aristotelian words "deliberation and decide" instead of "reflection and choice." *Federalist*, no. 14, 100 (stating that on "the act of your convention . . . you are now to deliberate and decide"). In a similar vein, the "Federal Farmer" told New Yorkers that "[o]ur true object is . . . to arm persuasion on every side, and to render force as little necessary as possible." Federal Farmer, in *The Complete Anti-Federalist* (see note iii), 2.8.93.
6. *Federalist*, no. 1, 27.
7. Oration Delivered at the Procession in Philadelphia, in *The Works of the Honorable James Wilson, L.L.D.*, 299.
8. See, for example, Tom Kuntz, "The Most Important Article in Our History," *New York Times*, September 5, 2004 (collecting quotations).
9. *The Anti-Federalist: An Abridgement, by Murray Dry, of the Complete Anti-Federalist Writings by the Opponents of the Constitution*, ed. Murray Dry, vii.
10. *McCullough v. Maryland*, 17 U.S. 316 (1819), 433.
11. *Cohens v. Virginia*, 19 U.S. 264 (1821), 418; and *Florida v. United States HHS*, 780 F. Supp. 2d 1256 (N.D. Fla. 2011), 1264 no.2.
12. See generally, Dry, *Anti-Federalist: An Abridgement*.
13. Eugene R. Fingerhut, and Joseph S. Tiedemann, *The Other New York: The American Revolution Beyond New York City, 1763–1787*, 215. Note that it was not until 1790 that New York and Vermont settled the dispute over Vermont's western border.
14. Federal Farmer, *Complete Anti-Federalist*, 2.8.68.
15. Brutus, *Complete Anti-Federalist*, 2.9.9.
16. Ibid., 2.9.1.
17. Cato, in *The Complete Anti-Federalist* (see note iii), 2.6.6.
18. *Federalist*, no. 1, 30.
19. Ibid., no. 31, 189–190.
20. Ibid., no. 14, 95 (mentioning that the "error which limits representative government to a [small] district has been . . . refuted in preceding

papers"); *Federalist*, no. 41, 260 (noting "[h]ow difficult it is for error to escape its own condemnation").

21. Letter to Henry Lee, Esq., in *The Works of Thomas Jefferson*, ed. Paul Leister Ford, 408–409.

22. Declaration of Independence, para. 2.

23. *Gertz v. Robert Welch, Inc.*, 418 U.S. 323 (1974), 340. This dictum has been quoted in hundreds of subsequent court cases. My own search using Lexis found more than 350. See, for example, *Milkovich v. Lorain Journal Co.*, 497 U.S. 1 (1990), 18; *United States v. Alvarez*, 617 F.3d 1198 (9th Cir. 2010), 1220; cf. *West Virginia Bd. of Ed. v. Barnette*, 319 U.S. 624 (1943), 642 (famously declaring that "[i]f there is any fixed star in our constitutional constellation, it is that no official, high or petty, can prescribe what shall be orthodox in politics, nationalism, religion, or other matters of opinion *or* force citizens to confess by word or act their faith therein" [emphasis added]). The use of the conjunction "or" suggests that even in the absence of coercion, public officials may not identify a political orthodoxy. I am grateful to my father for this insight; see Paul J. Upham.

24. Harry V. Jaffa, 9.

25. James Wilson, "*Lectures on Law*," in *Complete Works of Wilson* (see note vii), 105–106 (emphasis added).

26. See, for example, *Federalist*, no. 9.

27. See, for instance, Melancton Smith's comments: "The nation of Israel, having received a form of civil government from Heaven, enjoyed it for a considerable period; but, at length, laboring under pressures which were brought upon them by their own misconduct and imprudence, instead of imputing their misfortunes to their true causes, and making a proper improvement of their calamities, by a correction of their errors, they imputed them to a defect in their constitution; they rejected their divine Ruler, and asked Samuel to make them a king to judge them, like other nations. Samuel was grieved at their folly." In *The Complete Anti-Federalist* (see note iii), 6.12.7.

28. Brutus, *Complete Anti-Federalist*, 2.9.1.

29. *Federalist*, no. 2, 34.

30. Ibid., no. 71, 430 (emphasis added).

31. Ibid., no. 76, 457.

32. *Federalist*, no. 55, 343. Such a faith in the people is not exclusive to modern republics. As Professor Dry has pointed out, with reference to Aristotle's thought, "the case for political equality is based, at least in part, on the *superior wisdom of collective deliberation*" (Dry, *Civil Peace*, 82 [emphasis added]).

33. *Federalist*, no. 76, 457.

34. Ibid., no. 39, 236 (emphasis added).

35. Ibid., no. 1, 27.

36. Ibid., no. 11, 85.

37. Federal Farmer, *Complete Anti-Federalist*, 2.8.62.

38. Ibid., 2.8.74. Elsewhere, he celebrated the "strong advantages" American enjoyed "in the equal division of our lands, and the strong and manly habits of our people (ibid., 2.8.59).

39. Cato, *Complete Anti-Federalist*, 2.6.1.

40. Federal Farmer, *Complete Anti-Federalist*, 2.8.19.

41. *Federalist*, no. 3, 36.

42. Ibid., no. 31, 2, 32.

43. Declaration of Independence, para. 32

44. Ibid., para. 2.

45. Cato, *Complete Anti-Federalist*, 2.6.4.

46. Federal Farmer, *Complete Anti-Federalist*, 2.8.64.

47. A Citizen of New York, Address, in *Friends of the Constitution: Writings of the "Other" Federalists 1787–1788*, eds., Colleen A. Sheehan and Gary L. McDowell, 137, 153.

48. *Federalist*, no. 2, 34 (emphasis in original).

49. Federal Farmer, *Complete Anti-Federalist*, 2.8.69.

50. Ibid., 2.8.69.

51. Ibid., 2.8.1.

52. Ibid., 2.8.60.

53. Ibid., 2.8.1 (disavowing "any bias at all" except, perhaps, his "uniform federal attachments [and his] interest ... in the protection of property, and a steady execution of the laws" and stating that "I do not mean, hastily and positively to decide on the merits of the constitution proposed," and that "I shall be open to conviction, and always disposed to adopt that which, all things considered, shall appear to me to be most for the happiness of the community").

54. *Federalist*, no. 1, 30 (emphasis added). In response, Brutus wrote as follows: "He sets out with calling in question the candour and integrity [of his opponents]. The man who reproves another for a fault, should be careful that he himself be not guilty of it. How far this writer has manifested a spirit of candour, and has pursued fair reasoning on this subject, the impartial public will judge, when his arguments pass before them in review" (Brutus, *Complete Anti-Federalist*, 2.9.111). And with reference to the issue of standing armies, Brutus replied to Publius as follows: "The public will judge, from the above comparison, how just a claim this writer has to that candour he affects to possess. In the mean time, to convince him, and the advocates for this system, that I possess some share of candor, I pledge myself to give up all opposition to it, on the head of standing armies, if the

power to raise them be restricted as it is in the present confederation" (ibid., 2.9.114).
55. Cato, *Complete Anti-Federalist*, 2.6.12 and 2.6.20.
56. *Federalist*, no. 31, 189.
57. Ibid.
58. Brutus, *Complete Anti-Federalist*, 2.9.45.
59. Ibid., 2.9.98.
60. Sydney, *Address* in *The Complete Anti-Federalist* (see note iii), 6.8.15.
61. Cincinnatus in *The Complete Anti-Federalist* (see note iii), 6.1.35.
62. Melancton Smith, in *The Complete Anti-Federalist* (see note iii), 6.12.17.
63. Brutus, *Complete Anti-Federalist*, 2.9.9
64. Ibid.
65. Brutus Jr., in *The Complete Anti-Federalist* (see note iii), 6.3.7.
66. Cato, *Complete Anti-Federalist*, 2.6.31.
67. *Federalist*, no. 48, 305.
68. Ibid., no. 37, 244.
69. Ibid., no. 44, 278.
70. Ibid., no. 51, 319.
71. Ibid., no. 58, 358.
72. Ibid., no. 26, 164.
73. Ibid., no. 72, 437.
74. Ibid., no. 20, 133.
75. Ibid., no. 52, 324.
76. The earliest source I have found for this saying is from an anecdote told in 1936 by an American military officer, Lieutenant General Simon Bolivar Buckner: "Uncle Zeke was known in my Kentucky home town for his wisdom. One day a young friend asked him, 'Uncle Zeke, how come you're so wise?' 'Because I've got good judgment,' the old man replied. 'Good judgment comes from experience, and experience—well, that comes from poor judgment.'" "The Voice of Experience," in *The Reader's Digest*66.
77. *Federalist*, no. 15, 101.
78. Ibid., no. 38, 299.
79. Ibid., no. 15, 103.
80. Ibid., no. 38, 299 (remarking that "among the numerous objections and amendments suggested by the several States, when these articles were submitted for their ratification, not one is found which alludes to the great and radical error which on actual trial has discovered itself").
81. Ibid., no. 5, 45.
82. Ibid., no. 43, 272; and ibid., no. 45, 286 (discussing "ancient and modern confederacies"); ibid., no. 63, 384 (discussing "other popular

governments, as well ancient as modern"); and ibid., no. 52, 324 (explaining that "[t]he scheme of representation, as a substitute for a meeting of the citizens in person, being at most but very imperfectly known to ancient polity, it is in more modern times only that we are to expect instructive examples").

83. Ibid., no. 10, 72.
84. See generally, ibid., nos. 18–20, 118–134.
85. Noah Webster [A Citizen of America, pseud.], "An Examination Into the Leading Principles of the Federal Constitution," in *Friends of the Constitution* (see note xlvii), 373, 376.
86. Ibid.
87. Ibid., 373–374 (emphasis in original).
88. Cincinnatus, *Complete Anti-Federalist*, 6.1.37.
89. Brutus, *Complete Anti-Federalist*, 2.9.116; and Cato, *Complete Anti-Federalist*, 2.6.19 (indicating that the people should "attend to the history of mankind"); Federal Farmer, *Complete Anti-Federalist*, 2.8.178 (affirming that the people should "examine history attentively").
90. *Federalist*, no. 64, 390 (arguing that the Senators' six-year term "is such as will give them an opportunity of greatly extending their political information, and of rendering their accumulating experience more and more beneficial to their country"); *Federalist*, no. 72, 437 (claiming that presidential term limits would deprive "the community of the advantage of the experience gained by the chief magistrate in the exercise of his office"); Publius celebrated the Constitutional Convention because "some of the most distinguished" delegates brought to the deliberations "their accumulated knowledge and experience" (*Federalist*, no. 2, 35).
91. Federal Farmer, *Complete Anti-Federalist*, 2.8.147.
92. Noah Webster, "On the Education of Youth in America," in *The Founders' Constitution*, eds. Philip B. Kurland, and Ralph Lerner, 679–680.
93. Ibid.
94. "Notes on the State of Virginia," in *Works of Jefferson* (see note xxi), 64.
95. Thucydides, *The Peloponnesian War*, II.1, quoted in Dry, *Civic Virtue*, 89.
96. Cato, *Complete Anti-Federalist*, 2.6.5.
97. *Federalist*, no. 44, 99.
98. Ibid., 99–100.
99. *Federalist*, no. 9. Even here, this modern science would rely heavily on a consideration of experience, as the innovations he mentions (representative assemblies, judicial tenure of "good behavior, etc.) were decades-old (if not centuries-old) features of the English constitution. Ibid., p. 67.
100. Ibid., no. 2, 32.

101. David Micklethwait, 102 (quoting Webster) (emphasis in original).
102. Cato, *Complete Anti-Federalist*, 2.6.28.
103. *Federalist*, no. 68, 410.
104. Ibid.
105. According to the initial designation, the largest congressional delegation was Virginia's with ten representatives and two senators.
106. *Federalist*, no. 68, 410 (emphasis added).
107. Murray Dry, "The Constitutional Thought of the Anti-Federalists," (explaining that most of the Anti-Federalists "accepted the unitary office and the 'electoral college' mode of election"); *Federalist*, no. 68, 410 (remarking that the electoral college is "almost the only part of the system, of any consequence, which . . . has received the slightest mark of approbation from its opponents"); Federal Farmer, *Complete Anti-Federalist*, 2.8.29 (conceding that the election of the president and vice-president "seems to be properly secured").
108. Articles of Confederation. art. 5 (providing that "[n]o State shall be represented in Congress by less than two, nor more than seven members").
109. U.S. Constitution, art. 2, sec. 2–3. The First Congress proposed, as its first amendment, to increase gradually this "floor" to 200 members. "Amendments to the Constitution (Sept. 28, 1789)," in *Creating the Bill of Rights: The Documentary History of the First Federal Congress,* eds., Helen E. Veit, Kenneth Bowling, and Charlene Bangs Bickford, 3.
110. *Federalist*, no. 55, 340.
111. Ibid. Elsewhere, Publius explained that "the representatives must be raised to a certain number, in order to guard against the cabals of a few" but that "they must be limited to a certain number, in order to guard against the confusion of a multitude" (*Federalist*, no. 10, 77).
112. Articles of Confederation, art. 5 (providing that "[n]o State shall be represented in Congress by less than two, nor more than seven members").
113. U.S. Constitution, art. 1, sec. 2; the unratified "first amendment" would have further lowered this ceiling to one representative for every 50,000 inhabitants ("Amendments to the Constitution," 3).
114. Federal Farmer, *Complete Anti-Federalist*, 2.8.33.
115. Ibid., 2.8.136.
116. Cato, *Complete Anti-Federalist*, 2.6.38.
117. Federal Farmer, *Complete Anti-Federalist*, 2.8.27.
118. *Federalist*, no. 16, 109.
119. Declaration of Independence, para. 2.
120. Dry, *Civil Peace*, 82.
121. Ibid., 99.
122. Federal Farmer, *Complete Anti-Federalist*, 2.8.93 (emphasis added).

123. "Amendments Proposed by the New York Convention (July 26, 1778)," in *Creating the Bill of Rights* (see note cviii), 21–23.

124. *Chisholm v. Georgia*, 2 U.S. (2. Dall.) 419 (1793), 471–472 (opinion of Jay, C.J.).

125. Ibid., 463 (opinion of Wilson, J.) (stating that "the people of the United States" consisted in "the citizens of thirteen States, each of which had a separate Constitution and Government, and all of which were connected together by articles of confederation"); "Lectures on Law," *Complete Works of Wilson*, 432, 442 (defining a citizen as "one of the people" and including within a discussion of the "duties and rights of a citizen" as opposed to an alien, that "[t]he citizen under a free government has a right to think, to speak, to write, to print, and to publish freely . . . concerning publick men, publick bodies, and publick measures").

126. *Reports of the Proceedings and Debates of the New York Constitutional Convention of 1821*, eds., Nathaniel H. Carter and William L. Stone, 27–28.

127. New York Constitution, art. 7, sec. 3, 7–8 (guarantying religious freedom to "all mankind" and due-process rights to every "person," but the freedom of speech and press to "every citizen"). *

128. U.S. Constitution, amend. 1.

129. Ibid.

130. "Madison Resolutions (June 8, 1789)," in *Creating the Bill of Rights* (see note cviii), 11–12; it was a House select committee that combined these proposals into one provision that mentioned "freedom of speech, and of the press and the right of the people peaceably to assemble" (ibid., "House Committee Report (July 28, 1789)," 29–30).

131. Ibid.

132. Cincinnatus, *Complete Anti-Federalist*, 6.1.7.

133. Federal Farmer, *Complete Anti-Federalist*, 2.8.203.

134. Professor Dry ascribes this silence to the fact that the Federal Constitution was not designed to secure this freedom, which was already "enjoyed in practice" (*Civil Peace*, 72); this silence also no doubt arose from the fact that the absence of a constitutional guaranty for this and other freedoms was one of the most effective objections to ratification.

135. "The Virginia Report," in *The Mind of the Founder: Sources of the Political Thought of James Madison*, rev. ed., ed. Marvis Meyers, 229–243.

136. *Blackstone's Commentaries*, ed. St. George Tucker, 296–297; see also Virginia Constitution of 1776, Declaration of Rights, sec. 12 (declaring that "the freedom of the press is one of the great bulwarks of liberty, and can never be restrained but by despotick governments").

137. "Lectures on Law," *Complete Works of Wilson*,443 (emphasis added).
138. Ibid. (emphasis added). Wilson added, immediately after mentioning the citizen's freedom of speech, "[t]hus much concerning the duties and the rights of a private citizen. I next treat of aliens" (ibid.)
139. New York Constitution of 1821, art. 7.
140. *Bridges v. California*, 314 U.S. 252 (1941), 280 (Frankfurter, J., dissenting).
141. *Bridges v. Wixon*, 326 U.S. 135 (1945), 148.
142. *Citizens United v. FEC*, 558 U.S. 310 (2010) (affirming that the First Amendment protects corporations and leaving open the question of whether "the question whether the Government has a compelling interest in preventing foreign individuals or associations from influencing our Nation's political process"); Brad Smith, "Debunking the Citizens United Horror Stories: Episode 1: Foreign Corporations," Center for Competitive Politics, January 24, 2010, www.campaignfreedom. org/2010/01/24/debunking-the-citizens-united-horror-stories-episode-1-foreign-corporations/?pagename=debunking-the-citizens-united-horror-stories-episode-1-foreign-corporations, (purporting to debunk the concern but noting that under federal law, businesses incorporated in the United States but owned by foreign nationals would enjoy free speech rights pursuant to *Citizens United*).
143. A Lexis search of federal and state court opinions in the nineteenth century reveals that "freedom of expression," "liberty of expression" or "free expression" was rarely used to designate the constitutional freedoms of communication—and only in two cases before the Civil War: *Wardens of Church of St. Louis v. Blanc*, 8 Rob. 51(La. 1844) (affirming that "[t]he highest prelate of the church, in common with the most humble worshipper, cannot be molested on account of his religious opinions, and the free expression of them"); and *United States v. Lumsden*, Case, 26 F. Cas. 1013 (C.C.S.D. Ohio 1856) (No. 15,641) (noting the absence of "any law, state or national, forbidding assemblies of the people for any lawful purpose, or restricting the right of a free expression of opinion, either by speaking or writing").
144. *Milwaukee Social Democratic Pub. Co v. Burleson* 255 U.S. 407 (1921), 431.
145. Ibid., 431 (Brandeis, J., dissenting) (arguing that certain restrictions on the use of the mail "would prove an effective censorship and abridge seriously freedom of expression").
146. *Gitlow v. New York*, 268 U.S. 652,(1925), 664.
147. See, for example, *West Virginia State Bd. of Educ. v. Barnette*, 319 U.S. 624 (1943), 664; *Carpenters & Joiners Union v. Ritter's Cafe*, 315 U.S. 722 (1942), 725; and *Minersville School Dist. v. Gobitis*, 310 U.S. 586 (1940), 604.

148. Brutus, *Complete Anti-Federalist*, 2.9.1.

149. Cato, *Complete Anti-Federalist*, 2.6.5.

150. Ibid., 2.6.9.

151. Federal Farmer, *Complete Anti-Federalist*, 2.8.62, 2.8.64.

152. *Federalist*, no. 1, 28.

153. Ibid., no. 63, 382.

154. Ibid., no. 49, 314.

155. Federal Farmer, *Complete Anti-Federalist*, 2.8.125 (emphasis added).

156. Ibid., 2.8.3 (emphasis added); see also Cato *Complete Anti-Federalist*, 2.6.7 (attacking the Federalist "Caesar" who "shuts the door of free deliberation and discussion, and declares, that you must receive this government in the manner and form as it is *proffered*") (emphasis in original).

157. *Federalist*, no. 6, 49 (giving various examples of "private passions," including "the attachments, enmities, interests, hopes, and fears); cf. *Federalist*, no. 10 (seeming to distinguish "passions" from "interests").

158. Ibid., no. 10, 73.

159. Ibid.

160. Ibid., no. 15, 106.

161. Ibid., 104.

162. Ibid., 108.

163. Ibid., no. 10, 74.

164. Ibid., no. 42, 264.

165. Ibid., no. 3, 39.

166. See, for example, Federal Farmer, *Complete Anti-Federalist*, 2.8.69 (accusing the Constitution's proponents of using "mysterious veils," instead of speaking with "candor and firmness").

167. *Federalist*, no. 11, 83 (noting that "[t]he dissolution of the Confederacy would give room for delicate questions concerning the future existence of [certain littoral] rights"); ibid., no. 42, 266 (claiming that vesting the federal government with power to establish a uniform rule of naturalization would avoid "intricate and delicate questions" arising from disuniform rules).

168. Federal Farmer, *Complete Anti-Federalist*, 2.8.68.

169. *Federalist*, no. 38, 230.

170. Ibid.

171. ibid., no. 43, 276 (emphasis in original).

172. Ibid.

173. Ibid.

174. Ibid.

175. Ibid.

176. Ibid.

177. Ibid.

THE CONDITIONS OF POPULAR POLITICAL DELIBERATION   319

178. Ibid., 276–277 (emphasis in original).
179. See generally, ibid., 6–8, 48–66.
180. Ibid., no. 16, 109.
181. See, for example, ibid., no. 5, 47–48 (noting that in disunion, each state might be more "desirous to guard against the others by the aid of foreign alliances, than to guard against foreign dangers by alliances between themselves" and warning "how much more easy it is to receive foreign fleets into our ports, and foreign armies into our country, than it is to persuade or compel them to depart").
182. Ibid. (stating that in case of civil war, "recourse would be had to the aid of foreign powers").
183. Kent published and distributed abridgements of the Federalist Papers during the ratification debates in Dutchess County. Elizabeth Kelley Bauer, *Commentaries on the Constitution, 1790–1860*, 82; John Jay, as Governor, gave Kent his first judicial appointment (ibid., 84).
184. *People v. Ruggles*, 8 Johns. 290 (N.Y. 1811), 294.
185. Ibid.
186. Ibid.
187. Ibid., 295.
188. Ibid., 292.
189. Ibid., 291.
190. See Leonard Levy, 400–401 (explaining that in the early national period, anti-blasphemy prosecutions were "isolated" and "aberrant," for "[t]he American temperament looked askance at prosecutions for bad opinion").
191. *Federalist*, no. 1, 28 (emphasis added to "moderation," but in original as to "candor").
192. Federal Farmer, *Complete Anti-Federalist*, 2.8.2.
193. Ibid., 2.8.7.
194. Ibid., 2.8.3, 2.8.6.
195. Ibid., 2.8.60.
196. Ibid., 2.8.53.
197. Ibid., 2.8.25.
198. Ibid., 2.8.73, n.52.
199. Ibid., 2.8.58.
200. Cato, *Complete Anti-Federalist*, 2.6.48.
201. Ibid.
202. *Federalist*, no. 1, 29.
203. Ibid., no. 31, 190.
204. Ibid., 192 (emphasis added).
205. Ibid., no. 6, 51.
206. Ibid., no. 5, 46.
207. Ibid.

208. Ibid., no. 40, 243–247 (addressing this problem).
209. See text accompanying notes (ibid.).
210. Ibid., no. 57, 350–351.
211. Ibid., 351.
212. Ibid.

Bibliography

Bauer, Elizabeth Kelley. *Commentaries on the Constitution, 1790–1860.* New York: Columbia University Press, 1952.

Blackson, William. *Blackstone's Commentaries.* Edited by St. George Tucker. 5 vols. Philadelphia: William Young Birch, Abraham Small, 1803.

Buckner, Simon Bolivar Buckner. "The Voice of Experience." *The Reader's Digest.* Vol. 46, 1945.

Carter, Nathaniel H., and William L. Stone, eds. *Reports of the Proceedings and Debates of the New York Constitutional Convention of 182.1* Albany: Hosford, 1821.

Dry, Murray, ed. *The Anti-Federalist: An Abridgement, by Murray Dry, of the Complete Anti-Federalist Writings by the Opponents of the Constitution.* Chicago: University of Chicago Press 1985.

———. "The Constitutional Thought of the Anti-Federalists." In *This Constitution: A Biosentential Chronicle.* American Political Science Association and American Historical Association, 1985.

———. *Civil Peace and the Quest for Truth.* Lanham: Lexington Books, 2004.

Fingerhut, Eugene R., and Joseph S. Tiedemann. *The Other New York: The American Revolution Beyond New York City, 1763–1787.* Albany: State University of New York Press, 2005.

Hamilton, Alexander, James Madison, and John Jay. *The Federalist Papers.* Edited by Clinton Rossiter and Charles R. Kesler. New York: Signet Classics, 2003.

Jaffa, Harry V. *Crisis of the House Divided.* Chicago: University of Chicago Press, 1858.

Jefferson, Thomas. The *Works of Thomas Jefferson.* Edited by Paul Leister Ford. 12 vols. New York: Putnam's Sons, 1904.

Kurland, Philip B., and Ralph Lerner, eds. *The Founders' Constitution.* 5 vols. Chicago: University of Chicago Press, 1986.

Levy, Leonard. *Blasphemy: Verbal Offense Against the Sacred, from Moses to Salman Rushdie.* Chapel Hill: University of North Caroline Press, 1993.

Madison, James. *The Mind of the Founder: Sources of the Political Thought of James Madison.* Rev. ed. Edited by Marvis Meyers. Waltham, MA: Brandeis University Press, 1981.

Micklethwait, David. *Noah Webster and the American Dictionary.* New ed. Jefferson, NC: McFarland, 2005.

Sheehan, Colleen A., and Gary L. McDowell, eds. *Friends of the Constitution: Writings of the "Other" Federalists 1787–1788.* Indianapolis: Liberty Fund, 1998.

Storing, Herbert, ed. *The Complete Anti-Federalist.* 7 vols. Chicago: University of Chicago Press, 1981.

Thucydides. *The Peloponnesian War.* Edited by Robert B. Strassler. Translated by Richard Crowley. New York: Free Press, 1998.

Upham, Paul J. "The Pledge of Allegiance to the Flag of the United States of America: An Historical Report/Review." Unpublished manuscript.

Veit, Helen E., Kenneth Bowling, and Charlene Bangs Bickford, eds. *Creating the Bill of Rights: The Documentary History of the First Federal Congress.* Annapolis: Johns Hopkins University Press, 1991.

Webster, Noah. "An Examination Into the Leading Principles of the Federal Constitution." In *Friends of the Constitution.*

———. "On the Education of Youth in America." In *The Founders' Constitution.*

Wilson, James. *The Works of the Honorable James Wilson, L.L.D.* Edited by Bird Wilson. 3 vols. Philadelphia: Lorenzo Press, 1804.

Chapter 11

Tocqueville on Liberal Democracy and the Philosophy of Moderation

Paul O. Carrese

For Americans, who still live to some degree under the institutional framework and political principles of the moderate Enlightenment—embodied by the philosopher Montesquieu, and later best articulated by his countryman Tocqueville—it is good that moderation still has some standing in public life. It is regularly invoked by public intellectuals as a rare but essential ingredient in the discourse and self-government of a free people. The adage still employed in many American government textbooks, when explaining our political tendency toward adopting (eventually) compromises and balanced policies that are not fully satisfactory to any one view or party, is a football metaphor. Because of our complex order of separated institutions, federalism, and competition among parties and interests, American politics tends to be played between the 40-yard lines. What is largely missing is the intellectual or philosophical defense of this institutional and political moderation that informed our founding political science. The American Framers learned that political science from Montesquieu more than from any other European philosopher. Tocqueville later analyzed and expressed the philosophy of moderation perhaps more astutely than any other modern philosopher, drawing on his study of Montesquieu and of America. I first studied Montesquieu and Tocqueville, and seriously studied these issues, with Paul Nelson and Murray Dry at Middlebury College; and Dry identifies moderation as an essential virtue in his account of our freedoms of speech and religion. Both gratitude to my teachers, and duty to investigate a neglected yet important topic, compel a deeper look at whether there is a philosophy or principle of moderation.[1]

Voices both left and right, whether in politics or the academic study of politics, are mistaken if they suppose that moderation as a principle must be only half-hearted about the pursuit of justice or truth, even if that posture describes some who, in particular circumstances, call themselves moderates. For the Federalists and Anti-Federalists of the American Founding, as for Montesquieu and Tocqueville, moderation was not a mushy avoidance of conflict and thus a betrayal of either justice or truth. Rather, moderation was a liberal and modern adoption of the classical and medieval conceptions of political and intellectual balance in the Aristotelian tradition. As informed by Montesquieu, and explained by Tocqueville, the first American political science saw moderation not as a one-dimensional concept that sought a safe middle point on a line between two extremes. In the Aristotelian tradition as mediated by Montesquieu, true moderation was characterized by at least two dimensions—as an excellence or virtue that rose above opposing and false extremes, as in the peak of a triangle, toward an intellectual and political excellence found in a golden mean. Moreover, they understood in this broadly Aristotelian way that the true and just point was not necessarily the mathematical middle, but instead was farther from whichever point was the graver error or danger of the two erroneous extremes.[2] For example, separation of powers avoids the extreme of unified, absolute political power while also avoiding the opposite extreme of complexity that yields only gridlock; yet, separation of powers keeps farther from absolutism, and risks the occasional moment of gridlock. Philosophically, the modified Socratic dialectic of the Aristotelian tradition—broadly found in Aquinas, Montesquieu, and Tocqueville—avoids at one extreme a fanatical, absolute devotion to a single idea that forbids inquiry and debate but also avoids, at the other, pure skepticism or relativism. In the modern era, Montesquieu and Tocqueville saw the radical Enlightenment as occupying each of these rival extremes of single-mindedness and skepticism simultaneously, and thereby as abandoning the philosophical middle. The philosophies of Hobbes and Locke evince too much skepticism and relativism about larger moral and political truths that should guide political science and politics; in response, a moderate liberal philosophy should address moral principles and political culture as well as individual rights. Regarding the other extreme, Montesquieu and Tocqueville saw a methodological rigidity or single-mindedness in the radical Enlightenment—with its strict foundationalism in individual rights—and thus proposed a moderated, more complex political science and constitutionalism. These extremes of the radical Enlightenment occupied flip sides of a single coin, and while this kind of rationalist clarity became attractive to later thinkers and actors, the moderate philosophers warned that such a currency could not sustain a decent liberal civilization.

We should care about rediscovering these ideas of political-institutional and also philosophical moderation because this is the principle behind both the architecture of our politics and also the software originally designed to operate our hardware of separation of powers, federalism, and party competition. The last of these, a culture of faction, was accepted by Montesquieu and the Framers as a necessary evil in a liberal order, but one especially in need of moderation. Indeed, on the level of practice, today's academic and public concern with polarization or counterproductive acrimony in American politics and discourse is traceable in part to our failure to any longer study and teach the principle of moderation, of balance and the avoidance of extremes, that was intended to sustain our debates and deeds in politics. On the intellectual plane, there is growing awareness that our universities and disciplines are not intellectually balanced and thus not adequately searching for or discerning the truth, but instead are reinforcing self-segregated and self-selected paths of inquiry, especially but not exclusively in the humanities and social sciences. The two failures of moderation, in political discourse and practice but also in intellectual discourse, are related. However, those who worry about destructive polarization in our political practice are not so likely to see the intellectual imbalance that is a significant contributing cause to the phenomena they deplore.

To find our bearings, we can begin with a presumption about the evergreen insights of Tocqueville, namely, that *Democracy in America* arguably is still the best book ever written about America, and the best book ever written about democracy.[3] Intellectuals on the left and the right, and politicians across the spectrum, still invoke Tocqueville's insights and quote (as well as misquote or invent) passages from this great work. It is worth inquiring, then, about the signs of political and intellectual immoderation Tocqueville warned about when he assessed both America and modern liberal democracy a century and a half ago. We then would have reliable guidance on the deeper causes of these dimensions of immoderation, and a deeper argument for why we should reconsider moderation as both a political and intellectual virtue.

Montesquieu and Tocqueville on the Intellectual Virtue of Moderation

The Socratic tradition of philosophy more easily recognizes moderation as a supposed political and moral virtue, but we have difficulty even recognizing moderation as an intellectual virtue. In politics, we recognize the balancing of institutions or centers of power as found in separation of powers, federalism, and competition among parties or interests. There is still a slight memory that we understand these modes of political moderation through Montesquieu's philosophy above all, because Hobbes's liberalism never even addresses these principles, and Locke's offers only a simple separation of powers and nothing at all on federalism and parties. Still, our predominant thinking now is that if moderation has any value it is on the plane of politics, because the single-mindedness we find in Hobbes and Locke—not to mention Spinoza, Rousseau, Marx, or Nietzsche—is an indication of their philosophic seriousness. As for Montesquieu, the charge arose even in his lifetime that it is not philosophical complexity, but really just confusion, that we find in his sprawling efforts at intellectual moderation or balance. Shouldn't a philosopher be intransigent, uncompromising, clear, and single-minded in the search for the truth—or, as later moderns might urge, in seeking the most recent revaluation of our ever-changing values? If phrased another way, however, we might see the point about intellectual moderation as a virtue. Should a philosopher be dogmatic and fanatical in pursuing his favored views? Should a thinker impose a degree of clarity that does not exist in the phenomena, simply to meet an abstract theoretical test of rigor or purity? Understood this way, the roots of philosophical moderation are deep in our tradition. Ultimately, they are traceable to Socratic dialectic, and also to the dialectical method of the *quaestio* in Aquinas, which is integral to the substantive moderation he demonstrates in exploring the compatibility of revelation and reason. Consideration of Aquinas helps us to see that the most recognizable and characteristic forms of such moderation lie in the Aristotelian tradition, broadly conceived.[4]

The classic exposition of pursuing the mean as the method and principle of moral philosophy is, as noted, the *Nicomachean Ethics*. The complexity and care of that work reveals the fundamental challenge of this approach, because any analysis of ethics or politics that discerns moderation between extreme alternatives must persuasively define, and ground, the extremes as well as the spectrum connecting them. While Aristotle does not launch the *Politics*—the sequel to the *Ethics*—by announcing the same method and aim, the first work of the new discipline of political science is replete with arguments that the political good and justice are found in a middle between intellectual and institutional extremes. The *Politics* thus counsels that political philosophers and also legislators should avoid extremes about the status of gods, beasts, and humanity; about money, communism, and private property; and about unity, divisiveness, and pluralism, either in Plato's ideal polis or a more reasonably ideal polis. Aristotle thus defends polity, or the mixed and well-balanced regime, as one the three correct regimes. Moreover, while he states (at the close of Book 3 of *Politics*) that only aristocracy and monarchy are best regimes simply, he offers many suggestions throughout the *Politics* that a correctly structured and balanced polity also could be a regime of excellent rule.[5] Aristotle had not encountered the claims of the modern philosophers and especially the radical Enlightenment about new, mathematically precise foundations for utterly new sciences of moral philosophy and politics, yet already he counseled philosophical moderation. The *Ethics* argues that any science of human affairs (ethics or politics) should strive to attain only "the clarity that accords with the subject matter," and that "one should not seek precision in all arguments alike," implying that arguments about what is just or noble will be lost upon, or dismissed by, those seeking mathematical precision. Thus, "it belongs to an educated person to seek out precision in each genus to the extent that the nature of the matter allows: to accept persuasive speech from a skilled mathematician appears comparable to demanding [mathematical] demonstrations from a skilled rhetorician."[6]

It is no coincidence that Montesquieu sought to revive a broadly Aristotelian approach after the bold, rationalist claims of the radical Enlightenment, and after the political turbulence brought about by modern ideas of liberty. One king had been beheaded in England in the prior century, and Cromwell had shown the possibilities for republican despotism. Only a few decades after publication of *The Spirit of Laws*, a more radical regicide and revolution would engulf France. The architect of balance or moderation in modern liberal constitutionalism thus was keen to warn of a particularly virulent strain of philosophical dogmatism or fanaticism arising, paradoxically, from the conditions of modern freedom. Montesquieu's second portrait of England in *The Spirit of Laws* examines how a constitution of liberty shapes the mores and culture of its people, and it closes with a biting criticism: "In extremely absolute monarchies, historians betray the truth because they do not have the liberty to tell it; in extremely free states, historians betray the truth because of their very liberty, for, as it always produces divisions, every one becomes as much the slave of the prejudices of his faction as he would be of a despot."[7] Because Montesquieu was a historian as well as a philosopher—having published *Considerations on the Romans* in 1734—and, given his remarks throughout *The Spirit of Laws* about the prejudices and tendency to extremes among philosophers and modern thinkers, he seems to have more than historians in mind.[8]

Indeed, a main point of *The Spirit of Laws* is to educate philosophers and statesman about complexity and balance as principles of both political theory and practice.[9] Montesquieu's modern conception of moderation sought to capture the philosophic complexity he thought necessary to comprehend reality, and he declared this the key to his labyrinthine masterwork. The long-criticized complexity of *The Spirit of Laws*—30 books, in 605 chapters, stretching to 700 pages in a recent translation—sought to correct Enlightenment philosophy and liberalism by restoring an appreciation for the multifarious reality of humanity and politics. Montesquieu thought the analytical rigor of modernity had slighted the multiple dimensions of human affairs and the equilibrium—the moderation—evident in the very nature of things.[10] So it is that, only near the end of the reader's long, complicated journey through *The Spirit of Laws*, Montesquieu sounds the keynote to the work: "I say it, and it seems to me I have brought forth this work only to prove it: the spirit of moderation ought to be that of the legislator; the political good, like the moral good, is always found between two limits."[11] He seems to have postponed this statement until he had shown that he had granted the world its complexity and patiently observed it. Just a few chapters later he chastises both ancient and modern political philosophers (Aristotle, Plato,

More, Machiavelli, Harrington) as "legislators" who succumbed to their "passions and prejudices" by reducing all of politics to some one concept.[12] Once we see this principle of moderation at work in his philosophy we can understand why Montesquieu, not Locke, was the foremost philosophic influence upon the framers of the American Declaration and 1787 Constitution. Our constitutionalism is not simple but complex—blending liberalism and modern republican-ism but also elements of classical philosophy, Christianity, and classic common law.[13] Such moderation or balancing of diverse principles not only pervades the structures of our constitutionalism but also shapes the complexity of American life and thought, evident still today in our blending of single-minded principle and broad plural-ism, of individual rights and public purposes.

Once we place *Democracy in America* alongside *The Spirit of Laws*, the philosophical kinship is evident. This is not to say that Tocqueville saw himself as writing merely a philosophical footnote to his prede-cessor. After the French Revolution, and given the evident contrast between the relatively successful launch of American liberal democ-racy and the disastrous launch of the French version, Tocqueville saw the need to moderate Montesquieu's conception of moderation. That is, he recalibrates Montesquieu's modern conception to emphasize classical and medieval themes about the greater importance of mores as opposed to institutions for sustaining a decent liberal-democratic order. Thus, he more openly advocates the truth and importance of religious belief for democracy—even though Tocqueville himself seems to have lost his faith as a young man and could affirm only a philosophical truth about a transcendent divine mind, and, even though he feared for the eventual decline of religious belief under conditions of modern democracy and its materialism. Tocqueville also revises Montesquieu's moderation given his own perception, post–French Revolution, of a European world awash in philosophical ambition that may be doing more harm than good; a worry he voices even before the rise of Nietzsche and the avowed self-destruction of Western philosophy. He further moderates the Enlightenment by hiding his philosophical ambition and avoiding abstraction, thus adopting the pose of a thinker, a man of letters, a bridge between theory and practice who is wary of the pretensions of *philosophes*.[14] This philosophical moderation can be glimpsed in his opening to Volume Two of *Democracy in America*, adopting a Montesquieuan stance about the need to rise above parties and fads. Indeed, this is all the more necessary because he senses the winds blowing in favor of liberal democracy: "it is because I was not an adversary of democracy that I wanted to be sincere with it. Men do not receive the truth from their enemies, and their friends scarcely offer it to them; that is why I have spoken it."[15]

Tocqueville's Moderation: Liberty, the Soul, and Political Science

Democracy in America is, like Montesquieu's masterwork, a rich and complicated work of political philosophy addressing the dilemmas and possibilities of the moment while also seeking enduring philosophic understanding. Tocqueville generally endorses Montesquieu's philosophical moderation, which blends the classical quest for honor and prudence in politics with the modern concern for individual dignity and secure liberty. Still, while he shows his debt to Montesquieu in *Democracy* and other writings, his conception of moderation pulls his predecessor's thought in an ancient and medieval direction even while being more committed to equality in a more openly Christian vein. Thus, Tocqueville's political philosophy questions whether the predominantly negative or skeptical view of human nature and liberty in Montesquieu (and other liberals) can provide a decent politics of equality and liberty.[16]

Like Montaigne and Montesquieu before him, Tocqueville was an aristocrat and jurist; he was also, however, an advocate of the new conception of democracy, if a moderate one. The French Revolution posed deep problems for the meaning not only of aristocracy but also of law, right, and philosophy itself in the new democratic era. In *Democracy in America* he addresses these and other pressing issues but also opens the work by declaring a higher, philosophic duty of moderation: "This book is not precisely in anyone's camp; in writing it I did not mean either to serve or to contest any party; I undertook to see, not differently, but further than the parties; and while they are occupied with the next day, I wanted to ponder the future." His prefatory note to Volume Two, on speaking "the truth" to democracy because he is a friend to it, also notes that the first volume was praised for its "impartiality," and that he hopes the same is true of the sequel.[17] It might be said that Tocqueville's focus was literally on parties and the partisan contests, especially in France and Europe, but he makes too many references to philosophical views standing behind parties to justify this narrow reading. We also should query a related kind of narrowness regarding Tocqueville, practiced by recent communitarian and liberal theorists, who mostly use him to carry the standards of their schools—be it civic participation, equality, or individual autonomy and tolerance.[18]

If Tocqueville is to help us to see farther than we normally do in late-modern liberal discourse, one point of departure is his cryptic statement in introducing *Democracy* about "a mother thought that so to speak links all its parts." This seems to be not a single abstract concept, nor is it a usual variety of liberalism. In the Introduction, and elsewhere in the work, he emphasizes his concern with ensuring that the new "equality of conditions" remains a democratic liberty and not a democratic "tyranny," a kind of equality safe for, and that even will nurture, the "natural greatness of man" inherent in the human soul.[19] To undertake this analysis, and convey his judgment, *Democracy in America* follows *The Spirit of Laws* in comprehensiveness and complexity—examining institutions and laws (Volume One, Part One) but also political mores (Volume One, Part Two) and then ideas, sentiments, and private mores that both reflect and reinforce the politics of liberal democracy (Volume Two, in four parts). While Tocqueville does not make a declaration on a principle of moderation, as Montesquieu does, he nurtures a political science that seeks to nudge democracy away from its excesses (including especially its excessive attachment to equality and individualism) by reminding it of the aristocratic principles that preceded it. By so restraining democracy's drift, and praising balance and a proper middle ground, Tocqueville seeks to moderate its "dangerous instincts." *Democracy* thus opens by noting that in Europe since 1789 democracy was "adored" then "weakened by its own excesses" and then some sought to destroy it "instead of seeking to instruct and correct it."[20] He sketches a better democratic society marked by moderation regarding the rule of law, authority, and class relations; by the balance of individual interests and public duties; and, by the ability to avoid both tyranny and anarchy. If "less brilliant, less glorious, less strong" than some aristocratic alternatives, this properly balanced, elevated, and moderate democracy is more just to all persons, and this moderate ideal "would have taken from democracy all the goods it can offer" to modern peoples.[21] The Americans took steps toward achieving this moderate ideal: the superiority of the federal Constitution over those of the states is that it follows "a more just and moderate course," in that the federal Framers sought to temper and even counteract majority tyranny and the dominance of the popular branch.[22] Indeed, in each volume he pronounces on the highest achievement of the legislator-as-framer: "Each [kind of] government brings with it a natural vice" and "the genius of the legislator consists in discerning it well" so as to counteract it, which the American Framers did.[23] Thus, the "whole art of the legislator consists in discerning well and in advance the natural inclinations" of a given society to know "when one must aid the efforts of the citizens and when it would rather be necessary to slow them down."[24]

Because of the richness of *Democracy in America* in both scope and substance, the spirit of Tocqueville's philosophy resists reduction to one philosophical source or school. Nonetheless, he indicates which philosophers he thought he was developing, or correcting, given his bold opening statement that a "new political science is needed for a world altogether new."[25] This claim concludes his list of ways in which statesmen and philosophers must "instruct" democracy to moderate its beliefs, mores, and practical judgments. During the writing of both volumes of *Democracy*, and especially after 1835, Tocqueville read extensively in ancient, medieval, and modern political philosophy in the Western tradition. If he is offering a new political science not per se, but for a new egalitarian world, he does so amid study ranging from Plato, Aristotle, and Plutarch, to Thomas Aquinas, on to Machiavelli, Montaigne, Bacon, and Descartes.[26] Moreover, we know of his report to his friend and cousin Kergolay about communing each day with Pascal, Montesquieu, and Rousseau while writing *Democracy*. However, most discussion of this remark usually overlooks his final thought on the topic, which reinforces his commitment to philosophical conversation rather than pursuit of a singular doctrine: "A fourth is missing: you."[27] Much scholarship on *Democracy* cannot see this balance or moderation across schools or philosophers. For some, its attention to modern equality suggests the predominant influence of Rousseau; for others, Pascal or even Augustine; for still others, he is more a reactionary aristocrat than a democrat. These narrow readings overlook, in part, that his now widely cited report to Kergolay gives equal prominence, in fact, to his correspondent—a philosophic friend upon whom he depended for conversation to assist his insights and investigations, just as he did with Beaumont, his traveling companion in America. Tocqueville signals his capacity to employ earlier ideas to aid his understanding in new circumstances, and to develop new blends from diverse thinkers.

One need not dismiss Tocqueville's Rousseauean moments to consider that, by applying the method and spirit of both Montesquieu and Pascal to the new phenomenon of mass equality, *Democracy* attempts a modern version of Aristotle's balanced political science.[28] Montesquieu clearly informs the complex, massive structure of the work, as well as its opening chapter on terrain and climate, its emphasis on mores or political culture, and an Aristotelian typology of regimes adapted to the democratic era.[29] That said, Tocqueville's emphatic concern with the human soul in modern democracy, and his serious attention to religion and the transcendent, also echoes Pascal. The foundation for his analysis of American mores in Volume Two is a Pascalian skepticism about the capacity of Cartesian philosophy and modern secularism to address humanity's most fundamental questions.[30] Nevertheless, just as Montesquieu is more confident about reason than is Montaigne, Tocqueville tempers Pascalian or generally Augustinian doubts with a political science that can aid mankind in this new era. He adapts the Montesquieuan emphasis on constitutional forms and separation of powers, itself rooted in Aristotle's analysis of the different functions and offices in any regime. He tempers or balances Montesquieu's revised Aristotelianism with Pascal's larger questions about modern man and the modern project.

One fundamental departure from Aristotle that complicates this complex new science is Tocqueville's insistence that historical change requires consideration of political realities beyond the standard of an unchanging human nature. Is it anti-Aristotelian to argue that the power of mass democracy must be reckoned with if our nature is to survive such novel pressures and commotion? Tocqueville carries forward the Aristotelian concern with the human soul and its higher destiny only as much as is feasible for serving those ends in radically new conditions, which govern the kind of discourse his audience can either tolerate or comprehend. His neo-Aristotelian method combines observation of particulars with prescription in light of philosophic principles of natural right and constitutionalism.[31] This political science is more concerned with the higher potentiality of politics and the soul than is Montesquieu's new science, while nonetheless stating a necessity to depart from the ancients strictly defined. This yields Tocqueville's twofold stance toward modern liberal democracy—praise for the greater justice of basic equality, yet concern about the fate of human greatness and the soul itself.[32] Neither Montesquieu nor Rousseau, even given their concerns with the degradation of man in modernity, could state that in aristocracies one finds "inequality and misery" but at least "souls were not degraded" as they can be in mass democracy.[33] Tocqueville recommends neither the largely negative liberty of Montesquieu, nor the Augustinian detachment from politics of Pascal, nor the collectivist, historicist liberty of Rousseau's modern republic. Some elements of each philosopher, blended with something more, are needed in the new political science.

Justice and Moderation in Constitutional Democracy

Tocqueville warns that modern egalitarianism "lends itself almost as readily" to "the sovereignty of all and the absolute power of one alone" as it does to a politics safe for genuine dignity. His main fear is the power of modern equality to homogenize and enervate human souls, to produce not citizens but subjects who would "fall below the level of humanity."[34] On the basis of this mother thought, Tocqueville's political science practices the kind of statesmanship he commends to American federal judges, to "discern the spirit of their times" so as to "confront those obstacles they can defeat" while steering "out of the current when the flood threatens to carry [them] away."[35] This echoes Aristotle's argument that political science as a practical science must seek to achieve what good it can in light of both philosophic principles and actual circumstances.[36] Tocqueville thought equality was an irreversible fact of "the times" and was more just than hereditary privilege and prejudice, but he also insisted that a choice confronted mankind between equality in liberty and "equality in servitude."[37] If modern man is to secure liberty and whatever political virtue is possible, then statesmanlike steering is needed. This practical wisdom must be rooted in the philosophic ability to look beyond any current party and to speak stern truths to democracy in a spirit of friendship. Like Montesquieu, he sprinkles prudential advice amid his philosophic analyses. A striking example is his effort from the very opening of *Democracy in America* to elevate the democratic soul by linking liberty and religion but also to temper the opposing extremes of Christian reactionaries and rationalist atheists: "One still encounters Christians among us, full of zeal, whose religious souls love to nourish themselves from the truths of the other life; doubtless they are going to be moved to favor human liberty, the source of all moral greatness."[38]

Tocqueville offers such moderating advice because after defining a point of departure or fundamental principle for American constitutionalism in Volume One, and another for American mores in Volume Two, he warns of problems with each. The fundamental principle of our politics and constitutionalism is complex—the "marvelous combination" achieved by the Puritans of "the *spirit of religion* and the *spirit of liberty*." Indeed, it is a principle of balance and moderation: each spirit prevents the other from going to its characteristic extreme, and thus they "advance in accord and seem to lend each other mutual support."[39] However, he later notes that in Europe and America "religions are weakening" and "the divine notion of rights is disappearing."[40] The main cause of this decline is the "philosophic method of the Americans"—the point of departure for our mores, which he links with America's Protestant principles as well as Enlightenment rationalism. In this discussion that opens Volume Two, he identifies Descartes but also Luther and the "sixteenth-century reformers" as the root of this radically modern philosophy.[41] A philosophy that eschews authorities or traditions yields a rationalism that isolates individuals and cuts off succeeding generations from traditional reasoning and judgments. This blend of skepticism and progressive, historicist principles, openly embraced in the twentieth century as the American school of Pragmatism, now takes many forms that collectively dominate American law, higher education, and much of our politics, thought, and culture.[42] The paradoxical result of such individualism is that equally weak minds or souls look to the democratic mass, and to public opinion, for guidance: "The same equality that makes him independent of each of his fellow citizens in particular leaves him isolated and defenseless against the action of the greatest number."[43]

Tocqueville suggests no inevitability or Hegelian end of history for this modern drama, for democracy can yield either liberty or tyranny. Long before Nietzsche, Kojève, or Fukuyama, he grasped that any such endpoint entailed the eclipse of humanity, the "Last Man," but his own view is that a historicist repudiation of natural right is neither progressive nor humane. The unintended consequences of America's blend of pragmatism and skepticism include corrosion of the fundamental link between religion and liberty achieved in the original point of departure, replaced by a democratic inclination toward "pantheism." He thus foresees American Transcendentalism and its erasure of distinctions between the "microcosm" of the individual and the "macrocosm," its celebration of homogeneous man and democratic society, and its merging of humanity and divinity in a single existence.[44] He finds that this humanist tendency to consecrate our own comfortable opinions of the moment—a prescient critique of Rawlsian doctrines about liberal public reason and Kantian constructivism—ultimately yields a democratic "instinct for centralization" and centralized administration. Volume Two of *Democracy* thus steadily warns about, and concludes with a dramatic exposition of "what kind of despotism democratic nations have to fear." This new, soft despotism "reduces each nation to being nothing more than a herd of timid and industrious animals of which the government is the shepherd."[45]

When he suggests, in the opening of Volume Two, that Puritan liberty cannot counteract the skeptical individualism caused by democratic philosophy—since Protestantism is one seed of that philosophy—Tocqueville proposes two other antidotes. After explaining why Americans are deeply Cartesian but never read Descartes, he praises both English empiricism and traditional Catholic Christianity.[46] He contrasts the empiricism and attention to particulars characterizing English thinking with the French taste for philosophic abstraction and generalization, worrying that American thinking is becoming more abstract and rationalist. His endorsement of Catholicism in America deepens the point, because Luther's search for a radically personal foundation for faith similarly rejects the tradition and hierarchy implicit in English common law. Tocqueville had praised this traditional Anglo-American approach to law in Volume One, especially its American formulation, which blends respect for precedent and legal custom with concern for equity and natural right.[47] Moreover, his one thematic statement on rights implicitly echoes the classic common law view of Sir John Fortescue (fifteenth century) and Sir Edward Coke (seventeenth century), and implicitly excludes the Hobbesian, Lockean notions of self-preservation or interest. It recalls, instead, the terms of classical and medieval philosophy: "After the general idea of virtue I know of none more beautiful than that of rights, or rather these two ideas are intermingled. The idea of rights is nothing other than the idea of virtue introduced into the world of politics."[48]

This striking claim seems nonsensical or sloppy to many academics, because it seems to confuse diverse schools, philosophers, eras, and concepts. For Tocqueville, the intellectual balance or blending of classical, medieval, and modern views is deliberate, and indispensable to a political science that moderates. His claim arises in a section of *Democracy* discussing "the idea of rights" and "respect for the law" as among the five "real advantages" America derives from democratic government.[49] In one sense, these remarks develop the emphasis on judicial power seen early in the first volume, and they prepare for the striking emphasis on judging, law, and rights that follows.[50] That later emphasis explicitly falls under the principle of moderation, assessing "What Tempers the Tyranny of the Majority in the United States." By treating juridical topics in terms of virtue and beauty, and a legal aristocracy in terms of statesmanship guided by integrity, right, and liberty, Tocqueville pulls American law and democracy toward its highest potential so as to buttress the ennobling influence of a faltering point of departure.

Tocqueville reinforces these judgments with a further striking claim, made when pondering why the ancients could not discern "the equal right to liberty that each bears from birth." Yet the claim is not that modern philosophy first discovered human equality; rather, "it was necessary that Jesus Christ come to earth" to make it understood that all humans are "naturally alike and equal."[51] If Montesquieu can puncture the pretensions of modern liberal philosophy by noting that English liberty first was found in the Germanic forests, Tocqueville can credit Biblical religion, not the American Declaration or the French Declaration of the Rights of Man, with first teaching about equality.[52] His concern seems to be that modern rationalism and skepticism exacerbate the individual isolation that in turn threatens democratic liberty, human greatness, and human dignity. This understanding guides his choices in *Democracy*, both prudential and philosophical, about how to at once analyze and influence the soul of modern democracy. His concern with rationalism dictates an initial emphasis on the Puritan origin of American liberty, however flawed, instead of discussing the abstract doctrines in either declaration of rights. Because, however, the Puritan point of departure needs buttressing, he recommends in Volume One a complex constitutional order that balances and moderates democracy. This features a common law spirit and judicial enforcement of individual rights, as understood in a more virtuous, public-spirited sense. A moderate constitutionalism and conception of rights can be prime supports for both Christian mores and liberty. Abraham Lincoln, both in his formulations in the 1830s of threats to American liberty and decency and in his subsequent rhetorical efforts as President to address such threats, strikes similar themes about a "political religion" and civic spirit—not a civil religion in Rousseauean terms—that reconciles rule of law and religious devotion. Lincoln and Tocqueville both were lawyers deeply respectful of the classic common law tradition, marking this as a faith not in democracy per se but in a tradition of law and constitutionalism, medieval in origin and recently reaffirmed in America.[53]

Religion, Statesmanship, and Tocqueville's Deepening of Modern Moderation

At least since Aristotle chided his teacher Plato for claiming to contemplate city and soul while only speculating about the soul, the problem of philosophical immoderation has dogged political philosophy and political science. Today most political science either indulges reflection on abstract conceptions of justice without attention to the practice of politics and institutions, or, especially since Machiavelli, analyzes institutions and rational calculations of political actors with no reference to the soul and its proper ends. Aristotle, Montesquieu, and Tocqueville claim to moderate this dualistic tendency in political science by dialectically examining the mutual influence of laws and mores, constitutionalism and political culture. This political science seeks to understand human nature and its potentialities in the light of experience and traditional practical wisdom.[54] The temptation to separate inquiry about aims or values from analysis of institutions and political practice also is evident in scholarship on Tocqueville himself. To some he is a philosopher and quasi-theologian seeking eternal verities, but to some others, a sociologist bound by the problems and thinking of his times. Tocqueville seems to view himself as blending or balancing these approaches. This is evident in the way he opens the first volume of *Democracy*, and in the neo-Aristotelian analysis of laws and institutions he undertakes throughout the Volume One. Tocqueville's aim is to establish a moderate political science that steadily connects the particulars of politics with the universal and metaphysical dimensions of political and human life.

This effort at philosophical moderation is coeval with the opening declaration of the work about the need to found a new political science. The remainder of the Introduction then elaborates a concern about the extremes dominating Europe's transition to modern equality and democratic politics, and Tocqueville calls on all modern democracies to moderate their morals, politics, and philosophy.[55] Volume One, Part One carefully assesses the laws and institutions of American federalism and separation of powers, but gradually rises toward the theme emphasized in Part Two of that volume, that good laws alone cannot sustain a decent form of political liberty. The right mores and character in both citizens and rulers also are indispensable—indeed, are most indispensable.[56] Montesquieu's moderate political science had consciously departed from Hobbesian and Lockean liberalism to capture the full complexity of the physical, moral, and legal elements that, in their interactions, produce a certain political "spirit." He partially restored the Aristotelian concept of regime (*politeia*), that rule involves both moral character and institutions, but largely did so as a means to liberal security and tranquility. Tocqueville's famous attention to mores (*mœurs*)—which he capaciously defines as "the ensemble of moral and intellectual dispositions which men supply to the state of society," and which political scientists today might translate as "political culture"—marks his deeper turn.[57] He develops Montesquieu's attention to mores by recovering some Aristotelian and Christian-Aristotelian standards on right and regime.

In American terms, Tocqueville's moderate political science blends the Federalist concern with the necessary powers and constitutional order of good government with the Anti-Federalist concern for the moral presuppositions of self-government. Aristotle's Socratic, dialectical political science, which embraced both natural right and a regime's division into distinct functions—so as to balance inclusive participation with space for merit in select offices—is partially evident in Montesquieu but more fully so in Tocqueville.[58] Tocqueville endorses the American correction of Montesquieu's still largely negative liberalism, and *Democracy in America* more fully captures the American spirit by calling liberal democracy to appreciate those dimensions of the Biblical and Western traditions that moderate the quest for ever-greater equality and individual security. Appreciation for Tocqueville's philosophy of moderation reveals the troubling paradox of Montesquieu's political science: a fundamental orientation toward individual tranquillity and security permits the rise of rival extremes of individualism and majority tyranny, and these in turn undermine a stable liberal constitutionalism and mores meant to ensure tranquillity. Tocqueville saw the possibility, however, of moderating Montesquieu with those resources in the Western tradition that provide balance to his liberal conceptions of philosophy, humanity, and politics.

Indeed, scholars who perceive Christian concerns at the core of Tocqueville's philosophy also emphasize the importance of moderation in his thought. While duly noting his concern to moderate or balance democratic tendencies, this approach also can overstate the influence of Pascal and of other neo-Platonic minds (such as Augustine and Rousseau) upon Tocqueville's perception of the dangers to human greatness and the soul in modernity.[59] Moderation as an effort at philosophical balance—at avoidance of intellectual errors defined as extremes—has roots in Socratic dialectic; however, this disposition is not the hallmark of Plato's psychology, ethics, or politics, as best as one can glean those from the Socratic skepticism of the dialogues. Plato and neo-Platonism emphasize dualistic antagonisms between the high and the low, and the need for the high to vanquish or dominate the low. Equilibrium as an aim, and the means of achieving moderation to find the right ground between extremes, are hallmarks of the Aristotelian tradition, which broadly includes a range of minds from Thomas Aquinas—who is more moderate than much Thomism—to Montesquieu. The neo-Platonic and Christian reading of Tocqueville implies that there is little disagreement with Augustine or Pascal in Tocqueville's anthropology, ethics, and politics, or in his basic approach to philosophy. The difficulty, however, is to explain how Tocqueville can depart from Pascal and neo-Platonism generally by so strongly affirming the dignity of politics if his central focus somehow is the spiritual impoverishment of the City of (Modern) Man.[60]

Tocqueville's adaptation of Montesquieu's philosophy does not echo ancient or modern or Christian philosophy per se, but offers a modern renovation of the Thomistic harmonizing of philosophy and religion. While Tocqueville is a modern and a liberal of sorts, the extremes in these philosophies and phenomena led him to revive a medieval sensibility recast for modern dilemmas and possibilities. Montesquieu had prepared the way for this turn by defending the benefits and naturalness of religion, and especially Christianity, against modern irreligion as found in Hobbes and other philosophers.[61] *Democracy in America* further moderates Montesquieuan liberalism by prescribing a moderate dose of the Aristotelian and Thomistic concern with the destiny of the soul. Tocqueville sought to leaven liberal individualism and egalitarianism by restoring the higher potentiality of a politics and civil society gently guided by religious principles and practice, but he nonetheless consciously departed from the strict teleology of ancient political philosophy and medieval Christian political philosophy. Recent debates in Tocqueville scholarship about the true nature of his beliefs about religion, and its role in modern democracy, thus might be viewed differently in light of the tradition of moderation informing Tocqueville's thought. Is he a genuine advocate of the true light that Biblical faith and theology shed upon the human condition, regardless of the trials of faith and personal doubt that clearly dogged him personally?[62] Or is he a functionalist advocate of a civil religion, endorsing only utilitarian counsels either because of philosophic skepticism about faith or concern about the zealous, illiberal tendencies of religion?[63] If Tocqueville defines philosophy in the spirit of Montesquieuan moderation, balancing and blending ancient, medieval, and modern elements, then his endorsement of religion would indeed be moderate but in a way that transcends skepticism, functionalism, or a primary concern with the illiberal potential of faith.[64]

Tocqueville's famous attention to mores marks a more Aristotelian development of Montesquieu's attention to mores because for Tocqueville religion and the soul are primary concerns, not left in the background.[65] Here one wonders whether Tocqueville's moderate political science learned to blend Federalist concerns with constitutional government and Anti-Federalist concerns with the moral presuppositions of self-government by reflecting on the statesmanship embodied in George Washington's "Farewell Address."[66] Tocqueville may have learned from American practice about a theoretical correction to Montesquieu's largely negative liberalism. *Democracy in America* more fully captures the American spirit than either Montesquieu or *The Federalist* by calling liberal democracy to appreciate dimensions of the Biblical and Western traditions that moderate the quest for ever-greater equality and individual security. He moderates Montesquieu with those resources in the Western tradition that temper Montesquieu's conceptions of philosophy, humanity, religion, and politics.

Tocqueville's discovery that America's first point of departure, the equilibrium or moderate relationship between liberty and religion, is unstable or eroding leads him to endorse the moderate mode of Catholicism evident in America, but also more extraordinary remedies. These include a role for government in indirectly fostering and buttressing religious faith.[67] He knows it will be controversial to ask "the politicians" to "act every day" as if they believed in the soul's immortality, "conforming scrupulously to religious morality in great affairs."[68] His model for this remedy may have been Washington, for earlier he emphatically praises both "this great man" and Marshall's biography of him, and quotes the Farewell Address.[69] Indeed, he names only two models of American statesmen who guided their actions by fundamental ethical principles and resisted the clamor of majority opinion—Governor John Winthrop, and Washington.[70] For both models he draws on the analysis of these statesmen by another statesman, Marshall's *Life of Washington*. Winthrop, however, embodies the best and worst of America's first epoch, the Puritan fusion of church and state and the "bizarre, tyrannical," and shameful excesses in enforcing Biblical morality through penal law, both of which Tocqueville rejects.[71] What is needed as America continues its experiment is the more moderate and indirect, but powerfully sincere, education in religious principle embodied by Washington in America's second epoch. Tocqueville warns that such "great characters are disappearing" and that "the race of American statesmen has shrunk" during America's third epoch.[72] His new political science calls for statesmen educated in religious and constitutional principle who can inculcate, in a temperate way, the moderate aims of ordered liberty and the belief in the dignity of the soul's temporal and eternal destiny. In modern constitutional parlance, Tocqueville follows Washington in favoring the accommodationist view about religious liberty rather than a stricter, separationist view—namely, that the First Amendment ensures the separation of church and state but does not entail, or advocate, the separation of religion and politics.

Moderation in Understanding the Late-Modern World

The importance of understanding both Montesquieu and Tocqueville stems in part from the former's influence on the political science of the American Founders, and the latter's insight into and elevation of that political science. Further, we live in the world that the one philosopher helped to launch and that the other analyzed with uncanny insight. This is the world of modernity and liberal democracy as the dominant political, moral, economic, legal, and military phenomena across the globe. If we recognize this and turn to their philosophies, we must further grapple with the fact that this now-unfamiliar concept, moderation, was a central principle of the political philosophy that Montesquieu and Tocqueville developed. If scholars today tend to overlook this principle in these philosophers, they also tend to overlook the spirit of moderation meant to inform liberal, constitutional democracy. We might wonder, then, how much our dismissal of these views impedes the capacity for political science to aid citizens and statesmen in governing under our constitutional order. In particular, we should not be surprised that an American political science either ignorant of or actively repudiating its roots in philosophical and political moderation now fails to temper our destructive kinds of intellectual and political partisanship—or, even exacerbates such acrimony and gamesmanship.

It would be immoderate to imply that Tocquevillean philosophy—and its insights for theory and practice—are the final word about modern liberal democracy, let alone political philosophy simply. Moderation deserves rediscovery because the current condition of both theory and practice suggest that the old reasons behind the principles and forms of moderate liberal constitutionalism can appear cogent once again—in comparison to the bold alternatives proposed and tested in recent centuries and recent decades, and to the cycles of polarization these innovations have spawned. Montesquieu's philosophy provides particular insights given that it both predicted and shaped our world today, the world of complex constitutional democracies rising to prosperity and global power but troubled by moral confusion and spiritual decay. Tocqueville further explains America's likely preeminence in the era of equality and its exceptional attachment to religion and constitutional complexity, while also providing philosophical resources for the challenges posed to the soul and to societies by a dynamic, materialistic, and globalized life. Still, these strengths do not entail any claim to be a complete theory of human affairs. Rather, they reinforce a disposition and framework for sustaining Socratic debate about the strengths and weaknesses of liberal democracy, and for sustaining a healthy politics of liberty and equality that is open to civil debate about first principles, constitutionalism, and statesmanship. It is not immoderate to suggest that such an approach is necessary even if not sufficient. It is necessary for a healthy liberal democracy by encouraging fundamental philosophical discourse while restraining democratic dogmatisms and the cycle of rival extremes in theory or practice. The spirit of moderation warns against single-minded theories of justice, or narrow doctrines in politics or political science. It is the spirit, rather, of Socratic conversation, held together by certain principles and stances about justice, but not reduced to the quarrels of sects or schools.

Notes

1. "To preserve [speech and religious] freedom, at a time when any claim to a transcendent truth is suspect, we need to appreciate the importance of moderation. Moderation—a classical virtue—protects and preserves political freedom *and* intellectual inquiry"; and "we must acknowledge that our democratic protection of both the 'emotive' function as well as the cognitive content of speech, which protection includes flag burning or cross burning, does not encourage rational discourse . . . to pursue the rational life in our practical affairs and other inquiries as well, we will need recourse to one more condition, Socratic moderation." Murray P. Dry, *Civil Peace and the Quest for Truth: The First Amendment Freedoms in Political Philosophy and American Constitutionalism* (Lanham: Lexington Books, 2004), 10, 288.

2. This tradition was adapting the arguments in Aristotle's practical science (politics and ethics) that virtue is found in a middle between false extremes, with two crucial qualifications—that some actions or passions allowed no middle and were simply wrong (Aristotle cited, as examples, adultery, theft, murder, spitefulness, shamelessness, and envy) and that a virtue is closer to one extreme than to another rather than being mathematically in the middle. See *Nicomachean Ethics*, trans. Robert C. Bartlett and Susan D. Collins, 1106b37–1109b27, esp. 106b5–16, 1107a9–18, 1109a1–2.

3. See Harvey Mansfield and Delba Winthrop, editors' introduction to *Democracy in America* by Alexis de Tocqueville, xvii; an astute claim on the editors' part.

4. Among scholars viewing Aquinas in this moderate, dialectical vein are Josef Pieper, *The Silence of St. Thomas: Three Essays*; and Anthony Kenny, *Aquinas*.

5. See Peter Simpson, trans. *The Politics of Aristotle*, 1.2 (1253a26–28, p. 12); 1.8–11 (pp. 20–29); 2.3–5 (pp. 37–45); 3.11–13 (pp. 95–105), 3.17–18 (pp. 112–114), and 6.11 (or, in the traditional ordering of the books 4.11) (pp. 189–193). The modern interpretations closest to this view—arguing that Aristotle raises doubts about whether rule by a godlike one or few is still political rule if it completely excludes the many, and, on the positive side, that polity could be an excellent regime if structured to permit limited participation by the mediocre many, while having the highest offices held by the truly excellent—are Mary Nichols, *Citizens and Statesmen: A Study of Aristotle's* Politics (Savage, MD: Rowman & Littlefield, 1991), and Kevin M. Cherry, "The Problem of Polity: Political Participation and Aristotle's Best Regime," 71. *Journal of Politics* (2009): 1406–1421, which addresses scholarship for and against this view; see also Stephen Salkever, *Finding the Mean: Theory and Practice in Aristotelian Political Philosophy* (Princeton: Princeton University Press, 1990).

6. Aristotle, *Nicomachean Ethics*, 1094b12–28.

7. Montesquieu, *De l'Esprit des Lois*, in *Œuvres complètes*, 2:583. Subsequent references, against which I have checked the translation, cite book, chapter, and, where appropriate, page number in *The Spirit of the Laws*, eds. Anne Cohler, Basia Carolyn Miller and Harold Samuel Stone, 19.27, 333.

8. On avoiding "prejudices" and "sallies" (better as "striking features"), see Cohler, Miller, and Stone, *Spirit of the Laws*, preface, xliii–xliv; on no need for theorists to seek what is readily found, ibid., 11.5, 156; on the excess of reason, ibid., 11.6, 166; on prejudices in even great philosophers, ibid., 29.19, 618; on avoiding a theoretical "system" and finding a better, middle way, ibid., 30.10, 626–627.

9. See Aurelian Craiutu, "The Architecture of Moderate Government: Montesquieu's Science of the Legislator," 33–68. I pursue this same view in "Montesquieu's Complex Natural Right and Moderate Liberalism: The Roots of American Moderation," 227–250; and *The Cloaking of Power: Montesquieu, Blackstone, and the Rise of Judicial Activism*. See also David Carrithers, introduction to *Montesquieu's Science of Politics*.

10. Jonathan Israel's simplicity confirms this character of Montesquieu's philosophy: in his account Spinoza's rationalism is dominant, and

Montesquieu rarely appears. *Radical Enlightenment: Philosophy and the Making of Modernity 1650–1750* (Oxford: Oxford University Press, 2001).

11. Montesquieu, *Spirit of the Laws*, 29.1, 602.

12. Ibid., 29.19.

13. On Montesquieu' influence, and on complexity in the founding, see, for example, Paul Spurlin, *Montesquieu in America 1760–1801* (on his influence of the Declaration especially, see ibid., 116–120, 126–128, 137, 141–142, 152–157); Donald Lutz, "The Relative Influence of European Writers on Late Eighteenth-Century American Political Thought," 189–197; and Judith Shklar, "A New Constitution for a New Nation," 158–169. I discuss this in "The Complexity, and Principles, of the American Founding: A Reply to Alan Gibson," 711–717.

14. This is a main theme of Harvey Mansfield, *Tocqueville: A Very Short Introduction.* Other accounts of Tocqueville's philosophy that provide important insights about his moderation but see it more as confusion or ambivalence include Robert Nisbet, 59–75; Peter Lawler, "Tocqueville's Elusive Moderation," 181–189; and Aurelian Craiutu, "Tocqueville's Paradoxical Moderation," 599–629.

15. Tocqueville, *Democracy in America*, authors notice to vol. II, 400. On occasion I revise this translation, consulting *Œuvres complètes*, ed. J.P. Mayer; and *Democracy in America*, trans. George Lawrence, ed. J.P. Mayer. Subsequent references cite volume, part, chapter, and, where appropriate, page of the Mansfield and Winthrop edition.

16. Beyond other sources cited in this chapter arguing that Tocqueville is a philosopher, see Pierre Manent, "Tocqueville, Political Philosopher," 108–120.

17. Tocqueville, *Democracy in America*, introduction to vol. I, 15, author's notice to vol. II, 400. Norma Thompson emphasizes this Aristotelian quest for an intermediary between extremes in "Surveying Tocqueville," in *The Ship of State: Statecraft and Politics from Ancient Greece to Democratic America*, 125–136.

18. See Sharon Krause, "Honor and Democracy in America," 67–96, on this questionable tendency, and her own view of *Democracy* as a Montesquieuan effort to moderate liberalism. This section of the essay draws in part upon my chapter "Tocqueville's Judicial Statesmanship and Common Law Spirit," in *The Cloaking of Power* (see note ix), 211–230.

19. Tocqueville, *Democracy in America*, introduction to vol. 1, 14, 3, 5, I.2.7, 239ff.

20. Ibid., introduction to vol. 1, 7. See Paul A. Rahe.

21. Ibid., introduction to vol. 1, 9.

22. Ibid., I.1.8, 143–146; see also ibid., I.2.7, 239–242, I.2.8, 250–258.

23. Ibid., I.1.8, 129.

24. Ibid., II.2.15, 518.

25. Ibid., introduction to vol. 1, 7. Among other analyses of this claim see Harvey Mansfield and Delba Winthrop, "Tocqueville's New Political Science," in *The Cambridge Companion to Tocqueville*, 81–107; and Seymour Drescher, "Tocqueville's Comparative Perspectives," in *Cambridge Companion to Tocqueville*, 1–20.

26. See James Schleifer, *The Making of Tocqueville's "Democracy in America*," 26; Tocqueville reveals some of the range of his mature studies in "Speech Given to the Annual Public Meeting of the Academy of Moral and Political Sciences on April 3, 1852," in *Alexis de Tocqueville and the Art of Democratic Statesmanship*, ed. Brian Danoff, trans. L. Joseph Hebert Jr., 17–29. On his classical, humanist education prior to study of law, see André Jardin, *Alexis de Tocqueville, 1805–1859*; and "Education and Emancipation," in *Tocqueville: A Bibliography*, 57–64.

27. See Schleifer, *Making of "Democracy in America*," 25–26, citing "Letter to Kergolay, 10 November 1836," in *Œuvres complètes* (see note xiii), 13.1:415–418.

28. See Peter A. Lawler, "Introduction," in *Tocqueville's Political Science: Classic Essays*, especially on the Aristotelianism of his political science and its distinctive "view of greatness" (xi); see also Mansfield and Winthrop, "Tocqueville's New Political Science." Cf. Catherine Zuckert, "Political Sociology Versus Speculative Philosophy," in *Interpreting Tocqueville's "Democracy in America*," ed. Ken Masugi, 121–152, arguing that Tocqueville's political science consciously repudiates Aristotle.

29. On Montesquieu and Tocqueville, see Raymond Aron, *Main Currents in Sociological Thought*, 1:188–190, 200–201, 204–205, 210, 230; Melvin Richter, "The Uses of Theory: Tocqueville's Adaptation of Montesquieu," in *Essays in Theory and History*, 74–102; Anne Cohler, ch. 8; James Ceaser, "Political Science, Political Culture, and the Role of the Intellectual," (see note xx), 287–325; and James Ceaser, *Liberal Democracy and Political Science*, ch. 3.

30. Tocqueville, *Democracy in America*, II.1.1–7. See Peter A. Lawler, *The Restless Mind: Alexis de Tocqueville on the Origin and Perpetuation of Human Liberty* , esp. 7–10, 73–87. An Augustinian reading of Tocqueville is Joshua Mitchell, *The Fragility of Freedom: Tocqueville on Religion, Democracy, and the American Future*. Other works that find in Tocqueville a profound and sympathetic view of religion include Patrick Deneen, *Democratic Faith*; and L. Joseph Hebert, *More Than Kings and Less Than Men: Tocqueville on the Promise and Perils of Democratic Individualism*.

31. James Ceaser analyzes and defends Tocqueville's complex philosophy on these points in *Designing A Polity: America's Constitution in Theory and Practice.*

32. Tocqueville, *Democracy in America*, introduction to vol. I, 5, II.4.8, 673–6. For Raymond Aron and Pierre Manent Tocqueville's philosophy aims at liberty, animated by concern for the human soul and human dignity, but they do not find him a Christian or Augustinian thinker. See "Tocqueville," *Main Currents* (see note xx), vol. 1; and Pierre Manent, *Tocqueville and the Nature of Democracy.* See also Raymond Aron, "On Tocqueville," in *In Defense of Political Reason: Essays by Raymond Aron*, 175–178; and Lawler, "Was Tocqueville A Philosopher?," in *Restless Mind* (see note xxii), 89–108.

33. Tocqueville, *Democracy in America*, introduction to vol. I, 8.

34. Ibid., I.1.3, 52, I.2.9 301; see ibid., introduction to vol. I, 3, 6, 12, II.4.6, 665. See also Manent, *Tocqueville and the Nature of Democracy*, xii, xiv.

35. Tocqueville, *Democracy in America*, I.1.8, 147.

36   Aristotle, *Nicomachean Ethics*, 1179a33ff; *Politics*, 1288b10–1289a25.

37. Tocqueville, *Democracy in America*, I.1.3, 52.

38. Tocqueville, *Democracy in America*, introduction to vol. 1, 7. See Manent, "Democracy and the Nature of Man," in *Tocqueville and the Nature of Democracy* (see note xxiv), 67–81.

39. Tocqueville, *Democracy in America*, I.1.2, 43. Emphasis in original.

40. Ibid., I.2.6, 228; see also ibid., I.2.9, 281–288, 299.

41. Ibid., II.1.1.

42. See James H. Nichols Jr., "Pragmatism and the U.S. Constitution," 369–370; and Albert Alschuler, *Law Without Values: The Life, Work, and Legacy of Justice Holmes.*

43. Tocqueville, *Democracy in America*, II.1.2, 409.

44. Tocqueville, *Democracy in America*, II.1.7. See Lawler, "Democracy and Pantheism," in *Interpreting "Democracy in America"* (see note xx), 96–120; and revised in Lawler, *Restless Mind*, 33–50. In contrast, Sheldon Wolin's broad critique of Tocqueville includes praise for the Emersonian "Over-Soul" without noting that this is the very kind of pantheism and postrationalism Tocqueville criticizes; in *Tocqueville between Two Worlds: The Making of a Political and Theoretical Life*, 157–158.

45. Tocqueville, *Democracy in America*, II.4.5, 659, II.4.6; 661–663.

46. See ibid., II.1. 3–6.

47. Ibid., I.1.6, I.1.8, I.2.8.

48. Tocqueville, *Democracy in America*, I.2.6, 227. On the Platonic and Aristotelian definition of law as virtue, and its influence on the classic common law, see Ellis Sandoz, "Fortescue, Coke, and Anglo-American Constitutionalism," in *The Roots of Liberty: Magna Carta,*

Ancient Constitution, and the Anglo-American Tradition of Rule of Law,
ed. Ellis Sandoz, 1–21; and James Stoner, *Common Law and Liberal
Theory: Coke, Hobbes, and the Origins of American Constitutionalism.*
Fortescue cites Aristotle and Aquinas in defining law as virtue in "In
Praise of the Laws of England," in *On the Laws and Governance of
England*, chs. IV, V, IX, XIII, XVI.

49. Tocqueville, *Democracy in America*, I.2.6.

50. Ibid., I.1.6, I.1.8; and ibid., 1.2.8.

51. Ibid., II.1.3, 413.

52. Montesquieu, *Spirit of Laws*, 11.6, 166. See also Tocqueville's comment
in *The Old Regime and The Revolution*, vol. 1, ed. François Furet and
François Mélonio, trans. Alan Kahan (University of Chicago Press,
1998 [1856]), that while he had thought (in *Democracy in America*)
that the New England township was a unique form of political liberty,
he later discovered that such local self-government had long existed in
the ancient regime of France and Germany, and that a few vestiges still
survived; book 2, ch. 3, p. 129.

53. "The Perpetuation of Our Political Institutions," in *Collected Works
of Abraham Lincoln*, ed. Roy Basler, I:108–15; Gettysburg Address,
in *Collected Works of Lincoln*, VII: 22–23; for Lincoln's common law
pedigree see his dissection of *Dred Scott v. Sanford* (1854), in Speech
at Springfield, June 26, 1857, in *Collected Works*, II:401.

54. Ceaser, in *Liberal Democracy and Political Science*, argues that Aristotle, Montesquieu, and Tocqueville embody "traditional political science," which better explains and sustains liberty than do the extremes
of empiricism or utopian constructivism. He continues this argument
in *Designing a Polity*.

55. Tocqueville, *Democracy in America*, introduction to vol. I, 7–15.

56. Ibid., 1.2.9, 292–295.

57. Ibid., I.2.9, 305, n. 8; see also ibid., 1.2.9, 287.

58. Aristotle, *Politics*, 1297b35–1301a18; see also Ceaser, *Liberal Democracy and Political Science.*

59. On moderation and religion in Tocqueville, see Lawler, *Restless Mind*,
137–139, 142–143; and Mitchell, *Fragility of Freedom*, x–xi, 78–87,
132–140.

60. See Lawler, *Restless Mind*, 78–87, 141–158; and Mitchell, *Fragility of
Freedom*, 3–11, 22–28, 78–87.

61. See Rebecca Kingston, "Montesquieu on Religion and the Question of
Toleration," in *Montesquieu's Science of Politics* (see note ix), 375–408,
developing the testimony of the Dominican priest Lacordaire (*Œuvres*,
1880) and recent scholarship by Robert Shackleton and F.T.H. Fletcher
to argue that Montesquieu was sympathetic to Christianity broadly defined; see n. 4, 399–400. Compare the severe skepticism about

Montesquieu and religion in Diana Schaub, "Of Believers and Barbarians: Montesquieu's Enlightened Toleration," in *Early Modern Skepticism and the Origins of Toleration*, 225–247; Robert Bartlett, "On the Politics of Faith and Reason: The Project of Enlightenment in Pierre Bayle and Montesquieu," 1–28; and Thomas Pangle, *The Theological Basis of Liberal Modernity in Montesquieu's "Spirit of the Laws."*

62. In addition to the works by Lawler, Mitchell, and Hebert noted above see Doris Goldstein, *Trial of Faith: Religion and Politics in Tocqueville's Thought.*

63. See Catherine Zuckert, "Not by Preaching: Tocqueville on the Role of Religion,"259–280; and "The Role of Religion in Preserving American Liberty – Tocqueville's Analysis 150 Years Later," in *Tocqueville's Defense of Human Liberty: Current Essays*, 223–239; Sanford Kessler, *Tocqueville's Civil Religion*; and Aristide Tessitore, "Alexis de Tocqueville on the Natural State of Religion in the Age of Democracy," 1137–1152.

64. Scott Yenor argues that Tocqueville hopes for a return to genuine religious faith after the decline of Protestantism at the hands of pantheism and materialism, in "Natural Religion and Human Perfectibility: Tocqueville's Account of Religion in Modern Democracy," *Perspectives on Political Science* 33, no. 1 (2004): 10–17; see also Deneen, *Democratic Faith*; and Hebert, *More Than Kings.*

65. Tocqueville, *Democracy in America*, I.2.9, 275, 292, n. 8; see generally Ibid., 1.2.9, 275–288, 298–302.

66. See, for example, Tocqueville, *Democracy in America*, 1.1.8, 129, 1.2.7, 241–242, 2.2.15, 518. I discuss Washington and Tocqueville in "Liberty, Constitutionalism, and Moderation: The Political Thought of George Washington," 95–113.

67. Tocqueville, *Democracy in America*, 2.2.15, 17.

68. Ibid., 2.2.15, 521.

69. Ibid., 1.1.2, 30 n. 1, 1.1.8, 107, I.2.5, 217–220; 1.2.10, 320; see also ibid., 1.1.3, 46, 50, 52.

70. Ibid., 1.1.2, 42, 1.2.6, 217–220.

71. Ibid., 1.1.2, 39, 1.2.9, 283.

72. Ibid., 1.1.3, 50, 1.1.8, 130, 1.2.5, 188, 1.2.7, 246–247, 1.2.9, 265.

Bibliography

Alschuler, Albert. *Law Without Values: The Life, Work, and Legacy of Justice Holmes.* Chicago: University of Chicago Press, 2000.

Aristotle. *Politics.* Translated by Peter Simpson. Chapel Hill: University of North Carolina Press, 1997.

———. *Nicomachean Ethics*. Translated by Robert C. Bartlett and Susan D. Collins. Chicago: University of Chicago Press, 2011.

Aron, Raymond. *Main Currents in Sociological Thought*. Translated by R. Howard and H. Weaver. 2 vols. New York: Basic Books, 1965.

———. "On Tocqueville." In *In Defense of Political Reason: Essays by Raymond Aron*. Edited by Daniel Mahoney. Lanham, MD: Rowman and Littlefield, 1994.

Bartlett, Robert. "On the Politics of Faith and Reason: The Project of Enlightenment in Pierre Bayle and Montesquieu." *Journal of Politics* 63 (2001): 1–28.

Basler, Roy, ed.. *Collected Works of Abraham Lincoln*. New Brunswick: Rutgers University Press, 1953.

Carrese, Paul O. "The Complexity, and Principles, of the American Founding: A Reply to Alan Gibson." *History of Political Thought* XXI (2000): 711–717.

———. *The Cloaking of Power: Montesquieu, Blackstone, and the Rise of Judicial Activism*. Chicago: University of Chicago Press, 2003.

———. "Liberty, Constitutionalism, and Moderation: The Political Thought of George Washington." Ch. 5 in *History of American Political Thought*. Edited by Bryan-Paul Frost and Jeffery Sikkenga. Lanham, MD: Lexington Press, 2003.

———. "Montesquieu's Complex Natural Right and Moderate Liberalism: The Roots of American Moderation." *Polity* 36, no. 2 (2004): 227–250.

Carrithers, David, Michael Mosher, and Paul Rahe, eds. *Montesquieu's Science of Politics*. Lanham, MD: Rowman and Littlefield, 2000.

Ceaser, James. *Liberal Democracy and Political Science*. Baltimore: Johns Hopkins University Press, 1990.

———. "Political Science, Political Culture, and the Role of the Intellectual." Ch. 10 in *Interpreting "Democracy in America."* Edited by Ken Masugi. Lanham, MD: Rowman and Littlefield, 1991.

———. *Designing a Polity: America's Constitution in Theory and Practice*. Lanham: Rowman and Littlefield, 2010.

Cohler, Anne. *Montesquieu's Comparative Politics and the Spirit of American Constitutionalism*. Lawrence: University Press of Kansas, 1988.

Craiutu, Aurelian. "Tocqueville's Paradoxical Moderation." *Review of Politics* 67 (2005).

———. "The Architecture of Moderate Government: Montesquieu's Science of the Legislator." Part 2 in *A Virtue for Courageous Minds*. Princeton: Princeton University Press, 2012.

Danoff, Brian. *Alexis de Tocqueville and the Art of Democratic Statesmanship*. Translated by L. Joseph Hebert Jr. Lanham, MD: Lexington Books, 2011.

Deneen, Patrick. *Democratic Faith*. Princeton: Princeton University Press, 2005.

Drescher, Seymour. "Tocqueville's Comparative Perspectives." Ch. 1 in *Cambridge Companion to Tocqueville*. Edited by Cheryl Welch. Cambridge: Cambridge University Press, 2006.

Fortescue, John. "In Praise of the Laws of England." In *On the Laws and Governance of England*. Edited by Shelley Lockwood, 1–80. Cambridge: Cambridge University Press, 1997.

Goldstein, Doris. *Trial of Faith: Religion and Politics in Tocqueville's Thought*. Amsterdam: Elsevier B.V., 1975.

Hebert, L. Joseph. *More Than Kings and Less Than Men: Tocqueville on the Promise and Perils of Democratic Individualism*. Lanham, MD: Lexington Books, 2010.

Isreal, Jonathan. *Radical Enlightenment: Philosophy and the Making of Modernity 1650–1750*. Oxford: Oxford University Press, 2001.

Jardin, André. *Alexis de Tocqueville, 1805–1859*. Paris: Hachette, 1984.

———. "Education and Emancipation." Ch. 4 in *Tocqueville: A Bibliography*. New York: Farrar, Straus and Giroux: 1989.

Kenny, Anthony. *Aquinas*. Oxford: Oxford University Press, 1980.

Kessler, Sanford. *Tocqueville's Civil Religion*. Albany: State University of New York, 1994.

Kingston, Rebecca. "Montesquieu on Religion and the Question of Toleration." Ch. 9 in *Montesquieu's Science of Politics*. Edited by David Carrithers, Michael Mosher, and Paul Rahe, Lanham, MD: Rowman and Littlefield, 2000.

Krause, Sharon. "Honor and Democracy in America." Ch. 3 in *Liberalism With Honor* Cambridge, MA: Harvard University Press, 2002.

Lawler, Peter. "Tocqueville's Elusive Moderation." *Polity* 22 (1989): 181–189.

———. "Democracy and Pantheism." Ch. 3 in *Interpreting "Democracy in America."* Edited by Ken Masugi. Lanham: Rowman and Littlefield, 1991.

———. *Tocqueville's Political Science: Classic Essays*. New York: Garland, 1992.

———. *The Restless Mind: Alexis de Tocqueville on the Origin and Perpetuation of Human Liberty*. Lanham, MD: Rowman and Littlefield, 1993.

Lutz, Donald. "The Relative Influence of European Writers on Late Eighteenth-Century American Political Thought." *American Political Science Review* 78 (1984): 189–197.

Manent, Pierre. *Tocqueville and the Nature of Democracy*. Translated by John Waggoner. Lanham, MD: Rowman and Littlefield, 1996.

———. "Tocqueville, Political Philosopher." Ch. 4 in *The Cambridge Companion to Tocqueville*. Edited by Cheryl Welch. Cambridge: Cambridge University Press, 2006.

Mansfield, Harvey. *Tocqueville: A Very Short Introduction.* Oxford: Oxford University Press, 2010.

Mansfield, Harvey, and Delba Winthrop. "Tocqueville's New Political Science." Ch. 3 in *The Cambridge Companion to Tocqueville.* Edited by Cheryl Welch. Cambridge: Cambridge University Press, 2006.

Mitchell, Joshua. *The Fragility of Freedom: Tocqueville on Religion, Democracy, and the American Future.* Chicago: University of Chicago Press, 1995.

Montesquieu. *De l'Esprit des Lois.* In *Œuvres complètes.* Edited by Roger Caillois. Paris: Gallimard, 1949–1951.

———. *The Spirit of the Laws.* Edited by Anne Cohler, Basia Carolyn Miller, and Harold Samuel Stone. Cambridge: Cambridge University Press, 1989.

Nichols, James H. "Pragmatism and the U.S. Constitution." In *Confronting the Constitution: The Challenge to Locke, Montesquieu, Jefferson, and the Federalists from Utilitarianism, Historicism, Marxism, Freudis.* Edited by Allan David Bloom. Washington, DC: AEI Press, 1991.

Nisbet, Robert. "Many Tocquevilles." *American Scholar* 46 (1976–1977): 59–75.

Pangle, Thomas. *The Theological Basis of Liberal Modernity in Montesquieu's "Spirit of the Laws."* Chicago: University of Chicago Press, 2010.

Pieper, Josef. *The Silence of St. Thomas: Three Essays.* Translated by John Murray and Daniel O'Connor. New York: Pantheon, 1957.

Rahe, Paul A. *Soft Despotism, Democracy's Drift: Montesquieu, Rousseau, Tocqueville, and the Modern Prospect.* New Haven: Yale University Press, 2009.

Richter, Melvin. "The Uses of Theory: Tocqueville's Adaptation of Montesquieu." In *Essays in Theory and History,* 74–102. Cambridge, MA: Harvard University Press, 1970.

Sandoz, Ellis. "Fortescue, Coke, and Anglo-American Constitutionalism." Ch. 1 in *The Roots of Liberty: Magna Carta, Ancient Constitution, and the Anglo-American Tradition of Rule of Law.* Columbia: University of Missouri Press, 1992.

Schaub, Diana. "Of Believers and Barbarians: Montesquieu's Enlightened Toleration." Ch. 11 in *Early Modern Skepticism and the Origins of Toleration.* Edited by Alan Levin. Lanham, MD: Lexington, 1999.

Schleifer, James. *The Making of Tocqueville's "Democracy in America."* Chapel Hill: University of North Carolina Press, 1980.

Shklar, Judith. "A New Constitution for a New Nation." Ch. 11 in *Redeeming American Political Thought.* Edited by Judith Shklar, Stanley Hoffman, and Dennis Thompson. Chicago: University of Chicago Press, 1998.

Spurlin, Paul. *Montesquieu in America 1760–1801.* Baton Rouge: Louisiana State University Press, 1940.

Stoner, James. *Common Law and Liberal Theory: Coke, Hobbes, and the Origins of American Constitutionalism.* Lawrence: University Press of Kansas, 1992.

Tessitore, Aristide. "Alexis de Tocqueville on the Natural State of Religion in the Age of Democracy." *Journal of Politics* 64 (2002): 1137–1152.

Thompson, Norma. *The Ship of State: Statecraft and Politics from Ancient Greece to Democratic America.* New Haven: Yale University Press, 2001.

Tocqueville, Alexis de. *Œuvrescomplètes.* Edited by. J.P. Mayer. Paris: Gallimard, 1951.

———*Democracy in America.* Translated by George Lawrence. Edited J.P. Mayer. Garden City: Doubleday, 1969.

———. *Democracy in America.* Translated by Harvey Mansfield and Delba Winthrop. Chicago: University of Chicago Press, 2000.

Wolin, Sheldon. *Tocqueville between Two Worlds: The Making of a Political and Theoretical Life.* Princeton: Princeton University Press, 2001.

Yenor, Scott. "Natural Religion and Human Perfectibility: Tocqueville's Account of Religion in Modern Democracy." *Perspectives on Political Science* 33, no. 1 (2004): 10–17.

Zuckert, Catherine. "Not by Preaching: Tocqueville on the Role of Religion." *Review of Politics* 42 (1981): 259–280.

———. "Political Sociology Versus Speculative Philosophy." Ch. 4 in *Interpreting Tocqueville's "Democracy in America."* Edited by Ken Masugi. Lanham, MD: Rowman and Littlefield, 1991.

———. "The Role of Religion in Preserving American Liberty – Tocqueville's Analysis 150 Years Later." In *Tocqueville's Defense of Human Liberty: Current Essays.* Edited by Peter Lawler and Joseph Alullis. London: Routledge, 1993.

Chapter 12

John Rawls and EU Multiculturalism

Is Post-Enlightenment Rawlsian Liberalism Sustainable?

Giorgi Areshidze

Introduction: Obama's Defense of Ground Zero Mosque—An American Civil Religion?

In the summer of 2010, a controversy arose in the United States over whether it is permissible and wise to build a mosque a few blocks from Ground Zero in New York City. Clearly, the heated national debate had immediate significance to the American public whose views of Islam unfortunately are shaped in part by the events of 9/11. Recognizing the far-reaching importance to our understanding of the limits of religious toleration that this controversy posed, President Obama felt the need to announce his support for the construction of the mosque. In defending the plan to build the mosque, President Obama appealed to what seemed like a version of an American civil religion: after invoking the Pledge of Allegiance's vision of the American republic as "one nation, under God, indivisible," Obama went on to identify a theological basis for American liberalism by claiming that "we can only achieve 'liberty and justice for all' if we live by that one rule at the heart of every great religion, including Islam— that we do unto others as we would have them do unto us."[1] This statement, which was the earliest and the most articulate version of President Obama's position, and from which he later partly retreated,

presented a few critical assumptions and raised a number of important questions about the role, status, and character of religious commitment in the American regime:

- Was President Obama correct to cast the American regime as
possessing an "overlapping consensus" of a genuine plurality of
religious beliefs that agree on a substantive liberal vision of tolerance and justice, and that this shared vision constitutes a form
of unofficial civil religion, at least implicitly recognized by the
Pledge of Allegiance's reference to God?
- Was he correct to imply, in effect, that the protection of this overlapping consensus requires, not just the legal accommodation
of religious pluralism through separation of church and state,
but also the active moral commitment on the part of American
citizens, on the basis of their privately held religious beliefs, to
broad religious and tolerant pluralism in American society?
- Finally, and most importantly, should the United States, and
Western democracies more broadly, encourage religious minorities, including Muslims, to conceive of their citizenship in liberal
democracies in religious terms—and therefore to regard liberalism as sanctioned by and rooted in their own private religious
beliefs—or should the West present the requirements of liberal citizenship in secular, rational, or some other nonreligious,
terms?

What is striking is that in the wake of what seemed at first to be a
genuine crisis, it took very little time for the issue to disappear and
fizzle out. In a paradoxical way, and in a way that is compatible with
what Obama can be interpreted to be suggesting about the American
civil religion, the logic of the First Amendment, especially of its twin
clauses that commit the American constitutional polity to both free
exercise and disestablishment, exercised their influence on the debate. In reacting to the mosque controversy, conservatives refused to
question the legal right of the Imam and his supporters to build the
mosque where they wished to, focusing instead on the prudence of
constructing the mosque so close to a site that Americans continue to
associate with an act of horrific terrorism and, unfortunately, with a
radical ideological perversion of Islam. Precisely because the Constitution provided an absolute protection of free exercise that precluded
any official interference from the state, the critics argued, the Imam

and his supporters had even greater responsibility to reflect on the interfaith message that the decision to construct the mosque would send to their fellow American citizens. Not too long after the incident took on national attention, this constitutional logic of absolute First Amendment protections—which almost guaranteed the mosque supporters a judicial avenue to vindicate their claims in the face of any legal or institutional opposition—combined with broad public but peaceful opposition, created a fissure within the Muslim community itself, so that more than half of polled Muslims supported moving the mosque to another location or officially converting it to an interfaith community center. While the story receded from the national spotlight, the constitutional lesson that it contains is illustrative of the assimilationist logic of the American system of separation of church and state, and of its unofficial civic religion.

In sharp contrast with this picture of American constitutional disestablishment, consider the avowedly secular commitments of *laïcité* in France and Kemalism in Turkey. Their constitutional identities invest both of these states with transformative aspirations that explicitly commit the governments to aggressively policing the public sphere by constraining religious expression to a narrow private realm, with the aim of securing a distinctively secular national identity.[2] While Article I of the French Constitution affirms "freedom of religion," it also defines the state as "a Republic that is indivisible, *laic*, democratic, and social,"[3] a provision that has increasingly been interpreted to require a robust public secularism. Similarly, the Kemalist authoritarian origins of the Turkish constitution commit the state and the judiciary to the task of forging an economically modern, politically liberal and increasingly secular Western-oriented republic from the traditionally religious society that Turkey inherited from the Ottoman Empire.[4] In both cases, such a constitutional disposition implies not just the exclusion of religion from the secular public sphere, but also the direct intervention of the state in the private sphere with the aim of reshaping religious belief along secular lines.[5]

In its recent religious free exercise jurisprudence, the European Court of Human Rights (ECHR) has relied on these constitutional commitments to secularism to uphold the French law banning the wearing of the Muslim headscarves in schools, on the grounds that Islamic headscarves represent threats to the secular public order.[6] While other European states do not explicitly share with France constitutional commitments to militant secularism, the increasingly critical pressure that is being placed on European multiculturalism is pushing the EU toward a difficult choice: should the EU states follow the lead of the ECHR and adopt the constitutional model of secular imposition of France, or should they instead strive to emulate the American model of civil religion under disestablishment? In this chapter, I begin answering these questions by dwelling on the religious situation in the European liberal democracies, which, while they share the basic liberal commitments of the American regime, diverge considerably from the American model in their institutional approach to state-church relations. In the process, I hope to diagnose and evaluate some of the theoretical and constitutional shortcomings of both multiculturalism and militant secularism—the two constitutional postures that appear to be the most tempting institutional solutions for contemporary societies confronting the challenges of religious pluralism. The dormant questions of the foundations and limits of liberal toleration and civic identity that the controversy over the Ground Zero mosque brought to the fore, and therefore the challenges and rewards of liberal and religious pluralism, are much more vividly discernible in Europe than in the U.S.[7]

The Crisis of Multiculturalism and the Normative Foundations of the European Polity: Is Christian Secularism Possible without the Enlightenment?

If one ponders the experience of the European Union with religion in the public square in recent decades, one is struck not so much by the monolithic secularism of European liberalism but rather by the enduring political-theological tensions that European states are still struggling to resolve on the national and transnational levels. The French version of militant constitutional secularism is, after all, the exception rather than the norm within the broader pattern of diverse national church-state legacies in Europe.[8] Europe's multiple decade experiment with multiculturalism was conducted against the backdrop of a complex set of national identities and cultural and religious traditions, among them constitutionally protected state religious establishments and publicly funded (Christian) religious schools. While these traditional structural features of national identity and religious holdovers from Europe's past had already started to weaken with advent of cultural secularization, the combined pressure of political centralization and the growing challenge of ethno-religious immigration has in fact precipitated their resurgence as the basis of immigrant religious contestation against the European state. As Francis Fukuyama has observed, "[a]sking Muslims to give up group rights is much more difficult in Europe than in the United States, [. . .] because many European countries have corporatist traditions that continue to respect communal rights and fail decisively to separate church and state."[9] In the 1980s and 1990s, in particular, Muslim groups used the officially privileged position of Christianity in the political and educational institutions of England, Netherlands, and Denmark to contest the notion that European states are genuinely secular or neutral with regard to religion. While these efforts reached a critical juncture in the Rushdie Affair in 1989, when Muslims petitioned that the British blasphemy law be extended to protect Islam against what they perceived to be the offensive and libelous depiction of the Prophet Muhammad in *The Satanic Verses* (1988), their resilience went beyond the dispute over the publication of that infamous text: relying on the language of group rights and identity politics, Muslim groups have continued to demand similar levels of official enfranchisement of minority religious groups through state subsidies and religious instruction in public schools.[10]

These demands for religious equality and for political recognition had genuine force that fed into the multiculturalist wave, because, as the existence of the blasphemy law indicates, European states are emphatically not neutral, in their traditional and constitutional posture, towards religion, but instead legally sanction particular denominations of Christianity.[11] While the practical and policy consequences of Muslim assertiveness and the demands for "parity with native religions"[12] have varied depending on the competing national contexts in Europe (official multiculturalism in Britain and Germany, secular resistance in France and Belgium), the most important commonality is that the EU vision of neutrality has been effectively challenged under the pressure of religious immigrant lobbying that the state afford them with the political recognition and financial support that it already provides to Christian denominations. The challenge of Muslim immigration, therefore, illuminates the philosophical ambivalence in the constitutional identity of liberalism, not only in Europe but also in Canada, over the scope and breadth of liberal pluralism, and over whether liberal values should be defined on a Christian or a secular foundation.

The practical challenge to the secular identities of the EU states has been accompanied and exacerbated by a more profound and deeper internal philosophical questioning within the Western intellectual world of the soundness of the liberal constitutional order. The forefather of this philosophic attack on the theoretical foundations of liberalism was Frederick Nietzsche, who mounted a frontal assault on the rationalist enterprise of the Enlightenment as a misguided effort, rooted in a transfigured and secularized religious impulse, to reshape the human world through will-to-power.[13] In its contemporary anti-foundationalist form, this Nietzschean critique of the Enlightenment asserts that the political principles which liberalism espouses as being grounded in rational truth—the constitutional protections of individual rights and the separation of church and state—so far from being rationally demonstrable and defensible, in fact reveal liberalism's implicit bias towards a specifically narrow, materialistic, individualistic, and ultimately democratic way of life that is dependent for its spiritual and moral authority on a secularized version of Christianity: liberalism is at bottom not an outcome of rationalism, but of faith transfigured through history.[14] As an illustration of the anti-foundationalist desire to get beyond the rationalism of the Enlightenment, and its propensity to regard modern rationalism as a religious impulse, consider the following claim that Richard Rorty made in one of his last public lectures, delivered at a conference in Iran: "We anti-foundationalists, however, regard Enlightenment rationalism as an unfortunate attempt to beat religion at religion's own game—the game of pretending that there is something above and beyond human history that can sit in judgment on that history."[15]

From Rorty's perspective, while liberal constitutionalism may be defensible on traditional, historical, and even practical grounds, it does not for that reason exhibit any higher claim to reasonableness and therefore to human dignity than do other, non-Western and even potentially illiberal institutions and cultures. But while he is willing to embrace, and even to proclaim, the death of rationalism as a foundation of our way of life, Rorty does not follow Nietzsche, who, when he proclaimed the death of God and of modern rationalism, also rejected liberal democracy: "We argue that although some cultures are better than others, there are no transcultural criteria of 'betterness' that we can appeal to when we say that modern democratic societies are better than feudal societies, or that egalitarian societies

are better than racist or sexist ones."[16] For Rorty, the attempt to
defend liberal constitutionalism on the basis rational foundations,
which allegedly endows its political institutions with universal validity and applicability, is both futile and counterproductive. We would
be better off admitting that a rational universal defense of liberalism
is not feasible. Doing so would give us the freedom to acknowledge
that liberalism is based not on self-evident rational truths, but instead
on a peculiar (Western) historical experience that has bred a certain
form of conventional "light-mindedness" about theological questions which makes peaceful democratic existence possible. According
to Rorty, such light-mindedness (and the spiritual slackening and
herd mentality that it breeds) "may be a reasonable price to pay for
political freedom."[17]

As one can expect from the preceding short discussion, however,
Rortian anti-foundationalism finds it difficult to offer an intelligible
and satisfactory response to those religious believers who are not
willing to strike a similar historical bargain of "light-mindedness"
with liberalism, and who continue to insist that political life take seriously the moral demands of religion, especially in its revealed form as
the word and the law of God.[18] In light of this profound loss of confidence in the theoretical viability of their way of life, and their growing incapacity or Rortian unwillingness to defend liberalism on
rational grounds, it is not surprising that the European liberal democracies have come under increasing strain from precisely those citizens
who find the secular commitments of the EU states especially troubling and disconcerting. But, this picture is further complicated by
the fact that the antagonism between religious belief and European
secularism has been conducted not so much in terms of claims of
individual rights to religious liberties, as in the language of postcolo-
nial group rights discourse. Thus, Tariq Modood correctly points out
that even while they challenge the hegemony of European secularism
as a regime that publicly marginalizes, and implicitly deprecates,
spiritual and religious concerns, Muslims have been quite adept at
effectively appropriating the contemporary discourse of group and
ethnic identity in demanding official recognition from the state. In
doing so, by pursuing the postmodern European invitation to conceive and publicly articulate their citizenship in terms of their distinctive socio-religious identity, Western Muslims, in cooperation
with and encouragement from their European intellectual, legal, and
political facilitators, have transformed a legitimate claim to equality

and to individual religious expression and social accommodation within a liberal polity into a movement that aspires to transform the constitutional identity of that polity.[19] As a result, the widespread loss of confidence in the political program of Enlightenment rationalism—one that culminates in the sanctity of individual autonomy as the foundation of individual liberties and of human dignity—has converged, in the European instance, with the rise of Western postmodern multicultural language that is increasingly employed, with official state encouragement, to construct demands for legal recognition for ethnic and religious group autonomy or self-determination.

The policy outcome in response to this complicated set of pressures led to the regime of European multiculturalism, which entailed a genuine concession to the complaints against the mythical neutrality of liberalism. In a retrospective report on the government sponsored analysis that he authored in 2000 as the Chair of Commission on the Future of Multiethnic Britain, Bhikhu Parekh crystallized the policy wisdom of this multicultural approach by explicitly claiming that the acknowledgment of British diversity required not just the transcendence of a substantive vision of a good life (as some versions of classical liberalism would admit), but also the elevation of group identities over the cultural norm of individualism that heretofore formed the core of liberalism: "When we see Britain as a community of individuals and communities rather than as a nation or nation-state, we bypass [...] problems [... associated with national identity ...]. We appreciate its internal plurality, as well as the need to base its unity and cohesion, not on a common substantive vision of the good life, but on an acceptance of its cultural and moral diversity." Since citizens had "differing needs," equal treatment required "full account to be taken of their differences." Equality, the report insisted, "must be defined in a culturally sensitive way and applied in a discriminating but not discriminatory manner."[20] Multiculturalism, therefore, internalizes on a policy level the anti-foundationalist denial that liberalism requires a rational moral foundation, and it does so by deliberately constraining the state from making substantive cultural and moral demands on its citizens as individuals, and prefers to speak to them as deeply divided groups that can somehow still be expected to coexist in a peaceful and cohesive society. It was on the basis of this anti-foundationalist and post-Enlightenment understanding of the requirements of diversity that the EU sought to construct an accommodationist multicultural liberalism that leaves the citizens' religious identities intact in order to create a politics that is more protective of group autonomy, and in that sense more inclusive, tolerant, and just.

The results of the EU experiment, therefore, seem to provide an extremely vivid illustration of some of the key tension-ridden features of the post-Enlightenment paradigm of political liberalism. These approaches to liberalism range from the avowedly anti-foundationalist, such as the one espoused by Rorty, to the more dominant ones that interpret liberalism through the framework of "neutrality," which was the hallmark of John Rawls' *Political Liberalism* (1993). It is the latter approach, which aspires to secure an "overlapping consensus" within the framework of a genuinely neutral public space, that has been tested in the EU multicultural system. Signs of a crisis in EU multiculturalism are there to see for anyone who wishes to look. In a speech on "Multiculturalism and Integration" in 2006, Tony Blair succinctly summarized the attitude of many Europeans in the wake of 7/7 bombings: "We like our diversity. But how do we react when that difference leads to separation and alienation from the values that define what we hold in common? For the first time in a generation there is an unease, an anxiety, even at points a resentment that our very openness, our willingness to welcome difference, our pride in being home to many cultures, is being used against us; abused, indeed, in order to harm us."[21] More recently, Angela Merkel went much further when she announced that Germany's attempt "[to build] a multicultural [society] . . . has failed, utterly failed." The relatively moderate diagnosis of the problem by Blair and Merkel contrasts with the more extreme reaction to this failure that is discernible in the growing appeal of right wing anti-immigration political parties throughout Europe, especially in Netherlands and Germany. These groups wish to replace multiculturalism, and even potentially put into question the transnational integrationist aspirations of the EU project, with a rejuvenated nationalism that centers around Europe's closed Christian identities.[22]

In light of the failure of cultural and religious neutrality, the European intellectual elite has reached a rather paradoxical position: uncomfortable with either the rationalist or postmodern approaches to liberalism, some of the leading intellectual and religious figures in Europe now proclaim that liberal values somehow derive from Christianity. As an illustration, consider the strange convergence, from two drastically opposed starting positions, of Jürgen Habermas and Joseph Cardinal Ratzinger (later Pope Benedict XVI), around the common proposition that European liberal constitutionalism is rooted in a secularized version of Christianity, and that while Europe may owe to the Enlightenment its secular heritage, it cannot be said that that heritage is either rational or universal. Habermas, who seems to betray an extremely radical rationalist starting point by claiming to be "tone death in the religious sphere," still insists that reason cannot claim to know what "may be true or false in the contents of religious traditions."[23] But, at the same time, Habermas concedes the untenability of a secular position that complacently and unreflectively dismisses the claims that emanate from these religious traditions, on the one hand, and the insufficiency of a pluralistic position that simply acknowledges and celebrates the deep religious and moral diversity that they foster, on the other. Liberal societies should indeed be more inclusive of religious claims than they have been, but they must be so while simultaneously promoting a cohesive vision of liberal citizenship that does not rely on rationalism. Since it is futile to search for a rational and secular normative foundation for such a liberal vision of citizenship,[24] Habermas insists that what is needful is for liberalism to embrace a postsecular age in which it consciously turns to religion, and through the collective trust-building process of deliberative democracy, induces religious believers to acquire a stake in the secular state and therefore undergo the same process of secularization that transpired in Christianity.

But, in a paradoxical twist, Habermas suggests that such a process of mutual learning and communication through a strictly procedural conception of deliberative democracy will make the secularized "substance of biblical concepts," to which we owe liberalism, "accessible to a general public that also includes those who have other faiths and those who have none."[25] In his debate with then-Cardinal Ratzinger, Habermas had claimed that "philosophy has good reasons to learn from religious traditions," and elsewhere he has suggested that Christianity makes an indispensible contribution to liberalism: "Universalistic egalitarianism, from which sprang the ideals of freedom and a collective life in solidarity, the individual morality of conscience, human rights and democracy, is the direct legacy of the Judaic ethic of justice and the Christian doctrine of love. This legacy, substantially unchanged, has been the object of continual critical appropriation and reinterpretation. There is no alternative to it. Everything else is postmodern talk." But if indeed we owe some of our liberal values to "biblical concepts," then is Habermas not conceding Ratzinger's point about the importance of the theological legacy of Christianity for democracy's civic and moral health? Is he not conceding, in other words, that the neutral framework of "political liberalism" (whether Rawlsian or Habermasian) is not in itself sufficient to sustain liberal citizenship, especially among non-Christians, since liberalism relies on a prepolitical or preprocedural normative consensus around values that have emerged through a historical transformation (and secularization) of the Christian ethic?

If the preceding diagnosis is accurate, we are compelled to raise the following questions about the normative foundations of the liberal values of tolerance and separation of church and state:

- Does the "retreat of multiculturalism," and the continuing growth of unanswered religious commitments of immigrants in Europe, condemn the EU states to emulating the increasingly illiberal secularism of French laïcité in their effort to reconstitute their national identities? Are there no alternatives to good-natured but ineffective multiculturalism, on the one hand, and anti-religious and illiberal secularism on the other?[26]
- Or does liberalism, especially as it was articulated originally in early modern political philosophy, posses theoretical and practical resources that are exhausted neither by multiculturalism nor by aggressive secularism, resources that should give us hope as we confront an increasingly globalized and ethnically and religiously divided Western world?

Rawls and the Foundations of Multiculturalism in Post-Enlightenment Liberalism

In order to better articulate the assumptions that underpin the multiculturalist critique of the deficiencies of liberalism, I briefly turn to the political thought of John Rawls, and to his influential critique of Enlightenment liberalism. I turn to Rawls in order to show the ambivalent status of group rights, in particular the rights of religious groups, in the most dominant theoretical conception of liberalism that wants to self-consciously discard the Enlightenment assumptions that informed early modern thinkers. At the same time, I turn to Rawls because his theory illuminates both the motive behind, and

the preferred strategy of, multiculturalism as an alternative to Enlightenment liberalism. The modern Enlightenment was an effort of
rational theological reform, aimed at reinterpreting, and, in the process, enlightening inherited religious opinion in the service of liberal
political priorities and under the guidance of modern rationalism. A
central feature of this early Hobbesian effort was a rationalist assault
on revealed religion, in particular Biblical Christianity, as the source
of moral and political guidance for human beings, that aimed at in-
stilling a decidedly individualistic and secular worldview. But the Enlightenment evolved beyond Hobbesian absolutism and matured in
Locke's constitutionalism and disestablishment, which turned rationalism to the task of providing an increasingly tolerant, humane, and
liberal reading of the Bible as *a* theological source that could morally
support, spiritually enrich, and make more appealing, the rational
liberal individual rights that constitutionalism aims to secure. Rawlsian multicultural liberalism, too, wishes to extend the protections
of liberalism only to those groups that are tolerant and respectful of
others, and have accepted liberal priorities, but it wants to do so without relying on the normative character of Enlightenment rationalism
as it is applied to theology, including especially orthodox theology.[27]
According to Rawls, political liberalism aims to vindicate the claim
that "there is, or need be, no war between religion and democracy.
In this respect, political liberalism is sharply different from and rejects Enlightenment Liberalism, which historically attacked orthodox
Christianity."[28] The motive behind Rawls' break with Enlightenment
rationalism, and his attempt to establish liberalism as "a self-standing
conception of justice," not dependent on any contentious or divisive
religious or moral doctrines, is the desire to achieve greater consensus
than Enlightenment liberalism was able to secure on its own with the
help of modern rationalism.[29] Free-standing liberalism, from Rawls
perspective and from the perspective of multiculturalism, promises
to secure a greater degree of consensus among those who disagree on
comprehensive questions, including especially among religious believers, than does liberal rationalism. Like modern-day multiculturalist critics of liberal neutrality, the chief goal of Rawlsian liberalism
is greater inclusiveness as the condition for the legitimacy and stability of the liberal democracy.

   Although Rawlsian liberalism has been criticized for unduly bur-
dening religious claims, and even altogether banishing them from
public life,[30] Rawls himself was insistent about the persistence of

certain kinds of comprehensive and theological doctrines under political liberalism. Rawls insists that public reason in the liberal order must not appeal to justifications that depend on any one particular comprehensive doctrine at the expense of others, but he does not believe that democratic life can be sustained without such doctrines: "I assume *all* citizens to affirm a comprehensive doctrine to which the political conception they accept is in some way related"; "we *always* assume that citizens have two views, a comprehensive and a political view"; "*all* those who affirm the political conception start from within their own comprehensive view and draw on the religious, philosophical, and moral ground it provides."³¹ Here, Rawls's vision seems to be quite close to Habermas' vision of liberalism as a plurality of comprehensive, and potentially incompatible, private beliefs, that nevertheless overlap to form a consensus about the legitimacy of liberal politics.

But the political liberalism that Rawls has in mind is intended to be neither an uneasy *modus vivendi* (prudential political compromise) between individuals committed to incompatible beliefs and doctrines, nor a regime of "boutique multiculturalism" in which differences in beliefs are merely superficial and therefore ultimately unimportant. His critics have generally misinterpreted the strategy behind Rawls's "free-standing" liberalism as requiring complete separation or detachment from truth claims, because Rawls himself believed that the character of the consensus at the heart of the liberal order should reflect, and be morally supported by, the citizens' privately held beliefs. From Rawls's perspective, the resilience of privately held absolute beliefs and truth claims, both religious and nonreligious, as the foundation of individual allegiance to a democratic regime is not only unavoidable, but also necessary and desirable for a healthy and pluralistic society: "we want a political conception to have a justification by reference to one or more comprehensive doctrines," because only such a conceptions can provide the moral consistency, spiritual meaning and broad popular appeal to liberalism that rationalism alone is incapable of providing.³² Thus, while from the private perspective of the individual citizen, the legitimacy of political liberalism depends on its congruence with his or her privately held particular comprehensive doctrine, from the public perspective of freestanding liberalism, it is not important, which, if any, of these doctrines is true, so long as religiously devoted citizens abide by the liberal requirement that they "translate" their claims into the Rawlsian language of public reason.

In light of this paradoxical readmission of comprehensive doctrines into political liberalism, it becomes increasingly clear that
when Rawls says that his liberalism is "freestanding," he does not
mean that it is free of all normative foundations, but rather that he is
reluctant to attempt to provide such a foundation himself. Rawls
presents his "freestanding" liberalism as a fuller articulation of the
incomplete promise that Enlightenment liberalism was incapable of
fulfilling because of its parasitic dependence on rationalism, but in
presupposing private comprehensive doctrines for its moral support,
political liberalism seems to fail its own test of what constitutes a
"freestanding" political consensus. Instead, it appears more and more
clearly that instead of shaping such a consensus through rational
argumentation, the Rawlsian account presupposes precisely the
moral and theological consensus that he claims political liberalism is
more capable of achieving than Enlightenment rationalism. Consider
Rawls' admission that the only reason liberalism can finally aspire to
be freestanding is because historical progresses has freed the Western
democracies from the need to resolve the sort of religious and clerical
conflicts that entangled Europe in religious warfare: In the sixteenth
century, Catholics and Protestants did not possess "an overlapping
consensus on the principle of toleration. Both faiths held that it was
the duty of the ruler to uphold the true religion and to repress the
spread of heresy and false doctrine."[33] Our acceptance of toleration
after the Reformation emerged initially as a "modus vivendi," as a
grudgingly accepted temporary ceasefire between the hostile parties,
because it provided the "only workable alternative to endless and
destructive civil strife."[34] But as Rawls himself eventually acknowledges, this ceasefire or "reluctant" "modus vivendi" had to be transformed into a genuine cohesive moral vision that united the religious
parties in a reformed commitment to a tolerant and "reasonable"
Christianity, in order to make the intolerant views of sixteenth-century Catholics and Protestants a decided "minority" in our society.[35]
In depending on this historical transformation, Rawls' political liberalism loses its claim to embody a deep and genuine moral and theological diversity that he claimed it possessed. The inescapable
conclusion, then, seems to be that the "overlapping consensus" that
Rawls wants to see as the foundation for the social cohesion of political liberalism depends on our peculiar and therefore contingent historical experience, through which we have inherited toleration as a

legacy of liberalized Christianity, because Rawls himself insists that "political liberalism" does not take a rationalist stand on the deep theological questions that divided Catholics and Protestants. But, if we return for a moment to Rorty's critique of foundational liberalism, does this discovery not mean then that liberal constitutionalism is, at bottom, a "faith," and therefore, as Nietzsche proclaimed, an act of will-to-power, as distinguished from the universal political conclusions of unassisted human reason? If, as Rawls seems to imply, liberalism in fact unconsciously depends on such a theological inheritance of secularized and liberalized Christianity, then we are prompted to have an even more serious reason to ask how well liberal institutions can actually speak to religious believers, especially non-Christian believers, both within and outside of the Western world, who have not yet undergone—and for good reasons do not wish to undergo— such an intrusive process of secularization.

Having spotlighted what I believe to be the dependence of Rawls' framework on a specific sort of intellectual and spiritual conformism of comprehensive doctrines—that is, those that already accept the Rawlsian injunction to leave morally and theologically divisive issues in the realm of private opinion and to translate their moral commitments into publicly justifiable and therefore reasonable language—it behooves us to reconsider Rawls's relationship to the modern Enlightenment and Christianity. Rawls insists that liberalism cannot judge the truth or falsehood of any such doctrines, including those theological opinions that continue to dispute the truth and legitimacy of liberalism itself.[36] Political liberalism cannot adjudicate rationally between the various competing faiths that constitute a genuine plurality, on whose support Rawls claims liberalism continues to depend for long-term practical stability and for broad moral and psychological appeal. All that political liberalism can do is insist that devoted believers "reconcile" themselves to the historical triumph of political liberalism, by following the Rawlsian injunction to translate their privately held beliefs into the language of public reasons when they appeal to them in public. Rawls therefore simultaneously desires political liberalism to leave comprehensive doctrines, and therefore high-order disputes about moral and theological truths, intact, while expecting privately held beliefs to serve as the foundation of individual devotion to liberalism and public reason. Unlike Enlightenment thinkers such as Hobbes and Locke, however,

Rawls does not provide a blueprint for how this is to take place, and how inherited theological opinions are to undergo the process of "reconciliation" with and integration into the liberal order, for he desires to do away with the rationalism of the Enlightenment. Neither Rawls and his supporters, nor Richard Rorty and other critics of political liberalism, have paid sufficient attention to precisely *how* liberalism is to bring about such an enlightening transformation of illiberal religious beliefs, because they have not paid sufficient attention to how modern rationalism spearheaded the effort to bring about precisely such a transformation in the seventeenth- and eighteenth-century Europe. In the absence of such an effort of public civic education that can render inherited religious opinion compatible with rationalism, and thereby with public reason, the multicultural model of political liberalism is bound to run up against resistance from entrenched traditions and beliefs that see no deeper grounds for bowing to the authority of a mere aspiration to peace and overlapping consensus.

The foregoing analysis should help us grasp the profound challenges that European liberalism confronts in integrating Muslim as well as other ethnic and religious groups, and why "the old multiculturalist model," so popular during the last two decades, appears to be in retreat in Europe today.[37] Because European liberalism has tried break out of the relatively more consistent shell of Enlightenment liberalism, and the public expectations that this traditional version of liberalism places on religion, by shifting a new public discourse toward multiculturalism, it is finding it increasingly difficult to muster the intellectual, legal, and institutional resources to articulate the rational case for integration and toleration. More importantly, however, the practical deficiencies of EU multiculturalism that I have emphasized, and the avowed inability of Rawlsian political theory to speak to illiberal religious believers, compel us to reconsider the soundness of any policy approach that assumes that integration in a liberal order can take place without a prior transformation of religious beliefs. We also have grounds for reconsidering the feasibility of a liberal political theory that deliberately shuns confronting burning theological issues from the perspective of liberal civic rationalism. When we turn from contemporary liberal thought to the early modern Enlightenment in search of an alternative perspective on the role of religion in a liberal society, the most striking difference that comes to our attention is that the Enlightenment was directly engaged with such theological issues, and that it was preoccupied with advancing, and even grafting on to Biblical theology, a decidedly rationalistic civic ethos. In aspiring to establish a post-Enlightenment liberalism, contemporary liberal thought has exempted itself from the responsibility to engage in a searching and critical dialogue with revealed religion. It has therefore forfeited its obligation to confront and rationally assess, in light of a standard of justice discernable to human reason alone, the plausibility of the moral and political imperatives that revealed religion imposes on human beings. By substituting "metaphysical neutrality" for rationalism, political liberalism has short-circuited the dialogue that liberals cannot avoid engaging in if they are to offer compelling reasons to devoted religious believers for genuinely accepting liberal political priorities. The Enlightenment strategy, in contrast, was to foster precisely such a critical dialogue with religion, even if it required presenting liberal rationalism as a legitimate practical and theoretical antagonist against revelation and as a worthy object of mankind's devotion. In aspiring to answer the challenge that Rawls seems to have abandoned or eschewed—the *theoretical* challenge of revealed theology to reason—the Enlightenment first had to vindicate the capacity of modern rationalism to create a civic culture that could effectively solve the *political* problem posed by religious pluralism, above all in its illiberal form, to liberalism.

The Limits of Neutrality: Relative Merits of Assertive Secularism from Hobbesian and Lockean Perspectives

What is clear from the preceding account of the Enlightenment's divergent institutional and rhetorical approaches to religion is that liberal constitutionalism, if it is to outgrow the shackles of Hobbesian absolutism without seeking to destroy religion altogether, presupposes a serious effort of civic education and a mutually transformative learning process through which religion and liberalism become supportive of each other. It is clear that something like a process of transformation is already starting to take place in Europe vis-à-vis Islam in the twenty-first century, even as the European states diverge drastically in their institutional approaches to this effort. But this process, I argue, is partly hampered by two institutional developments which are based, in part, in pathological theoretical transfigurations of liberalism: the extremes of multiculturalism and secular absolutism. The French ban on the Muslim headscarves suggests that the appeal of the Hobbesian approach is very strong, and this temptation carries the risk of constraining liberal constitutionalism in a direction that is damaging both to religion and to liberalism. At the same time, even after the alleged demise of European multiculturalism, the persistence of the Rortian anti-foundationalism on the elite level of Western political, legal and intellectual thought constrains the state and, more importantly, impoverishes the intellectual resources of the leading secular and religious reformers who should be the key stakeholders and actors in a more constructive, transformative process of liberal civic education and religious transformation.

But if, as I have suggested earlier, Hobbes is not entirely a liberal, what does he have to teach liberals today? And more importantly, why is it necessary to turn to an absolutist thinker for assistance in theorizing about the contemporary situation confronting liberal democracies? We tend to regard the sanctity of the private sphere as being near-absolute, and therefore believe that the government must pass an extremely high threshold test if intrusions on individual rights of free speech and religious practice are to be legitimate. The incremental tests that the U.S. Supreme Court has developed to evaluate government intrusions culminate in the "strict scrutiny" test, and in order to justify violations of individual rights of speech and religion, the government must demonstrate a "compelling state interest," usually involving public safety, that can be achieved only through means that require the violation of such rights. Thus, from this liberal perspective, the French government's decision to ban the wearing of headscarves in schools appears patently illegitimate and intrusive because it violates the absolute right of individual to determine how they dress without involving clear issues of public safety. What is instructive, however, is that President Sarkozy did not even try to defend the ban on these familiar classical liberal grounds of legitimacy: he did not say that the wearing of headscarves in schools poses a potential public threat to the security of the state, nor that it should be banned because it somehow violates the rights of female Muslims who may be hindered from choosing not to wear it by cultural reasons. Instead, as Peter Berkowitz has correctly noted, Sarkozy defended the ban as necessary and legitimate because he claimed that the veil "runs counter to women's dignity."[38] In this case, France, an otherwise substantially multicultural society, was driven to transcend neutrality and officially embrace a substantive good, a "comprehensive doctrine," as part of its vision of a secular public sphere, by taking a stand on the meaning of female dignity. Yet in choosing to employ the intrusive power of the state to aggressively advance this secular vision of female dignity, France may be risking its commitment to competing substantive goods, including religious liberties, which have also come to define, and ought to continue to define, its constitutional identity.

Berkowitz is correct to claim that the First Amendment makes such a ban for similar reasons unthinkable in the United States, and that part of the reason that the French can actually implement this policy is because of the absence in the French system of government of similarly robust protections of freedom of religion.[39] Nonetheless, he does not go far enough in identifying the Lockean and Tocquevillean objections to a decision to implement such a ban through state policy. Surely he is correct that the doctrine of laïcité— which is inscribed in Article 1 of the French Constitution and officially sanctions national secularism in France—frees the French government from some of the considerable obstacles that the First Amendment imposes and that must be surmounted before government intrusion is justified in the United States.[40] While Sarkozy's defense of the ban may strike contemporary constitutionalist and First Amendment absolutists as a strange and even an illegitimate or extremely intrusive attempt by government to dictate the meaning of female dignity, Hobbes would predict that this kind of interference is inevitable even and especially in a liberal society that confronts deep religious plurality. The Hobbesian conception of liberal society sees permissiveness as depending on the existence of the religious and cultural climate that is conducive to toleration. Hobbes would predict, as he did in *Leviathan*, that such recurrences of sovereign authoritarianism are an inevitable facet of political life which dictate the necessity of absolutism in the first place, and that the particular danger in the doctrine of limited government (or of state neutrality, for that matter) is not so much that it would make the reassertion of absolute sovereignty impossible (since the power would be used when it is necessary anyway), but that instead it would make it appear illegitimate when the state was finally compelled to resort to pass judgment on private beliefs and religious practices. Would not Hobbes argue, therefore, that by allowing our contemporary assumptions about state neutrality to obscure the true preconditions and rational foundations of liberalism, we have unnecessarily constrained the legitimate and necessary scope of state action? Although we find Hobbes' solution to be unnecessarily repressive and authoritarian, and recoil from what is happening in France and Europe with trepidation, we should pause to consider whether our own toleration of competing sects in the U.S. stems not so much from our superior devotion to constitutional principles, as we would like to think, but instead from the fundamentally less confrontational nature of these sects themselves in their American manifestation, as Hobbes would probably suggest.

As much as a Hobbesian would point to the resurgence of what Christian Joppke has called "repressive liberalism" as confirmation of Hobbes' insights into sovereign absolutism, this approach to civic education and integration is neither the most effective, nor in the long term the most desirable, model for religious toleration that the liberal Enlightenment proposed.[41] It is not effective precisely because it is not sufficiently appreciative of the stark danger that Tocqueville perceived in the profound anti-religious radicalism of prodemocratic partisans during the French Revolution. Tocqueville warned that when Enlightenment employs the repressive power of the state as an antagonist of religion, it risks reducing its political program to a form of anti-religious secularism that is too shallow to satisfy either the human longing for freedom or the spiritual longing for self-transcendence. At the same time, such a repressive approach is not desirable because it does serious harm to liberal constitutionalism: as we saw in Locke, while a liberal regime must retain the capacity to protect itself, it must not exhaust its constitutional identity through a singular Hobbesian commitment to this-worldly security. Doing so does permanent damage both to the meaning and the power of constitutional government as well as to religion, and for this reason Europe (and modernizing Middle Eastern states) should be wary of emulating the aggressive model of French secularism on a broader scale. Uncovering the alternative Lockean and Tocquevillean options requires not merely transcending the policy assumptions of multiculturalism, but, even more importantly, asking afresh the questions that were posed by Enlightenment rationalism: What is the proper balance of religion and liberalism, and what is the foundation of the liberal values of toleration and equal human dignity that liberal constitutionalism is intended both to promote and to protect?

The Disharmony in the European Court's Religious Free Exercise Jurisprudence

Instead of leading to policy convergence among the EU nations, the waning of multiculturalism under the strain of continued Muslim immigration has resulted in significant institutional divergence among the EU states. The domestic reactions span a wide institutional and policy spectrum, ranging from the resurgence of militant secularism (in France and Belgium), to increasingly incentivized institutional accommodation (in Britain and Germany), through to existing traditional church-state establishments. While the banning of the wearing of the Burqa in France and Belgium underscores the long-standing secularist trends in these states with respect to the role of religion in the public sphere, the French model of laïcité does not, and should not, exhaust the institutional options that the EU states have at their disposal in the wake of the retreat of multiculturalism. Engaging in such highly symbolic but ultimately impulsive and insufficiently considered efforts to purge the public sphere of troublesome Islamic symbols—a development in which the European Court of Human Rights (ECHR) has been complicit—the European states are likely to marginalize, alienate, and thereby radicalize religious believers instead of bringing them into the liberal consensus that these believers can regard as being worthy of their devotion. In particular, French laïcité, even as it masquerades under the banner of equal treatment of all religions, in fact ends up targeting one religion in particular, Islam, and therefore violates the cherished principle of neutrality in its own insidious way. By embracing without hesitation what many commentators have called "militant secularism," therefore, the ECHR has played into the very critique of the "mythical" neutrality of secularism that leading Muslim intellectuals have already employed for several decades—even while they deployed that critique to encourage Europe's aborted turn to multiculturalism. French laïcité is too institutionally inflexible and insufficiently attentive to both the legitimate social demand for expression and recognition of religious belief, as well as the theological and spiritual requirements of a healthy liberal polity. It therefore is ill-suited to serve as a long-term policy model for civic education and religious integration.

As an illustration of this dilemma of secularism, consider the explicit dichotomy that the Italian Administrative Court had to construct between Christianity and other non-Christian faiths in arguing that the crucifix should be understood not as a genuine religious symbol, but rather as watered-down "cultural" remnant of a religion whose secularized and broadly tolerant message is the foundation of the modern secular Italian state: "Singularly, Christianity [...] through its strong emphasis placed on love for one's neighbour, and even more through the explicit predominance given to charity over faith itself, contains in substance those ideas of tolerance, equality and liberty which form the basis of the modern secular State, and of the Italian State in particular."[42] This observation is not incompatible with the view that, while Christianity can and should make an important contribution to liberalism, liberal tolerance has a rational foundation independent of any religion altogether, and that it is the rational foundations of liberal tolerance that require promotion by the state. But this is not the implication that the Italian Court draws, for it wants to employ the liberalized Christianity that it has read into the crucifix as an institutional vehicle that can carry the state-endorsed message of tolerance to other faiths: "It must be emphasised that the symbol of the crucifix, thus understood, now possesses, through its references to the values of tolerance, a particular scope in consideration of the fact that at present Italian State schools are attended by numerous pupils from outside the European Union, to whom it is relatively important to transmit the principles of openness to diversity and the refusal of any form of fundamentalism— whether religious or secular—which permeate our system." By implicitly relying on the dichotomy between liberalized, secularized Christianity and nonliberal Islam, according to which the former is projected as the foundation of liberalism while the latter is cast as a threat to liberal values, this sort of jurisprudential approach risks collapsing liberal toleration to the Rortian vision that equates liberalism with faith.

To be sure, in the *Lautsi* decision the Grand Chamber of ECHR dismissed the Italian Court's attempt to render the meaning of the crucifix in strictly Lockean and liberal terms, even as it came to a judgment that granted the Italian government a wide degree of latitude in determining whether to display the crucifix in the schools. However, because of their broadly inflexible attachment to a secular vision of liberalism—one that paradoxically, as I stressed earlier, views it as an inheritance of secularized Christianity—neither the lower Courts nor the ECHR have been willing to extend a similar courtesy of accommodation to Islamic symbols. Instead, the Court

has explicitly constructed a jurisprudential narrative that simultaneously judges Islam as being incompatible with liberal democracy,
while also rendering liberalism as requiring and permitting the state
to restrictively regulate religious expression (of Islam) in the public
sphere. Thus, in one of the judgments upholding the French ban on
headscarves that the ECHR issued in 2008, the Court interpreted
French laïcité in light of the militant anti-Islamist secularism of
Turkey's constitution, which is rooted in the Kemalist notion that traditional Islam is incompatible with democracy. Citing its decision
upholding the Turkish ban, the Court announced that it "reiterates
that the State may limit the freedom to manifest a religion, for example by wearing an Islamic headscarf, if the exercise of that freedom
clashes with the aim of protecting the rights and freedoms of others,
public order and public safety."[43] However, since in this case a genuine rationale of public order and safety was missing, the Court went
on to add that it was taking into account "the "powerful external
symbol" represented by wearing the headscarf "and also [. . .] the
proselytising effect that it might have seeing that it appeared to be
imposed on women by a religious precept which was hard to square
with the principle of gender equality."

The ECHR view is correct in implying that liberalism requires a
certain transformation of religion—a transformation that European
Christianity already has undergone. But the Court's decision to throw
its weight in favor of an explicitly militant secularism that still privileges secularized Christianity, and against religious accommodation,
is a strategic mistake that bodes ill for the capacity of the EU's constitutional culture to accommodate religion. In its church-state jurisprudence the ECHR should try to avoid needlessly antagonizing
those who already are committed, or are capable of being persuaded
to undertake such commitment, to a legitimate and peaceable public
role for religion within a democratic framework. A judicial commitment to what Gary Jacobsohn has called "ameliorative" or "militant"
secularism may turn out to be appropriate in circumstances where
the state's secularist commitments are in profound disharmony with
the broad socio-religious identity of its citizens—as was the case in
Kemalist Turkey in the early twentieth century, and India in the early
stages of its transitions to liberal modernity. Such a judicial disposition may actually be counterproductive, however, not just for
European liberalism, but for maturing non-Western societies such as
present-day Turkey and India.[44]

Notes

1. Barack Obama, Statement on the Ramadan Iftar in the White House, August 15, 2010.

2. Gary Jacobsohn, "If an Amendment Were Adopted Declaring the United States A Christian Nation, Would It Be Constitutional? Well . . . Let's Look at Turkey," 3. French Constitution of 1958, art 1.

4. Despite or perhaps precisely because of this strong secularist constitutional agenda, Kemalist Turkey has experienced a dramatic resurgence of political Islam over the last few decades. For a helpful overview of these assertive constitutional models, and of how constitutional courts have attempted to contain religious challenges to secularism, see Ran Hirschl, *Constitutional Theocracy*.

5. For a recent account of the Turkish state's contested attempt to develop and disseminate in institutions of public education a "modern Turkish Islam" as a means to countering political Islam and fundamentalism, see Umut Azak, *Islam and Secularism in Turkey*, 175.

6. Following the recommendation of the Stasi Commission, France's National Legislature passed a ban on "conspicuous religious symbols" in primary and secondary schools. The ban was signed into law by President Chirac on March 15, 2004. While the law does not mention any particular religion by name, and appears to be neutral on its face, it was widely understood that the ban was motivated by anti-Muslim animus and aimed specifically to target Muslim headscarves. The Turkish analogue to this law is even more aggressive insofar as it targets religious symbols not just in public schools, but in all educational institutions. ECHR upheld the bans in *Dogru v. France*, App. No. 27058/05, ECHR 2008. On the other hand, ECHR refused to strike down the display of the Christian crucifix in Italian public schools in *Lautsi and Others v. Italy*, App. No. 30814/06, ECHR, 2011.

7. The horrific attacks on the French satirical newspaper *Charlie Hebdo* by Islamic fundamentalists claiming to be avenging the magazine's offenses against Prophet Mohammed highlight the resilience of the challenges to European liberalism that are explored in this chapter. The latest attacks are but the most recent episode in a sequence of events stretching back over a decade that center on the clashing values of freedom of speech and respect for religious sensibilities: from the public assassination of the Dutch filmmaker Theo Van Gogh (2004) and the Danish cartoon controversy (2006), to the French bans on wearing the hijab in public schools (2004) and niqab or burqa in any public space (2010). As many have pointed out, the terrorists do not represent the vast majority of peaceful European Muslims, and the

version of Islam that they subscribe to is rightfully condemned by many Europeans of all faiths. But such attacks, even when perpetrated by a small minority bent on exploiting the most radical and illiberal interpretation of the Islamic faith, crystallizes difficult questions confronting European societies: How can the chasm between Islamic and liberal values be more effectively bridged? Are there limits to liberal tolerance of religion, on the one hand, and limits to the liberal commitment to freedom of speech and religion, on the other hand? How can European states more effectively integrate Muslim migrants (and their European-born children and grandchildren) and encourage liberal interpretations of Islam that are compatible with liberal principles of free speech and religion?

8.   For a helpful overview of the competing institutional arrangements in three European democracies, see Joel Fetzer and J. Christopher Soper, *Muslims and the State in Britain, France, and Germany*. Fetzer and Moser show that the institutional responses to Muslims in European states, and the degree of institutional multiculturalism they have chosen to adopt, have been driven by the legacy of church-state arrangements in each state: assertive secularism or *laïcité* in France, weak establishment in England, and multidenominational "corporatism" in Germany, have each resulted in a different strain of institutional multiculturalism.

9.   See Francis Fukuyama, "Identity, Immigration, and Liberal Democracy," 14.

10.   Daniel O'Neill, "Multicultural Liberals and the Rushdie Affair: A Critique of Kymlicka, Taylor, and Walzer," 219–250.

11.   See also, Jan Rath, Rinus Penninx, Kees Groenenduk, and Astrid Meyer, "The Politics of Recognizing Religious Diversity in Europe. Social Reactions to the Institutionalization of Islam in the Netherlands, Belgium and Great Britain," 53–67.

12.   Tariq Modood, "Muslims and the Politics of Difference," 100–115.

13.   Thomas L. Pangle, "A Critique of Hobbes's Critique of Biblical and Natural Religion in 'Leviathan,'" 25–57.

14.   A similar denial of rationalist foundations of liberalism, and the implications of that denial for the constitutional separation of church and state, are discernible in the writings of Stanley Fish.

15.   Richard Rorty, "Democracy and Philosophy," 16. Ibid. "We are sure that rule by officials freely elected by literate and well-educated voters is better than rule by priests and kings, but *we would not try to demonstrate the truth of this claim to a proponent of theocracy or of monarchy*. We suspect that if the study of history cannot convince such a proponent of the falsity of his views, nothing else can do so" (emphasis added).

17. Richard Rorty, "The Priority of Democracy to Philosophy," 271–273, 269.

18. Consider Rorty's unhesitating and impulsive dismissal of those who question, or even reject, liberal democracy on religious or spiritual grounds: "Rather, we heirs of the Enlightenment think of the enemies of liberal democracy like Nietzsche and Loyola as, to use Rawls' word, 'mad.' We do so because there is no way to see them as fellow citizens of our constitutional democracy, people whose life plans might, given ingenuity and good will, be fitted with those of other citizens. [. . .] They are crazy because the limits of sanity are set by what *we* can take seriously. This, in turn, is determined by our upbringing, our *historical situation*" (ibid., 266–267) (underlined emphasis added).

19. "Muslim assertiveness, then, though triggered and intensified by what are seen as attacks on Muslims, primarily derived not from Islam or Islamism but from contemporary Western ideas about equality and multiculturalism. While simultaneously reacting to the latter in its failure to distinguish Muslims from the rest of the 'black' population and its uncritical secular bias, Muslims positively use, adapt and extend these contemporary Western ideas in order to join other equality seeking movements" (Modood, "Muslims and the Politics of Difference," 109).

20. Bhikhu Parekh, "The Future of Multiethnic Britain: Reporting on a Report," 695.

21. Tony Blair, Speech on Multiculturalism and Integration (December 8, 2006). Anticipating the assertiveness that is starting to characterize official British discussions about national identity, Blair went on to add that "when it comes to our essential values—belief in democracy, the rule of law, tolerance, equal treatment for all, respect for this country and its shared heritage—then that is where we come together, it is what we hold in common; it is what gives us the right to call ourselves British. At that point no distinctive culture or religion supercedes our duty to be part of an integrated United Kingdom." But this insistence on shared values and identity only begs the question: Where do these values comes from? Do they possess a normative foundation, and is that foundation rational or theological? And how does a liberal state promote consensus around such values?

22. On his first day on the job in March 2011, Hans-Peter Friedrich, Germany's new interior minister, said, "To say that Islam belongs in Germany is not a fact supported by history." Alan Greenblatt, "Far-Right Parties Gain Ground in European Politics," 23. Jürgen Habermas and Joseph Ratzinger, *The Dialectics of Secularization: On Reason and Religion.*

24. Habermas and Ratzinger, *Dialectics of Secularization*, 11, 42. Habermas subscribes to a version of Rawls' "political liberalism," in this case described as possessing "a non-religious and post-metaphysical justification of the normative foundations of democratic constitutions."
25. Ibid., 45.
26. Christian Joppke, "The Retreat of Multiculturalism in the Liberal State: Theory and Practice," 237–257; and Tridafilos Triadafilopoulos, "Illiberal Means to Liberal Ends? Understanding Recent Immigration Integration Policies in Europe," 861–880.
27. For an extremely illuminating overview, see Judd Owen, *Religion and the Demise of Liberal Rationalism*.
28. John Rawls, "The Idea of Public Reason Revisited," part 4 of *Political Liberalism: Expanded Edition*, 486.
29. Ibid., 485.
30. Greenwalt 1988; Stout 2004; Weithman 2002; Wolterstorff 1997.
31. Rawls, "Public Reason Revisited," 12, 140, 147 (emphasis added).
32. Ibid., 12.
33. Ibid., 148.
34. Ibid., 156.
35. Ibid., 148.
36. Ibid., xxvii.
37. Joppke, "The Retreat of Multiculturalism."
38. Peter Berkowitz, "Can Sarkozy Justify Banning the Veil?" 39. Ibid.
40. Article 1 of the French Constitution (1958) states: "France shall be an indivisible, secular, democratic and social Republic. It shall ensure the equality of all citizens before the law, without distinction of origin, race or religion. It shall respect all beliefs. It shall be organized on a decentralized basis."
41. Christian Joppke, "Immigrants and Civic Integration in Europe," in *Belonging? Diversity, Recognition, and Shared Citizenship in Canada* (McGill-Queen's University Press, 2007), edited by Keith G. Banting, Thomas J. Courchene, F. Leslie Seidle.
42. These statements come from the original judgment of the Italian Administrative Court dealing with the challenge to the display of Crucifixes, in which the Court dismissed the challenges. The European Court reversed judgment, but in turn was subsequently reversed by the Grand Chamber of European Court. The Grand Chamber's judgment in *Lautsi*, which I rely on, gives a lengthy treatment of the Administrative Court's judgment (*Lautsi and Others v. Italy*, 5–7).
43. *Dogru v. France*.

44. See Gary Jacobsohn, *The Wheel of Law: India's Secularism in Comparative Constitutional Context*. Especially pertinent is Jacobsohn's discussion in chapter 4 of the manner in which the Indian Supreme Court has handled the Hindu demands for constitutional recognition of Hinduism as the official national identity of India.

Bibliography

Azak, Umut. *Islam and Secularism in Turkey*. London: Tauris, 2010.

Berkowitz, Peter. "Can Sarkozy Justify Banning the Veil?" *Wall Street Journal*, April 5, 2010.

Blair, Tony. Speech on Multiculturalism and Integration. December 8, 2006.

Casanova, Jose. *Public Religions in the Modern World*. Chicago: University of Chicago Press, 1994.

Dunn, John. *Interpreting Political Responsibility*. Princeton: Princeton University Press, 1990.

Fetzer, Joel L, and J. Christopher Soper. *Muslims and the State in Britain, France, and Germany*. Cambridge: Cambridge University Press, 2004.

Freedman, Jane. "Secularism as a Barrier to Integration? The French Dilemma." *International Migration* 42, no. 3 (2004): 5–27.

Fukuyama, Francis. "Identity, Immigration, and Liberal Democracy." *Journal of Democracy* 17, no. 2 (April 2006): 5–20.

Greenblatt, Alan. "Far-Right Parties Gain Ground in European Politics." *NPR Online*. April 27, 2011. www.npr.org/2011/04/27/135745530/far-right-parties-gain-ground-in-european-politics

Greenawalt, Kent. *Religious Convictions and Political Choice*. Oxford: Oxford University Press, 1988.

Habermas, Jürgen, and Joseph Ratzinger. *The Dialectics of Secularization: On Reason and Religion*. San Francisco: Ignatius Press, 2005.

Hirschl, Ran. *Constitutional Theocracy*. Cambridge, MA: Harvard University Press, 2010.

Jacobsohn, Gary. "If an Amendment Were Adopted Declaring the United States A Christian Nation, Would It Be Constitutional? Well . . . Let's Look at Turkey." Presentation, Conference on Religion and Constitutionalism, University of Maryland Law School, Baltimore, MD, February 2009.

———. *The Wheel of Law: India's Secularism in Comparative Constitutional Context*. Princeton: Princeton University Press, 2009.

———. *Constitutional Identity*. Cambridge: Harvard University Press, 2010.

Johnston, David. *The Rhetoric of the Leviathan: Thomas Hobbes and the Politics of Cultural Transformation*. Princeton: Princeton University Press, 1989.

Joppke, Christian. "The Retreat of Multiculturalism in the Liberal State: Theory and Practice." *British Journal of Sociology* 55, no. 2 (2004): 861–880.

Locke, John. *Reasonableness of Christianity*. Edited by George Ewig. Washington, DC: Regnery, 1965.

———. *Letter Concerning Toleration*. Edited by Mark Goldie. Indianapolis: Liberty Fund, 2010.

Macedo, Stephen. *Diversity and Distrust: Civic Education in a Multicultural Democracy*. Cambridge: Harvard University Press, 2003.

March, Andrew. *Islam and Liberal Citizenship: The Search for an Overlapping Consensus*. Oxford: Oxford University Press, 2009.

———. "Is There a Right to Polygamy? Marriage, Equality and Subsidizing Families in Liberal Political Justification." *Journal of Moral Philosophy* 8, no. 2 (2011): 246–272.

McConnell, Mitch W. "Establishment and Disestablishment at the Founding, Part I: Establishment of Religion." *William and Mary Law Review* 44, no. 5 (2003): 2105–2205.

Mintz, Samuel. *The Hunting of the Leviathan: Seventeenth-century Reactions to the Materialism and Moral Philosophy of Thomas Hobbes*. Cambridge: Cambridge University Press, 2000.

Modood, Tariq. "Muslims and the Politics of Difference." *Political Quarterly Publishing* 74 (August 2003): 100–115.

Obama, Barack. Statement on the Ramadan Iftar in the White House. August 15, 2010.

O'Neill, Daniel. "Multicultural Liberals and the Rushdie Affair: A Critique of Kymlicka, Taylor, and Walzer." *Review of Politics* 61, no. 2 (Spring 1999): 219–250.

Owen, Judd. *Religion and the Demise of Liberal Rationalism*. Chicago: University of Chicago Press, 2001.

Pangle, Thomas L. "A Critique of Hobbes's Critique of Biblical and Natural Religion in 'Leviathan.'" *Jewish Political Studies Review* 4, no. 2 (Fall 1992): 25–57.

Pangle. Thomas. "The Roots of Contemporary Nihilism and Its Political Consequences According to Nietzsche." *Review of Politics* 45, no. 1 (1983): 45–70.

Parekh, Bhikhu. "The Future of Multiethnic Britain: Reporting on a Report." *The Round Table: The Commonwealth Journal of International Affairs* 90 (2001): 691–700.

Rabieh, Micheal. "The Reasonableness of Locke, or the Questionableness of Christianity." *Journal of Politics* 53, no. 4 (1991): 933–957.

Ramadan, Tariq. *To Be a European Muslim*. Markfield, UK: The Islamic Foundation, 2000.

Rath, Jan, Rious Groenendijk, Kees Groenenduk, and Astrid Meyer. "The Politics of Recognizing Religious Diversity in Europe. Social

Reactions to the Institutionalization of Islam in the Netherlands, Belgium and Great Britain." *Netherlands Journal of Social Sciences* 35 (1999): 53–67.

Rawls, John. *Political Liberalism: Expanded Edition.* New York: Columbia University Press, 2005 [1993].

Rorty, Richard. "The Priority of Democracy to Philosophy." Part III in *Objectivity, Relativism and Truth: Philosophical Papers.* Cambridge: Cambridge University Press, 1990.

———. "Democracy and Philosophy." Editorial. *Kritika and Kontext.* May 2007. www.eurozine.com/articles/2007–06–11-rorty-en.html

Stout, Jeffrey. *Democracy and Tradition.* Princeton: Princeton University Press, 2004.

Triadafilopoulos, Tridafilos. "Illiberal Means to Liberal Ends? Understanding Recent Immigration Integration Policies in Europe." *Journal of Ethnic and Migration Studies* 37, no. 6 (2001): 861–880.

Weithman, Paul. *Religion and the Obligations of Citizenship.* Cambridge: Cambridge University Press, 2002.

Wolterstorff, Nicholas and Robert Audi. *Religion in the Public Square: The Place of Religious Convictions in Political Debate.* Lanham, MD: Rowman & Littlefield, 1997.

Publications by Murray P. Dry

Books

Same-Sex Marriage and American Constitutionalism, Philadelphia: Paul Dry Books, 2016.

Civil Peace and the Quest for Truth: The First Amendment Freedoms in Political Philosophy and American Constitutionalism. Lanham, MD: Lexington Books, 2004.

Edited Works

Herbert J. Storing, ed. *The Anti-Federalist: Writings by the Opponents of the Constitution*; selected by Murray Dry from *The Complete Anti-Federalist.* Chicago: University of Chicago Press, 1985.

Herbert J. Storing, ed., with the assistance of Murray Dry. *The Complete Anti-Federalist.* 7 vols. Chicago: University of Chicago Press, 1981. First volume also published separately as *What the Anti-Federalists Were For!* Chicago: University of Chicago Press, 1981.

Articles, Book Chapters, Essays

"The Anti-Federalists." In *Encyclopedia of American Governance.* 5 vols. Edited by Stephen L. Schechter. New York: Macmillan Reference USA/ Cengage Learning, 2016.

"The Separation of Powers." In *The Bloomsbury Encyclopedia of the American Enlightenment.* Edited by Mark Spencer. London: Bloomsbury Academic, 2015.

"The Same-Sex Marriage Controversy and American Constitutionalism: Lessons Regarding Federalism, the Separation of Powers, and Individual Rights." In *Vermont Law Review*, 2014, vol. 39, no. 2.

"Checks and Balances." In *The Encyclopedia of Political Thought.* 8 volumes. Michael T. Gibbons, ed.-in-chief. Hoboken, NJ: Wiley-Blackwell, 2014.

"The Mixed Character of Free Speech and its Implications for Public Schools in America." In *Vermont Bar Journal*, Fall 2006, vol. 32, no. 3, 32–38.

"'Brutus' and 'Federal Farmer'." In *History of American Political Thought.* Edited by Bryan-Paul Frost and Jeffrey Sikkenga. Lanham, MD: Lexington Books, 2003, 216–229.

"The First Amendment Freedoms and the Pledge of Allegiance." In *Addison County Independent*, Vermont. August 2002.

"Toleration and American Constitutionalism: The Case of Rights of Homosexuals." In *Courts and the Culture Wars*. Edited by Bradley Watson. Lanham, MD: Lexington Books, 2002, 79–97.

"Supreme Court Criticisms are Misleading." Community Forum essay on *Bush v Gore*. In *Addison County Independent*, Vermont. December 21, 2000, 5a.

"The Origins and Foundations of the First Amendment." In *Journal of Supreme Court History*, 2000, vol. 25, no. 2, 129–144.

"Herbert J. Storing." In *Leo Strauss, the Straussians, and the American Political Regime*. Edited by Kenneth L. Deutsch and John A. Murley. Lanham, MD: Rowman and Littlefield, 1999, 305–328.

"The First Amendment Freedoms, Civil Peace, and the Quest for Truth." In *Constitutional Commentary*, Summer 1998, vol. 15, no. 2, 325–354.

"*Brown v Board of Education* at Forty: Where Do We Go From Here?" In *Race and Ethnic Ancestry Law Digest*, Washington and Lee Law School, Spring 1995, vol. 1 no. 1, 8–16.

"Hate Speech and the Constitution." In *Constitutional Commentary*, Winter 1994–1995 vol. 11, no. 3, 501–513.

"Free Speech in Political Philosophy and its Relation to American Constitutional Law: A Consideration of Mill, Meiklejohn, and Plato." In *Constitutional Commentary*, Winter 1994, vol. 11, no. 1, 81–100.

"The Rehnquist Court Revisited: Conservative Revolution Stalled or Transformed?" In *Middlebury College Magazine*, Autumn 1992, 28–32.

"Flag-Burning and the Constitution." In *The Supreme Court Review 1990*. Edited by Gerhard Casper, Dennis Hutchinson, and David Strauss. Chicago: University of Chicago Press, 1991, 69–103.

"The Debate over Ratification of the Constitution." In *The Blackwell Encyclopedia of the American Revolution*. Cambridge, MA: Blackwell, 1991, 471–486.

"Free Speech and Modern Republican Government." In *Constitutional Commentary*, Summer 1989, vol. 6, no. 2, 351–366.

"The Rehnquist Court." In *Middlebury College Magazine*, Autumn 1989, 28–32.

"The Anti-Federalists and the Constitution." In *Principles of the Constitutional Order: The Ratification Debates*. Edited by Robert L. Utley, Jr. Lanham, MD: University Press of America, 1989, 63–88.

"Federalism and the Constitution: The Founders' Design and Contemporary Constitutional Law." In *Constitutional Commentary*, Summer 1987, vol. 4, no. 2, 235–250.

"The Case Against Ratification: Anti-Federalist Constitutional Thought." In *The Constitution: A History of its Framing and Ratification.* Edited by Leonard Levy and Dennis Mahoney. New York: Macmillan, 1987, 271–291.

"Anti-Federalism in *The Federalist*: A Founding Dialog on the Constitution, Republican Government, and Federalism." In *Saving the Revolution: The Federalist Papers and the American Founding.* Edited by Charles Kesler. New York: Free Press, 1987, 40–60.

"The American Founding: A Study Guide for a Seminar on the Framing of the Constitution and the Debate over its Ratification." In *The Blessings of Liberty: User's Guide.* Produced by *Project 87*, The American Historical Association and the American Political Science Association, 1987, 66–70.

"The Constitutional Thought of the Anti-Federalists." In *This Constitution*, Fall 1987, 10–14.

"The Constitutional Thought of the Anti-Federalists," and "The Constitutional Scholarship of Herbert J. Storing." In *Encyclopedia of the American Constitution.* Edited by Leonard Levy and Kenneth Karst. 4 vols. New York: Macmillan, 1987.

"Constitutionalism and Republicanism in the American Founding." In *Teaching Political Science*, Fall, 1986, vol. XIV, no. 1, 5–10.

"Choosing Rules for Selecting a Presidential Candidate: Lessons From the Founding." For *The New Federalist Papers*, circulated to newspapers by Public Research Syndicated, Claremont, California, August 1984.

"The Supreme Court and School Desegregation: *Brown v. Board of Education Reconsidered*." In *The St. John's Review*, Summer, 1983; also in *Middlebury College Magazine*, Fall 1983, 12–21.

"The Congressional Veto and the Constitutional Separation of Powers." In *The Presidency and the Constitutional Order.* Edited by Joseph Bessette and Jeffrey Tulis. Baton Rouge: Louisiana State University Press, 1980, 195–233.

"Pro" side of "Legislative Veto: Two Views." In *The Congressional Staff Journal*, September/October, 1980.

Testimony on the Congressional Veto before the Administrative Practice and Procedure Subcommittee of the Senate Judiciary Committee, 96th Congress, Wednesday, July 18, 1979. In *Regulatory Reform*, part 2, serial no. 96–28.

"The Congressional Veto, the Constitution, and Administrative Oversight." In *Congressional Record*, April 6, 1978, H2587–2594.

"Congress." In *Founding Principles of American Government: Two Hundred Years of Democracy on Trial.* Edited by George and Scarlett Graham. Bloomington: Indiana University Press, 1977, 223–257.

"The Unmaking of a President: A Study in the Preservation of our Political Institutions." In *Middlebury College Newsletter*, Fall 1974.

"The Separation of Powers and Representative Government." In *Political Science Review*, 1973, 43–82.

"Liberal Education and Political Life." In *Middlebury College Newsletter*, Winter 1970.

Reviews

Controlling the Law: Legal Politics in Early National New Hampshire, by John Phillip Reid (DeKalb: Northern Illinois University Press 2004). In *American Journal of Legal History*, October 2005, vol. XLVII, no. 4, 447–48.

The Constitution: A Biography, by Akhil Reed Amar (Random House, 2005). In *Legal Affairs*, November/December 2005, 66–71.

Separation of Powers in Practice, by Tom Campbell (Stanford Law and Politics, an imprint of Stanford University Press, 2004). In *Perspectives on Politics*, September 2005, 632–633.

From Parchment to Power: How James Madison Used the Bill of Rights to Save the Constitution, by Robert A. Goldwin (Washington, DC: American Enterprise Institute, 1997). In *St. John's College Review*, 1998, vol. XLIV no. 2, 125–135.

Fighting Words: Individuals, Communities, and Liberties of Speech, by Kent Greenawalt, (Princeton: Princeton University Press, 1995). In *Journal of Politics*, August 1997, vol. 59, no. 3, 951–954.

"National Standards for Civics and Government" (Calabasas, CA: Center for Civic Education, 1994). In *PS: Political Science & Politics*, March 1996, vol. 29, no. 1, 49–53.

Learned Hand: The Man and the Judge, by Gerald Gunther (New York: Knopf, 1994; Harvard University Press, 1995, paperback). In *The Review of Politics*, Winter 1996, vol. 58, no. 1, 194–196.

The Debate on the Constitution; Federalist and Antifederalist Speeches, Articles, and Letters during the Struggle over Ratification, edited by Bernard Bailyn, 2 vols. (New York: Library of America, 1993). In *William & Mary Quarterly*, 3rd series, vol. 52, January 1995, 209–212.

The Origins of American Constitutionalism, by Donald Lutz (Baton Rouge: Louisiana State University Press, 1988). In *William & Mary Quarterly*, 3rd series, June 1990, vol. XLVII, no. 1, 176–178.

The Authority of Publius: A Reading of the Federalist Papers, by Albert Furtwangler (Ithaca, NY: Cornell University Press, 1984). In *The Review of Politics*, Spring 1986, vol. 48, no. 2, 314–316.

SELF EVIDENT TRUTHS: Being a Discourse on the Origins and Development of the First Principles of American Government - Popular Sovereignty, Natural Rights, and the Balance and Separation of Powers, by Paul Conkin (Bloomington: Indiana University Press, 1974). In *American Political Science Review*, December 1977, vol. 71, no. 4, 1615–1616.

Constitutionalism, Executive Power, and the Spirit of Moderation:

Murray P. Dry and the Nexus of Liberal Education and Politics

Giorgi Areshidze, Paul Carrese, and Suzanna Sherry, eds.

In the spirit of Murray P. Dry, honored teacher and scholar of political philosophy and American constitutionalism at Middlebury College, *Constitutionalism, Executive Power, and the Spirit of Moderation* explores the nexus between liberal education and politics. Contributors ranging from former students to practitioners in the federal executive and judicial branches explore constitutional, legal, and philosophical topics while mirroring their teacher's blending of political and philosophical reflection. Part I, "The Role of Courts in Constitutional Democracy," explores the proper functions and limits of the judiciary and judicial decision-making in constitutional government. Part II, "Law and Executive Authority," reflects on the tensions between constitutionalism and presidential leadership in both domestic and international arenas. Part III, "Liberal Education, Constitutionalism, and Philosophic Moderation" shifts the focus to the relationship between constitutionalism and political philosophy, and especially to the modem modes of philosophy that most directly influenced the American Founders. The volume provides a valuable scholarly resource for specialists as well as a text that will be of use in undergraduate political science and law school classes.

Contributors

Giorgi Areshidze (2004) is assistant professor of political science at Claremont McKenna College, where he teaches political theory and American politics. His first book, *Democratic Religion from Locke to Obama: Faith and the Civic Life of Democracy*, is being published by University Press of Kansas in June 2016. *Democratic Religion* explores the modern Enlightenment's attempt to transform and liberalize religion through a comparative study of the philosophies of John Locke, Alexis de Tocqueville, John Rawls, and Jürgen Habermas. It then evaluates the ambiguous results of the liberal experiment in religious transformation in light of the theological dimensions of the statesmanship of Abraham Lincoln, Martin Luther King, Jr., and Barack Obama. Areshidze is currently writing his second book, *Crisis of the West: End of History, Clash of Civilizations, and the Challenge of Religious Fundamentalism*. Areshidze received his Ph.D. in political science from the University of Texas at Austin, and his BA in political science from Middlebury College.

Paul O. Carrese (1989) is professor of political science at the U.S. Air Force Academy, and co-founder and former director of its honors program. He has been a Rhodes Scholar, a research fellow at Harvard, a Fulbright Scholar at University of Delhi, and a fellow in the James Madison Program, Princeton University. He is author of *The Cloaking of Power: Montesquieu, Blackstone, and the Rise of Judicial Activism* (Chicago, 2003), and *Democracy in Moderation: Montesquieu, Tocqueville, and Sustainable Liberalism* (Cambridge, 2016). He has co-edited John Marshall's *The Life of George Washington: Special Edition* (Liberty Fund, 2001); and *American Grand Strategy: War, Justice, and Peace in American Political Thought* (Johns Hopkins, forthcoming).

Karl S. Coplan (1980) is professor of law at Pace Law School and co-director of its Environmental Litigation Clinic since 1994. Prior to joining the Pace faculty, he practiced land use and environmental litigation for eight years with the New York City firm of Berle, Kass & Case. As the principal outside counsel for Riverkeeper, Professor Coplan and the Pace Environmental Litigation Clinic have brought numerous lawsuits enforcing the Clean Water Act and other environmental laws (including *Catskill Mountains Chapter of Trout Unlimited v. City of New York*). Professor Coplan teaches courses in environmental law and constitutional law. He is recently the author of the chapter on citizen suits in *Environmental Litigation, Law and Strategy* (ABA, Cary Perlman, ed.) and the chapter on takings law in *Constitutional Issues in Environmental Law* (ABA, James May, ed.).

Barbara Kritchevsky (1977) is Cecil C. Humphreys Professor of Law and Director of Advocacy at the University of Memphis School of Law. She currently teaches civil rights and appellate advocacy. She has written extensively on section 1983 civil rights litigation and on the tort doctrine of negligence per se. She also supervises Memphis Law's Advocacy program and coaches teams in national moot court competitions. She holds a JD from the Harvard Law School and a BA in political science from Middlebury College. She is indebted to Murray Dry for introducing her to political science for the inspiration he has provided throughout her teaching career.

Kevin Marshall (1994) is a partner at Jones Day, where he assist clients with analysis, strategy, and advocacy involving novel or complex legal issues in federal and state courts, prelitigation including internal investigations, and before regulatory agencies. He received his JD from the University of Chicago in 1998 and clerked on the U.S. Court of Appeals for the Fourth Circuit and the Supreme Court (for Justice Clarence Thomas). Before joining Jones Day in 2007, Kevin was a deputy assistant attorney general in the U.S. Department of Justice's Office of Legal Counsel. He provided authoritative written legal opinions and other legal advice throughout the executive branch, on the Constitution, treaties, international law including the law of war, and federal statutes and regulations. He also testified three times before Congress.

Sean Mattie (1991) is an independent scholar. He majored in political science at Middlebury, then attended graduate school at Boston College (MA, political science, 1993) and the University of Dallas

(PhD, politics, 1999). His teaching assignments have included Ashland University, Hillsdale College, Ave Maria College, and Clayton State University. His publications include articles on prerogative and the rule of law in Locke and the Lincoln presidency for *The Review of Politics*, and on the political thought of Daniel Webster and John Quincy Adams for *History of American Political Thought* (Lexington Press, 2003) and *Modern Age*, respectively. Among his research interests are: themes of political philosophy in American political history and in literature; the rule of law; the separation of powers; and the political themes of Machiavelli in Shakespeare's plays.

Peter Minowitz (1976) is professor of political science at Santa Clara University, where he co-founded the environmental studies program—and arranged for Murray Dry to teach a class during Dry's 1997 sabbatical. In addition to *Profits, Priests, and Princes*, his 1993 book on Adam Smith (Stanford University Press), Minowitz wrote *Straussophobia: Defending Leo Strauss and Straussians against Shadia Drury and Other Accusers* (Lexington Books, 2009). Minowitz has also published articles/chapters about Machiavelli, Smith, Marx, Strauss, Frank Herbert, Harvey Mansfield, and Woody Allen; his current research focuses on Strauss and Nietzsche. Working mainly with Mansfield, Minowitz received his PhD in political science from Harvard University. He got his first "gig" at Mister Up's Restaurant in Middlebury, and still moonlights as a jazz pianist; among the many captivating singers he has accompanied along the way are Cecelia and Judith Dry.

James Morone (1973) is the John Hazen White Professor of Political Science and Public Policy and director of the Taubman Center for Public Policy at Brown University. Morone's first book, *The Democratic Wish*, was named a "notable book of 1991" by the *New York Times* and won the Political Science Association's Kammerer Award for the best book on the United States. His *Hellfire Nation: The Politics of Sin in American History* was nominated for a Pulitzer Prize and named a top book of 2003 by numerous newspapers and magazines. His *The Heart of Power: Health and Politics in the Oval Office* (written with David Blumenthal, MD) was featured on the front page of the *New York Times Book Review*. Morone's tenth book, *The Devils We Know*, was in 2014. He has also written more than 150 articles, reviews, and essays on American political history, health care policy, and social issues.

Suzanna Sherry (1976) is the Herman O. Loewenstein Professor of Law at Vanderbilt University. Her work focuses primarily on constitutional law and theory, and on judicial decision making. She is the author or co-author of eight books and more than ninety articles, essays, and book chapters. She is currently working on a book about judicial activism and an article defending the Supreme Court's traditional distinction between personal rights and economic rights. She holds a JD from the University of Chicago and BA in History from Middlebury College. She first encountered constitutional law and theory in Murray Dry's classes, which inspired her to go to law school and then into academia.

James R. Stoner Jr. (1977) is professor of political science at Louisiana State University, where he has taught since 1988. He is the author of *Common-Law Liberty: Rethinking American Constitutionalism* (Kansas, 2003) and *Common Law and Liberal Theory: Coke, Hobbes, and the Origins of American Constitutionalism* (Kansas, 1992), as well as a number of articles and essays. He was twice a visiting fellow in the James Madison Program in American Ideals and Institutions at Princeton University and is a senior fellow of the Witherspoon Institute of Princeton, for whom he has co-edited two books: *The Social Costs of Pornography: A Collection of Papers* (2010) and *Rethinking Business Management: Examining the Foundations of Business Education* (2008). From 2002 to 2006, he served on the National Council for the Humanities. He earned his AB from Middlebury College and his MA and PhD from Harvard University, all in political science.

David R. Upham (1993) is associate professor of politics at the University of Dallas, where he regularly teaches courses in political theory, American politics, and constitutional law. His research and publications have focused on American constitutional history, especially the history of the Fourteenth Amendment. He holds a JD from the University of Texas School of Law, a PhD in politics from the University of Dallas, an MA in political science from Boston College, and a BA in political science from Middlebury College.

Ayşe Zarakol (1999) is a university lecturer in international relations at the University of Cambridge and a politics fellow at Emmanuel College. She holds a PhD and MA from UW-Madison and a BA from Middlebury College, where she took many classes with Professor Murray Dry. Ayşe was previously an assistant professor at Washington

& Lee University and an International Affairs Fellow with the Council on Foreign Relations. Ayşe works on East-West relations in the international system, problems of modernity, rising and declining powers, and Turkish politics in a comparative perspective. In addition to her book *After Defeat: How the East Learned to Live with the West* (Cambridge University Press, 2011, and in Turkish with a new introduction with Koç University Press, 2012), she has published in journals such as *International Studies Quarterly, International Theory, Review of International Studies, European Journal of International Relations*, and *International Relations, Journal of Democracy* and in edited books.

Index